A JOURNEY TOWARD
THE LIGHT

A JOURNEY TOWARD THE LIGHT

On Waves of Challenges
- spiritual stories about
often hard but mostly
Blissful search for the Truth

Andrew Mirosław Bukraba

authorHOUSE®

AuthorHouse™ LLC
1663 Liberty Drive
Bloomington, IN 47403
www.authorhouse.com
Phone: 1-800-839-8640

Credit: Title page Dan Drewes

Editors:
Maheshwari (Shauna R.)—USA
Patricia P.—Argentina/India
Olga Serebriakova—Russian Federation
Mary Sanders—USA
Final and major editor: David Williams-Zaanta (Mahabodhi)—England/Germany

Published by AuthorHouse 05/19/2014

ISBN: 978-1-4969-0529-1 (sc)
ISBN: 978-1-4969-0528-4 (hc)
ISBN: 978-1-4969-0527-7 (e)

Library of Congress Control Number: 2014907223

This book is printed on acid-free paper.

CONTENTS

Who Is The Author?

H is real name is Traveler because, for many incarnations, he was traveling in search of the Only Truth. Recently, though, people are calling him—Andrew, so possibly he is Andrew. Some call him Rascal, so he must be one, at least for now. He is also known as Woodpecker because this was his last profession. But actually he, himself, is trying hard to discover who he really is.

Andrew Mirosław Bukraba a.k.a. Traveler a.k.a. Raskal a.k.a. Woodpecker—was born in 1944 in Lithuania, in a town known as 'Rome of the North'—Wilno (Vilnius)—in a family from the clan Gasztold bearing the crest Szeliga Odmienny (Different). One of his ancestors came to Poland from Asia: a general who defeated Genghis Khan. After being knighted by the King, he was appointed for life as Podskarbi Koronny (Minister of Finance of Polish Kingdom). He was the first big landlord in Europe who granted freedom to his feudal subjects and divided his land equally among each of them.

Andrew graduated in Poland with a Masters Degree in Soil Science. In the Polish Army he was in a rank of Leutenant a commander of a tank platoon. After his studies he worked at the University, Polish Academy of Science, and later for the government both Provincial and Central. He worked and lived in eight countries—hot and cold, and visited, on his search for the Truth, many more. He is an experienced rock climber and mountaineer, pistol, rifle and AK-47 machine-gun marksman at Olympic level, but recently only shooting at sport targets. He is also a high mountains skier and martial arts fan; a life-long hobby that has served him very well, when needed, in a few difficult situations.

He emigrated illegally to Sweden escaping the clutches of Communism, then moved to England and later got permission to settle in Australia. He has been a free and uncompromising seeker of the Truth throughout his entire life. Andrew is a writer of short stories and poems. He spent a few years in a Indian Hindu ashram than a few years in South Indian town of Tiruvannamalai and now is back to his Old Cold Country thinking where to go next—perhaps Venezuela would be challenging enough but different way.

Author on the slopes of Arunachala.
In a background Tiruvannamalai Arunachaleswarar Big Temple.

PREFACE

Namaste,

These stories are dedicated to You Dear Reader, You who are an individualized projection of the Oneness, You, who are predestined, by making, before incarnating on Earth, the conscious choice, to have an opportunity to read them. If this statement is at present for You too enigmatic I guarantee that later its meaning will become clearly understandable. I'd like also to add here that these stories are also, maybe even especially, dedicated to those who will not have a chance to read them because they live in a suppression of freedom and often are not even aware that they are having Free will projections of the Oneness. Met on my Path Light Bearers have assured me that those last mentioned will not be ignored but accessed and spiritually elevated in a more subtle way then rest of humanity.

It is rare that a single journey will be just that—only one. Usually, any journey involves smaller ones that end up making, together, "the" journey. So it is with this book. Some are physical—many are not! We can travel with our physical bodies and we can also travel with our Astral bodies.

Almost all the journeys described involved "chance" meetings, logically almost impossible to be mere coincidences, with beings (both of this physical world and from other realms) who shared with the Traveler profound, and often hard-to-believe or accept, facts and advice on how to proceed to the next "journey".

Some readers may have to alter their preconceptions of how the world is, and even re-evaluate their deep-rooted beliefs, if they are to take full advantage of the wisdom contained in this amazing book. This book is for bold individuals who are not afraid to confront reality as it is. Therefore, it may not be for everyone?

People are usually more comfortable with their old beliefs and concepts, and have an instinctive fear of anything new or unknown.

Some of the following stories are on the brink of controversy but are not controversial. My intention is to steer old beliefs and alert Readers to understanding that you, by being strong and fearless have nothing to lose but everything to gain; Freedom, Wisdom and Love. That is why this collection of stories contains many challenging and radical ideas. When reading this we must also be aware that the discussed theories, opinions, beliefs and experiences are not only possible interpretations of discussed topics, facts and evidence. The Truth 'has many faces'. Many will not even want to know what I say and will choose to put their heads in the sand like an Australian ostrich does when sensing approaching danger. F. Nietzsche said not without a reason: **'People don't want to hear the truth because they don't want their illusions destroyed.'** But it is sometimes necessary when intending to progress, to be able see Truth, to destroy what is outdated or false.

I encourage You, the Reader, not to avoid confrontation with presented ideas, information and their interpretation but to examine them and come to your own conclusions and judgments. I also like to warn you Dear Reader. In these stories you may find scattered pieces of Truth which You may assemble like a puzzle with the help of meditation into the full picture. The Truth is easy to understand once It is tracked down and uncovered. Truth is unbelievably simple! The point is to discover It! For success in this task, attention and intelligence is needed. So this text is not for entertainment. To understand Truth is without the slightest doubt a very liberating experience, albeit a very dangerous one. The Truth is a most lethal weapon against the Dark Forces known to all sentient beings living in the vastness of the Universe. Truth is capable of destroying false beliefs established through thousands of years of indoctrination. It can turn upside down cultures based on false foundations, reset morals, ethics and paradigms. It was and is considered illegal by most rulers either 'elected' or those who inherited their royal status. As we can see throughout human history that knowers and preachers of Truth were and are always punished by death—usually by the cruelest methods available. I, as the author of the following text, hope that this warning will not frighten off the Readers but rather ignite a curiosity in them prompting them to dive 'head down' into these stories. I wish all the readers to be brave and dare to learn something from this intellectual and spiritual adventure. Each time a person broadens his understanding he is sending an indestructible wave of energy to the Universe. Those tiny waves assemble into a mighty 'tsunami' of awareness which in time will destroy the dominant powers of oppression, annihilate illusion and expose deceit, liberating humanity. But You Dear Reader, are advised not to continue reading if you find it too uncomfortable, or too conflicting with your present belief system which You have chosen as valid, or are not ready to evaluate at this stage of your life. If you choose to read this book to the last page, please do so with an open mind, contemplating the depth of those messages which are hidden between the lines and seek the energy encoded in the key words.

I, as the author of these stories, was firmly assured by the Siddhas of Arunachala that they are committed to raise the curtain on illusion—Maha Maya, which has obscured humanity's understanding for millennia. They want to reveal, in these turbulent times more than ever before, the liberating beauty of the Truth and They invite Readers to undertake a journey of investigation into Its mysteries, a journey into the strange and wondrous world of Love manifested as Truth.

I wish You all to attune to Sat, Chit, Ananda–Truth of Existence, Consciousness and Bliss and realize for now and ever that **Tat Twam Asi**—Thou Art That!

The author.

ACKNOWLEDGEMENTS

I would like to convey my gratitude and thankfulness for all the people and body-less beings who helped me in countless ways to make those stories ready to be presented to the readers. I appreciate the support of my friends who motivated me to persist and overcome my linguistic limitations and also the critics who tried to discourage me but only ignited in me a fire of rebellion, prompting strong determination not to give up at any cost and to go against all odds. I would like to thank my editors whose work was very challenging but who managed to succeed despite my unending changes, additions and often difficult to follow Slavic way of expression.

I thank the Russian anglers from Brighton pier in Melbourne for sharing their experiences from Siberia. This allowed me to combine my personal perspective on this subject with a memory of a few others who went through GULAGs.

I would like to thank all Light Bearers whom I met in this life in many countries and feel sorry that some I did not recognize at the time because I was not ready to see though appearances. Particularly I missed a 'clochard' sitting on the steps of Keleti Railway Terminal in Budapest whom I ignored but who drew the attention of my lady partner at the time.

Swami Chinmayananda—A Photo given to the author by Swami.

I would like especially to thank all the Gurus I encountered on my way: Swamis, Siddhas, Avathutas, Fakirs and Sadhus of Poland, India, Fiji, Sri Lanka and Greece, Free Men and Bards of Russia. I am in great debt for sharing with me your Wisdom, providing me spiritual guidance and, when needed, moral support. Particularly I would like to thank Swami Chinmayananda for continuing for a few weeks in dreams His teaching of Advaita Vedanta, night after night, even after He took Maha Samadi in a far away country.

I would like to express my gratitude to all dogs with whom I shared life: Żuczek 1 & 2, Niluś, Głodny and Raja. They were, by example, my greatest teachers of loyalty.

I would like to thank all of you for giving me an opportunity to understand, sometimes through contrast, what integrity is and, being so equipped, how to begin this uncompromising Path towards the Truth; and for giving me the strength to go through the ultimate test.

I would like to thank my life partner of many incarnations, my soul-mate, a twin-flame for her pure love, support and for accepting the role of my last but most significant Guru.

And at the end I would like to express my deepest gratitude to All-What-Is for giving me glimpses of The Oneness I never imagined as possible, and for the permission to settle in one the of most important spiritual centers of this planet.

THE LIGHT BEARERS

I t all happened once upon a time long, long ago, when television was not yet invented, and even the radio was not commonly used. The children in those days were never bored. It all happened in an auspicious year of a Comet. The black magicians were predicting the end of the world, but for one young boy it was just the beginning—a turn in a very, very interesting life.'

Spring reigned in all its beauty throughout the high country. It was just after the snows had melted, and the milky coffee colored waters had departed to the distant sea through the mighty rivers. The mountains breathed the invigorating spring air and still retained on their tops some white patches of snow. The brown bears had awoken in their caves after their long winter-sleep. They were now rebuilding their strength, eating the easy-to-catch rainbow trout, which were abundant in all the rivers and streams. The wandering white clouds were moving slowly like pilgrims, passing between the peaks, occasionally combed by the dark cones of slim spruce trees. The narrow, long cultivation fields formed gigantic steps descending down the slopes to the green valley. Through the meadow between the boulders flowed a crystal clear, rapid stream. Its green banks were decorated by clusters of yellow marsh marigolds; above all dominated a volcano, many millions of years old, which had died long ago. Spreading out for miles, the chain of mountain ranges covered the land like an enormous octopus. The feeling of serenity was all-pervading.

On the porch of a tiny wooden house situated near the stream sat two people—a boy, maybe ten years old, and an old tattered man with long silver hair and a fluffy beard, who in spite of his advanced age was still full of vitality. An indefinable optimism and warmth radiated from him. The old man smiled all the time through sparkling gray eyes; he was an Old Traveler. The boy and the old man had never met before, but talked like only the best of friends can talk, meeting again after years of separation. The Old Traveler earned his living

1

by fixing aluminum pots. He looked up over a pot, which he was repairing, and smiling softly at the boy said,

"You, my young friend, will become a Traveler like me; ahead of you is a long, very long journey. You will go on a quest to find what you, in fact, already have in its fullness. You will adopt this as a name and be called Traveler. Soon you will forget what I am saying, but your destiny has to be fulfilled in due time. The sun of many countries will burn your face. Your feet will endure the cold of snows and the heat of desert sands. You will cry for Freedom, believing that you are hopelessly bound, but you will not be able to get it a second time, because you are already Free. To understand this will take you more than forty years of intensive, hard searching. The secret of Freedom is in the fearlessness. You cannot be fearless and experience Freedom as long as you believe that your body, which can be harmed, is you, and that you own anything. It will take time, but you will learn to give up everything, and to live as a Witness—to respond rather than to react. You will learn to be Nothing, and to surrender to The Highest. You will attain a state of 'darkness,' as I call it. The waters of events will fall on you but you will never get wet, like a duck in the rain. The praises and abuses of people will not affect you. You will learn to work hard and through free will, not from a feeling of duty. A Free Man is not an idler at all and he has attachment neither to his work nor to the fruits of his actions. You will have an incredibly intensive, fascinating, but also very difficult life. Those who hate the integrity of free people will sometimes try to kill you. But do not worry, you are protected! On the way you will meet a few Light Bearers. Some you will not recognize, some you will. Ultimately, your Eternal Guide will find you and call you. Through Him you will find a way to Silence. You will receive the teachings of Wisdom, inexpressive in the human language. Gradually, you yourself will become a Light Bearer. Look around you! Listen! Words, words, unending empty words! The restless minds have to express themselves externally in cascades of mostly meaningless sounds. There is no exception, no escape from it. It is a chain reaction. Ignorance can only be communicated by words. The deeper the ignorance, the more words are necessary to express it. Wisdom, on the contrary, can only germinate in Silence. Only in Silence can it grow and mature, and only in Silence can it be transmitted to those who are able to stop the chatting of their minds and plunge, with confidence, into the calm waters of Silence.

"Words, words, words. What can be said by words? Only trivial things! Those who think they know, know nothing, but talk a lot. Only he, who knows that he does not know, knows IT. But most of the time he keeps silent. What can he say? To whom can he speak? Silence, all pervading Silence is shouting in its eloquence the Wisdom of a Single Truth. IT speaks to him who is in Silence, to him who does not want to know any more. On what can he even meditate? What can he gain by another thought? Why should he create another illusion? Silence of Existence is singing the praises of the Eternal One, The Highest. Is it not better to listen to it, just to be? This is the Highest Knowledge, all else is better to ignore and to consider as worthless. Silence, Silence, Silence. In IT the universe disappears, time loses its power. Existence and nonexistence become dreamlike illusions. Pain and pleasure, darkness and light seem to be only a modification of the mind. What is the mind? Is it not only a parade of thoughts? Then, it is unreal and ceases to exist when we stop thinking. The Highest has to manifest the ideas projected by the mind. It is a law of creation. Thoughts are seeds of creation. From thoughts things are born! There is no other way for individuals to live in the illusions, or to stop thinking and transcend them. But for the Witness, the highest Bliss is in the witnessing of Beingness, not in interacting with the illusions of unreality and the endless creations of uncontrolled thinking. The decoration of the stage is not necessary. Why does the Real have to act on the stage of unreal space and time? He is The Real. Is it not better to give up all and be, just be? BE HIM? Is there anything on Earth He can gain? What can make Him more Him? He Is, and this is the Highest Truth. To be in Silence, to live eternally in Peace is the highest achievement a human can aim for. Never think that you are weak or limited. It is a gravest sin. You are the Greatest!

"My boy, now you do not understand much of what I am telling you. Never mind, you are still pure. My words are the seeds, which will slowly grow on this fertile soil. Many years will pass until you understand all of it, many more until you live it in everyday life. You are really a lucky one. You will meet face to face with The

Highest, who is going to incarnate on this planet soon. You will be born again. You will have three parents. It doesn't make any sense, does it? Wait, when your hair is silver, as mine is now, you will have grown into the shape SHE preset for you in the beginning of Time. Are you surprised that I am saying She? Wait, the future will show you some surprising things. Then, you will neither ask for anything, nor search any more. You will rest in Peace, working hard, and be totally satisfied with what life will give you. Now, my boy, sit facing our Father Sun and let us be quiet for a while. I am using too many words. Now, let us talk in Silence. When I am traveling through the mountains, the forests and the fields of golden rye, I talk in Silence to the fields, to the trees, and to the animals, and they talk back to me. One day you too will learn this language of Silence, this language of Love Divine. You will understand its whispers in everything you see and meet on your way. You will merge in The Oneness."

The rays of the Sun sinking towards the west warmly caressed their faces. The Old Traveler, externally withdrawn, was abiding in dimensions not accessible to mortals. On his face was painted an expression of Bliss, an expression of union with The Highest. The boy felt a warm river of Love from both the Old Traveler and the Sun, flowing toward him and filling his heart. In this brief experience of Silence, he was initiated by the Silence and he became a Traveler.

The doors of the little wooden house opened and an old lady appeared. She was slim, simply dressed, with a very pale face. Her silver gray hair was neatly combed and tied up at the back of her head. She smiled toward them and stood silently watching the boy, waiting for the Old Traveler to come back from his glide into Eternity. A feeling of serenity and Peace surrounded her. The boy was surprised to see her. It was clearly expressed on his face. He had lived for a few years just two houses away, but had never seen her before. His friends had often said that an old lady, who never buys any food and is rarely seen outside, lives in that small house. He obviously hadn't believed them. He thought the house must be deserted since its window shutters were always closed.

"This is your Older Sister," said the Old Traveler, regaining his normal consciousness.

"You will meet her again in the future. She is crystallizing here to permanently abide in Peace. She is my wife. We met more than sixty years ago and, because we were predestined to get married, we did. At the same time we chose not to start a family but rather to go on a quest in search of the ultimate Truth, to find out what is this secret of Life the philosophers are talking about. She is a Traveler too, but she travels differently than I do. She travels without going out of her house. We live separately but meet again every five years. This is our last meeting. Our time is almost over. Soon we will rest in our Eternal Abode, and give a testimony of our lives to The Highest. She will be born again on Earth, but I will stay and work in the Higher Dimensions of Existence. Now, my friend, you go back home. Your mother is anxious about what has happened to you. She is waiting with your supper."

Years passed. The boy continued his studies and in his free time, during every vacation and on weekends, he explored the villages and small towns near and far. Something was pulling him to go out and travel. He traveled on skis through snowy mountains in winter and on foot across mountain ranges in summer, reaching remote settlements where often there was no electricity or drivable roads. He felt at home everywhere and didn't hesitate to enter any house. Surprisingly, the people were not astonished to see a young boy appear out of the high forests and white, snow-decorated rocky peaks which were full of wolves and bears. They welcomed him as their own along with a dash of curiosity. They accepted him in spite of the fact he used the language of educated people, not at all fluent in a mountaineer's dialect. Evenings were spent sitting and talking, surrounded by men a few times older than him. They listened to him attentively, never interrupting and with a respect usually given only to the elders.

He was talking about mysteries of Existence; about the all-pervading conscious, intelligent and eternal energy, about the oneness in diversity. He was using simple words, trying to express that which cannot be expressed, that Single Truth. Following his words in their minds, the old villagers would effortlessly drift into that state where they experienced a glimpse of their oneness with cattle, pigs, fruit trees, fields and horses. His speech was not introducing anything new, only synthesizing and defining their preconceptions and expectations. They all lived so close to Nature that in fact no clear boundaries existed. They were simple in mind and pure in heart, these folks who greeted strangers and friends humbly but with dignity, saying, "Let Jesus Christ be praised for ages and ages." He was listening to their stories about a powerful, perverse negative spirit, called by the mountain folk Mamoona, who led people weak in character to the dangerous domains of sin, who harmed animals, who threw hail on crops ready for harvest, and who made women crazy and desirous for useless modern things. Though still a boy, he shared their supper breaking dark rye bread with the elders in communion of fellowship and brotherhood in God, as only a man does in this high country with a man. They asked him often for advice in family matters and farm problems, and advice was given. His lack of experience due to his young age was not a hindrance. The Old Traveler's wisdom was speaking through him. He was a channel only—knowing nothing he knew much. The boy and Old Traveler traveled separately, but the boy served as the Old Traveler's assistant and apprentice.

Years again passed by. The little boy became a man. He had almost forgotten all about The Oneness, the Single Truth. He was traveling a lot now, from one end of his country to the other. He was also traveling to other countries, but now he was not talking to people about Existence and Consciousness. He was exploring the fields not accessible to boys. He became interested in the enjoyments of the senses. Often, however, feeling guilty he escaped from himself into the unconsciousness of drunkenness and after awakening felt even guiltier. In trying to balance himself, he often suffered.

More years passed by. He felt all the time that something was missing, that this was not what he really wanted. He finished his studies and, climbing the ladder of his career, became more and more influential, and more and more dissatisfied. Having a position in the government, in one of the ministries, he was subconsciously waiting nonetheless for a call, a signal to go, to leave behind all of it and to meet the

Unknown. Many times he was 'on the chariot', many times under. He was experimenting with life, searching for his limits. A few times he balanced on the edge of death. Strange, but never was he in the paralyzing possession of fear. The words of the Old Traveler shared in his childhood acted like a protecting shield, promising the unavoidable. The people in his country say, "Who is going to be hanged can't be drowned." It is very true, destiny has to be fulfilled. What has to happen will happen and nothing can happen before its time.

And then this happened when he was forty-six years old. It happened after twelve long years of worldwide wandering; after he had left his office, the acquisitions of his life and even his country. He lived in many places, in several countries, on a few continents. He had worked in so many very different fields that he could no longer keep track of them all. He met his Guru, his Eternal Guide. He met face-to-face, as predicted by the Old Traveler, the Living God. He met the manifestation of The Oneness, the Incarnation of The Highest, the Super Light Bearer. It was a lady from exotic Brazil. He was stunned. There were no thoughts, only Silence. He instantly recognized in Her eyes that well known Golden Light of Divine Love. He had seen it a few times already in the eyes of the Light Bearers whom he had met on his way. But never before had he seen eyes that were an access-gate to Infinity. The search had ended. Four years later he stopped being a Traveler. He became a Dweller in Her abode. In this haven, hidden from the materialistic-minded rabble, he met again many of his relatives, some from the time before this birth: The First Sister, The Older Sister, Hidden Brother, Brother Lyon, and many, many younger ones. Some of them were already Light Bearers, but the Guru did not yet activate their eyes. They were waiting patiently for His command and, in the meantime, they did the same work which they had done before becoming Light Bearers. Some of them wore colorful clothes, some white, but all could recognize each other while others were not aware of their state of unconsciousness. Now he was happy, fulfilled and satisfied. There was nothing to want any more and nothing to search for. The memory of the words he had heard in childhood returned and now he understood what they meant. Now there was no need for more words. He entered the Silence to absorb the final timeless teachings. His son had become a Traveler. Now it was his turn to enter The Path, to go on a quest, to search for what he already possessed in its fullness.

Because it is a never-ending story, we can easily imagine the future. All that will happen already has happened many, many times, long, long ago. The sacred flame has been passed from the beginning of Time by the Old Light Bearers to the young boys and girls, who in turn have become first Travelers and then Light Bearers themselves.

Let us dream the continuation of this story: Years have passed; The Dweller's hair has become silver, as once was that of an Old Traveler, many, many years before. He was fully satisfied. Working, he was at rest; resting, he worked intensively. In the crowds he was alone, in solitude he lived in the Presence. One day, his Guru called him and said,

"Go on, son. Continue to talk to your brothers. Show them the way to The Light. Give them back what was given to you." He prostrated, smiled and left. Going, he was not going. Where could he go? He was one with Everything and so he walked back to his beloved mountains to cross again the ranges, to break the dark rye bread with his brothers. He again became a Traveler, an Old Traveler, but now he was also a Light Bearer. On the way he talked in Silence to the wolves, lizards, snakes, squirrels, rabbits and deer. He talked to the trees and the animals, to golden rye, and he talked to the volcano, dead many, many millions of years ago. They all understood him well as he was speaking the universal language of Love. In response, Love and more Love was projected. It all happened again in an auspicious year of a Comet. The entire country flooded, but this time it was not the flood from fast melting snows, but the flood of Love in The Oneness of Existence. After a life-long search, he realized that he knew nothing but that he had become a perfect channel for Her who was Everything, who was the Highest Manifested. Now he was totally fearless; he was a grown Free Man.

One warm spring afternoon he met a young boy, seated on a rock and lost in thought. It was on the bank of a small river filled with crystal clear water flowing fast between the boulders. Its green banks were decorated by clusters of yellow marsh marigolds. He recognized him immediately. It was a boy who had been predestined to become first a Traveler and, at the conclusion of his life, a Light Bearer. The Old Traveler sat on a stone next to him and, smiling softly with his eyes said,

"Do you recognize me? You can't! I am you. You are who I was and you will become who I am now. Sit with me for a while my son. Let us be in Silence to sow the seeds. Do not ask questions. There is no need for words."

And they sat for a while in the warmth of the setting Sun. The Silence initiated the small boy. He became a Traveler. The boy felt very peaceful and happy, like being reunited with his best friend after a long separation. From a distance they did not look like separate individuals, their figures blended with the surrounding boulders, homogeneous uniformity of Existence. It was almost perfectly silent; only in the distance a Guru-Bird chanted his usual mantra: Guru, Guru, Guru . . . Guru, Guru, Guru.

THE MAGIC TOUCH

It was a Saturday evening in early January, on the sandy coast of the Arabian Sea, in the South Indian state of Kerala. The weather was warm and humid as usual, but a gentle cooling sea breeze gave some relief, especially to those few who had just arrived in the tropics. From time-to-time the bluish lights of gigantic fireflies illuminated the darkness under the coconut palms. It looked as if they were trying to reach the stars that filled the Indian sky. The ashram atmosphere, saturated with the Guru's presence, was charged with His Divine Energy. He was giving *prasad* in the meditation hut to all of the residents. A long queue of waiting people emerged from the darkness and disappeared into the light of the doorway of the small thatched hut. All were silent, and seemed to be contemplating the special privilege of being fed by the Incarnation of The Oneness, by Love Divine wearing a human body, by their beloved Guru.

Hidden from peoples' eyes, in the shadows and under a dense bush growing near the meditation hut, stood a visitor from the far away Down Under. He had just arrived a few days ago. He had never before visited India and the ashram, but from the first moment he felt at home or rather 'back home'. In the late afternoon he learned from the others that *prasad* was given by the Guru on Saturdays and then only to the ashram residents who fasted on that day. He realized that he would not be allowed to receive any *prasad*.

At that moment, due to his emotional state, this became an almost unbearable tragedy. He experienced a strong conflict between his total identification with life in the ashram, and his formal status as a visitor. It created agonizing pain. This manifested externally in uncontrollable waves of tears and a temporary loss of interest in everything around him. His body, shaken by the convulsions of his crying, was only breathing sporadically. He was, in fact, suffocating like a fish out of water.

After a while, the distribution of *prasad* ended and he heard chanting. The Sanskrit *shlokas*, although not understandable to him, sounded familiar, and subconsciously created a slight relief from his sufferings. Somehow, the chanting miraculously had a sedating effect on his nerves. It sounded like an echo of something long ago forgotten, but, nonetheless, still his very own.

Ashramites started to leave the overcrowded meditation hut. Suddenly, one of the Western residents, known to the visitor from the Guru's Down Under Tours, walked to the very spot where he was hiding. Somehow, appearing not at all surprised at seeing the dark figure under the bush, she sat down quite naturally as if everything was very normal:

"Would you take some of my *prasad*, please? We can share it, can't we?" The visitor automatically took some of it in his hands. He was so surprised that he could hardly manage to say 'thank you'. All of it was so shocking and so unexpected. It was like the final act of a drama being magically directed by some invisible author.

The sweetness of the prasad was unbelievable! It was heavenly nectar and it had come to him in such a special way. He felt as if the Guru had given it to him personally. But this was not the last act as he had previously thought. A few minutes later he noticed some movement among the ashramites who stood at the entrance of the meditation hut. It was the Guru Himself coming out! The visitor sank deeper into the shadow of his bush. He did not want to be in the Guru's way, or to be noticed by Him in his present, miserable state. To his astonishment, the Guru headed directly towards him. He was nearly paralyzed from exhaustion after his long cry, and now he was stunned by the Guru's sudden approach. He was not able to prostrate. He just stood there, motionless, like a wooden post, feeling like an utter idiot. The Guru gently touched his chest at his heart, and rubbed his right arm in one deft motion—The Guru did not stop nor say a word as He passed him on His way to the mango grove to have a bit of rest after another very busy day. The visitor could not see the Guru's facial expression because of the darkness, but he felt that HE was smiling lovingly and with full understanding of his mental state.

His reaction to this magic touch was instantaneous. His feeling of being shipwrecked, alone in a hostile exotic world, unwanted, unrecognized, and totally useless, had vanished immediately. The feeling was unexpectedly replaced by a warm sensation. A feeling of love for the sake of love was germinating in his heart. It was the bliss of happiness and gratitude for the Guru's all-knowing compassion, and for the miracle of the instant healing of his bleeding heart. The Guru's touch was also silently promising:

"Wait. Be patient. At the right time you, too, will queue with your brothers and sisters for my *prasad*. Do not worry. You belong here. You are my son, but it is not your time, not yet. Wait, son, wait! All will be fine."

Now calm, he meditated for a long time under the coconut palms. The mighty waves of the nearby sea, beating against the sands of the shore, loudly confirmed the Guru's silent promise, implanting into his subconscious the truth about his destiny: "Om . . . you belong here. Om . . . be patient. Om . . . what has to happen will happen. Om . . . the Guru is with you always. Om . . . Om . . . Om . . ."

In the beginning of December of the following year, a new *ashramite* was standing in a long queue waiting to receive the Guru's Saturday *prasad* for the first time. He was concentrating deeply on every detail of this new experience. It was the same man who once stood crying under a dense bush in the darkness of the night close to the meditation hut, where the Guru was giving *prasad*. Now his turn had come! He knelt in front of the Guru with great respect and devotion. The Guru quickly put *prasad* on his plate and looked straight into his eyes. Again, He did not say a word, only smiled lovingly, but he understood the language of the Silence:

"You see, all is well. I told you, you belong here. In the end, you have come. It was not too long, was it? Now concentrate on the present. Do not think about the past or imagine the future. Do your sadhana. Do not worry about anything. I will take care of you. I am with you, always."

Another loop of time had closed. A successive battle in his struggle for FREEDOM had been won. Now, he lives directly under his Guru's protection and guidance. There will be more battles to fight, but now he is aware that he is not on his own. The Guru is walking the Path with him, step by step . . .

THE SIGNPOSTS

This year the winter in Europe was much more severe than since the end of WWII, and the meteorologists called it 'the winter of the century'. The snow and cold paralyzed the Northern part of the continent causing great damage. Even human lives were lost. Nature had started to punish the selfish and irresponsible humanity for years of misusing their knowledge and contaminating the entire planet. In England the snowstorm hit the London-Glasgow highway, freezing to death twelve travelers in their cars unprepared to face such extreme conditions, while stuck on the road in broken down vehicles for more than 24 hours.

His house built near Warsaw, the capital of Poland, was nice, cozy and warm. The central heating had made the two-story dwelling a pleasant abode for its few inhabitants: his mother, wife, dog and himself. He had just returned from his office tired and upset, and, to relax, he sunk into the warm water of the bathtub. There he thought:

"What is the purpose of living such a life? Why must I pretend that I am doing something sensible, whereas in fact I'm only drinking tea and coffee, smoking cigarettes, gossiping, calling friends, and visiting nearby bistros and cafés to break the monotony? What is the sense of going to meetings where there is no need to find any solutions for the problems because everything is arbitrarily decided in advance by Communist Party leaders, who receive their directives from Big Brother in Moscow. The functioning of this government is a masquerade, a play performed to fool the free World, to pretend that here is a real democracy; a pantomime of puppets suggesting that this is a free country, ruled by the working class, as the official Marxist propaganda says. What will be the end of my solitary games of trying to straighten up the country's economy, when I'm against the stupidity of the system and the servility of my superiors? Am I not on the doorstep of calamity? I am under constant surveillance by the UB (the Poland extension of the Russian secret police – KGB) who keep a close watch on my every move, my contacts and my words. Is it not the right time to leave this game and earn my living, even with my hands, working with a hammer, brush or a spade?"

These thoughts passed through his mind. He was no longer interested in being in the game. He was fed up to the point of a break-down, and prepared to make a full stop and finish this idiotic involvement, this madness. He wanted to free himself and be able to make decisions about the directions of his life, to find a higher purpose of existence, if there was such a thing. Some time ago he had read a book given to him by his aunt entitled: "Humans Yesterday, Today and Tomorrow." In it there was a promise: "Those who really, sincerely strive for Freedom will be called at the right time and guided to Freedom. The

Masters of the White Brotherhood are watching the entire human race. Not even one single person will be left unnoticed."

He didn't know which way to go. Life in this communist ruled country was boring, hopeless and very dangerous, especially for one in his position. He knew this from years of experience. He had the feeling of false security, even while playing the games and calculating the risks. He never played cards but had the character of the poker player, and he even liked to sometimes extend himself to the point of danger to test where the limits were. But still he was moving in the circle of the known. It would be good to have a sign, a message from the unknown Master, if such a one exists; which way to go, what to do. Stay here and continue bluffing that he is above their reach, or run away in time to save his neck and meet the Unknown.

Suddenly he found himself covered by something. He jumped up frightened, splashing water. UB? No! On his head was a large bath towel, which had fallen down from the shower curtain rail installed over the bathtub. Obviously it hadn't fallen by itself! He realized that it was the color of *kavi*—the color of red-orange bricks—the color of the clothes Indian renunciates or *sannyasins* wear. Was it a sign? Yes!! It was a message from the unknown Master!! He decided to start preparations for leaving the country, for his escape from the domain of the totalitarian communist regime, from the grasp of demagogy and the gloom of masquerade. He had already made one such attempt, but unsuccessfully. He had done this in an incredibly naive, childish way.

"This time I can and I will succeed", he thought. This was not a dead slogan. He had already paid the price to know that it was a magic formula that works. He was not attached to anything or anybody. He deeply loved his mother, the Tatra Mountains and his country Poland, but felt somehow detached and free to go. Maybe the seeds sown long, long ago by the Old Traveler in tattered clothes on the banks of the Small River had started to germinate, having been watered well by the unhappiness from this kind of life. Maybe the words he had once heard when lying on a bark, under the logs of trees cut down for making paper printing propaganda, "You have been born to become

Free." Words heard once in far away country were accepted by his subconscious mind and now started to bear fruit. Who knows?

A few years passed. After long and exhausting, but very interesting wanderings and work in Sweden and England, he found himself in remote Australia. There he started his own business and earned his living as a tradesman, mainly renovating old colonial, Australian heritage houses—using a hammer and a brush!! There he dissolved amongst the thousands of immigrants from every possible country in the World. He had come from Europe with his wife and a child born in London, a brilliant and very sensitive boy. After two years on this new continent he bought a few books at a garage sale about spiritual matters. Strange, but the books attracted his attention in spite of the fact that he was unable to read English. He didn't know the language well enough and he didn't have the time or money to study it. Gradually, with the help of a dictionary, he managed to read, 'In Days of Great Peace' by Mouni Sadhu and 'Initiations' by Paul Sedir translated by Mouni Sadhu. The first one was a diary of one European-born seeker, who wandered through France, Brazil and Australia, where he settled after WWII. He visited and spent a few months with Ramana Maharshi, a contemporary Indian sage who unfortunately died in 1950. With a mastering of the language his study in this field intensified. He started to meditate and practice *"Atma Vichara"* as advised by Sri Ramana.

A few years later he met a great Vedantin, Swami Chinmayananda, and after receiving some scriptural teachings was directed by him to his next Guru. All of this was too mystical, too foreign and frightening for his wife, who developed a strong aversion to everything connected with India and its philosophy. It reactivated a dormant conflict between them. Gradually the conflict between his involvements in scriptural studies, spiritual practices and his wife grew into a confrontation. Her negative attitude and disturbing behavior reached the point where he started to entertain the possibility of a separation, in spite of his love for his son. He felt that the conflict, with the frequent arguments, was more damaging for the boy than the eventual lack of his close proximity.

One evening he was having a bath after a hard day's work. The idea of separation was hanging at the back of his mind. He was not yet confident about what was the best thing to do. He wasn't certain that separation would be the best solution, but he was prepared to pay any price to be able to continue his now intense search for the key to the secret gate to the Land of Freedom. He was tough and had already survived twenty years of a mostly unhappy and conflict-ridden marriage.

"It would be good to have a sign from my Guru." he thought. Suddenly something fell on his head. He lifted it, and it was again a bath towel, and again it was of a *kavi* color. The sign had been repeated after more than fourteen years. The decision had been made. He didn't dwell on the problem anymore but accepted it as his destiny.

A few years passed. He was on his own and already legally divorced. For a while, the powerful *Maya* still deluded him, but his Guru had saved him and he stayed single. His business started to be more and more successful and new and tempting possibilities and gates had opened. At the same time a strong pull towards complete renunciation manifested itself. His surrender to his Guru became very deep after unconditionally following the advice given to him to stay on his own. He started to think about finalizing his worldly affairs and going to join his Guru's ashram. Again he was not sure if this was just another trick of his mind, another delusion. It was a very difficult decision. He was aware that even in the World he could live a very spiritual, disciplined life and progress well. Not everyone can live in an ashram and not everyone should. His Guru was visiting Australia every year and from time to time he would visit Him in India or join Him for a World Tour. In fact he didn't have even the slightest desire to live in India, but felt clearly that his destiny was to serve his Guru in the way He chose for him, and be where He wanted him to be.

"It would be good to have a sign", he thought again.

The weather was miserably windy and cold, a typical early spring day in the Australian state of Victoria at the end of October. He was feeling claustrophobic, locked in his apartment, so he decided to go for a walk along the beach of a large bay, on the banks of which his town was located and which stretched for more than fifty kilometers. It was Sunday. On the way toward the sea he passed the industrial suburbs. The streets resembled those of a deserted town— no people. After he parked his car he directed his steps toward the beach thinking, again,

"My Guru is far away, I'm on my own; how can I know if I really should aim towards complete, total renunciation, or start to organize myself anew? Time is running fast. In a few years it will be too late. It would be good to have a sign from my Guru, or if not I must write a letter and ask for advice." Just then a gusty wind brought from under his feet a new, clean handkerchief. It was *kavi* in color—the color of renunciation!!! (Later he checked: none of the shops in Melbourne sold handkerchiefs in this color.) What could he say now? Was it not a very obvious sign from his Guru? What was left was only to ask his Guru to accept him as a disciple and allow him to stay permanently with Him. But it would only be a formality. The sign was too clear to have any doubts.

His Guru was coming again to Australia in late November. He decided to go to Brisbane to meet Him when He arrived from Singapore on the early morning flight. He rented a motel room with a friend from the Guru's *satsang* group in Melbourne and spent the evening with an Indian couple from Seattle, USA, who had come here for the Guru's Australian tour. They talked about the mysteries of their Guru and His Divine Love, and finally he found himself at the airport the next morning before 5:25 a.m.

The Singapore jumbo-jet landed. When the customs area sliding doors opened he noticed his Guru some ten meters back in a long passage carrying two, very large, heavy suitcases. He dropped them on the floor and made a calling gesture. His reaction was automatic. He ran, pushing aside the security guard who tried to stop him, and after prostrating at Guru's feet took His luggage. His Guru smiled lovingly, patted his back and said,

"You have done well. It's good that now you don't have to live in your van."

"How did He know?" It is one thing to talk with friends, who are also the Guru's followers, about how He knows everything that happens to His children all over the World, and quite another, to experience His omnipresence and full awareness when it happens to oneself. It was a shocking statement, as in fact just one month before the Guru's arrival, he had rented a one-bedroom apartment. Following his Guru's advice when separating from his partner and having no money, and because of a large job he was involved in was not yet completed, he was homeless for a few months, living partly in his van and partly in the renovated building.

The Guru traveled from Brisbane and along the ocean shore to Byron Bay—the Australian climatic haven in New South Wales, close to the border with Queensland. It is the capital of the alternatively living people. When the group arrived there the tropical weather was humid and hot.

On the last day of programs, there was a *Guru Bhava*, and he sat at the back of the hall and watched his Guru giving *darshan*. Young hippies showed up, and compared to the other Australian centers, they showed little emotion. They were nice, smiling, but somehow withdrawn, spaced out. Maybe it was an outcome of the excessive use of marijuana and other drugs in this community. Watching the parade of people and his Guru's unending projection of Love to His children, who are mostly rejected by the conservative Australian population, his mind slowed down. There were only residual thoughts left about his Guru's Divinity. In this state he joined the queue for *darshan*. The program was ending. He was not prepared to ask his Guru anything there and then. He preferred to wait for the programs in Melbourne, or even the retreat at Mornington Peninsula. But things happened as they were preset to happen. He asked! His Guru only smiled, and looking deep into his eyes nodded His head in confirmation. He almost swooned from happiness. Something fell from him like a heavy but invisible armor, which had paralyzed his freedom. It had happened! There was no return! "The bone-die is cast" as Cesar once said, crossing Rubicon. He felt relieved. Guru, by accepting him, confirmed that he was not dreaming about the direction of his destiny. Being incurably naive he thought his worldly games were over. Later he said to his friend,

"I am in!!" but the friend didn't take it seriously, thinking perhaps this was some craziness brought about from tiredness and emotions.

Who would have known how the perverted mind would soon find a way to put him into a doubting, confused state. The Guru left for Mauritius and Reunion Island. Then, in his confidence there appeared first a scratch, then a crack, where the seed of doubt started to grow, suggestively whispering all the time:

"Do you know for sure what the Guru meant by this gesture? He didn't say anything! Indians have different body language. When they say, "Yes," they make a gesture by moving their heads in a way, which in the West we can understand as, "Who knows?" You didn't talk things over in detail. Even one senior Swami from Guru's group said that now in the ashram there is a committee which decides about such things, and it's not as easy as one might think. His friends from the Guru's *satsang* group also tried earnestly to nourish his doubting mind, saying that many people wanted to go and stay there, but they all returned. That ashram life is not for people like him, that what he needs is a girlfriend. There were even a few propositions made to him, as a man being single is something difficult for others to allow. They were also saying that the Guru says: "You are my son" to everybody, and he shouldn't imagine that in his case it meant that he was His disciple. Even if he goes, it's guaranteed that after a few months he would be back. After such brainwashing he became restless again. What to do? Maybe his Guru really didn't mean,

"Yes." Maybe he was dreaming. Maybe all of them were right. He knew from earlier life experiences that common beliefs are not necessarily right, but how to find out what was right? Write a letter? The best thing would be to receive a clear sign.

One Full Moon night, after a long meditation, he drifted into a deep refreshing sleep and dreamt very vividly, in panchromatic colors, about a very special meeting. His old Advaita Vedanta Philosophy teacher, Swami Chinmayananda had come, but not as before to take him to the mist saying: "Forget her (his current lady partner), now let us talk about serious things", and continued his teachings. This time he had come to communicate something. He saw only the head and the torso of the Swamiji, but from up close. Swami's face was beaming the Golden Light of Love Divine. He who was always so serious was this time laughing happily, and not only with his facial expressions but also with his eyes and even hair. He had on his forehead a huge, round, gold *chandanam* mark, and in the middle of it a *kumkum* dot. It was activated and worked as the mind's antennae. They communicated effortlessly in a direct mind-to-mind language. He asked the Swamiji if he had brought him a message from his Guru. Swami, extremely happy answered,

"Yes, you guessed."

"Is it the truth that my Guru has accepted me as a disciple and promised to lead me back home?" Swami almost exploded from immense happiness, and jumping slightly shouted,

"Most certainly, YES! You are booked for a trip to . . . . !" What a relief! Now nobody, but nobody can question the fact! The Guru's will is unquestionable. It is final, as it is the law for the disciple to obey his Guru. But what was this experience? Was it a dream? It was irrelevant, because he felt in his whole soul that it was a true message from his Guru!

When the Guru came back the next year to Australia he was ready to go to India. To make all this clearer, he had a brief conversation with one senior Swamini. He wanted to find out the details of the conditions for his joining the ashram.

"Why are you so worried about all of it? Everything will be fine. Just come. Our Guru knows what's in your heart." she said. That was all.

His worldly games were over; the Grand Game has started. In this game, his Guru was his coach and the captain of the team, which he just joined. How could he have any doubts now? How? He was not after *kavi*, ochre or any other color of clothes. He was after The Freedom heard about long, long ago in many statements in many countries but never fully comprehended, and most of all, he just wanted to serve his Guru without any personal expectations.

People say that we are totally blind amongst the labyrinth of beings, things and happenings. This is not true! The signs on the road are always provided to everyone. It is up to us to see them and to act accordingly. We have to be alert and one-pointed. If our mind and senses are on the objects of enjoyment, we will obviously ignore the signs and even not notice them at all. Then we will feel blind, and the arrows of merciless *Maha Maya* will make us suffer the pain of our own mistakes and cravings. Sometimes we will notice and understand one sign and miss the other, like a stag on the rutting ground and in a mood of mating can't notice the approaching hunters. For travel on this road we can't get The Automobile Club insurance against the highway hunter—the killer called Maya. Our only protection and assurance of safe travel is *shraddha*—attentiveness and alertness, and *viveka*—discrimination.

THE STEPS

E veryone wholeheartedly welcomed the break in the miserable monsoon weather. The day started beautifully; from early morning it was clear and sunny. Through the gentle blue sky a single cirrus cloud moved towards the North. The greenery of the trees looked fresh after being bathed in so many days of rain.

The evening of this magnificent day was a culmination of the creator's mastery in manifestation of Mother Nature's beauty. The lowering Sun was now not more than 20 degrees from the horizon. He was painting everything in pastel colors: the clear sky, white clouds, and even the faces of people. The sky, beginning on the horizon with a warm orange color, changed to gold, light yellow and milky blue with a pure blue-blue at its zenith. As one looked up from the horizon, it formed a three-dimensional dome. The firmament was decorated in the Southwest with massive clouds of deep dark navy blue. Those clouds rose from the sea, forming great monuments, their formation homogenous in color and density. It gave the threatening impression that it was a hundred-meter high tsunami wave, which can be formed during a strong earthquake at the bottom of the sea.

There was no visible transition between the water and the cloud. It covered only one fourth of the sky, but it was overwhelming, dominating one's vision, strongly contrasting the gentle soothing shades of the sky. Moving in the background were small, pure white clouds of almost the same size and shape which created an even stronger contrast against the sky. They resembled a squadron of supersonic jet fighters and racing Formula-1 cars with wings as stabilizers. At the front of this busy stage hung a regular shaped, single row of bigger clouds of dark bluish-gray color. It provided a sort of border, like a folded-up theatrical curtain, preventing any of the illusionary vehicles, which ranged themselves backwards, from crossing the screen of navy blue cloud.

The continuation of it all towards the North looked like something from a totally different set-up. The sky was an orange-reddish color with a single row of very distant stratocumulus clouds on parade. They moved in the opposite direction, touching the horizon like a procession of penitents, bent under the weight of their sins on their way to their ultimate destination of final punishment at the sea. But it was only the wind in the high altitudes which caused such deformities.

In the North, at a distance of some forty kilometers, rising up from the plains and above the clouds, were mountains overgrown by primordial tropical jungle. The mountains were of a gray navy-blue, not as clear and intense in color as the 'tsunami cloud' in the Southwest. They stood like posts from where the columns of clouds, in shapes of heavy army vehicles, rushed west towards the imaginary battlefield. They were starting their trip from their hiding place behind the mountain range and speeding to meet cloud jets and racing cars. Now, for the observer, it became clear why the jet squadrons placed themselves in a back-to-front position. They didn't want to confront their enemy, as they became aware that they were both made of the same small particles of water. It was their common substratum so they couldn't be an enemy to each other. What a pity it is that people can't understand such an obvious and simple revelation! The jets had to follow the orders of General Wind, but were consciously prepared to retreat at any moment. People, on the contrary, commonly don't follow the orders of their leaders, but are always ready to take offensive force on others, who are usually weaker from their own point of view.

Such a fascinating play of colors and richness of shapes as seen this evening had never before been observed on such a scale, or in such definite contrasts or in so many strange shades. Some colors were so intense that they looked as tangible as solid matter, while others were so gentle and soft that they were perceived intuitively rather then through the senses. There was also a feeling that additional dimensions, unknown to human science, were participating in this performance. They could not be directly perceived by our senses, mind and intellect, because they were not built by the creator for the understanding of the subtle and softness of God's manifestation. Nevertheless it was a definite, almost spiritual experience. On the landscape, in the sky and on the clouds were seen colors which are not normally visible to the human eyes, or distinguishable from their neighbors on the visible part of the light spectrum.

The Observer remembered how, long ago, on one hot, windless day, when he was still fighting his war in the world called 'making a living', aimed at securing a simple existence; he was painting the inside of a swimming pool with a roller. All the vapors of the epoxy paint condensed to such an extent that the place where he was working became a deadly trap, a gas chamber. After some time, he realized that everything around him looked very different. He straightened himself and gazed with amusement at the sky, which was saturated by an unusual purple-like color. The background had a silvery and transparent underlining, and appeared to have the depth of a few inches of thick clear glass. It shimmered like light reflecting on the surface of powdered galena crystals. Somehow he knew that it was exactly how the bees saw the sky. He realized that if he stayed there longer, breathing the poisonous fumes, it would be his last experience of the beauty of Earthly colors. He climbed out of the swimming pool onto the neatly cut short green-green grass of the lawn, and lost consciousness in its moist softness.

The memory of a dream in the intoxication of epoxy vapors came to him. He was walking up steps leading straight to the top of a very high mountain with his lady partner, whom he loved very much. The mountain dominated the plains like the famous Fujiyama in Japan. Its slope, from the middle to its peak, was covered with snow and ice. It was a fantastic experience. He liked to be free and in the open air. People say that the greatest step is the one which leads outdoors. He had always wanted to know exactly what they meant. They walked barefoot. They were in tune, complementing each other in most situations. They both enjoyed being with one another, climbing the steps of their Path together. But from the very beginning of this ascent, they understood that they were walking the Path together, yet each alone. On the Path there was no friendship, partnership, companionship or even relationship. The pains and rewards on the way had to be experienced and finally consumed personally.

She knew it no less then he and did not try to invade his inner world. She knew that they belonged to each other in only a very limited way, always retaining their freedom. When they reached the snow-line half way up, she stopped and turned back. He stopped too and following her gaze looked down on the plains. They stood there, both motionless and silent, contemplating the beauty of the long, fork-shaped narrow valley. Visible along its floor were strange dwellings of some unknown beings. He thought that it must be a different planet or a different dimension of existence. The dwellings were very modern, like small, clear bubbles of transparent Plexiglas. They were located in unspoiled Nature. There were no roads or power lines. The valley was in the shade, and inside the dwellings light was shining; but the light didn't come from any particular source. The space inside the dwellings radiated a light, which was gold-orange in color. Along the valley drifted a streak of thin white smoke or foggy mist. All was saturated by colors, which he had never seen before. Maybe they were astral world colors, and now he could see them, being in a dream-state. It was beautiful, calm and cold. The fresh colors went through all objects, right into their insides. Those colors were breathable. Yes, breathable, even from great distances! He inhaled the cool calmness with unimaginable delight.

His lady partner pointed at a small house standing on the side of the valley. It was a small simple cottage built from wood, in the style of the Australian Gold Rush. It looked, in contrast to the other dwellings, very earthly. She said, "I feel cold. My feet are frozen. I would like to go back and live in that house." He didn't answer. It was obvious. She waved the problem aside with her hand, as if an annoying mosquito, impatiently, like driving away the memories of the past, and started to walk down the steps. After a few steps she stopped and turning back asked,

"Are you really going there to freeze? Do you really want to die? There is nothing there, only light" He again kept quiet and started to slowly climb up, feeling no pain, no cold and no sadness by the separation. He was thinking: "Is it really so easy to become free from worldly attachment?"

Closer to the summit the snow on the steps became warmer and all was submerged in an intense bright white light. Its source was at the very summit. Its rays were pleasantly warm but not burning. He walked higher and higher, ascending; she walked lower and lower, descending. She was on her way to the house of her dreams; he was on the Path to Light. As he was going up the steps, the perception of The Presence became more and more intense until it started to be felt as a touchable substance. From the plains, if she so wished, she could see him entering the Source of Light. He dissolved himself in It, dematerializing his body, and he became The Light, as hydrogen in a thermonuclear fusion is converted from matter to radiation. But, in his case, it was not a lethal radiation but, on the contrary, the radiation of Life and Love.

She was sitting on the porch of her small cottage, resting after working in the flower garden. Now he was The Light and from the heights, he fell on her face as the gentle rays of the Sun. She said to her dog,

"How nice it is to rest sitting in the sun and watch our own garden." The dog wagged his tail, confirming the truth of his owner's statement. The light fondled her face gently, and with love warmed her hands and feet. She said to the dog,

"I like autumn weather so much. The sun is so gentle and pleasantly warm. I feel like being with him who has gone to the Unknown to meet certain death."

He returned from this glide through past experiences and again gazed with utter wonder at the Divine Drama performed by Nature in the sky. The colors used for decoration were not simply colors but had many additional properties such as coolness, flatness, height, depth, elasticity, brittleness, sweetness or acidity, softness or hardness, and even depth. It was worth it to be born in this low yet beautiful material dimension, and to go through the hardships in life in order to be allowed to witness its multi-leveled Reality. It didn't matter that the experience couldn't be explained in human language, which is so limited in its possibilities of expression. The experience was not for sharing, so much as for living it, and it reminded him that he too was a part of this whole, that his existence depended on Nature. He remembered a poem he once composed. In a few simple words, he thanked the entire creation for maintaining his physical form, and he also thanked the creator for the wonders of his conscious life:

Thank You
I bow to you my brother trees,
I bow to you sister plants,
I bow to you father dust under my feet,
And the light from the sun,
And the air from the wind,
And the water from the rain.
Thank you all for your sacrifice,
Thank you for being here to meet my needs,

Thank you for supporting my existence.
I am one with you in the inner nature.
I am in the greatest debt to all of you.
I am your humble servant.
Let me always be ready
To do what has to be done.
Let me always see and remember
The Oneness pervading the World.
Let me see no diversity
In the multitude of its forms.
I love and accept all
As The Oneness is lovingly accepting me
As Its extension,
As Its son.

It was time to go back to the present limited reality. Darkness veiled the landscape. Another performance was starting. The stars and the Moon, in the Silence of their appearance, taught the lesson of Infinite Existence, of the Eternal un-changeability of spirit and the vastness of changeable matter spread throughout boundless space.

SEARCHING FOR THE LIMITS

In Northeast Poland, the kingdom of a thousand lakes—Mazury, Autumn is always spectacularly colorful. It is no wonder that it's commonly called 'Golden Autumn'. The trees, before losing their leaves for the winter, become colorful bouquets. Some have reddish colored leaves; some gold, some yellow, and some remain green much longer, giving a healthy contrast to the landscape. The birds, which are now migrating to warmer countries, are having frequent meetings and loudly quarreling while discoursing on their strategy for the long flight.

Meer and Yur were friends, united together by the common tendency to look for opportunities to explore some still existing mysterious things, and by trying to find out how far they could stretch the safety lines of their lives. Meer was on school holidays while Yur ended up

27

on a full semester placement at one of the University Research Farms located on the former property of the late admiral Keatling—Hitler's famous and favorite navy leader. The farm spread over a vast area covering a few lakes, hills and many hectares of cultivated fields. It was surrounded by a dense forest full of wild animals like foxes, deer, wild pigs and bison—Eastern Europe's version of the buffalo.

The Keatlings' residence is a palace that survived WWII and the vandalism of the 'heroic' Red Army passing through. The Admiral's collection of old paintings had been robbed earlier and had probably ended up as wrappers for the bare feet of the uncivilized Russian soldates (Rus.: soldiers). The residence was in the typical Eastern European baroque style, a two-story building full of staircases, small and large rooms, with parquet floors and marble mantle pieces around the open fireplaces and covered by a copper-sheeted gabled roof. There were also stables, cowsheds, storehouses, a mill and a distillery. But the most exciting object for those two was a mausoleum for the former owner of this property, who sadly would never use it. Externally it looked like an eighteenth century solid bower. Inside, behind very heavy forged steel doors, on a podium made from polished black marble, stood a real coffin. For fun Meer and Yur would show it at night to the new girls in residence from their University, who had been placed here like Yur. It was real fun to scare them. First, before the party arrived, Meer would enter the coffin and wait in the deathly silence, relaxed. After everyone was inside the mausoleum, the coffin lid opened with a squeaky noise and Meer began his performance, imitating the hellish noises, screams and howling of the suffering soul of the Nazi admiral. Obviously the result was prearranged. The candles somehow went out and the girls, deathly afraid, looked for safety on Yur's very masculine chest. In such a terrible situation Yur could easily play his role as their heroic protector and comforter.

One Sunday morning both fun and adventure hunters met again, as Meer was able to come on his motorcycle and stay there for the weekend. The weather was fantastic. The sky was clear with no wind. It was promising to be another marvelous day. The difficult question: "What to do?" was drilling their restless minds. As they walked slowly along the beach at the area closest to the mansion, where a small island sat in the middle of the lake, Meer spotted a pheasant. It was a bird imported not long ago from South America and bred on government farms. It would later be released on the potato plantations to clear the Colorado Beetle from them, a very aggressive and rapidly multiplying large insect. Its larvae could destroy tens of hectares of potato plants overnight. The birds were doing a much better job than the American imperialists' pesticides, which were harmful to Nature. The bird itself was very beautiful, about one third the size of a chicken, it had colorful navy blue and orange feathers on its neck and tail, contrasting with the brownish background of its body. Too heavily built for its small wings, the poor thing could fly a maximum of up to ten meters and even that was very low. It was mainly a walking bird.

The sight of the bird, a wonder from another continent, which had probably escaped from the Research Farm enclosure, awakened in both of them a dormant hunting instinct, stored in their subconscious from the times of their early incarnations as hunting tribal humanoids. The hunt started with complete determination and desperation not to give up, but to kill, kill, kill at any expense! Using long sticks as spears, they both tried to hit the bird, which waited patiently about 3 or 4 meters away, and when the deadly weapon was nearly touching its body, it took a step or two forward and then flew several meters away. It seemed as if the bird was fully conscious of playing with them, testing their patience and the depth of their killing *vasana*. Maybe it was not a bird but an *avadhut* who assumed this form in order to help them exhaust this ridiculous tendency. But in those days none of them knew anything about *avadhutas* and *vasanas*. In the meantime the running, throwing spears and disappointment repeated one after another for hours. Well after noon, Meer proposed they give up. There was no point in continuing since no progress had been made in the hunt for so long.

They decided to have a swim. On the bank of the lake lay an old wooden log. It was three meters long, half rotten and partly submerged in the water but it could still float! The idea to use it as a canoe to cross the lake to the island was for them as natural as it was silly. Using a pocketknife they cut off a long, wooden stick, solid enough to be used for rowing, and climbing on the log they immediately started their journey towards the unknown, small, uninhabited island. The log, heavy from the water almost saturating it, along with their weight, sank a few centimeters deeper, but still kept afloat, imitating the canoe of a Neanderthal cave man or rather a mini submarine ridden astride. Fast rowing did not result in fast travel. The heavy vessel moved majestically slow, like a gigantic transoceanic container carrier.

After one hour of hard paddling they arrived at the island. The exploration was a complete disappointment. Nothing interesting—no ruins, no wrecked tank not even a German bunker—only weeds, trees and a lot of ants. Exhausted after their trip, they climbed a tree overhanging the water of the lake. It wasn't possible to sit on the ground, there were ants everywhere: small, large, red, black and yellow. While they were recovering from their ordeal and having a smoke, the weather rapidly changed. In no time a wind started to blow gustily from the direction they'd come towards the opposite bank, which was overgrown by lake cane. The cane was more than one hundred meters in breadth, indicating that the lake continued in that direction as swamps. There was no chance to land there. They decided to try to cross the wind and head towards the cliffs along the road overpass. It was a greater distance but on a direct line to the palace. The wind had made the water choppy. From the island the waves didn't look too bad, only some sixty centimeters in height, but when they embarked upon their log they immediately understood that it was impossible to go together. The log sunk deep enough for the waves to reach their heads. After a short discussion they decided that one of them would stay on at the mercy of the ants, and the other would try to go and send some help. They threw a coin to choose who should go. Meer got the eagle and left the island on an uncertain trip. He was determined to overcome the difficulties and bring his friend to safety by sending a rescue party.

The wind was gradually increasing and the temperature had dropped. Meer was rowing furiously but after half an hour, immersed in cold water to his chest and exposed to the strong, cold wind, he started to slow down. The wind was pushing him to the left, towards the swamps. He was fighting hard, knowing that he was fighting for his life. He was already on the edge of death from hypothermia. There was not much of a chance to survive. He was up against a strong wind, waves, fatigue after the earlier hunt, and now the long and exhausting rowing, cold water and hunger as they had only had a light breakfast in the morning. He landed in the cane field, dense, more than two meters high giving him no visibility. First he tried to use the cane plants to pull himself across the wind to the safety of the bank, but his attempts were in vain. The strong wind pushed him deeper and deeper into the cane and the sharp stalks cut his palms like razor blades. There was no other way than to try to do the almost impossible—cross the swamps. Meer remembered stories from the past told to him by his father about the war, when Sweden had invaded Poland. A small group of Polish warriors had to deliver an important message to the king, so they crossed the swamps by laying flat on the pudding-like black mastic, and pulled themselves along inch by inch by holding onto the moss and the small plants. Not all of them reached solid land. One moment of panic and the smallest mistake would result in being swallowed by the swamp. He now imitated those brave ancestors who had been determined to go through any trouble in order to win freedom for their beloved fatherland.

He slowly inched his prone body towards the dry land. His hands, bluish from the cold, had difficulty getting a good grip on the plants. But he was hard on himself. He was trying to save his life and was determined not to give up. A few times his legs sunk a bit deeper into the semi-liquid swamp endangering his life, but he didn't panic and pulled himself up again. It took him about one and half hours to cross one hundred meters of swamp, which to him was an eternity. Finally he reached dry land. This haven was covered by soft green grass and felt hard under his feet. Exhausted to the point of collapse, he didn't even notice that his body was covered with leeches, which were sucking his blood in delight, but making him even weaker. He started to run towards the palace, if we can call his limping gait a run. It really was a strange run to watch. His whole body was stiff from the cold and his movements were very limited. But nobody saw him, except perhaps the hidden pheasant, which had eluded him earlier. After thirty minutes of this limping run he reached the palace, where Yur's friends were already getting ready to start the search for them. At first nobody recognized Meer; his hair was filled with moss, around his neck hung lake weeds, his skin was bluish-white, and he generally looked like a person who had drowned in the lake at least a week ago. On top of all that there were leeches hanging from everywhere. When they did recognize him the first question was, "Is Yur drowned?" Meer couldn't talk. He was short of breath and trembled uncontrollably from the cold, but somehow he managed to tell his story: "On the island with the ants."

An expedition was sent immediately to rescue Yur in a five-meter long aluminum boat. Meer was taken to the bathroom, washed, and then given a glass of vodka and a big mug of hot black tea to drink. After the cleaning and life-giving drink, the nurse on duty, an ex-serviceman, started to remove the leeches from his body by burning them with his cigarette. He counted forty-four, just like the year in which Meer was happily born into this fascinating World. Meer was then covered with a warm blanket, and drifted off to a refreshing sleep. He had again reached his limit and again won, after balancing on the edge of death, escaping from it thanks only to his strong determination, and maybe to an avadhut who had assumed the form of a colorful bird.

A year later both friends took up winter rock and ice climbing in the Tatra Mountains. This was another domain of unlimited possibilities, offering many chances to experience those blood-freezing emotions. Meer was more eager to take the routes beyond his experience, proficiency and strength. Yur liked to imitate him, and in spite of his fear would sometimes agree to participate in something fairly crazy. They had very poor quality belaying gear, as next to nothing was available on the market those days in Poland. This handicap and also the lack of special clothes increased the risk of their adventures, as in the Tatra Mountains the weather is unpredictable. Even in the middle of summer the temperature can drop below zero and it can snow.

Meer was already acclimatized after staying for over a week in the mountains. He did a few single climbs and took part in a rescue expedition for a German man who had fallen from the tourist track sixty meters down and got stuck in deep snow on the ledge of a four hundred meter high wall. The unfortunate tourist called for help for more than twenty hours, and spent the freezing night, at—18degrees C, unprepared and walking in a deep trench which he had dug for himself in the snow. The snow was deep around him, up to his neck, and it was almost impossible to locate him on this massive wall. Meer discovered his location when wandering alone on a neighboring mountain, less than one kilometer away.

Yur arrived, full of enthusiasm and energy and wanting to catch up but lacking the necessary acclimatization. Their choice for the next day's climb was as irresponsible as scary: the South wall of Death Turnia. It was a famous, difficult wall rising from the stony high valley 280 meters up at an angle of 85 degrees, with many overhangs. It was a clear granite rock with no vegetation, only an occasional bunch of brave grass growing in tiny cracks. It was their good luck that there was not much snow and ice as the entire wall was exposed to the winter sun. The climb for the first 40 meters was a routine one; the belaying stand, the partner up ahead, belaying, climbing to the partner on the stand, change and again climbing first, and so on. But then, about half way up, Yur reported some weakness in his body, dizziness and a lack of self drive. Considering Yur's state, his gradual deterioration, and the lack of an abseiling rope, backing up was more risky then proceeding. Meer decided to climb without being belayed to Yur as he had become more and more mentally withdrawn and physically weak and could not participate.

Some parts of the climb were not too bad for this adventurer. He would ignore the extreme height and concentrate on each point in the actual climb. They had already more than140 meters of air under their feet when Meer found the small, yellow, high altitude flower growing on a twenty-centimeter wide ledge. Only one single flower on this gigantic stony wall! It was a beautiful flower with silver mesh on the stem and leaves. This kind of plant can survive many weeks without any water and stay for a few months under the snow and ice. The Brother Flower, moved by the gentle breeze was silently saying, "Hi, you are a Traveler, but are now on a long by-pass. Never mind, all roads lead to the goal. Don't give up—fight your battles. Remember that you are not alone. There is something ever-present guiding and protecting you. Do you feel it here on this wall? It is everywhere! Go up and do not lose your determination. If you think that it is impossible to win you will lose, if you have faith in yourself you will survive and stay alive. Go brother human, go! Be brave!"

It was already afternoon. He started to climb again, aware that now he was fighting a battle for their safety, for their very lives. Yur, attached to the belaying stand, was passively gazing in deep apathy at the rocky valley. He seemed not to be even interested in watching his partner climb. Meer, in order to have at least a minimum of protection, was climbing only half the length of the rope, twenty meters, then hammering into the wall as many pitons as possible to reduce the length of an eventual fall, which is always double the distance from the last piton to the climbing person. After he had set up a new stand, he abseiled down to undo Yur as well as remove as much hardware on the way as possible: pitons, carbines and wire slings. Then having Yur on one end of the rope, he climbed up the same way but this time using the rope as a handrail and sliding the self-locking knot on a sling attached to his homemade harness. After reaching the top belaying stand he had to pull up a semi-conscious Yur. This was done by putting the rope across his back while he was in a crouching position and stretching his legs to a standing position, then securing the rope on a lockable carbine by a special knot to prevent it sliding down under Yur's weight. In this way Yur was lifted to the top belaying stand inch by inch and again tied up to it. This was repeated again and again. Yur was able to cooperate only a little bit but even this was a great help for Meer. Yur tried to always face the wall when Meer was lifting him up.

At one point Meer found a real challenge. Above him was a slab of granite, which had separated itself from the main rock but was still hanging on a small ledge, which lay over the very high 'nothingness'. There was no possible way to go over it as it was high and at a very sharp angle, and there were no steps or holds to use to climb it.

Usually the leading climber used his partner as a ladder to climb over it. Meer understood that his only chance was to jump up and grab the edge of it and then lift his body up. But a thin coat of ice glazed the edge. Having neither choice nor time to waste, Meer jumped. He hung from his right hand and waited for the ice to melt under the heat of his hand. Below him was air, a lot of air and a semi-conscious partner at his mercy. He knew that the rope was not good enough for long falls as it was already fatigued. After some long minutes he started to feel the roughness of rock under his fingers. He lifted himself up and sat on the edge of the slab breathing heavily. He had again won a little battle. There were still 40 meters to the top of Death Turnia. He lifted Yur slowly to safety. They reached the summit well before sunset.

They had climbed the Southern wall of this difficult mountain with such a suggestive name, and there was no death at all. There, on the summit, Meer, relaxing after the struggle, started to feel very tired, even exhausted. Suddenly the world around him started to swirl and he lost consciousness, falling face down on the snow. Strangely Yur now quickly started to regain his strength and he in turn was able to help Meer to get up. Later an expert told them about Tatra Mountain's phenomenon that a strong wind from the North could create a semi-vacuum on the Southern slopes. This was the cause of many accidents and even the deaths of some very experienced and fit mountaineers. Their climb down the North Slope was not difficult as it was only the advanced tourist track.

Again Meer had tested that special charm of reaching the limits of the body pushed by the mind to the extreme, and again proved to himself that even an average person like himself can perform impossible tasks when his mind is focused, determined and backed up by strong faith: "I can and I will!"

We should agree, dear readers, that this discovery was worth the price of suffering and struggle, but we don't encourage anyone to do the same. We can agree that the mind, under the control of the will, can lead the brave ones not only to safety in an emergency but ultimately to indescribable Freedom, in total and permanent union with the

Highest, this ever-present and all-pervading something about which small, Yellow Brother Flower had talked on the almost vertical, solid granite wall of Death Turnia.

The question for us remains unanswered but always open:

"Would we go and fight the battle with our own mind?" The prize is incredible but the task is very tough. It may help us to remember what Brother Flower said,

"If you think it is impossible you will lose, if you have faith and determination, nothing is impossible."

THE LESSONS

During the first years after the Second World War, it was as normal, for children in Europe, to play with explosives and abandoned firearms lying everywhere, as it is now common to watch TV or go to McDonald's for a Big Mac. The boys, who were obviously attracted to all this army junk, had great fun, although they were also exposed to great danger. Luckily TV was not yet invented, so no child was ever bored.

One small blonde boy was also playing. Many of his friends had lost their hands, and sometimes even their lives. He had more luck, because he had only burned his eyes. The blast from the explosion burned his face, blinding him at the age of four. A week later doctors discharged him from the hospital as a hopeless case, and he started to learn how to go about in permanent darkness. It was a sort of play, this experience of the invisible world, to move and to find needed things. But he remembered well how the world looked and could imagine what was happening when he heard sounds or smelled fragrances. A family friend who was a Christian priest came and composed a prayer for him. It was a nice, poetic, very humble declaration of surrender, of acceptance, and a few words of gratitude for the awareness of his conscious existence. He liked its words. They flew with love towards God, about whom he'd heard the priest talking to his father:

"Everything is in the hands of God. This terrible accident may become one day a blessing for the boy. We don't know what He is intending to do with him. We should have faith and do our duty well. Not even one hair can fall from his head without the will and knowledge of the Heavenly Father."

The boy repeated this prayer as a mantra all day long. He accepted his fate without rebelling and feeling sorry for himself. What could his complaints change? It had happened and it was his fault. The boy had wanted to blast the hollow pear tree stump in the garden. The gunpowder line had not worked as it should have. It had probably gotten moist. He went to the stump to check what was wrong. Inside, a tiny spark was slowly crawling along the fuse. Why he blew on it, he could not explain. It just happened. When he recovered, his eyes were like hard-boiled eggs, but it was not painful. In darkness, he saw the Light and felt the Presence. He talked to It. It became his closest friend, his only companion during his lonely days when his parents were gone to work. He offered his prayers to this Presence; he shared with It all his small happiness and pains. People say that God comes to see us in our houses without ringing the bell. But in the small blonde boy's case, He came in the form of Presence, announcing Himself by a loud, thunder-like explosion.

A few months later, the boy noticed a difference when his mother was changing the dressing on his face. It was the difference between the window and the wall. The difference was in the intensity of the darkness.

"What does it mean?" He thought. It meant that his eyes had started to see light! He didn't tell this revelation to anybody, because they would say that he was, as always, imagining it. He was already known as a person with a greater imagination than knowledge. For him, it proved to be the truth that the darkest hour is just before the dawn. Gradually his eyesight returned to normal. In time, his vision even became exceptionally sharp. Years later he reached Olympic standards in shooting targets, but because of a particular complexity in the situation, he was never able to use a sporting rifle for long, and instead got familiar with the Russian made machine-gun, AK-47 'Kalashnikov'.

The doctors in the hospital could not believe this. From a medical point of view, it was not possible.

"Probably it's not him but his brother," they thought, but he didn't have a brother. It was in a communist country, where miracles couldn't happen, as it would undermine the indisputable authority of the communist ideology, which is based on a godless philosophy of dialectical materialism. Who there, in those days, knew anything about the power of surrender, or of accepting fate with a boldly lifted head? Who was brave enough to even think that behind everything is Him—a Father, and that He decides? For Him nothing is impossible.

A few years later, this once blind, blonde haired boy became a high school student. Because of his independent nature, he could not accept the golden rule of his teachers:

"Do as I say, not as I do, and as most students do, then you will be accepted by others as well as by me." He was asked to change schools. He had to travel eighteen kilometers every day to attend school in a different town. Every day he walked two-and-a-half kilometers from his home to the railway station and then two-and-a-half kilometers to school.

One morning he was late for his train. From the road he saw it leaving and started to run. He was fast, and good in sports. The last two train carriages were for cargo. He tried to jump onto the steps of the last one. Unfortunately a guard was there. The guard tried to kick him to prevent him from unlawfully jumping onto a step. This boy hardly ever gave up. He decided to run further and jump onto the platform at the front of the second cargo carriage, hoping that from there he would be able to go safely to the passenger carriages. He did it in an air-borne marine style jump. Breathing rapidly, exhausted after the run, he was resting on the platform when the hit came. Because of the boy's disobedience, the infuriated guard had stopped the train by activating the emergency brakes. The boy was not holding on and lost his balance. He was thrown onto the greasy carriage bumper, as he put both his arms around it, while his legs, hanging down, were dragging on the line. His school bag fell under the train. After a while and because of the bulkiness of his winter overcoat, he lost his grip and fell under the train, hitting his head on a steel track. He lost consciousness. Now he was lying across the line, awaiting his destiny—to be cut in half. After a fraction of a second something made him open his eyes. The large silver wheel was rolling slowly toward him. He had no doubt that it was his end and accepted it as his unavoidable fate, which he had no chance to escape from. He lost consciousness again, but his body, answering to some unknown, mysterious command, contracted, forming a fetus-shaped ball as he rolled between the tracks. The train stopped. There was a lot of shouting and whistling. The white steam enveloped the entire station. He regained consciousness and, after finding his school bag, ran to safety into the milk-like steam. He was anxious about what would happen if the guard caught him. But it was not his time. Not yet.

Time passed. He went through many bumpy experiences but, in spite of the conviction of his teachers that he was a hopeless student, he finished school, passing the matriculation exams as second in his class. A few years later he was in the third year of his University studies. It was Easter vacation. He used every vacation as a great opportunity to go to his beloved mountains. This time he decided to go to Czechoslovakia and see the highest of the Tatra Mountains. The landscape there was so rigid, so stony, with one thousand meter high walls rising from bottomless valleys. It was difficult to believe that it was really in Europe. The elevation was not so great, but the peaks looked like real Himalayan giants.

The spring was very sunny, but up high there was still a lot of snow and ice in the gullies and chimneys of the slopes and cliffs. Snow, which melted during daytime and froze at night, seemed to be built of billions of small sugar like crystals. He was with a friend. They had climbed a peak called Vysoka (in Slovak—high). Now they were descending towards the Slovak High Country and a charming small town named Stary Smokovec (in Slovak—Old Dragon's Dwelling).

His friend and hiking partner was waiting thirty meters below him, unsure of how to proceed, as below him there was a cliff. But he was not aware of this, and deliberately entered a strip of icy snow and started to slide down, pretending he was skiing. It was fun. He was good at skiing, but this time he only had his hiking boots on. Suddenly he lost his balance and fell. The ice was now like polished glass going down at a forty-degree angle. He immediately tried to stop sliding by using his elbows, but without success. The sliding became faster and faster; first at thirty, then forty, then at the speed of fifty kilometers an hour. He noticed that the strip of ice and snow ended in a cliff, and realized that he was sliding towards certain death. He was holding two cameras in his hands. He didn't panic. He knew it wouldn't help. He had already done everything to stop this deadly ride. There were holes in the elbows of his jumper, which was torn. His elbows were bleeding. There was nothing to do but accept his fast approaching destiny, and watch this 'movie', the last in this life. He calmly accepted that he was going to die. Soon. Very soon! Now! He shouted to his partner who stood paralyzed watching the unfolding drama:

"Go away, don't try to stop me or we'll both die!" Being on the edge of the cliff his partner could easily imagine the outcome of the situation.

Then something extraordinary happened. In an instant, he found himself standing on the very edge of the cliff. He saw too, very clearly, the bottom of the cliff. He even thought that someone falling there would have a long fall, and dwelt for a while on the idea of how it would be to fall with outstretched arms like some sky divers do. He looked up and noticed someone sliding fast in the gully towards the edge of cliff. He was shocked when recognizing himself. How it is possible? He thought. I am here and my body is sliding there on the ice?

Then he noticed two boulders forming a step in a gully on the very edge of the cliff. The snow had melted around the boulders, forming a gap of about thirty centimeters wide. He realized that there might be a slight chance to survive if he could manage to put his legs into those gaps. It was silly to imagine that it was going to be easy. Sliding so fast, the chance was probably one in a million, or even less. He also knew he would badly break his legs if he miraculously succeeded with this feat.

In an instant he was again back in his body, sliding towards his unavoidable destiny. From this moment on he was practically unconscious of what was happening to him. He was like a lifeless corpse, controlled externally by some mysterious force. Later he didn't remember anything. The boy awoke from the shock, hanging head down from the edge of the cliff, still holding the two cameras firmly in his hands. "Where am I? Is it Heaven, or still Earth?" he thought, and started to crawl back from this precarious position, which was suitable only for bats living in the Tatra Mountain caves. He wondered which leg was broken. He felt a pain on his forehead because he had hit the rocks with it. "It must still be Earth. It's too small a pain for Hell and in Heaven there's no pain at all."

"A miracle? Again a miracle?" Both legs were unharmed. How was it possible? At such speed even high carbon steel would break! He didn't know that 'Father' had already incarnated again on Earth in a far away tropical country. He didn't know that he was predestined to meet Him and let Him guide him. He didn't know that he would work for Him, which was why he couldn't die so soon, in spite of his appointment with Yama, God of Death, as recorded in his astrological horoscope. 'Father' in the Guru's body still needed him for some reason and wanted him to stay for some time on this planet called Earth.

Some years later, after already meeting the Guru, he was getting ready to leave a worldly life and join His ashram in India, and there complete the jobs which He advised him to do. Three days before his airplane was to leave, he broke his right arm. It was a very bad fracture. The doctors joked,

"It's the best X-ray of the year. It couldn't be better! Bones are in powder!" It would take a few operations, a bone graft from his hip, and a long and only partial recovery. He was told that he would never be able to work as before with his hands. He again accepted it. He didn't feel sorry for himself, but rather waited with curiosity for what the Guru would give him to do now. Unexpectedly he was asked to write an article intended for the Guru's birthday souvenir. Surprise! He? But he knew so little English! He started to write using his left hand, for how could he refuse? Was it him? Certainly not! It was his Guru, his eternal guide, his way, vehicle and destination, working through him! Some of his associates laughed saying it was utter craziness and that he was on his way to the mental asylum, but he didn't mind their comments. At first, his story was published in the ashram's monthly magazine and later translated into many languages.

He was crying from happiness, from love for the Guru, from the love in his heart germinating towards all beings. The Guru agreed to his joining Him in the programs in Singapore, and then to stay permanently in His ashram in India. He had pins, bolts and stabilizing bone bars sticking out of his hand, he was in plaster and bandages, but he was the happiest person, not only in his town but also probably on the entire Earth. In spite of being in a hospital bed, he could already work for Him. There was nothing more to want. He had learned some of his lessons. No doubt more would come. Let them come. But he was on the highway to Freedom. He was on his way towards the Guru hidden in his heart.

SADHANA ON WHEELS

Traveling with Guru on a bus tour caravan across the hills, mountains, and plains of the Indian subcontinent is a unique, exotic and spiritually rewarding experience. Frequenting the presence of an Avatar is, in itself, an intense sadhana, and traveling in the vastness of India is equal to doing hard core tapas. Sometimes the buses have to cover a distance of over 500 km per day. This can be an exhausting experience, and especially exhausting for those who are only visiting India.

In our own countries, we often live in air-conditioned houses and work in air-conditioned offices. Refreshing cold drinks are readily available straight from the refrigerator, as well as savory meals from a favorite bistro or restaurant. In the extreme tiredness of many hours of travel in the heat, squeezed in between boxes of books and sound equipment in an already overcrowded bus, thirsty due to a shortage of safe drinking water, with a minimum of food, and very often experiencing the discomforts of colds or stomach disorders so common in the tropics, our real inner personalities manifest themselves externally.

Under such conditions, attachment to bodily comforts and needs are so strong that we can easily forget our Satguru's oneness with all creation. We often do not remember that, according to His teachings, everything is Him dancing on a screen of space as myriad forms of individuals and things. The unreal is only a reflection of the Real in the medium of time and space not more permanent than a picture in a mirror.

Guru is in the full awareness of His identity with The Oneness. He, for our sake, has manifested Himself in a form appearing similarly limited as our own human forms. We forget that if He is The Oneness, He is also the food we consume, the air we breathe, and the bus we are traveling in. We are Him also. Our fellow traveler standing for many hours, between seats because of the lack of sitting space is Him, too. Before meals we chant: "Brahman panam, Brahma havir . . ." and immediately after the chant we eat, then we throw our leftover food on the floor of the bus, and let it rot there together with the discarded paper wrapping and abandoned, dirty clothes. We are all on a spiritual quest. Aren't we? We are living in diversity but trying to experience unity in The Oneness. We want to find our Guru in our hearts. How can we expect to achieve this if we allow ourselves to travel in a dirty, smelly bus because of our bodily fatigue and lack of mindfulness? Is it possible to gain mental stability and purity— conditions indispensable for spiritual progress—without keeping a high standard of external cleanliness and order of the things we use?

Our minds automatically attune to vibrations from our external surroundings. We are living in the state of delusion, in the state of unconscious sleep, as Guru used to say, but at least, theoretically, we know about the Truth of The Oneness. Let us remember it always and be alert and respectful to others, and everything we use. Let us start anew our great journey towards the Guru within us by keeping ourselves, and the buses we are traveling in, in clean order.

One day, I hope we will meet together in the Unity of Peace of The Oneness, and that we will get there in spotlessly clean "buses". Happy journey, brothers and sisters, towards our Ultimate Destination!

Best wishes from your younger brother.

Bus Cleaner

RETURN

Clinical death.

S eemingly nothing could have predicted such a turn of affairs. The heart operation proved to be successful and after two days Jan was transferred from the Intensive Care Ward into a General Ward. His heart failure happened in the evening, when after having his supper Jan was dozing, covered with a few blankets. The ward was cold, because in spite of being late Autumn the central heating was not yet functioning. The hospital tried to save, for really cold weather, its modest reserves of their allotment of coal and coke. The nurse on duty, who brought some medicine to his neighbor, discovered accidentally that Jan was not showing any signs of life. She set off an alarm and all went on high alert. The doctors, without the slightest delay, started reanimation procedures. Jan was connected to an EKG monitor and they started electric heart massage. In the meantime he was connected to an artificial heart-lung machine. Attempts to save him started as the normal routine always used in such cases, hoping that his brain had not suffered any permanent changes caused by lack of oxygen due to suspended blood circulation. His body did not respond at all to the medical procedures and Dr. Fisherman, his surgeon, almost lost hope of bringing him back to life.

There, where he regained consciousness was quiet and still. Jan felt neither pain nor cold. A pleasant sound of calm, gentle music was coming from all directions. Strange indeed was this music. Never before had he heard anything similar. It sounded like a full of wonder whisper of Nature over the splendor of the Creator. It was like the joyful voice of all Existence; happy because of its immensity in boundless beingness. Jan, hovering under the ceiling, noticed below, the body of a middle-aged man lying on a hospital bed covered with blankets. To his great surprise this stranger was himself. For Jan it became obvious that this something that lay there like a bag of sand was only his body and he himself was separated from it, and existed totally independently.

Meeting Light-Being

He started to ascend. At the beginning it happened slowly, but with the lapse of time the speed of this movement became almost infinite. Contours of the ward faded away and melted into a dark homogenous substance. After a while, this substance formed a sort of tunnel-funnel. Besides it, nothing existed. Jan was surrounded by an absolute vacuum of nonexistence. Strangely, in spite of it all he did not feel terrified or even anxious. He was enveloped in an unbelievably deep 'coat' of peaceful fulfillment. By the power of intuition he knew that everything was as it should be.

After some time he noticed a light at the end of the tunnel. It wasn't a normal light that came from the sun or from an electrical lamp. It was an ever-present light. Even though he had only seen it at the end of the tunnel, he felt that it must also permeate darkness. Having no better word, Jan described this light as golden. It was a pleasantly warm light, favorably disposed and tolerant. It was also a very loving light. Jan wanted to reach it as fast as possible. He felt that there was his place; that from there he had come and there he had been unconsciously aiming all his life. When he reached the end of the tunnel he understood that this light was not a physical manifestation but The Presence Itself. He felt happy as never before. It was It! For this he had waited long years during his life on Earth. The Presence-Light enveloped him and filled his very beingness with Love Divine. Jan lost himself in delight of Bliss of this ultimate union. Only one thing, that he was still conscious, remained. It was a feeling of experiencing undisturbed existence in full awareness.

Light-Presence transformed Itself into a form of a man dressed in white. His face radiated with Divine splendor. Jan, knowing not how nor when, found himself on His lap. There he was cuddled with incredible love, like a small baby by a parent. In spontaneous dazzle he understood that He is God, that He is The Creator of Infinity, that only for his sake assumed a form of a Divine Person being not a person. He understood that he had known Him from the beginning of time, which meant eternally, that his life is happening just in Him, that he isn't a separately existing human, that he is a part of a Whole without a beginning and end, a part which is itself this very Perfect Entirety.

Surrounding His golden aura resounded softly in sweet Silence:

"Son, it is good that you have come. Always remember that I do exist and that I love you. But it isn't yet your time for a return home. You must go back there where you were living and finish what you have started. Your dear ones still need you."

His mind was absolutely still. He knew that whatever He told him would be only his warmest desire to follow and he would do it without a second thought.

"Let it be, as You wish," answered Jan in the language of Silence. "I also love You immensely." No word passed between them. All communication was on a level of passing thoughts directly, mind-to-mind; however all was very clear and easily understood.

Suddenly all faded in the lackness of shapes. Now all space filled a dense, milky fog. Jan slowly walked through it but did not know where he was or to where he was going. The memory of meeting The Absolute in a human shining body stunned him but at the same time assured him that there, on earth, is nothing worthy of his regret. Real happiness was only here, and here was also his real home.

In the fog appeared a tall man. He was dressed in a robe which was so long that it touched the ground. It was loose, airy and the color of fire. The man's head was covered with long but rather thin hair and his beard was fluffy, as are beards on old sacred church paintings of middle-aged Christian saints. His face radiated a joy usually felt at the sight of dearest ones. Jan immediately recognized in him his Old Teacher. Seeing him he also became visibly glad. How he could forget him? Through many incarnations they were bound by friendship and had deep respect and love for each other.

"My dear friend, it is so enjoyable to meet you again. By God's grace we once more have a bit of time to have a short 'class'. Your Guru wishes that you see now a 'film' of your entire life. After you evaluate your past actions we will briefly analyze some more important issues concerning your future." They sat on a bench, which had emerged from the fog.

Talk with a Teacher

Teacher embraced Jan, pulling him with love towards his chest. The fog disappeared and instead, before his eyes, materialized a bluish, transparent pane. It reached to the sky. Moving pictures started to appear on the pane. Because the projection was four dimensional, including time, Jan started to live his life again while fully participating in it.

Despite the awfully fast speed, he felt as he did when all those events took place in his life. Time now had a different value. In a few minutes, maybe even seconds, Jan experienced again the full forty years of his existence on Earth. He was a child who was wandering around his parent's house, peeping on the private lives of caterpillars crawling, on the lives of vegetables, and on lizards hiding under rocks. He was a boy who tried to converse with dogs, cats and household birds: ducks and geese. He started to attend school, his first love; a rendezvous on the bank of a river and in a cemetery. Kisses and caresses. Conflicts with teachers, who disliked him asking questions. They all tried hard to subjugate his independent nature and force him into 'normal' boundaries. He was now a grown man and married.

His boring job was not chosen freely. Political authorities nominated him County President. Birth of his son. Tragic car accident. Death of son and his wife. Loss of drive to continue life. Depression. Sudden burst of uprising against an unfair political system and marshal law. He who always refused to support the ruling country's 'red burgoos' while trying to earn a living is now condemned as a former member of the Communist party. Forced immigration. Wandering through foreign countries, scraping together pounds and dollars. Difficulties with adaptation to Western mentality—often even discrimination. Collapse of communism in Eastern Europe. Return to his own country. Starting a new family and birth of a daughter. Own business. Stress. Heart disease. Operation. Death.

The Teacher moved on the bench and inquired: "Are you pleased with all you just now saw? Why do you think that life is not square with you? That was you who by your own thoughts, actions and feelings in the present and previous incarnations created circumstances, which were so painful. We call this karma. It is not a punishment for wrong doings but simply interdependence between causes and results. So the future can be programmed and modeled by controlled attention on desired outcomes, focused thoughts and monitoring our emotions, as they are indicators if we are on a 'right track'. Despite the persistent claims of many partly enlightened people, we all have the unquestionable freedom to make choices. No Higher Power predetermines the events of our lives. We all make agreements with others before incarnating regarding major events to have opportunities to learn certain lessons, but when we are on Earth we can act in many ways in each 'preset' situation. So the results can be very much different. We all belong to this same unimaginable reality, which has 'roots' in higher dimensions but also manifests as the material Universe. Life there, on Earth is only a sort of school. By being exposed to challenges, we grow into, deserved by all, the status of sons and daughters of The Absolute—divine beings. We pass many stages and levels during our lifetime. We return to Earth life after life to correct failed 'exams' and to heal ourselves from ridiculous tendencies and desires. If we look on our existence from a perspective of Truth Absolute then we realize that individuality is simply an illusion. God wanting to experience His unending Existence 'dressed up' Himself into a body of the Universe, created from Himself. Everything is Him! This illusion is very misleading. We do not feel our divinity and oneness with the entire creation because we build around our Inner Being—The Self impenetrable shield of thoughts, desires, beliefs, attitudes and prejudices. It is called ego—personality. Ego has its own intelligence and is capable of pretending it is the very Self. Those who voluntarily get rid of selfish desires, start to respect others' beliefs as equal to their own, develop an attitude towards others of love and respect, drop prejudices and start to consider the entire world as their own and all beings as their most close relatives, will become blessed tools of God's will and His Grace will 'nourish' them and empower them continuously. They will serve the world expecting nothing in return. They will not take to heart praise nor abuse of selfish and ignorant relatives in The Oneness. The very privilege of helping those who are in need or who suffer will be their source of immense delight.

"Your Guru wants you to comprehend this and, during the remaining span of your life on Earth, strive to practice this in day-to-day life. Know that after physical body death nothing can be taken to astral worlds. There one goes only with the treasure of good merits, which 'is' in his heart. In the future you are going to be given an opportunity to not be attached to neither things nor people and learn to selflessly serve them. Accept this chance! But now go back. Your family is in an agony of fear. They worry that you are dead, your daughter Maja and wife love you very much. I know that you also love them but please also try to express this more clearly and more often. People need assurances that they are loved more than they need air to breathe! Unexpressed love is like candy remaining in a wrapping paper or in a glass jar with a lid closed on it. It is obvious that no one can lick candy through a wrapper or through a glass jar. All know that candy is sweet but testing it is not possible. Go now! Go my dear! You have a lot of work ahead of you".

Jan got up, turned towards his Teacher to thank him for giving him instructions, but where they were seated there was no bench and already no Teacher, only dense, impenetrable fog saturated by whirling heavenly music as before they met.

Meeting his son and first wife.

Jan started to walk ahead. In the fog human shapes of a woman and a boy appeared, Jan instantly recognized his first wife and son. They also recognized him.

"Daddy!" said the boy with excitement. "I am so happy to see you again. I love you so much. Don't be sad that we went away. You understand now that we still exist. We are here even more alive than there on Earth. Our accident was pre-planned. The suffering you experienced after the accident was necessary for you to make the next step on The Path of spiritual development. We agreed with mummy to help you and sacrificed one of our incarnations. It was fantastic!"

"Be happy Jan" said his first wife. "Try to care more for those who are now closest to you. Try to find more time to spend with your daughter. I also love her! We are all one huge family—we belong to the same group of souls. Always remember this. Now go. On the other side of the bridge is a dimension of no return and we must go back there. Your time has not yet arrived." Saying so she turned, showing him a bridge over the abyss. Strange was this bridge. It was made of flowers and smoke of fragrant incense. It appeared to have no strength, but when Janek's first wife and their son entered, it did not collapse, only started to pulsate a greenish light, like a faulty neon light over the shopping mall.

Jan wanted to cross it and stay there permanently. It was so peaceful here. There was no fear about future events and the past was remembered without grief. Even thinking about past enemies did not raise negative emotions like hatred or envy. The past was remembered as something unreal, like not so good dream from sleep at night. Why go back? For what is business and money? There on Earth is only unending struggle, only 'swimming' in 'muddy waters full of sharks'. Not even one moment of peace! Continuous stress! Plenty of worries!

"Don't delay, go now, go!" the voice of his first wife sounded from the bridge. He looked forward to check if the road, on which they advised him to go, existed. The road existed; sandy and wavy. Jan decided to obey and started to walk. Being-Light also told him that his time of return is not due. He wanted to tell his first wife and their son at least goodbye, but where the bridge on which they were standing was, was only a bottomless abyss. The bridge built of flowers had disappeared.

Coming back

Dr. Fisherman turned to the nurse in charge of the Intensive Care Ward and said:

"Thank God he is coming back. I caught another 'fish'". On the EKG monitor reappeared a dancing red line—showing heart activity again. After a while, the doctor switched off heart support. Jan opened his eyes. Around his bed people were standing. There were doctors, nurses and his second wife with their daughter Maja. All of them were smiling towards him with sympathy. His daughter said, wiping her tears:

"My daddy! I love you so much. We were so afraid that you would pass away. You were not breathing at all! We just arrived to visit you and here was such turmoil. All were running around and connecting you to some machinery."

"What happened?" asked Jan. "Why do all of you stare at me? I only had a strange dream! Did I say something when dreaming? But it was ONLY a dream! Wasn't it?"

"Mr. Jan, I must tell you the truth." said Dr. Fisherman. "According to what is known to contemporary modern medicine, you were dead and should have stayed in this condition forever. Usually human brains stop functioning after being deprived of oxygen for four-five minutes, but you were not breathing for at least eight or ten minutes, so you should be 'officially' dead for eternity. What were you 'dreaming' about? Please tell me. Did you dream about meeting someone? Have you seen some light?" Jan did not reply, but only looked straight into Dr. Fisherman's eyes.

"Is it possible that he knows? Maybe it was not a dream?" Thought Jan. Whatever it was he did not want to share with anyone his personal experience of death, meeting Light-Presence and his strange return to life. Who would believe that he is not hallucinating? They would only make fun of him! But now he knew that potentially he is also this Golden Light and that there, not here, is his real home, that there is much better.

Story of Maja.

A few years passed. Jan continued to run his modest, petite company. His heart did not cause him any more trouble. He was more relaxed and dedicated more time to his family. He wanted to catch up after years of being in a mad hurry—a 'rat race'; years when he rarely had any time for playing together or even loose talks. Often now he sat with his daughter in front of a fireplace telling her stories or listening to hers. She had an incredible imagination and was able to tell such stories that if they were written down and published she would soon find very dedicated readers and her stories would be as famous as those of Andersen. Once Jan decided to tell her about his strange experience in the hospital. Daughter was listening with great attention. This time she did not disturb him by asking hundreds of questions, only watched him strangely and with warmth in her eyes. When he finished, Maja embraced daddy and kissed him on both cheeks declaring with feeling:

"I also know this Being-Light! I also once ran towards this light which is a Person. Do you remember daddy last fall when I had a bad flu and was laying in fever? For a few days the fever would not subside and at the end I was so exhausted that I started to freak out and lose consciousness. First I was lifted up to the ceiling and from there I watched my sweating body spread on a bed. I believed that it must be a dream but after some time I found myself in a tunnel, moving fast towards the end, far away. At the end of it I saw light, growing stronger and stronger as I moved closer and closer. When I finally arrived I realized that this light was in fact a Light-Being, which radiated love. Light-Being was talking to me but now I do not remember a word. I also don't remember how this Being looked; I only remember a golden light radiating from It. Later, on a green-green meadow I met your mum, Grandma Teresa. I never met her in my life because she passed away before I was born, but there I recognized her immediately, like I knew her before for a really long time. She told me that a few years back you, daddy, lost your son from a first marriage and your first wife. She told me that I must go back. If I die now you would not survive again such tragedy and die of a heart attack. She told me that you have an assignment to do, something very important, and must stay alive for many more years. So I agreed to return, though I really wanted to stay there and the decision for me was not easy. There it was so nice, clean and peaceful. There a fever did not disturb me! Dearest daddy, all this is real, it is truth that we never die. It is impossible that two people have such similar dreams. Light-Being exists and loves us very much; Light-Being loves us truly! We all are His children! One day we will all return there where is our real home. There is no need to be afraid of death. This is nothing bad. It is liberation from our warmed up, often ill and problem causing body; it is liberation from suffering on Earth. There no one ceases to exist. It is only a shift in dimension, a change of 'address' to a higher level of unending existence. There a soul rests, for a while, enjoying unimaginable happiness. It is Heaven. But all or almost all, after a long or short rest, return to Earth to continue learning new lessons and perfecting their minds. Is it not fun? I like it!"

A Fair in Leipzig.

One more year passed. Jan decided to participate in the Commercial Exhibition in the German town of Leipzig held there in May. He had something unique to demonstrate to the European community. His business developed an electronic device that detects weak infra-sounds, which the Earth's core generates before tectonic tremors occur. This kind of device could save the lives of many miners. Until now Jan was only selling it in Poland, mostly to coal mines in Silesia.

In Leipzig Jan met a friend from his University who had immigrated to Canada and also had recently decided to return to his fatherland. Friend also owned a small company in Poland and came to Leipzig to present his device of an innovative design measuring light temperature. Friend told Jan that last year in Seattle, USA he met a Guru from India whose disciples considered as being an Avatar—an incarnation of God. Guru is an embodiment of love, compassion and kindness. Jan's friend told him that Guru, who once a year makes a worldwide tour visiting Japan, Singapore, Australia, Spain, Finland and England will soon have public programs in July in London.

After returning from the Leipzig fair, Jan started preparations for a full family trip to London. He booked a room in one of the small hotels in Kensington; his wife and daughter applied for passports. In the middle of July they left in the early morning from the Warsaw airport Okęcie on a flight to Paris. There they visited the Notre Dame Cathedral, the Louvre and in the evening took an express train under the La Manche (English Channel) to London. They arrived at night, had dinner in a nearby pub and, after good night's rest, they went for a walk to Bishop Park, which is on the Northern side of the Thames River. Maja was delighted walking among the immense variety of flowers growing on numerous flowerbeds. The weather was fantastic—middle of summer. Guru's program was going to start in three days. He decided to show his family the most important attractions of this big cosmopolitan town. He knew London from times of his exile. They visited the British Museum, the Gallery of Wax Figures, Westminster Palace and Parliament with the Tower of Big Ben. In the evening they enjoyed listening to the famous tenor Pavarotti. After the concert they went for a Mexican burrito in Trafalgar Square and talked with hippies splashing water from a pond with fountains under the Nelson monument. The next day they took a boat trip on the Thames River to see a bit of London's panorama and do some shopping in the famous exclusive 'Harrods'.

Meeting Guru.

On the afternoon of the third day was Gurus' first public program. Jan knew the location as the organizers had sent him, on his request, directions. It was in an old Masonic Hall in Kew. The air in the hall was saturated with the smoke of oriental incenses.

On the floor, a few steps into the entrance doors, was a silk cloth, and on it a huge brass plate, a jar with water, a smaller plate with some flowers and a carefully folded white cotton towel. A group of white dressed people chanted with devotion and concentration the Sanskrit mantra: Om Shivayari Namaha . . . Jan and his family took seats close to the stage, which was spread with strange musical instruments and many microphones on low stands. The chanting of the mantra increased in intensity. After a while they noticed at the entrance a massive person dressed in white. His face was dark brown—almost black. It was Sat-Guru, known to Jan from a photo sent by the program organizers. Behind Him they noticed a few people wearing red trailing attire. Many devotees from many countries on six continents, as the organizers informed Jan, considered Guru as the embodiment of Divine Love and the most humble person who ever lived on Earth, and also the greatest. Jan looked on this as in a trance. He forgot where he was and who he was and why he was even there. He had no doubt. The Guru radiated the same Light that he had met on the 'other side', from where not many returned. The Guru stepped on a brass plate and closed His eyes. Kneeling in front of Him a young girl poured water on His feet from a jar, dried them with a towel and placed on each foot a magnificent burgundy peony. Another person started to wave a flame of burning camphor in front of the Guru. Another person hung a garland made of white and red roses and carnations on the Guru's neck. When the Guru turned towards the stage many hands stretched towards Him. The Guru touched some, walked slowly distributing smiles to both sides and exchanging looks. Occasionally He made to some, in plain English, personal remarks.

Just before Guru entered the stage He noticed Jan timidly standing with his family and walked straight towards him. He placed His palm on Jan's chest where his heart was and asked with a concern in voice:

"Isn't it painful anymore?" Jan was not able to respond. He was standing like a pillar of salt from Biblical Sodom. His throat contracted in a spasm and he was only able to look with wide, surprised eyes.

"How does He know Polish?" Jan thought, stunned.

Going into big business and visiting India.

It was a foggy morning. Jan parked his 'Škoda' sedan in front of the Post Office and went to check his mailbox. He found there a bill for his Internet connection, another bill for a TV license and an invitation from an engineer friend for his son's wedding in Białystok. In his mailbox was also a very elegant envelope from England. On the top left corner was a sticker with the name of the sender: Safety Equipment Specialists R.S Thompson & Co., Glasgow, UK.

A contract to supply a huge number of his detectors to England was signed two months later after a banquet in an executive suite of the 'Forum Hotel' in downtown Warsaw. A month later Jan accepted a similar offer from the United States and South Africa. Money started to pour into his company bank account in large quantities. Jan's family could now afford to travel without skimping on other expenses. They decided to visit India. His daughter Maja wanted very much to see the Guru's ashram.

They landed in Mumbai. India welcomed them with warm and humid weather. It was 39°C. The air was sticky from humidity, smoky from a burned pail of rubbish on the side streets, and some other unidentified fragrances. They stayed for one night in the small hotel 'Arjuna' and Jan immediately went to the Central Railway Station to book sleeping class tickets on 'Malabar Express' to Trivandrum, the capital of Kerala state for the next day. Maja and his wife went out to buy some fruits and a couple of bottles of drinking water. They walked carefully on the bumpy pavement towards a few small shops visible in the distance. Maja, with her gaze fixed on this exotic world, stumbled and almost fell into a smelly open drain gutter in which black pigs were dining on waste. Luckily her mother supported her in time. On the pavement one big gutter slab cover was missing, creating a dangerous trap for pedestrians unfamiliar with it. Lethargic sacred cows moved about on the streets, trying to find something edible but mostly ended up eating waste papers, banana skins and even plastic shopping bags. Hungry, mangy dogs slipped by under peoples' legs. Before the first small shop was a sick woman with a leg the size of one belonging to an elephant sitting on a wooden box. It was almost equal in size to the rest of her body. The woman was mumbling something, stretching her hand towards passersby—expecting alms. Maja cuddled to her mother terrified and asked:

"Can anyone get this disease?"

"I do not know." answered mother. "I never saw anything like this myself; I only read that it is called elephantitis."

They bought bananas, oranges and apples. Returning towards they hotel they met a man ill with leprosy. Maja almost vomited when a dirty ragamuffin stretched his rotting, fingerless deformed hand close to her face. Mother passed him ten rupees.

"I wouldn't like to live in such a country. How dirty is everything here, how many terribly sick people." commented mother.

"But only think mum; Guru was born here not without a purpose. He chose to be close to those poor people. They need Him more than people from different, richer countries. Maybe all those people are sick from lack of love?"

"What comes to your mind? How can people be ill from lack of love?" replied mother but somehow with lack of conviction in her voice.

"Maybe Maja is right?" She thought.

Visit to Guru's ashram.

When the taxi brought them to the Gurus' ashram, Guru Bhava program was on. It was late afternoon. Monumental Hanumans's Mountain, Rumassala, which was in the legend Hanuman, Monkey King, brought from Sri Lanka to provide healing herbs for Rama's ill wife, Sita, was bathed in the reddish light of the setting sun. The many-thousand crowd of devotees who came there for a special *dharshan* were flowing in all directions in search of food, drinking water, toilets and a place to rest. Jan and his family were provided a room with a private bathroom in one of the few residential buildings. From their window they saw the marvelous view of the Arabian Sea and the coconut huts of the neighboring fishing village. On the left side, between tall coconut palms, stood the ashram temple building, richly decorated and painted in bright colors. From a distance was heard the rattle of an electrical generator. At five the *bajans* started. The Guru was sitting in front of sanctum sanctorum with His face towards the ashram inmates and devotees seated on the temple floor. Around Him were swamis dressed in orange/red and *brahmacharis* dressed in yellow or white. In front of each singer was a microphone on a stand. Most of them held strange musical instruments. The Guru was concentrating with closed eyes. Instructions were given, with closed eyes, to the swami playing an Indian box harmonium. The Guru was leading songs and the others repeated each verse a few times. The Guru held the fingers of both his hands in divine *mudra* and occasionally shouted in ecstasy: "Krishna, Krishna, Krishna or Shiva, Shiva Shiva . . ." His voice, full of devotion, sounded from gigantic speakers:

Transcribed from Malayalam:

"Life is a short dream. It last only for four or five years. Why you are in a hurry—o man? Your unending wild desires will fade with age. Know what is your relationship in the Oneness?"

Jan listened to *bajans* holding his breath. In spite of not understanding a single word from the songs, somehow the melody was talking to him and his heart was melting from a spontaneously awakened love towards all Existence. *Dharshan* started after *bajans*. Jan seated himself, as was advised, close to a chair on which Guru was seated. He watched an unending parade of people. On most faces were 'painted' adoration, rapture, enhancement and fascination of Guru's unique charm and radiating unconditional love. Hours were passing. Jan saw suffering people who approached Guru crying but departed with smiles of hope, carrying in their hearts assurances that everything will be well, he saw couples asking for the blessing of having a child. He saw children whom Guru initiated into writing by guiding their tiny fingers on a plate with raw rice to fashion letters of the Tamil or Malayalam alphabet, depending on their parents' ethnicity. Many people approaching Guru were from other countries. Some were here for the first time, some had been there before and Guru recognized them and asked questions. All wanted something. Guru was giving them pinches of calm and composure, seconds of desirelessness, wise advice and guidance. Guru was soothing their restless minds, healing hurts and bodily alignments, advised, directed to go in the right direction and to do the right action. Sometimes it was done by a touch, sometimes by a few words but mostly by the most powerful Language of Silence. So passed the night. It was close to 7 AM. The queue for *dharshan* was ending. By the time Jan noticed, there were only six people left to meet Guru. Jan closed his eyes and started to meditate. Suddenly, he felt someone look, like the physical touch of a hand. He opened his eyes and noticed that Guru was making inviting gestures towards him. Jan got up, hissing from the pain of numbed legs and limped towards the end of the queue.

The fragrance of rose oil and the warmth of Guru's body brought back memories from the 'Other Side' of Existence. Now there was not the smallest doubt, now he knew it with certainty. It was Guru who presented Himself to Jan as a Light-Presence and asked him to go back to Earth and continue life in his body. Guru existed simultaneously everywhere. This was a fact. He also loved him truly.

"Guru-ji, what do You want me to do? What is this work which you told me about 'there' my Old Teacher?" thought Jan, gazing into Guru's eyes.

"Son, whatever you do, you do for yourself. Help to organize an ashram in Poland. Remember that I am always with you and that I love you. Do not drink so much coffee because your heart trouble can reappear! Reduce also the salt in your food. Meditate regularly." Jan was overtaken by a wave of warmth. He realized that something was fulfilled and he got accepted to the inner circle of those who serve Guru directly. "So I will be useful in Guru's mission, spreading His Love!" thought Jan.

"I will do as You say Guru-ji" Jan said in a low voice, knowing that it will be so. "Now, after my 'return', my life belongs to You," he whispered.

Guru's wish is materializing.

The farm in Zapadłe was unbelievably neglected. The previous owner, PGR (Government Farm) Rybno was not the best manager. A park with two hundred year old oaks and linden trees surrounding an eighteenth century Renaissance nobleman's manor-house looked like a primordial forest from the times of Piasta Kołodzieja (Legendary ruler of Poland before first King—Mieszko I), who were first known to historians as rulers of the country, which later become known as Poland. The palace, after the passing of 'heroic' hordes of the Soviet Red Army, itself looked worse than anyone could imagine; empty vodka bottles on the floor, the remaining sections of marble fireplaces with chipped mantle pieces, sticky, filthy parquetry 'decorated' with cigarette ends and rotting potatoes, partly glassless windows sealed with pieces of plastic foil, and graffiti on the walls. Other buildings on this farm were in even worse condition. They qualified for immediate demolition rather than repair. Weeds were growing freely on once cultivated fields.

After Communism in Poland collapsed, the Director of this once government owned farm, Mr. Mordacki, purchased the entire property for a symbolic price and continued to neglect everything except the distillery. Most of the time he was completely drunk. He drank with suicidal determination. Now there were no more inspections from the Association of Government Farms, no more visits by black 'Volga' secretaries of Communist Party bringing orders to 'intensify production', 'strengthening the unity of the working class' and transporting cow manure to fields to 'stick a knife into the backs of the world's imperialists'. He took care of the distillery as he would his own child. He was a genius when it came to alcoholic beverages, and quickly learned how to make, better than the Hungarian original, plum vodka – Ślivovica. Only this gave him a decent income and provided 'heavenly' delight for his drunkards' palate. Cultivating fields and everything else was too troublesome so he ignored the comments of local people. He simply had no heart for all of this.

Now the distillery had burned down. Mr. Mordacki had no insurance and no savings to pay compensation to those workers who were injured in the boiler explosion, so decided to sell his farm. In this way the Zapadłe estate entered the property market. The price was very low because it presented miserably. Jan bought the farm. Now he had real money and could afford it. Once when he passed through Zapadłe and saw a "FOR SALE" sign, something made him stop the car to see the property. The purchase decision was surprising not only for his family but even for himself. It happened like he was under a spell of some invisible force. Jan decided to offer this farm to Guru and after bringing it back to its former glory, organized there the nucleus of a future ashram. He got in touch with his friend from Canada, who introduced him to Guru, and few other friends from America, Australia and Western countries of the European Union.

The idea to create an ashram in Poland aroused much great enthusiasm in all. They published an appeal for financial support in the Polish national and in exile newspapers. In Guru's followers' monthly bulletin 'Guruvani', the project was described in detail with a map on how to get there. Donations started to arrive. Money for the restoration of the palace was gathered in only three months thanks to the generous contributions of a few business people. Many volunteered to provide professional service and labor. People were even offering family heirloom jewelry, paintings of famous artists and antique furniture.

The interiors were restored to their original distinguished look and décor, introducing only the innovation of central heating. Elevation was stripped of deteriorated render and plastered anew, using high quality German acrylic render. The roof was retiled with Bohemian terracotta tiles imported from the Czech Republic, gutters and downpipes were, as a heritage building deserved, replaced with pure cooper ones. The park was rebuilt by landscape architects. Most of the cultivated fields were converted to orchards where small wooden cabins were located. These cabins were intended for ashram visitors who wanted to spend some time in silent seclusion and not be uninterrupted when practicing their *sadhana*. An auditorium for four thousand people was also built in the first year.

Guru coming to Poland.

The day of Guru's first visit to Poland arrived. At the International Terminal of Okęcie Airport in Warsaw waited a fairly big group of devotees, newsmen from national papers and the Channel One TV crew. The plane from Amsterdam landed on time. Guru went through customs surrounded by his closest chelas. He was radiating, as usual, goodness and love. Guru went straight into the middle of His Polish Devotees—His spiritual 'children'. Dr. Fisherman placed a garland made of wild flowers from the rice fields close to the ashram on His neck. The first *satsang* was conducted during the evening of the same day in the newly organized ashram. Sounds of *bajans* were carried by the wind all over the village fields and meadows, crossing the waters of a nearby lake and reflected by birch scrubs:

'Come, come my dear children, you who are the projections of All-What-Is. You are eternal sparks of life unending . . . .'

All surroundings were listening to the sounds of the *bajans*; barn-swallows drawing zigzags on the reddening sky, storks from their new nests on the ashram barn, villagers-neighbors returning home from toiling in the fields. Even cows in the ashram cow shed stopped making their sounds of satisfaction, 'moo' and even stopped chewing hay and listened attentively. Maybe they also knew who arrived and was now leading *bajans*.

Ashram activities

Two years passed. The ashram was developing speedily. It quickly became a center of spiritual training for seekers of Truth. Now there were over forty permanent residents. The ashram was frequently visited by an enormous number of Poles, Czechs, Hungarians and Russians. Even Scandinavians were not rare. At the ashram courses of *hatha yoga,* meditation were conducted, sacred writings of Hinduism were discussed and explained, and the philosophy of *Advaita Vedanta* lectured. Each evening residents and visitors sang Guru's *bajans.*

But the most important activity which the ashram initiated was work with law-breakers serving long terms in local prisons; work aiming on the felons' spiritual rehabilitation. A group of trained volunteer-instructors regularly visited a few large prisons and conducted courses of yoga and meditation. The results of this were astonishing. The tension in hard core criminals was relaxing; they stopped harboring hatred and aggression towards the normal community and were gradually healed of the desire for other people's money and possessions. After assessing the result of the ashram's work with criminals, the Ministry of Justice agreed to conduct an experimental rock climbing camp in the Tatra Mountains.

Jan, being a bit experienced in rock climbing, also went to a camp. The Tatra National Park Management allowed them to set up a camp in the Valley of Five Lakes close to the tourist chalet 'Murowaniec'. Janek's friend, who was an army officer, arranged for tents, sleeping bags and stretchers. The group called themselves: 'Free Men'. Participants divided themselves into two groups. 'Highland Robbers' was the name of the group with Janek as one of two instructors, the second group was named 'Plainsman' with Jurek 'Skunk', a veteran of Tatra climbs and rescues, as a leading instructor (famous for a stinking smell due to never taking a bath except from the heavy rains on a mountain cliffs). The weather was magnificent; gentle wind from high ranges and unobstructed sun. All participants enjoyed this adventurous sport.

Janek's partner on a rope.

The camp was scheduled to end the next day. Last climb! The choice was: Stanislavski Path on Small Kościelec, with difficulty rated II+. It was not a difficult path. 'Highland Robbers' were climbing along the South ridge of Small Kościelec. On it was an overhang, which even the beginners usually passed easily. Jan was leading, hammering hooks into cracks in the rock, hanging tape-loops on projections and attaching carbines with belaying rope going through them. Above a flat slab with a razor sharp edge was the overhang. Janek considered this part as too easy to arrange another belaying point. On top of that he did not have the long tape-loop needed in such a situation. After Janek on a team belaying rope was Mark 'Furrier', a young murderer from the Eastern Polish town of Łapy. Five years back he stabbed his grandpa when the old man refused to give him money for drinking. Unfortunately in doing so he made a hole in grandpa's fairly new sheepskin coat. When after receiving his prison sentence, and the inmates asked why he was imprisoned, Mark innocently explained: "§525 (murder—in Polish Codex of Crimes)—For making a hole in my grandpa's sheepskin coat." When a less intelligent prisoner, surprised that he got fifteen years of separation from his buddies and family for such a small thing, he happily clarified: "Accidentally in the overcoat was this dammed grandpa." That's how he acquired his nickname.

Accident.

Jan braced his climbing Vibrams boots against a rock and, holding from underneath the overhang, lifted himself high enough to grab a hold known to him from a previous climb. When his palm firmly grabbed hold he started to lift himself up searching with his other hand for another hold. Suddenly the ridge stood in front of his eyes. The hold, used by the followers of rock climbing pioneer, Stanislavski for over forty years, had chipped off. Jan fell straight down on his back on a slab, which was on an angle, hit his head on a rock, and then unconscious, he rolled down. He fell five meters with a jerk of the belaying rope, hit on a pendulum cliff and fell further. The razor sharp edge of a slab cut his rope like a tiny stalk of grass and Jan flew in a free fall towards a scree-covered base of the Western Cliffs of Kościelc. Now unattached to his belaying rope Mark 'Furrier', terrified, who was following Jan pulled the belaying rope towards himself, swearing. On the end of it was no one! There was no instructor! In a panic he whispered.

"O cholera! O kurwa! (Polish swear words) Now is the end of everything. I am damned! Nobody will believe that it wasn't me who killed him."

On the screes under the cliff, on a huge boulder, Janek's body was spread. It was lying like an offering on a cult altar of a Pagan God to be eaten by vultures. A woodchuck, interested to find out what made such a strange sound, crawled from under the stones and, realizing what had happened, announced to Nature by his loud whistle that one more of Its sons fulfilled his worldly duty and was allowed to return Home.

Jan immediately recognized where he was. Such a joy! He was again there to where he belonged, where there is no pain, no suffering, no stress and no worries! Now he eagerly waited for a Light-Being. Now he knew who It was. Light-Presence appeared from his left side.

"O that is you, my son! Very good, very well! Now you can stay here. Are you happy? You did not waste your life. So many people benefit thanks to your work. Now you will have more time to analyze your life and plan how to improve yourself. Most of your major karmic debts are already paid off. Go now into your 'residence'. First you must create it by imagining how it looks. Rest! Soon you will have to return to Earth. This time you will be born as a girl, a daughter of a very pious Brahmin family living in Kanya Kumari in South India, on the very end of the Indian peninsula. After you finish your study you will join your Guru nearby ashram as *brahmacharini*. There you will be given a chance to attain Liberation. But now go, go and have some healing 'sleep'." Saying so, Light-Being showed Janek a Tatra Mountains style villa, which had just materialized close by. In its main door stood his Old Teacher, waving a hand towards him urging him to hurry. Now Jan was happy. He finally returned to his real house. He said nothing but only prostrated in utter surrender towards Light-Being. Is it possible not to want that which Light-Being wishes?

In the evening, the Tatra Mountain Rescue Team of eight, under the command of Jaś, son of Kierdos of Łopalona (Pol.: Burned), carried Jan's body down using pine resin torch-lights and a tough canvas on bamboo. The body was placed under the back walls of the chalet 'Murowaniec'. The body was terribly damaged, so as to avoid tourist agitation they covered it with branches of kosówka (Pol. Dwarfish, bushy mountain pine). The 'Free Man' group was gravely silent.

A few participants were seated in tent corners silently crying and drying eyes with heavily tattooed hands; others were doing their *japa mantra* or meditated on the uncertainty of human life.

Despite this sad and tragic accident, rock climbing and meditation camps continued in consecutive years as highly effective in rebuilding criminals' mentality. Thanks to them, many hard criminals learned solidarity, responsibility for partners of a team and sometimes, for the first time in their life, tasted a real sporting challenge. They also learned about inborn divinity and the possibility of attaining Liberation, regardless of earlier committed transgressions. Many understood the existence of deeper than material meaning of life and never returned to the path of delinquency and crime. Guru regularly visited the ashram in Zapadłe.

Maja meets Geeta.

After graduating from medical studies in Warsaw, Jan's daughter went to London for a postgraduate course. A year after she was awarded a PhD she joined Guru's ashram as *brahmacharini*. For the first two years she worked in the newly created free hospital in Zapadłe, specializing in treating AIDS patients from all over Europe. Dr. Deepak Lal, from the famous Kerala *ayurvedic* clinic was there using his unique formulation 'Kari-Ka' to heal the early stages of this dreadful disease. Advanced stages, already incurable, were given relief from pain and the mental agony of fear. After two years Guru transferred Maja to his Indian ashram under the slopes of Rumassala Mountain. There Maja completed the *śhjastra* course and was formally initiated into *brahmacharia*. Already wearing yellow robes, she was sent to Tamil Nadu where in the mountains of Utti, Guru created the Institute of Medical Sciences and the adjoining hospital, specializing in the treatment of leprosy.

There Maja met Dr. Fisherman, who after reaching retirement age moved to India and committed himself to researching the biochemistry of blood in the state of *Sahadja Nirvikalpa Samadhi* in Guru's Institute. This idea came once to the mind of a house painter who had no medical knowledge. Once his client, Dr. Rahochy a

Hungarian neurosurgeon told him that a few minutes of interrupted blood circulation in a patients' brain forms unrepeatable changes due to lack of oxygen leading to unavoidable death. The painter immediately deduced that if yogis, during prolonged *samadhi*, stop breathing for many hours and even days, when even their hearts stop pumping blood, in spite of all of this nothing happened to their brains—no changes, no death—that yogis' bodies must produce under controlled conditions a substance that protects their nervous system and averts damage. This was a very promising subject. Millions of people's lives could be spared, giving them the chance to live lives less egoistically and animalistically but rather to a large extent caring more about others. Maja had a glimpse that this was her life mission and joined Dr. Fisherman as an assistant. Was it really her life mission? Only Light-Being knows because He knows everything. It was half an hour to sunset. Time for meditation. Maja switched off the gas spectrometer and went to the hall passage. The marble floor of the Institute reflected on its waxy sheen sunlight coming from the windows. From speakers installed in a false ceiling sounded the vibrant voice of Guru:

"Let life creek flow happily and continuously towards the Ocean of Transmigration. Let beings grow in Wisdom . . . .'

Maja thought about her father. "Many years have passed since the accident, but I remember him like I saw him yesterday. How he was dedicated to Guru! Now he is there always wanting to return, but maybe . . . he incarnated again." In the Laboratory Reception she met Geeta. She was a very young *brahmacharini* from a very pious Brahmin family from Kanya Kumari. She was taking a nursing course In Guru's Institute and in her free time helping in a laboratory. Last week she went for a few days to visit her family. Her father suddenly became seriously ill.

"OM Namah Shivaya. ഓഗീതാ,വെല്സിമേ,ഹൗആളരെയു? (Malayalam Fon.: *Oh, Geeta, niñgal vaño! Swagatam! Sukham* āno?" ("OM Namah Shivaja. O, Geeta you are back! Welcome! How are you?")

"I am well. What about you? What has happened here?" "Nothing special."

Geeta and Maja sat on a bench close to artificial rock formations opposite the main entrance. They both felt great sympathy towards each other. Even Maja's poor knowledge of Malayalam was not a serious hindrance in their warm and friendly relationship.

"Maja-ji സിസ്റ്റ—(Mal. Fon.: ĉceci =Mal.: Maja sister).What was your father doing before he met our Guru?" Geeta asked suddenly.

"He designed and later manufactured some electronic devices. I do not know exactly what they were. Why are you asking?"

"I do not know myself. Strange, but often I feel that we are from the same family. You are so close to my heart like no other person, even much closer than my siblings."

"Geeta you are right! Are we not spiritual daughters of the same Guru? Is not our real family the biggest family in existence? It is full of God's splendor Totality of Beings!" Down Geeta's cheek ran big tears. In thoughts she shifted to the time when Guru accepted her.

"Good my golden daughter. Come! After all you belong here. I will give you the biggest family in existence. Are you not my daughter?"

From the Institute speakers came the voice of Guru:

"Wake me up, o Guru that I will sleep no more in illusion of Maya. Let my only desire be to achieve Liberation. Let not a grain of this world create in me attachment . . .'

RETROSPECTIONS

You do not remember me, my Darling. You think I am a stranger. But when I first met you, I called you by your old name. It was not intended, not at all. It came out of my lips automatically, spontaneously, as something obvious, something well rooted in my subconscious. Somehow, I intuitively recognized you because you are you and you will always remain you. We both know that in fact we are not two but one, but, in spite of that, we don't yet experience it in our day-to-day life.

We have been growing together for a long time; step-by-step, year-by-year, life after life. We are still growing invisibly, until one day we will merge into The Oneness, and then continue to live in eternal unceasing happiness. We will dissolve our small individualities and become one with everything.

How is it possible that you don't remember those happy days when we were together, watching the snowy peaks of the Caucasus Mountains? Sitting on the verandah of the chalet we drank black tea from cups made of fine china. We called it 'Цай' (in Russian Cyrillic, pronounced: 'chay') and drank it without milk and sugar, along with a wild strawberry jam on tiny plates. We were Ved-Russ (not Russians as we talk about very, very old times not even known by mainstream history). Now we call it 'chaya' and have it sweet and with milk. Strange, but the similarity of words is amazing. Anyway, I think that tea made this way is spoiled. For me its taste is still revolting, but what can I do?

You forgot our Ved-Russ homeland meadows, spread with breathtakingly beautiful wildflowers. There we dived deep, deep into ourselves in a fruitless search for bliss. We experienced a short lasting pleasure of union, but not lasting happiness, nor bliss. In vain was our desperate effort to find it in a worldly relationship. We didn't know that we were looking in the wrong direction. We also didn't know that we were imprudently building a cage of attachment, and in this way were voluntarily enslaving ourselves.

You don't remember how, much later and in another country, we discovered for the first time the sweetness of freedom from attachment. We, who this time were filthy rich, somehow managed not to get spoiled by our wealth while living in both internal and external comforts. We, who had it all: palaces, servants, tropical farms, coffee plantations, the most expensive cars and an extremely profitable precious stone mine on an old volcano, we lived a detached life. We loved each other, and I bet we were even detached from ourselves. In those days we didn't even theoretically know the secrets of The Oneness, we had not even heard about spirituality, but somehow, intuitively perhaps, we lived according to its principles. There was no fear in us of losing anything, nor the slightest desire to gain something we did not yet possess. We were for the first time almost happy. We accepted anything and everything which The Oneness sent to us as our share in life, and we didn't forget to pass God's gifts on to those who were not so fortunate and in need.

We were at the peak of our health, prosperity and contentment when the fatal car accident happened. We fell off a cliff while driving our beautiful cabriolet Silver Shadow Rolls Royce. This put a full stop to our lives. I guess there was nothing more for us to learn in that life, so there was no purpose of continuing it. We were called for a rest.

After a short holiday in the higher worlds, we have come back to this material plane of existence to finish, this time I hope, our long journey. There are still some vasanas (tendencies) in us, which have to be exhausted and eradicated.

I am very proud of you, my Darling. Your intuition showed you the right way quickly, as it always did in the past. I have not been so good, and have shamelessly diverted from the Path many times to experience painful lessons. But do not think that I am totally hopeless. I'm not! I am earnestly trying to catch up, and I have a serious reason to hope for success. But this is a secret.

There is no need to say more. All that has any meaning was already said long, long ago. Now I am not even searching for you. We don't have to be together in our perishable forms to continue to be one. Why risk another fall? You have to follow your Guru; I will stay with mine. In fact internally they are one, but still I am very pleased that you once met my Guru. HE is very special, unique. The scriptures and my Guru say that we pervade the entire Universe. We live as all which can be thought of. Our beingness is pulsating in the stars.

Those stars which you liked so much to watch with me as we walked hand-in-hand at night along the dark streets and boulevards of our beloved Petersburg.

The dogs of human agitation bark at us sometimes, but we will remain unaffected, unconcerned. We are riding on a cloud of Peace on the infinite ocean of Eternity towards The Oneness. Is it not more enjoyable then riding on a 'trojka,' our once favorite vehicle for going out on day trips to the woods during the bitter-frosty Russian winter? Never be upset. There will always be some ignorant brothers and sisters along our way, like those wolves. Not all can grow in understanding equally fast, but they too have the right to exist and try to do their best. Do you remember the Petrovska Forest? One of our three horses broke its leg, and we were surrounded by a pack of wolves. I had only three bullets in my sporting rifle, and there were more than twenty wolves. Our death seemed to be certain. There, for the first time, we met the Incarnation of The Oneness. It was in the form of an old hermit who came out of the woods, waddling in the deep snow. In a soft voice he said to the wolves. "What is it all about? Don't you know my children? This is not their time, not yet. You rascals have no right to break the Law!! The horse with the broken leg will be yours. Now go, and come back after some time for your dinner." The wolves bent their heads in great respect, and ashamed went into the forest howling. Obviously we didn't recognize Him that time. He smiled towards us and said, "Clear the road my children. Leave your injured horse here and go in Peace. I will meet you later." We never met Him again in that life.

Who could only guess that He would become, in a different country, on a different continent, a Guru. Who could predict that one day He would say in a strange but nice language,

"Oh, you have come. Welcome back home. You belong here. I have been waiting for you. Why was it so long? Where were you wandering? Now it is time to finally end this aimless ramble. Stay here and be at Peace. Forget the past, do not imagine the future. Nothing has ever happened to you. There is no time; it too is only a part of the illusion created by the mind. Learn to master your mind. All this was only a dream. Wake up, son. What can you gain by watching the shadows? Make peace with the past and wake up. It is your time to wake up. Then, do not drift into the unconsciousness of duality. Stay wide awake. Your darling one is also only a shadow created by your own mind. You called her into existence by your restless thoughts. She had to manifest herself because you imagined that through her you would find happiness. The Law of Karma is always in operation. Be alert to what you are thinking about. Work, but remember that you are not the doer. I act through you, and the fruits of your toil belong to ME. You will soon find who you really are, and live forever in Happiness. I love you, son. I always have been, and always will be with you. I have no other place to dwell than in your heart."

Today is Monday. I can't do my work well. My face is swollen. I have been crying in bliss most of the night. I am such a limited individual, a little particle of cosmic dust, and when the feeling of The Presence comes I drift into blissful intoxication. I know that I am allowed to drink this Ambrosia. This is our Natural Drink. I don't understand how I earned this right in the past, but the fact is I can have it now at no cost whatsoever. I admit that by the Law of The Oneness the state of Peace is automatically creating a state of Bliss. Let us be in it if such is the will of The Highest. Do you experience it too? I am sure you do. You probably started to drink this Divine Wine much earlier than me, and by now you are totally addicted to it. You are? I am so happy to hear this! This is the only addiction which does not bind and enslave people, but on the contrary, sets them Free.

It is raining. The rain is drumming on the metal roof of my workshop. They say that it's the monsoon. They're wrong! This is not rain but the tears of unending Bliss of the Highest, who assumed the form of the clouds. Something is howling on the roofs and on the tops of coconut palms. They say it is a wind. No. They are wrong again. How can they not recognize what it is? It's not the wind but the Lord Himself, who is playing on His flute a charming melody of Freedom. He is calling His darling children home. He is floating on the waves of Eternity, touching the trees, caressing the sweating heads of his little ones laboring hard to earn a simple living and the right to return to their parental abode. Do you, my Darling, my shadow, hear

Him? Listen to the tunes of His Divine Flute, and contemplate His Omnipresence. His face is blue so you can't see Him in the sky. But be sure, He is there! This is the only thing in this entire world that is certain. He is everywhere. Only He exists. Only He is Real.

Someone is passing by. His face is apparently glowing for no reason from an internal light, so strange but familiar too. From where do we know this Golden Light? Stop for a while; look! Don't be in a hurry. We will all manage to reach the appointed place at the appointed time. Look deep into his eyes. You will be surprised by what you see! There is a clear reflection of the Real Light of the Lord. If you look carefully you can see Him standing there surrounded by an aura of Golden Light, playing HIS magic flute to awaken his children from the dream of their separateness from Him. Can you see? He is smiling at you, my Darling. Do you see Him? How great and wonderful is this world of His creation! Our efforts and sacrifices weren't futile, were they? Certainly they weren't. Let us continue to walk towards our home. I hope we will soon meet there, where all roads meet at the end. Good luck on the way my darling non-existing in Reality companion and friend. I feel that you will be there first. If so, please wait for me, wait patiently. I am on my way. I will come soon. I promise.

PRASAD

T he fiery sun was nearing the colorful western horizon, almost touching the waters of a distant Arabian Sea. Another warm day in South India was approaching with dignity its glorious conclusion. The clouds, moving slowly across the sky, resembled a parade of *sannyasis* going to pay a humble tribute of respect to the Eternal One.

Traveler strongly felt that he was simultaneously an actor and spectator of this Divine Drama, played endlessly since the beginning of time. The years of worldwide wanderings, filled with painful and joyful experiences, faded into unreality in his memories of the past. He didn't even know if he'd ever left this sacred land to which he belonged, perhaps from past incarnations. He was not even sure if the memory of foreign countries, the magnificent rocky mountains full of an indefinable but almost touchable Presence, people of many make-ups and from different nationalities, the immense vastness of the snow covered fields of a Siberian 'Nothingness, frozen in anticipation of awakening to the freedom' and if the nightmare of adversity under the totalitarian Communist suppression, were only figments of his exuberant imagination, a dream, or if he had really experienced them. In fact, feeling deeply relaxed, he didn't even care to find it out. He was enjoying to the fullness of his being his presence here and now. All that was and all that could eventually happen, had lost its attractiveness and allure. He merged almost completely into the surrounding Existence; living as Its extension and differentiating from It only in the intensity of manifestation of a Life Force, but not in Its quality. He listened attentively to the speechless eloquence of Nature, absorbing Its timeless Wisdom through all the pores of his skin.

Across the dense jungle, filled with countless varieties of tropical trees, bushes and plants and full of the sounds of humming, flying, walking and crawling brother creatures, a long row of white clad figures moved slowly in utter silence. They were following the Guru, beloved in all countries and continents by millions of His devotees; *Satguru* of many and incarnation of the Divine Creator of all small and great beings; His children from the three worlds. Being an Incarnation of the Eternal One, a physical manifestation of The Oneness, He was hiding in the form of a human body. He is a *Maha-avatar* disguised as a simple carpenter's offspring. A row of people were climbing the hill towards the spot chosen by Him for the evening meditation.

Guru walked straight to the top of the hill, where a mysterious small lake, with a spring in its middle, was located. It was a sacred lake; a very special one called *Vishnu Thirta*. Its existence will probably always remain a mystery. Geologically it doesn't fit into scientific logic. It lies in an approximately one hundred-meter diameter bowl of brownish lava, on a hill built from sedimentary rocks. Ancient legend says that, shortly after the time of creation, gods landed on this hill in a chariot of fire, which melted the top of it. It is an almost perfect imprint of a large disk-like weapon of destruction of the mythological

God of War. The people say that eons ago, impenetrable to human memory, shrines and hermitages were built on the banks of its sacred waters where great yogis and illuminated sages dwelt, oblivious to the unstable world, absorbed in contemplation of their oneness with the ever peaceful and unchangeable Reality.

At the present time an ancient banyan tree grows on its south bank. It is huge, with massive branches stretching more than half way to the Vishnu Thirta center. From a distance it looks like a silent gesture of begging for mercy; an external expression of its hopelessness of immobility, loyalty, and surrender to the will of the Highest. Maybe it is an incarnation of one of those *sadhus* who lived there long, long ago. Maybe he suddenly failed on the eve of Self-Realization. Maybe, just on the threshold of final Liberation, he was skillfully tempted by a charming, passionate *gopi*, full of love, with silky soft skin, dark, lingering eyes and perfectly rounded hips, and now he is paying so high a price for a few minutes of animalistic passion. He has to wait patiently, century after century, for the end of this long life as a banyan tree. But nevertheless, he is on his way to final emancipation, and we can hope he is exhausting his last remaining *vasana*.

Under the banyan tree, an old yogi sits day and night. In front of him burn a few wooden sticks to repel kusu—mosquitoes. The owner of this jungle, Mr. Hamsa, told the Traveler that the yogi would cook once a week for the community he hosted there and for this was getting one meal a day for the rest of week. Under the British the yogi worked as the local postman. The yogi, being immersed in samadhi, ignored the passing Guru's party.

The group sat down on the sun-warmed rocks on the East side of Thirta pond and surrounded their Guru. Everyone faced the sunset. Before meditation the Guru started distributing prasad. It was puffed rice mixed with crushed nuts and sultanas. The Traveler watched His face. The Guru wore different masks and expressed different emotions to those approaching Him for prasad. Was He acting according to their needs, mental state and level of surrender? His face was continuously beaming Love, Compassion and a powerful Spiritual Energy. The Guru radiated invisibly, but more intensely than the sun whose last rays gold-plated His face making it look like a living bronze statue of an ancient God. In fact, He was the real God Himself disguised as a mortal.

When the Traveler's turn came, he knelt in front of Him and respectfully waited with open palms for his share. But the Guru was in no hurry. He looked deeply into his eyes. The Traveler felt that in the blink of an eye all the contents of his mind, hidden to the world, were scanned and evaluated. The Guru smiled, expressing at the same time a deep concern about his shortcomings with a mischievous promise of some unexpected surprise. Speaking directly, mind to mind, He said,

"Would you, son, accept from me everything I want to give you? You were called back home, but now you carry a big load. To be able to cross the gate you have to free yourself from the ballast of your old useless habits, give up all desires, and eradicate attachments. I will help you, but remember, the operation of the cleansing will be painful. Will you freely accept the pain? You are now identifying yourself with so many labels, you have so many expectations. Are you ready and strong enough to become Mr. Nobody? Could you live without expecting anything from anybody and desiring nothing? There is nothing on the entire Earth that can make you, the Real You, more real than you already are. Are you afraid to completely empty your mind from accumulated preconceptions and memories of the past? Are you brave enough to be smaller than the smallest particle of dust on the country roadside, to lose all significance and individuality? You are dust. Admit it and become eternally Free. Ignore the transitory, illusionary manifestation of the World and of your body. Wake up! Stop dreaming, son! Just Be!"

He placed a portion of the *prasad* on his open right palm. The Traveler humbly bowed down in silent acceptance of his Guru's *prasad* and silent instructions, moved a few steps backward and walked towards the spot where he was previously seated. He was a bit intoxicated from the excess of shakti and felt like he was spiritually vaccinated against the charms and tinsels of the worldly material existence. Soon he was slowly eating the *prasad* received from his Guru. He sat gazing in wonder at the living God who acted in this incredible, Divine *leela* for the sake and benefit of those whose destiny allowed them to come into close proximity with Him, and to live submerged in His overflowing grace.

Suddenly he discovered the reason for the Guru's mischievous smile. He nearly broke his tooth. Between nuts, sultanas, and puffed rice was a piece of stone, the size of a fairly large chenna (chick-pea). Maybe it was a chip from this mysterious brownish lava bowl of *Vishnu Thirta*, or maybe He brought it from the other worlds. Anyway, it was intended to be his special *prasad*. It didn't raise any doubt as whether to eat it or throw it away. For the Traveler it was clear and obvious. Just a few minutes ago he had, in his silent treaty with his Guru, accepted, without asking questions, anything and everything He would give him in the future. Now he had to eat the stone. His Guru was smiling, watching him secretly. Only He knew the *sankalpa* which He had implanted into the stone. The Traveler swallowed the stone, not without difficulty as he didn't have any water to wash it down.

When the meditation started he drifted effortlessly into the warmth of Loving Silence, leaving behind the unreal world, the ever-troubled body, and the restless, pervasive mind. He clearly felt that something new and previously inexperienced was sprouting and slowly growing in his innermost enclaves. Like a new chip in a computer, the stone charged with the Guru's grace opened new circuits of energy flowing into his consciousness, permanently reprogramming him. It started to convert his inexhaustible life energy into invisible but perceivable radiations of Love Waves. From now on he would be living as its powerful source. It would be accessible to all he met and who were ready to absorb it, directly proportionate to their openness and willingness to accept the Unknown. Some of his younger brothers and sisters will possibly, from time to time, misunderstand the light in his eyes, thinking that it is an external sign of his especially warm feelings towards someone in particular. It had happened before, to his own surprise, when he presented to three female ashramites his poem, "I Love You To Love" and where all three ladies, without hesitation, identified themselves as the objects of his love. Sorry

Babes! Anyway, with the passage of time, they too will gradually realize that those rays of Love are not creating attachments, have no preferences and no aversions. They manifest spontaneously because such is the Guru's will. In fact, the person who deserved to be loved by the Traveler was a person of unmatched spiritual height whom he met six years later.

During this warm, spectacularly orange colored sunset, the Guru commenced a new epoch in the Traveler's life. This evening he absorbed so much of this auspicious color that his subconscious became fully saturated with it, and soon he was able to break free from his worldly bonds. In a few months he was able to settle permanently in his Guru's ashram. This evening he entered the path leading directly to the fulfillment of his destiny. From now on, day-by-day, month-by-month, year-by-year, he will shrink away from identifying himself as an individual until finally he will become perfect nothingness. It will happen as fast as he will allow his *Satguru* to cut off the chains of his mental bonds and attachments, destroy the overgrown toys of his desires, and burn to ashes his habits and harmful tendencies. Its speed will relate directly to the depth and sincerity of his surrender. Nothing in nature can appear from nothingness, and nothing can disappear into nonexistence. The energy from the negative qualities of his character, destroyed in the sacrificial fire of surrender, and the heavy load of worldly bonds and desires, will be converted by his Guru into powerful Love Waves, enabling him to work selflessly for the benefit of others.

The Traveler intuitively knew that it was a deadly serious game, and the venomous, multi-armed octopus of Maya would try intensely and persistently to divert his attention from the ultimate goal. It would present him with all sorts of tempting baits to swallow. The Traveler was determined to be watchful and not fall into the bottomless traps set by Maya, and later have to live a long, long life as a banyan tree. There was no other choice for him but to play the game with all his strength and attention, offering the results of this struggle to his Guru, and relying faithfully on His mercy.

He was aware that the key to his Divine Parent's House would be given to him only when he managed to become less than dust. It was a very difficult condition. His greatest enemy, the thorny, touchy, deceitful, cunning and arrogant ego would not be willing to give up easily. But there was great hope for success in this battle too, as he was guided by the best possible Guide—his Guru, mightily armed with all necessary Divine weapons to destroy and annihilate the revolting abomination called his ego.

When he opened his eyes again, it was already dark. At night, under the infinitely reaching Indian sky, full of sparkling and blinking stars, the feeling of being a part of the Whole was much clearer and more obvious than during the day. His spiritual brothers and sisters were still sitting motionlessly in meditation. They didn't look like recognizable individuals, only dark shapes and silhouettes blending with the surrounding lake, boulders, shrubs and bushes. They all looked like huge clusters of crystals, interconnected by the invisible Golden Thread of Existence and united with their Guru—Love Divine.

In this moment the Traveler had his first blissful glimpse of his cosmic anonymity, his vastness, a small sip of the nectar of Nothingness. In this enchanting mood his blissful tears flew through the rocks of brownish lava to the waters of the lake, mixing with those of his predecessors. Vishnu Thirta accepted this offering in the silence of The Oneness and the Totality of Things, as it had lovingly done for the past millennia. Guru sealed the scenario by concluding the meditation. He whispered His usual mantra: Shiva, Shiva, Shiva. Slowly all left the banks of *Vishnu Thirta*. Again the dense silence became all-pervading, witnessing impartially the unending Divine Drama played on the medium of space and time by the Eternal One—the formless manifestation of Him.

RESCUE

It was a day not much different than any other day in the last few months. The sun in the morning rose in the East and now, after performing all its day duty, was content, and already descending towards the horizon for its nightly rest. From temples, churches and mosques near and far, were heard sounds of evening prayers spreading all over the swampy landscape their monotonous Hindu chants and melodies of devotional songs. It was externally peaceful, but an internal tension, which was steadily growing, living with less and less optimism, less and less faith, culminated. He had already learned in the last few months to live in a void, but what he experienced now was something totally different. The void was not hostile. It was simply the emptiness of nonexistence.

This day he touched the bottom of condemnation and reached the limits of his mental endurance. It was dark there, cold and inhospitable. But this darkness was, on top of this, very aggressive. There he was very lonely and could not feel The Presence at all. He wanted to leave there immediately; to run away from this terrifying place of no life, no love, no future and no Truth, but his legs were immobilized as if glued to the black, swamp like surface of it. He wanted to shout out for help, but there was no air to carry the sound waves; only deadly silence and the darkness of absolute emptiness. Nonexistence. Is it the beginning of madness? In his mind sounded the echo of a long-forgotten song from a vast and absolutely empty far-eastern country in which the once flourishing, arrogant Red Empire turned into one gigantic concentration camp called, due to its isolation: 'Planet'. With cold, crystal clean air, it was beautiful, eminent and monumental, but also indifferent and moonlike, due to ecological devastation. The landscape's appearance enhanced its unreality. From there it was so far from the civilized world that most camp inmates did not believe in its existence. There, in the not so remote past, thousands of prisoners of state, terribly isolated and lonely in their suffering, unbelievably humiliated and physically abused and tortured, were dying, mercilessly slowly, in the horrible agony of cold and hunger. Those people enslaved by totalitarian regime were digging there for gold and uranium so needed by imperialistically minded leaders of this godless communist enterprise to buy Canadian wheat and to finance, communist system expansion, initiating uprisings and civil wars in third world countries to secure their influence. He started to croon:

«Называется 'Чудесной
Планетой'
О, вудь преклята Колымо
Волей-неволей
долженствуеш соити с ума
Обратной дороги уже нет . . . »

"Called 'Wonderful Planet'
O be damned Kowyma
Willy-nilly you have to go mad
Return road does not exist . . ."

Suddenly a soft voice of Silence whispered:

"Open the door, which is on a page 44 in the book lying on your table. I am waiting for you. It is your time".

"Hallucination? Bitter joke? Who is calling?" Still doubting that the way out of this hell can really exist, he looked with disbelief at the faded, soft cover page of an Indian economy edition book. It was a recorded testimony of a Free Man of this century living in the North of Kerala just a few decades ago. What a silly suggestion! What can I find in this book? Is it not so, that even ancient scriptures declare that the human language can't express the Truth? I am not interested in anything else! All are false facades only: friendships, love, dedication and words. Puffed up balloons! Dirty rubbish! Slogans! Real is only the Darkness. It is the same here or there where we are aiming. It is all pervading, has no nationality. It is as certain as death, our only real friend and liberator from this world of pain on whom we can always rely.

But having no other alternative and feeling heavy like a lump of lead, he sat down and opened the small book to page 44—his 'lucky' number. Two sentences and . . . suddenly, without the slightest squeaky noise of rusted-for-millennia hinges, the Door opened itself! Seen through it were fantastic landscapes: the sky, the Sun, trees and grass all pulsated with the Presence bathing in the Brilliant Golden Light of Love Divine. Not even a trace of the Darkness! In fact it all was Him playing a game of hide-and-seek with the innocence of a child. He looked on a wall. The wall was Him too. On the wall hung a huge picture of his Guru. He walked towards it and looked closely into His eyes. The photo was still pretending that it was only a piece of paper, but the eyes were really alive. Even the printing process could not take away their vibrations of Love brilliance . . .

Then he understood that He is also him, that He always was, that He is everywhere and everything is Him, even the Darkness and the Void, and that suffering and nonexistence were simply mere illusions, that it was only a tiring dream. In fact, real was only Existence without boundaries and beginning in an Eternal Bliss of Natural State where neither desires nor aims exist and an observer himself is nothing else but a Lasting having a bath in Eternity.

Subdued thoughts, subdued words, only Silence impenetrable whispered in thundering speechlessness a WORD from which once upon a time all of it began, a word which no one can ever repeat, a seed word.

LOOPS IN TIME

The spring in the Grampians was a symphony of wild flowers and of trilling birds. Some of the plants there are unique and some common, but all are very beautiful.

Andrew and Shanti decided to go there for the first time. They wanted to experience this symphony themselves and most of all they wanted to be together. Something was pulling, something was inviting. They knew something was approaching. They felt their destiny would be fulfilled. They were like two sides of the same coin; differences forming a unity; attached to each other, from the past, and from a time before this birth—desperately searching.

The five-hour trip, made in their tiny toy-like car, passed by as if in the blink of an eye. She was reading 'Towards the Goal Supreme' aloud. They listened to Sanskrit Geeta chants, both in love and in a meditative mood. Time did not exist. They lived in the Eternal NOW. They just were, but most importantly they were together. A large snake crossed the road. He stopped the car. The snake disappeared. Was this an illusion? Maybe it was a warning not to play in the lower chakras where the Kundalini serpent is dreaming. Again on the road, speeding towards the mountain, they were both the Mutants, going to visit the Real Peoples' Land, the Sacred Land given to humans during the Dreamtime.

The rock was magnificent. Dark-gray and beige with brown strips going vertically down, marking the way the water flowed. It looked smooth from a distance but was coarse to the touch, with many horns, loops and holes, which provided a good grip. The winds and the rains had been carving it through the millennia. Now it was a rock climber's heaven. They passed a cave with Aborigine rock paintings. Some fifty-thousand years ago, a tribe of Real People hunted kangaroos and camped here. Primitive windscreens, made from gum-tree branches and wallaby skins, surrounded each family site. Children played and climbed on the rocks. The Earth was in a pristine state. The men, after the hunt, were resting. They were gazing with love on the flat landscape toward the sacred Arapiles, which were raising high in the distance. Their monumental cliffs and ranges broke the monotony of the plains like hard, strong shouts break the silence, announcing victory after the successful hit of the boomerang. The women were cooking.

Andrew was climbing first, giving Shanti brief instructions on how to do it safely. He was very experienced. She was discovering, by doing, these dimensions that were new for her. Andrew felt a strange familiarity here. The warmth from the sun-rock was as his own. He was part of it; he belonged to it. He felt as though he once more possessed Dreamtime understanding. He nearly recognized the steps and the holds. Time had disappeared. He was again in his teens— wild, happy and one with Nature. He understood its silent talk. He talked to it too. He loved it. He felt that here he was at home, like when he was black, in a previous incarnation as an Australian Aborigine. Shanti too, felt that it was a sacred ground. She was silent, quiet and moved with deep respect. After a while she stopped and touched the face of the cliff; dark, monumental.

"Do not talk," she whispered. "Don't disturb it. Maybe it's a sage in deep meditation having chosen this form to last longer through time."

The sun was going down to sleep. They sat separately on the Western slope to meditate. Orange-red light from the setting sun was silently repeating the Eternal Gayatri Mantra and painting their faces. All time became condensed in an instant.

When they finished, she pointed down towards the plains to the tops of the moving gum trees playing with the wind.

"Look, he is there spreading the seeds," said Shanti. He took her hand and they started to walk towards the car.

"Mister Wind is gone," she said sadly. "Andrew, I know you will one day go too. You will be called. Now you're only resting on The Path for a while." She smiled gently in reverie but with sadness.

"Maybe I will go," he answered. "Who knows? Shanti, let's live in the present time. I like to be with you! I think we have some more karma to work out together. Please don't try to guess the future."

It had been very silent. Only in the distance, the "OM Bird" started its evening chant: OMmmm, OMmmm, OMmmm . . . The echo coming from the cliffs was repeating; OM, OM, OM . . . When they reached the car it was already dark. It was time to go back to the 'reality' of their life in a Big Town.

They drove in silence, contemplating the ripples of time, the loops in time, imagining the unimaginable, absorbing the Wisdom of the Silence, and memorizing the teachings of Mister Wind. The smooth roads led them towards the Big Town where they lived, and towards their unavoidable destiny. Was it necessary to break the Silence with words, which mean so little? What can words change? What can be expressed by words anyway? Only trivial things! What has to happen will happen. Why miss The Now? What is now will, in a second, be a dead past. The future, on the other hand, will take care of itself.

Seen from the distance, the reddish lights of the Big Town and the smoke moving over it made the impression that it was not a place of human dwellings but a hell. In fact it was a hell, created by the greed, anger, lust and jealousy of the restless people inhabiting it, the hell where almost all worship money as the only God. But the big town was on their path, and an important experience waited for them there. Without it, it was impossible for both of them to continue the journey.

ON A SWING

It was early morning. The priest had just finished mass; the parishioners had all left the church. Everyone in the small village was busy running after their own affairs. Since the Russian Czar Katharina had died, everything here had become stagnant. During her reign, a small wooden villa on the grounds of an Eastern Orthodox Christian nunnery had been used as a meeting place for her and some selected young officers to exhaust her lustful desires. The graves of those unfortunate lovers are numerous in the local cemetery. They all died unexpectedly after a short romance with her—the Empress. The village, poetically called Pink Slope, was barely accessible as the vast area surrounding it was a dangerous swamp. Only two dirt tracks led to this Byelorussian retreat. The buildings of the old nunnery and adjoining church had walls more than one meter thick, like a real fortress. After the communists took over, the nuns left and the buildings became the home of the Agricultural Technical College with a boarding house for students—those future agronomists.

There was nothing around to break the boredom for the young boys. One of the most popular ways of spending free time was drinking vodka, wine or a home-made, strong alcoholic drink called 'bimber,' and afterwards getting into stupid fights. Drinking here was considered normal. Everyone drank: Workers, teachers, policemen, and priests. The boys' girlfriends were proud of them when they drank like real men.

On a bench behind a huge column in the church sat a boy. Close to a side altar hung a picture of Mother Mary, which was supposed to be responsible for performing miracles. The boy was waiting for the priest to go back to the presbytery; and, after a while, when he was certain that no one was left inside, he slowly rose from his seat and climbed the marble steps of the altar. On both sides of the picture of Mother Mary were tall display cases with devotional offerings. They were mainly silver or amber symbols of hearts, legs and arms given to the miraculous picture by those who had been cured by their faith in it. The boy started to carefully select pieces, which were hanging in the densest areas, where no one would easily notice if one was missing. He collected three or four silver hearts and left the church.

That same afternoon, after class, he went on foot to a nearby town. He knew a shortcut through the swamps. Jumping from one small bunch of grass and moss to another, he crossed the marsh. He reached the town faster than he would have on the regular track. It was a risky, deadly game. The slightest mistake would be the last. The black pudding of the swamp would suck in an unskillful jumper with a smack. But he liked to take risks. It raised the adrenaline and created a sort of euphoria.

It wasn't difficult to cash the scrap silver at the small and only jewelry and watchmaker shop in town. The money he received wasn't a fortune, but it was just enough to buy a bottle of cheap fruit wine and have a couple of mugs of beer in the tavern before going back.

The evening was cold. He walked quickly along the roadside towards the campus. In the darkness it was not possible to go through the swamps. The beginning of the road was drivable, because between the town and the Pink Slope there was another village. On both sides of the road were fields. He was walking fast. Being hungry, since he missed his college dinner, he felt more intensely the warmth of the alcohol from the beer circulating within the blood in his body. There were no people or vehicles passing by. In this remote Byelorussian country, no one was brave enough to be out at night near the swamps. People believed that at night huge, human scalps with glowing, blue eye-holes, sitting on spider legs, were wandering around and would attack anyone who came close to their domain, sucking their blood.

Because it was getting colder, he decided to open the bottle of wine and add the alcohol to his body. He did it by hitting its bottom with the fist of his right hand through the folded jumper. The poorly fermented wine, under such treatment, produced so much carbon dioxide that the pressure of it pushed the cork out. Soon he had a good sip of it. Strong wine warmed better than beer. The cold was not so disturbing now. He loved the feeling. His mind was razor sharp and alert, but his body was deeply relaxed. After a while, the critical faculty of his mind was so poisoned that he didn't realize that he was crossing the 'barrier of safety' and entering the state of drunkenness. He finished the bottle very fast.

The stars in the black sky were exceptionally bright. The temperature was rapidly dropping, as often happened in late autumn on clear nights. It was called a radiation frost. The heat from the ground and lower parts of the atmosphere were escaping to outer space through infrared radiation. The trees, the electrical poles and the stars started to sway like a raft on a wavy ocean. Walking became more and more difficult. His balance was badly affected by the liquor. Suddenly he totally lost control and fell onto the frozen road, backwards, hitting his head badly. Getting up he thought, "Why does it always happen this way after drinking wine? Being drunk from vodka people always fall forward on their face."

It was impossible to proceed. The only logical thing to do in this situation was to rest. On both sides of the road the fields were plowed for the winter; and stored snow barriers, forming V-shaped huts waited to be assembled into a sort of fence to prevent the road from being covered by the snow when it was windy. Slowly, murmuring complaints because of his hurting head, he crawled on all fours under one of the huts. The grass on the roadside was crisp, already frozen in the subzero temperature, but the heat from the alcohol was so strong that he didn't care. He lay down on his back, with his hurting head sticking out a bit from under his shelter. Soon he drifted into the unconscious sleep of drunkenness.

A few hours passed when he suddenly opened his eyes. The stars were now so close; they seemed nearly accessible to the touch of the hand. He forgot where he was, who he was, and why he was lying on the frozen grass gazing at the sky. Actually, in his miserable state, he was enjoying pure beingness. The poisoned mind was sleeping, but awareness of his conscious existence remained.

Suddenly, all the stars started to move like dust particles inside the pipe of a vacuum cleaner, crashing into each other and then condensing into small light balls, which became smaller and smaller, constantly increasing in speed until becoming only a spark of golden light. He could not move. He was paralyzed, waiting. He felt that something extraordinary was happening. The spark entered his body through his chest and settled in his heart. In the same moment, the firmament of stars exploded into a myriad of lights, like the fireworks on New Year. The stars immediately returned to their original positions, forming constellations. The Milky Way was back, crossing the sky. But now he saw it in a different way. His consciousness expanded, embracing the entire Universe. He experienced a glimpse of The Oneness of himself with all of creation. Waves of love flowed over him and he became again intoxicated, but this time in a very different way. The tears of Bliss of the Union started to fall like a waterfall, forming little ice crystals on the frozen grass.

This state did not last long as the cold started to disturb him. After a while he got up. He recognized the road, remembered what had happened and started to cry again, but this time not from Bliss but rather from great shame. He was devastated after realizing that he had done something unforgivable. He had stolen offerings given to Her, whom he had already started to serve as a two year old baby. He had done such a crime so he could become drunk because he was restless and unhappy, and She, knowing the need of his heart, paid him back by giving him Bliss of Cosmic Awareness.

His mind started to recall the story told to him some years back by his parents. When WWII ended in 1945, the Soviet Union didn't leave the Eastern Polish territory of Lithuania. The Western Allies, the USA and England approved all of it by signing with Stalin the famous Yalta Pact Treaty. The town where he was born remained under the brutal rule of the communist Red Empire. Most Polish people tried to get permission to go to central Poland, as a gradual, perfidious denationalization had immediately started. Thousands of people were transported to Siberia and Kazakhstan. The people already knew about the killings in Katyń, Starobielsk and Ostaszewo by the Russian NKWD, predecessor of the KGB, of over 14,000 Polish officers, priests, university professors, medical doctors, lawyers and other educated people, and the Polish people were in a panic.

His parents, after receiving permission to repatriate, joined a group of priests, because his uncle was a local Catholic bishop and most of the priests were his parent's friends. They traveled in a cargo carriage and took with them only their basic, personal items. The trip to Poland through the Soviet Union's border was not long. In those days, railway lines on the Lithuanian and Byelorussian territory were still standard size, as in the rest of Europe. They were later made one foot wider, a typical maneuver of the Russian Empire to make their vast territory less accessible to possible aggressors. There was no need for them to disembark, and then re-board the train at the border. Half drunken NKWD officers who boarded the train did the customs and military check.

He was only 2 years old. His mother was holding him in her arms. He was interested in everything and watched the soldiers and NKWD commander searching his carriage, looking for contraband—forbidden by 'revolutionary' law—items of religious cults, memorabilia of the life of Polish bourgeois society, books and valuables. Rolled in a Persian rug was hidden a very old, famous picture of Mother Mary. This picture was the goal of many pilgrimages, a picture that had cured thousands who were incurably ill; a picture of the Holy Mother whose grace and love had cemented the broken lives of countless devotees for centuries. It was a picture of Mary from the Sharp Gate (Mary of "Ostra Brama") in Wilno—"Rome of the North."

The NKWD officer in charge, arrogant in his drunkenness, staggered around the carriage, swearing and scolding his soldiers. Standing on widely spread, unstable legs, he started to chat with the little boy. The smell of alcohol mixed with the stink of herring and dill cucumbers hit the face of the little one. The foreign language did not sound friendly. Nobody expected from him, who was so peaceful, so kind and always smiling, and who was only two years old, to take a deep breath and hit, with his tiny fist, the red and sweaty face of the officer. The officer was so surprised that he started to laugh hysterically and shout at the boy,

"What do you think? Who is in command here?" The next hit came as unexpectedly as the first one. More confident after the first time, the boy hit his enemy's face with such an impact that the officer's NKWD hat fell onto the floor. The officers and comrades watching the boxing performance burst into uncontrollable laughter. The officer lost his temper and his mind. Humiliated by the little Polish boy, he became even redder in the face. He quickly retrieved his hat and opened his pistol holster. His hands, trembling with anger, handled the gun with difficulty. He shouted, hoarse from anger,

"You Polish pig, I will kill you, I will smash you to pieces!" He put the barrel of the pistol on the boy's forehead. Now it was only a matter of seconds until the sound of a shot would announce the end of the life of the two-year-old hero.

One comrade, seeing the stupidity of his superior's behavior and risking disciplinary punishment, pulled his hand up just in time. The shot sounded like thunder, but the bullet missed the little boy's head by a few centimeters.

"Are you crazy Comrade?" said the soldier. "Do you want to fight a war with a baby? Cool down! You are completely drunk. Don't make an idiot of yourself." The officer, in spite of his drunkenness, realized his mistake. He put his pistol back in the holster, pulled down his uniform jacket and said with a sour smile,

"You have won my boy. If you want, I will not check your carriage. You and your companions are free to go to your Poland. It seems to me that you have been born to become free." The officer saluted and left the carriage with his soldiers.

For the college student, it was much too early to know that his destiny was already preparing him in such a strange way as to become totally dedicated to the Divine. Even before his birth, the configuration of the stars showed his life to be interwoven with It. He didn't know that one day he would leave the charms of worldly life and go to serve It, in Its present manifestation on Earth. He was not the first man to go from the gutter of life to the radiant heights of *Brahmaloka*, to become an amazingly clean lotus flower and Eternally Free. Sage Vyasa, before he became one and before composing the epic of the Mahabharata, was a highway bandit killing merchants for profit. But now, the college student was walking towards his boarding College, crying, with a headache, and feeling more wretched and unhappy about himself than before.

LETTER TO MY LITTLE SISTER

My Darling Little Sister,

I know you feel sad. You feel lonely. Your life is not the easiest one. But try to cheer up. Relax. Take it easy. Don't worry so much. Everything is as it is. It is not in our power to change the world. You are, despite all adversity, very, very good. You can easily become even better. Go step by step until you are the best. Never rest! Put a bold face on difficulties. Look at all as a great gift, a great opportunity to grow stronger and to become wiser. Do not row upstream! Conserve energy! Just float freely watching the 'banks of the river of life'. Be the Witness! I will tell you a secret which will help you a lot. I think you should know it. I will tell you how to meet our Guru whenever you like. Close your eyes. Calm your mind. Look into the dark space in front of you. This space is full of light. It is The Golden Light of Divine Love. He is there! He Himself is this very light. Tune into Him; talk to Him. He will listen to you carefully. He will cry when you cry and smile when you smile. He is always ready to take all the heaviness from your shoulders. His only desire is to make your mind calm and peaceful. He wants you to be free from illusion, to wake up. He wants you to rediscover the Real You!

I know you like to be cuddled. It's very relaxing. But actually you're being cuddled right now. He always cuddles you from within when you're sad, when you feel down. Little Sister, you are the Princess of the Universe. You are His Golden Daughter. You are born from Peace, and Peace is your birthright. Wake up my Sister! You own all of it. There is no need to beg. You are That!! You have just forgotten. So be always calm my Sister.

It's autumn and it's windy. You say you hear the wind. Listen, it's not the wind. Listen carefully. It's Him, our Divine Guru. He's whispering how much He loves you, how dear you are to Him—you, Golden One. You say it's hard, it's difficult? You say He's not with you when you're suffering, when you're in pain? Look back; look at the sand behind you! How many sets of footprints can you see? One only! Just one! Do you know why? You still think you are on your own? No! It's He who walks The Path with you step by step and is carrying you when it's hard, when it's difficult, when you're going through the torments of life. It's only thanks to Him that you can make it so well.

You often think Our Guru is far away in Japan, Europe, or in the USA. How can it be so? It is not true! It is spring. Look at the apple tree. You say it is only a tree. Look closely. Look at the blossom. It's Him wearing a gown with a dash of pink. He is everywhere, and everything is a form of Him. In fact, I don't know the place where He is not.

Dry your tears Little One! My Sister, there is no use in being sad. It's all only a tiring dream. Nothing from outside of you can affect the Real You. Wake up and be at Peace, be happy! Happiness is your Real Nature. Smile my Little Sister! A smile is your birthright too.

You say I am gone, I am far away. Why are you so sure? Where could I go? Look down, look under your feet. What do you see? Dust. I am there! Dust I am. Where am I not? I am everywhere you go. I only assumed this form for a while and you call it by a name, but soon I'll go back Home. Maybe I wanted to be with you once more as your brother. Maybe I wanted to once again see and contemplate the orange-red disk of our Father, God Sun, rising up and conquering by His light the darkness of the night.

Never look into mirrors my Sister, they lie. It's not you who looks back from the glass. It's Maya, showing only your temporary costume. To see yourself, the Real You, look into your heart. He is there. He is your real Self. Our Guru, having no fixed place to live, dwells in the hearts of all His children. He lives in your heart too. Remember this and be very gentle, be humble. You are as great as you are humble.

Words express thoughts. They have a power of their own, not only in sacred mantras, but up to a certain extent all words. Always take a deep breath, my Sister, or maybe even better two or three, before you utter a word, which can hurt someone, which can cause pain. Words can even kill, not less-successfully than a gun. Please remember what our Guru says, "When you are hurting another being, you cause harm mostly to yourself." There are no others. All exists in The Oneness. Your lips were designed to say only words which soothe, which calm those who are in pain and who suffer. Always be aware of who you really are and act accordingly. My Little Princess Sister, try to imitate a lion, not a fox. I hope you remember the enlightening story that Guru once told us.

I have full trust in you my Sister. I know that at the right time I will meet you again there, where 'I' cease to exist and 'I-I' as the Self start to shine. Now I have to go. My destiny is calling me. Maybe there is some work to be done and our Guru has chosen me for it? Let us see! I won't try to change the ways of the world. No! I will struggle to change only myself. Support me in your prayers as I support you in mine. Be well my Sister. Think only positively and keep your head high, very high, but without even a trace of pride. Grow; grow my Sister to become, as soon as you can, my Big Divine Princess Sister! I know you can, I believe you will.

With all the Love I have.

I am always with you; I am always under your feet.

Your Brother, Dust

LETTER TO MY OLDER SISTER

My Dearest Older Sister:

Here, in Australia, it's now winter. The nights are cold and sometimes foggy. In the dense, milky fog everything looks as if it is in a different dimension. I like to walk in the fog doing my japa. The fog makes me feel like I'm wrapped in the white clothes our Divine Guru wears. Somehow, during such moments, I experience His presence more intensely, and in a more intimate way than when I am close to His manifested form. The world then becomes nonexistent. Only I, this little I searching for the way to merge with Him, and in Him, exist in eternal identification with The Oneness.

Often in the morning, everything is covered with white frost. It looks so beautiful! It reminds me of my old country in Eastern Europe. It brings back memories of the time when I was speeding in a tank across the frozen plains of Belarus, firing a gigantic gun, learning to protect my Fatherland. In those days, instead of repeating my mantra, I was shouting commands into a short-wave radio, and directing a platoon of 'iron turtles'. How silly! We were learning to kill!

You, my dearest Older Sister, can't even imagine how pleased I am to find that you now live in Peace. I danced, blissfully intoxicated with happiness, when our Father Sun moved majestically over the vast Australian soil and whispered to me the great news: the God Sun Himself, who colors the western firmament, dyed you too in orange-red. By this He has confirmed your inborn right to be called His Divine Daughter.

Be well, my blessed Sister. Be in Bliss. Himalayan snowy peaks go through such transformation as yours twice a day, but remain white. You have grown up in white; now you will permanently abide in the color of fire. From Peace you have been born with serenity as your nature; in Peace you now live; and in the Peace of The Oneness you will eternally merge. Please accept your younger brother's humble salutations to you . . . to the Peace within you.

Actually, you are younger than I, but nevertheless, you are my Older Sister. Mysterious are the ways of our Divine Parents. I doubt if we will ever be able to fully understand THEM.

Now, on this remote continent, when I hear the waves of the Southern Ocean repeating the sound . . . Om . . . Om . . . Om . . . I know that you, too, are constantly chanting the sacred mantra. This supports me in my struggle for Freedom, and sends me the ammunition of patience and strength. I am in great debt to you. You, my Older Sister, set for me an example of an ideal spiritual aspirant, and by this you have helped me immensely. By being as humble as you are, you have earned the right to the highest respect a human being can be given by his younger brothers and sisters. My salutations to you!

Your firmness, persistence, discipline and determination on the path is, for me, the priceless proof that I am on the right track, traveling on the right train. I do not have to be in your Holy Presence to benefit from your Peace. Its power now crosses long distances because our Divine Guru works through you more intensely than before. Thank you very much, my Older Sister, for giving me your helping hand. Do not worry, I will always remember our Guru's advice, and I will be firm. There will be no more diversions from the Path. I have been born to become Free, and I will fulfill my destiny. I am so confident because our Divine Guru has promised to take me back home, to guide me to the Him within me. There is not the smallest doubt! I will return one day to our Eternal Abode, thanks to His grace, in spite of my many faults and mistakes. Nevertheless, I must say that some of my sidetracks have proven to be very beneficial. They became a rare opportunity to exhaust a few deep rooted vasanas, and at the same time, enabled me to see through my own eyes the emptiness of this Maha Maya world and its false charms.

Words express so little; why write this letter at all? Love knows no distance, nor boundaries, nor limits of time. I am with you always. Every day I come to you in the food you take, and every day you walk on me. I have already told my secret to our Little Sister: I am dust. I exist everywhere, nourishing plants and ripening fruits, as you also do. We are made from the same substance; yet from a pinch of this dust a diamond has emerged. That's you.

Because you are so close to our Divine Guru, you will now and always be in Peace. Wait for me! I am trying to come back home soon. Please pray for me that when the time loops close, I will be determined and brave enough to stand face-to-face with my destiny and, with my head held up, assume the privileged sacrifice, embracing the pain with love. When my time reaches its conclusion, please do not be sad . . . smile, knowing that I am already free and will remain free.

Please be so kind as to tell our Divine Guru how I love Him, how dear He is to me, and how grateful I am for everything He has ever done for me. Thank Him for the endless and sometimes severe tests and corrections, for the scolding, and also for the affection He has given me with unimaginable love. Please tell Him how closely I feel Him, deep, deep in the innermost enclaves of my heart.

I'd also like to tell you how playful our Divine Guru is! He has come to me a few times in dreams to correct my endless mistakes. He has appeared to me sometimes in the garb of an old Jewish lady, and then as a retired carpenter, and even again in the guise of a little girl. His attempts at disguise were in vain! My love for Him helped me to recognize Him immediately. The luster of His eyes cannot be forgotten, and only He can look so serious and at the same time smile with His eyes. We both laughed freely, like two little children, from the happiness of meeting each other.

My dearest Older Sister, please give my love and express my great respect to all of our Brothers and Sisters who live in the ashram, and those whom you met while touring with Our Guru. My heartfelt greetings to all who live with the Divine Light glowing in their faces in the Temple of Peace. My best wishes, also, to all of the younger ones still anxious and sometimes angry, but, nonetheless, earnestly searching for the key to the inner gate of the most sacred of temples.

Be well and in lasting Peace, Divine Solar Princess . . . my Older Sister. Let our Guru's grace, in which you are immersed day and night, be your best friend and closest relative; may it be your food and water, as well as the air and the light showing the path. Please accept once more, my salutations. I prostrate to your Holy Feet.

With all my love to our Divine Parents within you,

Always at Their service,

Your younger brother,

Dust

P.S.
Enclosed please find a small present. I am sending you a unique flower, which I found long, long ago and brought here. This flower was growing magically, in spite of all logic, on a vast and far away snow-covered nothingness where freedom was a bitter joke; a place where loudspeakers were blaring freedom, praising songs all day, but where people were afraid to speak freely. This flower grew in a place where the people preferred to 'speak' with their mouths closed and even avoided eye contact because a look could sometimes say much more than mere words.

This is the flower of the Smile of Freedom. Do not be uncomfortable that I am giving this to you. You deserve it. Inhale its fragrance. There is no other flower like this one in the entire universe. Let it be with you forever. Let the Smile of Freedom always blossom on your face, and give support and rays of hope to those of our Brothers and Sisters who still dream that they are living enslaved in chains of individuality.

LETTER TO MY INDIAN BROTHER

My Dear Divine Brother from the Holy Land of Krishna:

It is early morning now. The sun is rising. The darkness of the night is giving way to the light of day. All creation is waking up to enjoy a magnificent new day. Our Brother Birds are singing in ecstasy the triumphs of the Eternal One. Let's join them and be happy!

You, my Brother, are the Chosen One. You know the Truth. You see Him and only Him wherever you open your eyes. You know that you, yourself, are Him. Our Divine Guru has told you this, the most secret of secrets. You are the substratum of all that exists. Now, you are trying hard to experience it for yourself, to live it.

Dear Brother, please do not be angry with me for writing this letter to you. I know that it is entirely my fault. I have white skin, speak with a funny accent, possess many unnecessary items you have never seen before and, to top it all, innumerable faults. All of it, sometimes, irritates you. I am very, very sorry for causing you such discomfort.

You see, we are basically the same, but we have been molded in different ways, because we were born in different countries, in different cultures. I was born in a northern country very far from here, where temperatures during the winter can drop to—35⁰ C, and everything is covered with a thick blanket of snow, often more than one meter deep. I was raised in a culture very different from yours, with a different mentality.

My country was suppressed by a totalitarian communist regime with a materialistic philosophy. Our freedom of speech, freedom of movement, and even our freedom of independent thinking, was restricted. To mention God was a crime!

I was born at the end of the cruel German occupation during WW II and, as a baby, endured the take-over of our land by the brutal and barbaric Russian Red Army. Now I am a Traveler on a quest of my inner-most Self, visiting your warm land. I really admire it. It is a land that has been sanctified over the millennia by the presence of saints and sages.

I have been living in different countries on different continents for many years, and I never tried to imitate the ways and customs of the local people. I think it would be strange and miserably foolish. Why now, living in India, should I adopt an Indian name as you suggest? Would it make me spiritually greater or more advanced? How could it help me? A name is only a label. Changing the label of a bottle does not affect its contents. I try to improve my contents! Why should I eat food as you do using my hands, if I have the option of using a spoon as I have done my entire life? Is it so important? Does it have any deeper meaning than just "local custom"? I find it inconvenient and unhygienic, and feel resistance in doing so.

You, my Dear Brother, practice many rituals that are unknown and foreign to me, and you observe many traditional ways of dharma. It all belongs to your culture and I respect your culture deeply. But, many of these things have no universal application. Oftentimes, customs tend to originate due to the hygienic requirements of a particular country. I don't think it's all very important spiritually, as it all belongs to the realm of the phenomenal world.

I am very, very sorry if I make grave mistakes. Please forgive me if I am not following your customs strictly. But, I get the impression that you too think that as a Westerner I am not included in your dharma. You walk into my living quarters wearing sandals, but you want me to be barefoot in a storeroom—where nails and screws are scattered on the floor—that you think of as a temple?!!

It also seems to irritate you, when I openly speak my point of view, which may vary from yours. I think it is okay to be or to think differently. We have here the opportunity to learn a lot from each other. We have very different backgrounds, and extremely different experiences and education. The truth is that nothing is final, nothing is definite. Everything is relative, and our little truths can be seen in many ways, depending upon the angle of our point of view.

I do not know much about your traditions and customs because I have just arrived here. But I am happy to share some of my ways with you, ways that have worked for me in the past.

When we open ourselves to the Unknown and accept strangers with all their differences, considering them as our own extensions and sometimes as our own reflections, we can live in peace without irritation, while at the same time improving ourselves by learning from their faults or mistakes. We are as great as we are humble; we are as expansive as we are broadminded. Let us relax and watch the rising sun, singing our Divine Guru's praises together with our Brothers, the Birds.

The day is going to be warm. Let us enjoy it in unity. It is His intention for us to adjust, to adapt to each other, to forget all prejudices; don't see insignificant differences as separating us, instead see the many similarities that also exist. We will gradually become ONE and then we will merge in Him. Not only you—me too! You have no other choice but to accept the fact that you can pick only your own friends, but your relatives you simply have, and they are as they are. Some are more difficult to get along with, like me, but our Divine Guru has chosen all of us. Please do not call me an outsider, a stranger, because we both belong to the same family. Remember that we are both His children. Unity is Peace. Let us live in Peace and Unity.

I have patiently waited for more than forty years for the Berlin Wall to fall—more years than you have lived on this planet. Please, be as patient with me. We should be careful and not build new walls in our minds. Now is the time to destroy the barriers that are dividing humanity. The New Age of Awakening to the consciousness of The Oneness is quickly approaching.

Please accept the plate given to you from my hands when I serve food on our Guru Tours; my hands are as clean as yours. You only imagine that we, who come from the West, don't wash them after using the toilet. My hands have already served thousands in the past. Please allow me to serve you, too. This is my way of worshiping The Oneness in form of our Guru.

My Brother, I love you because this is the language of the heart that I understand. Only through the language of the heart can we communicate freely. I do not know your language at all, nor do you know mine. English, the language we try to communicate in, is a second language for both of us. Unfortunately, neither one of us has a good command of it.

Our Guru, being Divine Love Incarnate, has shown us how to love selflessly. He has also blessed us with the faculty of intuition to detect the intentions of others. Now it is up to us whether we use it or not.

Let us imitate our Older Brothers and Sisters whose faces are shining with the Light of Love and Peace. We, the beginners, can't even imagine how internally content they are, how light their hearts and how blissful their feelings. They, Our Dear Ones, are fully open to the flow of Love Divine. Even though they are living in the same phenomenal world as us, they are living as Free Beings. Let us try hard to be as they are—Free.

I don't expect anything from you, not even to accept the fact that I am your brother, chosen by Our Guru. I only wish for you to open your heart so Love can flow. You say that daily chanting is the most important practice on our Path. I'm sorry. I don't agree. It seems to me that the most important thing to do is to cry daily from intense love and from devotion. This is more purifying than anything else. I see that you sometimes suffer. I see in your eyes some insecurity mixed with a bit of fear of the unknown coming from the Western. And, I see a dash of pride because you can communicate verbally with our Guru while I can't. I believe that when our bhakti is strong, there is no room for fear, and the internal Silence of Love is more eloquent then the most fluently spoken Malayalam. Strong bhakti always results in total acceptance, total surrender to Life.

Everyone wants to be respected. We do too, my Brother, but we can't demand respect. Respect must be earned. You know, perhaps much better than me, that, when we strictly follow the Guru's teachings and personal instructions as given to us and are pure in our hearts, respect will automatically follow. Respect cannot be assured by title and position, by place of birth, by the clothes we wear, nor by the years spent in an ashram; but rather by utter humility and respect paid to our co-travelers on the great journey of life.

We should be very, very discriminative, and see each situation separately as a unique experience happening for the purpose of our spiritual growth. We can't store ready-made labels, poised to stick them on a particular situation if they fit a model we are familiar with. When things are difficult, we also need to avoid using a simplified, escapist explanation: "Nothing happens without the Guru's will." This is perhaps true, but it doesn't relieve us from our duty to resolve the problem. We have been given the faculty of *viveka*—discrimination—and our duty is to use it.

We cannot, and we should not, always ask the Older Brothers' permission to take the next step. Please understand that independent thinking is not a hallmark of disobedience to those higher in the hierarchy of life. I would say that it's a symptom of mental maturity. Even if we make mistakes on the way, it is okay. Actually, it's very beneficial, as we will grow to not repeat the same mistakes in the future. This is one of the rules of the game we are now in.

One thing is not clear to me at all, my Brother: Your reactions to my suggestions, ideas and inventions, aimed to speed up and improve the quality of work for our Guru. Although I lack formal technical education in some fields, I have fresh ideas that come from a mind that is not pre-programmed, and out of extensive life experiences gained in numerous countries. In the past, I often found new, simple and unconventional methods for improving things. This worked quite well for many years and benefited many people. Some of the problems I have pointed out are so obvious that in Western countries they're now backed by legislation. So to me it sounds very strange that you, who are like me working for the same Guru, reject most of my suggestions, ideas and inventions, and smiling ironically say:

"No problem. We're in Kerala, not in the West. Here capillarity does not exist even on Ernakulam swamps." But often the future shows that a problem of capillarity existed, and by not reacting properly or straight away, it caused a financial loss to the Guru's project, as well as work delays. For example, moisture rising by capillarity in ground floor slabs evaporates and causes extensive corrosion to equipment. In the West, ignoring a problem instead of solving it is not acceptable. Doing so would ultimately result in bankruptcy. So, I really don't understand your attitude. It really doesn't matter who finds the right way. After all, we are not competitors in business; we are equal disciples of Him—Our Guru. Remember that we are both His sons. Or maybe you think that you are more of a disciple than I am, more equal as in the story of the pigs in "Animal Farm"?

In our case, there is no need to show off. We should not be concentrating on being noticed or praised by our elder Brothers and Sisters, but on doing our Guru's work to the best of our capabilities. Don't we believe that our Guru knows our hearts and attitudes?

It really is not important what color the clothes we wear are. It is our state of mind that matters. Look around. Under the plastic hat, wearing a dirty shirt, you can find a man with the smiling eyes of a sage. He is not even thinking about having an asana or something else in kavi. He is doing what he has been doing all his life, but he's detached from it. He has no concern about blame or fame, he is Free and fully aware of his internal, indestructible wealth. Can you recognize him? He is just passing by. He is also our Older Brother though not an ashramite. If you relax and smile, he will respond immediately, returning a benign smile. He will be happy that you are progressing well, that there is no tension, no anxiety in you.

I have one more request. Please don't use my bath towel and then throw it into the bathroom corner. This is very unhygienic. In this hot, humid weather, it increases the risk of spreading skin diseases that are so common here in the tropics. It is much better to wash your own towel and have it ready for your own use. This is possible, even with our busy lives filled with hours and hours of *sadhana* and karma yoga.

You, Brother, are at home; you are in your own country, but that does not give you the right to go through my personal belongings and letters without my permission. You see, everybody's right to privacy is as sacred in the West as temples are sacred in the East. Believe me; it is very offensive to intrude on someone's privacy. I do not want to be rough with you, as you're not too tough with me when, in my ignorance, I break the rules of your customs. Nevertheless, such behavior as yours is not acceptable, and it makes me feel very, very uncomfortable.

I am not irritated, because I know it is a result of your child-like curiosity. I only feel sad that, after over fifty years of having all my personal things always in the open, even while living under a communist system, where the secret police would violate our private lives, I now have to keep everything under lock-and-key because of your curiosity and lack of respect. If you are so interested in seeing foreign goods and my letters in Slavic language, please feel free to ask me. I would have great pleasure in showing you everything, all that life has given to me to use, and even translate the letters to English. There are no secrets and nothing is hidden from you.

I hope, my Brother, that you will not take my comments negatively. I hope that one day we will meet at the Golden Gate of The Oneness, and that you, my Brother, will arrive there before me.

Always in Our Guru's Service,

With all my love for Him in you,

Your younger brother Old Brother-Traveler

LETTER TO BROTHER GILGAMESH

Dear Brother Gilgamesh:

I, Uru, your brother and companion for many thousands of years, and a few incarnations, am sending you my salutations, and would like to express my greatest respect and love. Let the praises of your glory always be sung by all the beings in the three worlds.

You have many names, but please do not be surprised that I am using this one. It is my favorite of your names. You have been using this name during your most spectacular life on this planet. Amazing, indeed, were your deeds on Earth during the period when you were here as Gilgamesh. I am very, very proud of you. Brother, you have become a legend! But now very few remember that you ever existed!

We were both born here. Our mother was Goddess Nin-Sun. After being educated and trained by our human father, a King on the intergalactic station, you returned to Earth to rule for over 750 years. This was an enormous sacrifice on your part, because you were so eager to learn more, to explore; and yet, you, of your own will, decided to give up your aspirations and, obeying the request of our father, you returned home. As you know, our parents had chosen me to take part in a trans-galactic expedition. It was a very long mission, lasting well over fourteen-thousand Earth years.

We visited many solar systems and landed on countless planets. We investigated many mysteries of the Universe. We also had the great pleasure of having the most beneficial meetings with a number of intelligent beings from civilizations spread all over the vast regions of infinite space. All of this kept my mind very busy, but sometimes I stayed alone in the navigation cabin of our space ship. Then, I was able to gaze into the dark infinite space, separated only by thick Plexiglas windows. I was watching the slow movement of the stars while the ship was traveling at a speed of forty-six times the speed of light. Very often during such moments I was thinking of you, my Brother.

Our anti-matter guns blasted apart the small particles of matter that were on a collision course with us. Because of our traveling speed, hundreds of years passed by on Earth while I experienced only minutes. I did not know anything about you. I have been thinking that maybe you incarnated again on one of Saturn's moons, and were meditating on The Oneness, trying hard to merge into It.

I have missed you, my Brother, very, very much. I haven't seen you since we went our different ways a week after you were established on the throne as King of Earth. Thank you, my Brother, for giving your capital city the name Ur, the root of my name.

I have often thought about our homeland, planet Earth. I knew that the Golden Age, with its entire spiritual splendor had already ended, and that Earth was diving deeper and deeper into the eon of Kali Yuga. Earth will face many negative consequences like, for example, increased ignorance, selfishness, hatred, wars, crime and indulgence in sensual pleasures. Humans will also start to try to find happiness and bliss—so much desired by all beings in the Universe—in the wrong way. They will turn to intoxicants, tobacco, opium, alcohol, hallucinogenic drugs and so on, similar to the evil and degenerate inhabitants of planet Pluto.

I have also been anxious knowing the kind of trouble that can be caused in the future due to the rapidly increasing population of migrants from Mars. It was our fault. After they lost the war and were searching for a new homeland in their gigantic liner ships, instead of finishing them off we allowed them to settle on Earth. We knew that Martians have an inborn desire to conquer, to fight wars. They also have an inborn tendency for cruelty.

Luckily, our father comforted me saying that The Oneness would be sending a great soul to Earth, who would start a new religion in Asia, where the Mars holocaust survivors had settled due to our too hasty permission. This man, a teacher of the Law of The Oneness, will be known as the Buddha—the Enlightened One. He will teach a lesson of love, forbearance, patience and nonviolence.

I have always wondered why Earth had become a home for so many races from remote parts of the universe: black-skinned people from Sirius B., Eskimos from Andromeda, and the most recent, yellow ones from Mars. However, after traveling for so many years through our Galaxy, I realized that our case is not an exception. A mixture of intelligent beings, sometimes looking very different and with predominantly human-like bodies, inhabit most planets. Physiologically they differ incredibly due to the conditions in which they live. The Oneness is always providing Its children with the most suitable bodies.

By mixing individuals from different races at different levels of development on one planet, the Oneness is providing favorable circumstances for teaching lessons of mutual acceptance, as well as opportunities to see in each other the similarities while disregarding the insignificant physical differences. This is the same exercise the Oneness has prescribed for our planet. This exercise, which has been going on for thousands of years, will soon be intensified—travel will accelerate and there will be an increase in the migration of people from various races and nations. Soon, in some countries, eighty-percent of the population will be composed of migrants. Gradually, the entire Earth will adopt one language as it was in the beginning of the present Wave of Life.

Before the end of the Dark/Iron Age, Earth will begin to awaken to spirituality; to the tendency to follow the Law of The Oneness; not degenerating but growing into our Natural State of Godhood. People's intelligence, dimmed in the Dark/Iron Age, will start to flourish once again. At this time, many Great Ones will incarnate on Earth to help us. We both will have an opportunity to once again meet and spend time together with the Great Ones: first in a small family, and then after a while under the guidance of one of the Great Ones—a Satguru—an aspect of The Oneness, the Incarnation of the Divine in human flesh. He will be known worldwide, and have many ashrams filled with spiritual aspirants from all possible countries.

Our advanced civilization collapsed due to the Earth planet being hit by a huge planetoid. A gigantic tsunami of more than a thousand meters high washed away everything humans created. Now in the fifth Wave of Life humans will discover anew what was known long ago. Fifteen thousand years passed. I have already been serving on Earth for a few incarnations after my return from the expedition. You, who have been resting for so long in higher dimensions, will soon come to live on Earth. You will come to Earth in the usual way; falling from the sky in a metal and crystal capsule as a flash of bright light, like a meteor. You will enter the soil with the rain and then as minerals from ash as a plant. You will be given a human birth as the son of the man who will eat this plant—be prepared for a surprise . . . me?!? Is it not incredible? Only The Oneness knows why.

Anyway, welcome back Brother-Son. You are most welcome. But that is enough about private things for now. Let me tell you a little bit about our discoveries during the expedition.

We gathered all possible data on spiritual knowledge, one area that interests both of us; from all the planets we visited in our Galaxy. I believe we saw and copied the oldest writings on the subject. These writings were imprinted on golden plates in order to preserve them through time, and were recorded from Sutras, which existed long before them, having been first memorized by beings unknown to us. We estimate that these plates are at least six-and-a-half billion years old, but we can't estimate the age of the Sutras.

How we found them is quite amazing. We were cruising in our planetary shuttle when our spaceship experienced severe mechanical difficulties. At first, there was nowhere for us to make an emergency landing, but all of a sudden a planetoid came into our sensor's range. While our robots were making the necessary repairs, I decided to take a walk on the planetoid's rocky surface. The gravity was so weak that I had fun making thirty meter long jumps.

After a while, in the reddish light of the local sun, I discovered an entrance to some artificial caves. On the portals, carved in solid rock was a drawing of some unknown planetary system and a likeness of human-like beings and some type of strange symbolic writings. As soon as I touched the door, it opened. Inside the cave, soft and pleasantly glowing lights were running off of solar panels.

The hallway led me to a square room containing a clear glass case that housed the golden tablets. There was nothing else. I found that the text was long enough to provide the computer with sufficient data for translation.

This and other discoveries we made have provided solid proof that the Law of The Oneness has been known from the 'beginning of Time'. What humanity is now rediscovering was known even before the creation of the Earth and after it cooled down enough to support the most basic forms of life. The First, Second, Third and Fourth Waves of Life were at least as much aware of the existence of The Oneness as being all-pervading and the substratum of all, and set by IT the Laws of Nature. In different times it was called by different names but being universal and eternal, IT always remained the same. The words in which the Truth about The Oneness were explained were only chosen to suit traditions, location of the planet, and the stage of advancement of its inhabitants.

It seems to us that the knowledge about The Oneness always comes directly from The Oneness Itself as an illumination in meditation. It is given to those who have evolved in consciousness rather than their contemporary brothers and sisters; to those who, by purifying their bodies and minds, have become open for receiving the revelation and the flow of the ever-present grace of The Oneness.

There are planets with highly advanced spiritual civilizations, where all live in perfect harmony with Nature. Unfortunately, there are also planets living in a state of confusion, as is the case with our Earth during the Dark Age. Then there are planets where the inhabitants know the Law of The Oneness, but who are rebelling against IT due to great arrogance, as they want to be equal with the Oneness while still retaining their individuality. They are putting forth enormous efforts to develop their technology because they want to attain immortality through an artificially controlled balance. The individuals there live a long life, almost eternally; but if they accidentally die, they have to start again the soul's evolution nearly from the beginning as primitive forms of life: bacteria and even viruses.

In your incarnation to come, my Brother, you are predestined to have the same compassion as the great masters, living in the small colonies of sages on one of Saturn's natural satellites. One day you will say;

"If it were possible, I would work out the karma of Satan, the leader of the rebels myself. I would make him Free because he too is a son of The Oneness and our brother. Now he is living in great fear, unable to reverse his wrong ways. He thinks that the price for Liberation is too high—to climb the ladder from the bottom, to grow in the darkness blindly looking for a direction in the labyrinth of manifested things and beings for billions of years, growing slowly and painfully into the State of Godhood." Only you could offer such a sacrifice. My humble salutations to you my brother from the past, and my future son!

It seems to me that you are on your way to becoming a spiritual giant, but you will have to pay the price for it. You will have to grow up struggling with difficulties, tension and anxiety. This time your dwelling place will not be a royal palace. You are by nature sensitive, and very early in your life you will want to help others, but your first duty will be to grow strong and knowledgeable. Do not waste time; there will not be much to be idle. You will have to learn what is necessary for the age and ignore the obstacles. The rest will come to you when the time is right. The Oneness will constantly guide you.

We have so much work to do. Our Divine Guru has already incarnated on Earth, and is waiting for us. The cycle is ending and many of our brothers and sisters are in great need of help. In the near future, you will have an exceptional opportunity to exhaust your tendency to help.

By the beginning of the third millennium, a magnificent and rare event in the Universe will happen in our Solar System. Our sun will receive a brother. It is already traveling through the vastness of dark cosmic space, and will soon be visible by the telescopes of the observatories. Both suns will form a binary system, something that is not so rare in certain parts of the Galaxy. Obviously, this will create many disturbances in Nature, especially in the beginning. There will be significant changes in the conditions on all the planets, changes in orbits and exposure to solar radiation. Our Earth will move into a new orbit positioned where the asteroids are now located. We will lose the moon as a satellite, but will soon gain a smaller satellite, which is currently orbiting another planet. Many people will die, but continuation of the human race is guaranteed. It will not be the end of the World.

The transformation of the nature of people from egocentric, greedy and lustful to selfless, loving, spiritually inclined and pure-minded will start before the great planetary changes take place. This will be a slow, gradual process with a possibility to progress faster. Those of us who see the need for change, who are ready to renounce petty desires, identifications and attachments, and who are ripe fruits on the tree of life, will be guided and trained to become as free as the Great Ones are. Those who are not afraid to lose their individuality and who merge in the Oneness will be called by one of the manifestations of The Oneness.

We are, my Brother Gilgamesh, very, very lucky. The Oneness is going to reward us for our past work. We are both predestined to directly serve, although in different ways, our Divine Guru, who is the incarnation of The Oneness. This is a great and rare privilege. It is certain that if we play our part well and sincerely, the gate to our spiritual growth will open, leading to our merging in Him and fulfilling our ultimate goal of evolution. We have been waiting for this opportunity for billions of years and during innumerable incarnations. Let us always be aware of the value of our present chance and not miss it. Many will meet our Guru and all will benefit, but only a few will be able to totally, and unconditionally, surrender to His Holy Lotus Feet. We will be amongst those few, and ours will be the final reward.

Now I have to finish and start preparing for a long journey. I am going to leave my country and go to a Great Island in the West where I will meet you. There, this mysterious plant containing your soul will grow. There I will meet you. What more can I say? I am very pleased that we will meet, and I am very curious as to how we will be together. We have no choice but to accept what has been predestined for us by the Oneness.

Please be patient with me. In this life we are going to be simple and humble people, neither poor nor rich. During your childhood and youth many desires that will be impossible to fulfill will manifest. It is unavoidable as long as your subconscious mind is saturated by experiences from your long life as a King of the World. We will have no servants, no treasures. Try to control your desires and concentrate your energy on getting ready for your mission. Gather strength, and please accept my different ways and separate destiny. It will hurt because of attachment, but remember we are always together; we are in the same game, Brother. Let's have faith in the Omnipotent and play for the jackpot.

Now it is time to put into practice what I have learned on my expedition. I'd like to share it with you. It is of incredible wealth. Earthly science has not discovered it yet, but there is a much greater speed then the speed of light. The Oneness will show us how to glide on that speed on the Ocean of Eternity. Let's travel together to the core of Existence, to the most distant, almost inaccessible place in all creation—our own Self, hidden in our hearts.

The cosmic wind is howling between planets, touching moons, cooling suns. Listen, my Brother, to its whispers. It is not a wind of cosmic particles speeding through the infinity of space. It is the music of the Divine Flute of the Eternal One. HE is playing the melody of freedom for us. Let us dance in ecstasy to the timeless tune "Hava nagila, hava . . ." like your one hundred-eight wives danced during your coronation ceremony. Listening to the melody of the Divine Flute will help us to avoid getting tired when difficulties come, and we will not become upset when our ignorant companions and relatives start trying to stop our endeavor, or at least to slow it down.

I love you more than myself, but love cannot be fully expressed through words. Please try to find it hidden between the verses. If you start to feel sweetness in your throat and if your eyes become watery—that is it! You are on the right track. Go further, slowly, systematically, and you may find the Real Bliss ahead of you in the land of the Unknown.

The starting bell for the game is due now. Be ready, be well, and see you soon on the stage of life.

Please accept my blessings.

Your brother, friend and father to be,

Uru

GARDEN

How sweet are the fragrances in Your Garden, Guru! How joyful is its serenity. How many of us already rest there? Eden. Is the Garden of Eden and Your Garden the same? Those few who are sitting under the widely spreading boughs of the eternal, indestructible Peepul Tree, which grows on Earth but whose roots are in Heaven (mystical tree symbolizing that we are living on Earth but our real home is in another dimension), are crying intoxicated in illuminating Bliss—others are standing ready to serve, waiting for your call.

O Grand Master Gardener! You are incredible!! You are the best Gardener of the Universe. Expecting us to come, You planted Those Trees at the beginning of time. Following Your wish they became the first Preceptors. Now they are huge and give the shade of security and stimulating fruits of Knowledge, surcharged with Your spiritual power of The Only Truth. How grateful we are for all Your gifts so abundantly offered to us with Your Divine Love. Eating Your godly prasad we became Love Itself. Eons have passed as we've crawled towards the Light, unhappy due to our erroneous understanding of our relationship with others and with the world. Now through a mutual feeling we understand what Love-Light is. Now we can better appreciate the depth of Your Silent Love, this, what Compassion is, in its absolute fullness. So we too, through the Silence, try to say more than we are able to say using words. We are whispering in Silence how dear You are to us and how we love You so very much.

The restless wind of the mind raises waves on the infinite ocean of Consciousness. They assume shapes corresponding to respective desires and imaginations and . . . . then individuals are born. They interact, play together for a while and subside, as turbulent waves do after a storm. The minds and the intellects can function only when located in three-dimensional space and exposed to time. But where is time in Your Garden, Guru? In Eternity the causality does not exist. Then, there is no need to brood more over the future, as it has no power over us! Here we live in the NOW! Are there also any distances? For them to be a duality is needed, but in Your Garden there is only the all-pervading Oneness. When the Presence of the Absolute is manifesting Itself distances and time can't be measured. Nothing is even happening; all simply is. It is here and now. All has its being, its existence in You, Our Guru, who are for us God of Gods, all in all, road and vehicle, beginning and end, direction and final destination, hidden in the innermost enclaves of Your darling children's hearts, their own majestic Self!

What more can we say, Guru? Let us be in Your Garden forever and ever. Let us rest or work as You choose for us. We are Free! Tornadoes possibly will pass; a few of us may get uprooted or dry up but we, we will stay to grow! We want nothing and nothing can harm us. Don't You wish us to be as humble as ordinary grass is? Aren't we the offspring of the eternal Peepul Tree? We are the seedlings of Your own selection! Now we are small, but who can have a doubt, under Your care, nourished by the ambrosia of Your love we will become just Those Trees! From us is made Your Garden, the place of no time, Garden of Eden . . . .

FORCE FIELD

The conscious life existing on inhabited planets goes through unending mini and maxi cycles, just as the planets themselves. Those changes are induced and controlled by the activities of centrally located suns. Enormous masses erupting in thermonuclear reactions as lumps of tremendously heated plasma are simply bodies of highly intelligent super-beings, whose lives are not comprehensible for those of us who live for a few brief years in our limited tiny microcosms of planetary systems, within a small division of temperatures. Both a planet and its inhabitants are powerfully influenced by the position of an orbit around the Sun and its position on the trajectory around the center of a Galaxy.

The first mentioned factor is a cause of the mini and the second of the maxi cycles. The maxi cycles are called Life Waves or Yugas. Often when they close, there is no clear memory of the past eons and once flourishing civilizations, and no systematized knowledge is inherited by the successive Waves of Life. This is the case of once flourishing Atlantis and Lemuria. Usually, the end of a cycle is accompanied by massive geological changes where continents are almost completely turned upside down or immersed in the water of the oceans.

Accidentally discovered artifacts of vanished civilizations with hints of its advancement give headaches to the archeologists, as they don't fit the established theories of the evolution of living species; from monkeys through the Neanderthal to our predecessor, the Cro-Magnon man. Amazing information about distant and astronomical facts invisible to the naked eye, medical interventions utilizing natural immunological powers preventing rejection of transplants by the use of hormonal secretions of pregnant females, descriptions of flying machines—vimanas, interplanetary travels, a million year old nanotechnology found in the Ural Mountains, and weapons of mass destruction mentioned sometimes as secondhand knowledge in the ancient scriptures like Mahabharata are all interpreted as religious symbols and ignored as a source of information about the glory and fall of our predecessors.

Each civilization emerging from the darkness of time believes that it is discovering for the first time the Laws of Nature and the mysteries of the mind. It believes that it is developing new technologies, wireless communication, space travel and means of repairing body organs of their members. Only mystics, unnoticed by the general public tirelessly repeat that in fact there is nothing new under the sky that has not already existed long, long ago. Who wants to listen to them? We are too busy conquering whatever we can reach with machines and instruments of our own creation. Now we are deeply immersed in heavy materialism. The symptoms of our degeneration are too obvious not to be noticed. The Earth is going through the most negative division of the cycle called the Kali Yuga. This is a dark period when human morals decline and attunement with the Cosmic Intelligence is interrupted. Our utmost attention is focused on raising the level of technology and increasing luxuries with our mad consumption.

Gradually, as the comforts of life get more and more sophisticated, and as mechanization and automation reduce the need for hard labor, sometimes, on planets with beings at an initial stage of evolution into galactic civilized society, the cancer of selfishness and arrogance grows, degenerating and disabling its inhabitants' minds and bodies. The memory of such unfortunate beings diminishes and unhappiness increases, unavoidably inviting a psychosomatic illness to infest the egocentric population. Crime and suppression explode as an outburst of terrorism, i.e. cruelty of state-sponsored torture and racial discrimination. When the core of denizens immerse themselves up to their ears in dense ignorance, they naturally lose the faculty of discrimination between what's Real and what's illusionary, becoming fond of evil ways of behavior.

When in uncontrolled greediness, they start to violate and rob Mother Nature; they abuse or mass-murder other brotherly creatures, depriving them of their deserved right to live in harmony in The Oneness. Also, when beings start to blindly search for a commonly desired happiness through intoxicants, deviations and unbridled, licentious sex-orgies—often with children—God reincarnates again on such a planet. The Unlimited, assuming the form of a mortal, He, All-Pervading, Omnipotent and Omniscient, walks barefoot on the sandy roads of a Jordan Valley, circumambulates a stony track under the slopes of the sacred hill of Arunachala, or wades in tropical backwaters of the South Indian swamps. He, ever silent, speaks a local human language. By what He says as well as by His life's examples and self-accepted suffering, He teaches the degenerated population the right way of living an honest life, and how to progress spiritually to regain the Natural State. Those manifestations of the Highest are called Incarnations or Avatars. There have been many such appearances on the surface of the Earth, and many on other planets. Mystics also say that the luminosity of Avatars created an immense, mighty and powerful spiritual energy field around the Earth. In fact it always existed. Only the sporadic presence of Great Ones activates it, making it easier and more readily accessible to us. It is a source of inexhaustible strength for those who eagerly try to reach the Ultimate. We can call it by different names: Ma-Force, Force Field, I-Current, or Ocean of Love. It doesn't matter what name we use. It's obviously helpful to call it by the name which brings back to our unusually scatterbrained minds the memory of our Guru's form, God or Existence of Cosmic Intelligence. It would allow us to attune faster to the object of our meditation.

The most important thing is that the Force Field exists and can be utilized by anyone at any time and at any location. It supports us and can even save us in times of confrontation with the forces of darkness; in times of almost irresistible temptations; in the hours of a dark void when our faith is shaken to its foundations; when nothing remains to hang on to. We can always call on it by using the name we decided to adopt for it. There is no doubt. It will respond promptly. This field envelopes the entire planet and most probably extends into infinite space where it interconnects with similar fields around other planets, forming a spiritual tissue of Infinity and providing a super conductive medium for Conscious Presence where information is transmitted in the quantum way, instantaneously, amongst all parts of Existence regardless of any distance.

There is no place where the Presence is not present. It supplements the verbal teachings left by Masters for humanity, and there is not too much of what we say that thunders in Silence more powerfully than Silence itself. It is a Godly gift to those of us who are looking for a way out from the labyrinth of physical and mental misery, not knowing where to go or whom to trust. When we mentally submerge in it, we will experience in an instant a calmness of the Bliss of Eternity, as well as an indifference and detachment from worldly affairs. It will open for us a door to Immortality and the powerful knowledge of Wisdom. It automatically neutralizes the toxins of negativity projected into the atmosphere, and disarms weapons of hatred, lust, jealousy, greed and other lower feelings.

We are all children of The Highest. We have an incontestable right to tap into this powerful Current-Field for our uplift. But we must remember that, being equipped by our Father with the power of discrimination, we are obligated to use it wisely. We should solve, with the help of the Force Field, only problems surpassing our capacities, exceeding our strength and overshadowing our abilities. We should never abuse it for gaining selfish ends. We are infinitely weaker in comparison to Incarnations and Masters in their full awakening to their oneness with The Reality, but even we can and should replace the resources of this Reservoir of Divine Force used by us. We should, in deep concentration, chant three times daily, morning and evening, with a sincere intention in our hearts to contribute to the well-being of our brotherly creatures inhabiting our beautiful blue-green planet Earth: Lokah Samastah Sukhino Bhavantu . . . Om Shanti, Shanti, Shanti (Let All Beings of This and Other Worlds be Happy . . . Peace, Peace, Peace . . .)

One of the Laws set up in operation by The Creator is: 'Only when you freely give you can freely receive.' We should remember it, and also the fact that the Force Field is a property of the Totality of Beings to which we belong. We should respect It as equal to The God-Creator, whose extension or form of manifestation, in fact, It is.

ETERNAL TAJ MAHAL

My dearest Lord Shahjahan,

Already more than three centuries have passed since I left you my Lord, taken away from this world by the merciless Yama, God of Death. I left you in grievous sadness, you and all of our fourteen children we loved so much. Not being physically with you and not being able to serve you and please you, I lost the purpose of my existence. But I did not cease to exist! You, my dear husband, you were the center of the universe for me, and serving you was my only desire. My love for you had no boundaries, no limits.

I very much like the Taj Mahal that you have built for me. It's great! Even celestial beings from the world where I now live admire it. It is magnificent! But it did not make me happy my Lord. Not at all! I could not bear your sadness, your despair. Looking at your beard, which had become white overnight, my soul was in an agony of pain. Your suffering was torture for me. I prayed day and night to Yama for his *darshan*. Centuries passed. In the meantime your body has rested next to mine in our Taj Mahal. My prayers at the end bore fruit. Yesterday Yama appeared and said,

"Mumtaz Mahal, I am deeply moved by your patience and perseverance. Ask and I will grant you a boon."

"Please tell me, O Yama", I said, "What is the path leading to everlasting happiness on Earth as well as in Heaven? Please enlighten me on this matter. Does such a path exist at all?" In the beginning he did not want to tell me anything and offered me other boons. But after a while, when I demanded that he keep his promise, he said:

"Mumtaz Mahal, I did not want to tell you because this is a secret that mortals should not know as Earth is an abode of sorrows. This secret opens the gate to immortality. I will lose the soul of who discovers this Truth. But listen Mumtaz Mahal, listen carefully. You deserve to be told. You are not an individual, not a separate existence. You are the Self—Eternal Deathless Cosmic Consciousness incarnating as a multitude of beings and things. You are as a drop of water from the Ocean of Existence, one with it. All of this is you. You exist as It, as Him. Being human, you live in that cage of a mortal body and you think it is you. The intellect, of which you are so proud, manipulates you by creating desires. Your mind entertains desires as thoughts and that is how trouble starts. Thoughts, by the law of *Maha Maya* must in due time manifest themselves as things, as experiences on the physical plane. Various desires popping in from the intellect are determined by your *vasanas*, which are stored in your inaccessible, subconscious mind. Your mind can enslave you or set you eternally free. The choice is yours. To break this wicked circle you need to stop thinking, but this is not possible. The mind's nature is to wander. Instead of struggling with your mind, you can occupy it with thoughts of God in any form you like. Repeat His name, think of Him, Him only. Meditate on Him. You become what you persistently think about! Your desires will gradually die, as well as all your attachments. You will enter the highest plane of existence, The Realm of Bliss—inaccessible even to the lower Gods. Your ego will gradually dissolve and you will stop identifying yourself with these transitory sheaths: body, mind and intellect. You will start to live, experiencing your Real Nature—Infinite Eternal Existence. You will enter the realm where I, Yama, God of Death, cannot execute my duties, the realm where death does not exist. You will realize that you never were born and that you will never have to die. Your life as Mumtaz Mahal was a dream only, which your own mind created. You will become an Awakened One". So saying, Yama left in a hurry, because a major earthquake was approaching and he was going to be very, very busy for the next few days.

Now you see my Lord, despite our love, which was really the greatest possible to be experienced by humans, we missed the point. We lived and died as mortals do and our great happiness was balanced by equally great suffering despite us being very wealthy. If we had used our energy, determination and dedication on contemplating God and Him only instead of cultivating attachments to each other, we would certainly have already attained the state Yama spoke of. This would be our Taj Mahal of Bliss—Eternal and Indestructible. My Lord, the time for us to incarnate again on Earth is due soon. Please promise me, you whom I loved so much, to remember Yama's teachings. Try to wake up from Maya—ignore the illusion. Direct all your love to Him, do not search for me, and do not think of me! Be detached! Maybe this time I will have white skin and speak a foreign language. It really doesn't matter. If I meet you in the next life, I will serve you as I did before, but I will remember who we really are. I will try not to create an attachment to you, my Lord, in whatever form you manifest. Meditate on Him, Him only. I will do the same, and when we reach the goal, we will become one forever, and our everlasting Bliss will be our Eternal Taj Mahal.

With all my love and from the very bottom of my heart, in Him, to you,

Your once loving wife,

Mumtaz Mahal

DARKNESS

A small boy walked across the huge vacant lot, holding a long stick in his hand, like a biblical shepherd on the hill of Palestine in the times of Prophet Abraham. A gentle breeze from the nearby lake ruffled his long, straight blonde hair while he loudly sang his song. The words had no meaning for those who might accidentally hear it; he was improvising only for himself and didn't care about anyone else's lack of understanding. For him, the sound was important; it had deep importance and significance. Through it he expressed his immense gratitude for his existence, for his ability to see again and for the beauty of the world. Only two years back he was blind and living in permanent darkness; but then a miracle happened. Now he could see well and, having an observant nature, he saw a lot more than many others. Walking across the block covered by the rubble of bricks and broken pieces of concrete and overgrown by weeds—tall thistle, nettle, pigweeds and wild poppies—he discovered at almost every step something new, something interesting, and something fascinating. Here an asparagus was growing through the rubble, there a cluster of fragrant violets, and further, growing in the bombed out area where a few years back had stood a hospital, were magnificent, deep purple moist peonies. And over there, on the big, shiny, green horseradish leaves, there was an orange caterpillar with black dots on its sides and short bristly hair growing all over its body.

The day was too short to see everything in his wanderings. He knew the area well. At the end of the site was a river with straight grassy banks. He called it 'The River Full of Milk', because after the rain it always became milky. It was not especially wide but a very deep, fast flowing river—very dangerous. Coming close to it, he always remembered that a few careless boys had lost their lives here while skating in the wintertime on the thin ice. Further up this river was a high embankment and a cobbled road on top of it. On the meadow, under the embankment, stood the greatest attraction for the boys: a real German 'Tiger' tank! It had rolled down, losing its ability to maneuver because of a broken caterpillar when the aggressor's army had hurried back toward its 'Reich', running away from the rapidly advancing 'Red Soviet Army'. Sadly, he could very rarely go there, as his parents didn't like him to play on it.

The boy stopped. Under his feet, amidst the ruins, he noticed a partly uncovered concrete slab with a metal flap. In the flap there was a small hole. The boy knelt and looked though the hole: Darkness. From inside came a stream of cold air. He shouted into the hole:

"Ho . . . Ho . . . Ho . . ." Deep down the echo answered, "ho . . . ho . . . ho . . ." The boy started to throw small stones into the hole and to listen to the sounds coming out of the darkness. After a few seconds, the stones falling into the water made a splash. He started to feel some indefinable fear, like after disturbing the deadly silence of a tomb. He stopped his play.

It was the very beginning of March. The weather was terrible—snow mixed with rain. One day the boy almost lost his life. Partly melted ice on River full of Milk cracked and he fell into the water. Luckily he managed to grasp a dry weed overhanging its bank and pulled himself up but he developed pneumonia.

The boy tossed and turned in his bed. The fever, reaching forty-two degrees centigrade, had made him semi-conscious. He started to rave. Though not sleeping, he saw visions, like tiring nightmares. It was like watching a sequence from a science-fiction film and being in it as an actor. He was being squeezed like an unborn baby in his mother's womb, locked in a ball made of an alloy of glass and metal. It was very thin, black and semi-transparent, but still an extremely strong prison. It was suspended in outer space and he saw, magnified, as if in an astronomer's telescope, stars, constellations and galaxies in the form of disks and spirals. Far away from him pulsars blinked regularly like Earthly lighthouses on the coast of the sea. A million light years away, quasars and supernovas vomited matter overheated to the state of radiation. He saw in the center of each galaxy the frightening monstrous 'naked peculiarities', called 'Black Holes.' by Western astronomers. They greedily swallowed any matter: planets, cosmic dust, meteors, comets and even huge suns. All that came closer than its 'horizon of happenings' fell into it, disappearing from this dimension and entering it again later in a different time and a different place, as matter projected from quasars. Space was full of Presence. IT was not visible, but he felt IT as something All-pervading and Real.

The boy struggled to break free from his prison, which separated him from The Presence, and prevented his communicating with IT. In vain were his desperate attempts. His small prison was built with the ultimate craftsmanship.

There was not much chance to get out of it, and not much chance to recover from his illness either. In those days, antibiotics for a lung infection were not available and he had not been born a Hercules. To make things worse, the family doctor, the gentle and very knowledgeable Dr. Hans Hoffman, had been arrested by the U.B. (Pol.: Urząd Bezpieczenstwa—Security Office), an extension of the famous Russian KGB. He was German and, in order to take over his apartment, someone had decided to get rid of him by making false accusations. Now, poor old Dr. Hoffman was locked in a deep dungeon, with sadistic experts from the U.B. torturing him with electric shocks and red-hot iron rods, beating his arthritic body with rubber truncheons, trying to force him to tell where he had concealed the 'Wecka' jars filled with gold coins he had received during the war from the Jews he had healed illegally. The doctor could not give any evidence of the location of a treasure he didn't have. He rarely had any money, as he seldom charged for his services. His work as a doctor was his mission and not a way to get rich. He had probably never even held a gold coin in his whole life.

When some relief from the fever came, the boy opened his window to try to catch some fresh air. It was another opportunity to see some of the still remaining and unknown wonders of the world around him. Maybe this was his last day? Why miss the chance to learn the secret of the spider building its web on a fence with the precision of an experienced engineer. Why not listen once more to the words of the song coming from the omnipresent street loudspeakers: «Солнышко над городом Сталин» (Sun over the town Stalin—short for Stalingrad = город—town of Stalin). The communist propaganda 'machine' shouted slogans all day long to saturate the subconscious minds of the children and adults. Some adults, knowing the truth, simply ignored it. But he believed the world existed only because Stalin wished it to be so; that the Sun would rise tomorrow only because Stalin instructed it to. The blonde boy also believed that Stalin was more than a human, that he was omniscient, omnipotent and everlasting. He believed that Stalin knew the contents of every child's heart, every single thought of every single man. The most uplifting message was one he had heard many, many times, that Stalin loved all people, as if they were his own children.

The small, blonde-haired boy obviously didn't know that Stalin had ordered to be built an extensive system of Siberian concentration camps, some of them meant for the children of Soviet Union citizens who were opposed to the totalitarian authority of the Communist Party, and therefore had to be destroyed. He didn't know that Stalin exterminated almost 12 million peasants in the Ukraine who refused collectivization. It was too early for him to know that on Stalin's command over 16,000 Polish officers, teachers, doctors, priests and lawyers were shot dead by the NKWD—the predecessor of the KGB I Katyń, Starobielsk and Ostaszewo. He didn't even know that his own father was a prisoner of a Lithuanian intern camp, from which most inmates were later passed onto the Russians for execution. He had escaped his ill fate only in the last moment using a clever trick. In those days, children didn't know about terrible tortures in the U.B. dungeons, or the terror of deportations to Siberia. He didn't even know why his sympathetic Dr. Hoffman wasn't coming to see him. In those days, even the most loving parents didn't talk openly in the family about the true face of communism, which, through propaganda, elevated their leaders almost to god-hood. The risk, that indiscriminate children might say something at school or to other children in the neighborhood, was too big. The fate of such incautious families was doomed. In this political system, the rules for survival were to keep quiet and do what they (the communists) told you to do, and not to praise communism itself too much either, as those who were real communists, real believers, had been destroyed first. The best way was not to show any emotions.

It was the 5ᵗʰ of March, 1953, only few days to his birthday. He felt it like darkness covering his vision. "Is something terribly wrong?", he thought. The door to his room opened and his mother entered. She had a long break between classes; she had come to see how he was. The school where she was working was only a few hundred meters away. Her face was shining like the sun. "Stalin nie żyje," (Polish: 'Stalin is dead'), she whispered, like it was the best news, but made no comment. But now the streets were silent. No songs dedicated to uplifting communist progress 'комсомольцев' (young members of Soviet organization called Consomow) and the labor champions, no hymns in praise of our Father, Josef Stalin; only silence.

The boy could not at first understand the meaning of her statement. This was something so impossible; it could not happen. It was equal to saying, "The sun has fallen into the lake." He asked, "Mum, what did you say?" She calmly repeated, "Stalin is dead. He died this morning of a heart attack. They announced that at twelve o'clock there should be one hour of total silence. The trains, factories, cars and buses all stopped. Now it is 12:30 p.m. At school, all are standing like wooden posts, gazing dully at his photos hanging everywhere on the walls. Those who wore badges with his likeness attached a black ribbon to it. Let us see, something may change. There is hope."

Suddenly he understood. Stalin had died. The boy closed his eyes. It was the end of the world! There was no reason to continue his life. Even the sun would not rise tomorrow. The entire world would die in total darkness. "That's why I had such dreams and visions", he thought. The tears started to roll down his cheeks. His whole body participated in his extreme grief. The boy's mother, not fully understanding his state, tried to calm him down but without success. Soon she had to return to school. The boy cried without stopping all afternoon and all night. In the morning, when he saw the first rays of the sun on the tall poplar trees growing on the bank of the lake, he stopped. Something was not right! The sun was rising in spite of the fact that Stalin was dead. This was a turning point in the boy's illness. He got better and after a while recovered completely. Maybe it happened for a purpose so he could know from firsthand experience the real falsehood of this godless system, and promised himself to never again believe that someone could be like God.

A few months later the family doctor, the sympathetic Dr. Hoffman was released. He came home in bad shape, and probably for the first time in his life was upset. The 'treatment' he had received in the U.B. 'clinic' was cruel beyond imagination! He had not supported Hitler's aggression on Poland, the country he considered his homeland, the country where he, as well as his father and grandfather were born. He quickly sold his humble belongings and, being a German, used his right to immigrate to the 'Federal Republic of Germany'— Bundesrepublik Deutschland.

As summer started, the initial work on the vacant lot opposite the boy's house began. Huge bulldozers and digging machines moved rubble and prepared the foundation for a new building. The government decided to build a new hospital. They uncovered underground areas of the old hospital undamaged by the bombing. Amazingly, three live Germans were found. They looked like a few hundred-year-old hermits, with long white hair, pale faces and very slim bodies. All of them became blind when forcibly taken out of their underground darkness. One died immediately; the other two were taken to the hospital. One survived and told his story. He had been a nursing assistant. When the bombing started he was in the cellar's storeroom fetching some medical supplies for his ward. The building collapsed and he, along with four others, became trapped underground. There was a huge supply of canned food, and an abundance of water and air. After some time, two of them died. This had happened in 1945. Later on, he lost track of time and didn't know how many years had passed. He didn't know that the war had ended one year after the rubble covered them. He was very afraid of Russians. The German also said some strange things; people repeated what he said with disbelief and fear. He claimed that the darkness is full of Golden Light and an all-pervading Presence. He was diagnosed as a serious mental case and quickly sent back to West Germany where his family still lived, never expecting him to return.

After some time, the small boy's family received the first letter from Dr. Hoffman reporting that he was almost well and had been given wonderful assistance from the German authorities. He complained that he had been forced to leave his country, Poland, due to the situation. He mentioned the miracle of the three men found in the hospital ruins, as the case had also become well known in Germany. The newspapers had interviewed the only survivor. Dr. Hoffman said in his letter that he believed that this man, after so many years in darkness, had started to experience Light, and that this Light must be a form in which God's Presence can be sometimes experienced by humans.

It was too early for the small boy to understand what his old friend was trying to say. Everything in the universe occurs at the right place and the right time. But the small boy believed the words of gentle Dr. Hoffman; he knew the doctor never lied. He knew from his own visions during the past feverish episode and having been at the edge of death, as well as from the time when he was blind, that darkness in fact is not dark at all. It pulsated intensely with light, a very special light. Only one thing the boy could not accept—Dr. Hoffman's comment that the light is the Presence of God. He knew from his teachers that God does not exist. That He was invented by the clever clergy to manipulate and exploit the common people, to keep them in the darkness of ignorance of the 'real' materialistic and scientific vision of the world. At this stage of his life he believed them.

CLOSING CIRCLE IN TIME

After running away from Poland, afflicted by Communism, I spent over two years in England. Finally I was allowed to settle in the free world. My choice was Australia, to be as far as possible from this sarcastically called 'the best political system in the World'— communism. But everything there was so different; mentality, food, climate and life style. In the beginning, communicating with the people became a problem, as I had never studied English in depth. All my skills in that language were developed by attending a two months' course in London and a one month's course in Melbourne, after arriving in Australia.

But a few words of promise from a small and mysterious book, 'Man's Past, Present and Future' which I got to read from my aunt, still echoed in my consciousness: **"Those who sincerely desire to grow in spirit will be found at the right time, called and guided . . . Not a single soul will be left unnoticed . . ."**

I wanted nothing else! That was why I had left my country and a promising career. I wanted only to find the 'Secret of Secrets', the source of unending happiness. Now I had no country of my own, no permanent dwelling. I became Mr. Nobody, a tiny particle of dust on the road to Freedom. But strangely—I felt that the entire Universe had become my home! Wasn't I a child of The Oneness? Still, I was patiently waiting for a call, feeling all the time the guiding protection of an unknown Master.

My time was filled with struggling to make a living in this new and somewhat hostile world of Western business until, one Saturday afternoon, when driving home from work I passed a sign on the road that said 'Garage Sale'. In the past I'd seen signs like this here and there and always ignored them. This time some irresistible power forced me to return and see what was for sale. A middle-aged, typical Australian 'mate' from the hippie generation of the 60s, was selling his humble bachelor's belongings, intending to try his luck in prospecting for gold in the wilderness of the vast Australian continent. Finding at first nothing of any use for me, I started searching in a few cardboard boxes full of books, spread all over the lawn. Despite the fact that until then I'd never wholly read a book in English, for some reason I selected three books which drew my attention: 'Initiations' by Paul Sédir (translated by Mouni Sadhu), 'Concentration', and 'In days in Great Peace' both by Mouni Sadhu himself.

And it happened! With the help of a dictionary, I read the entire text of 'Initiations' word by word, sentence by sentence. This book made such an impact on my mind, that ever since I felt as if I was living in a dream. So . . . great Masters DO EXIST!!! They are not illusions created by exuberant imaginations! THEY ARE REAL and, are watching over all of humanity, ever ready to pick up ripe souls, ready to guide to Freedom and Immortality the humble few who deserve their care.

I immediately realized that the first step towards conquering my restless mind was to develop concentration. So, I started to read Mouni Sadhu's next book, 'Concentration, a Guide to Mental Mastery', with great interest and determination. When I came to his statement: "If you, dear reader, have any habits like drinking or smoking and can't control them, then reading this book further is of no use as you are a slave of your habits and can't even dream about controlling your mind. So please close it now and pass it on to your best friend!" This was on my 40th birthday, and I was a chain smoker. Without much deliberation I decided immediately to give up this harmful habit, which I had cultivated for well over twenty years. I wanted to read this book to its end, sensing that in it is a key to The Path. I thought that there was no obstacle which could stop me from doing it. The desire to be master of myself was so strong that giving up cigarettes in one day, from 80 to zero, was effortless and without any of those side effects my doctor had warned me about.

I started practicing prescribed exercises wondering where I would find a living link to The Path. Then I discovered that Mouni Sadhu, in his 'Preface' to 'Initiations', mentioned that the translation of the book was made in Melbourne, Australia. I thought there ought to be a chance that he was still around and so, I started a systematic investigation.

Unfortunately I missed Mouni Sadhu by nine years. But in the process I discovered his grave in Springvale's cemetery called Necropolis. This cemetery is as beautiful as any first-class botanical garden could be. The vast cemetery area is organized in sectors according to different faiths, and all sorts of decorative trees and shrubs grow on the banks of artificially made creeks and waterfalls. A common 'economy' section called Cassia has walls made out of artificial stone, two meters high with 4—5 rows of niches for the ashes of cremated people. Mouni Sadhu's niche was in a top row and numbered 451.

It was here that I came upon a bronze plate on the wall of the niche containing his ashes. Inscribed on it was: "MOUNI SADHU greatly missed by all his friends", along with the year of his birth 1898, and the year of his Samadhi—1971. Checking with the Cemetery Administration, I found that here too he was registered under the name of Mouni Sadhu. The address of his last residence also did not provide any link to his original name.

It was probably Mr. Gangopadhyaya, President of the Ramakrishna Mission, Australia, who directed me to Ms. Vera Rundus—a Czech lady, well known as a hatha yoga teacher, in the suburb of Melbourne called Brighton. I was directed to her as having been once associated with Mouni Sadhu who had regular meditation classes in her educational facilities. So, on one rainy afternoon, we met in her school of yoga. One other person who also knew the departed Sadhu participated. He was an old, retired high school teacher. Our meeting formally scheduled for half an hour turned into a satsang that lasted over four hours.

We talked about The Path. What did I find out? I learned that Mouni Sadhu was probably Polish or Russian. This is also supported by a number of books in Russian, which he quotes in the bibliographies of his books. Mouni Sadhu completed his higher education in France. There he learned about Sri Ramana Maharshi from Paul Brunton's book "A Search in Secret India" given to him in a park by an unknown-to-him lady. Later, as an engineer, a specialist in building power stations and high voltage lines, Mouni Sadhu worked in Brazil where he formed a group of seekers following the Maharishi's teachings. There he also wrote a small book, "The Direct Path", which was translated into Portuguese, printed, and later personally offered to the Feet of The Master. On perusing it page by page, Bhagavan noticed a quotation from Adi Sankara's spiritual classic "Viveka Chudamani", and asked Mouni through the translator to add a footnote regarding this source, in the next edition. Sometime after World War II, Mouni Sadhu immigrated to Australia and settled in Melbourne. From there he made his only trip to the abode of the Great Rishi. All people who were associated with Mouni Sadhu believe that, during this short visit, being a ripe soul, he successfully completed in Bhagavan's

Presence his lifelong sadhana. Ms. Vera Rundus also informed me that in Melbourne Mouni Sadhu formed a group of Ramana Maharshi's devotees called the "Arunachala Group". It was located in the suburb of Burwood. I also found this information in a small printed note, in one of the books "Theurgy" by Mouni Sadhu, which I bought on a later occasion. Living in Melbourne, Mouni Sadhu, who continued his profession and worked with the Electricity Commission of Victoria, was also helping a few schools of yoga by conducting classes on meditation and spiritual unfolding.

Both Ms. Vera Rundus and the old teacher told me that there was some evident dissonance between Mouni Sadhu and Paul Brunton. Towards the end of his life, Paul Brunton, being a famous writer, started to claim that Ramana Maharshi had become worldwide famous only thanks to his book "A Search in Secret India" where two chapters were dedicated to living on Arunachala, Sage. As this led to some confusion in the mind of his readers, it was met with strong disapproval by Mouni Sadhuand and temporary rejection of Paul Brunton by Ramanashramam. There was in fact some brief written correspondence between the two regarding this matter, after which Mouni Sadhu scrupulously refrained from making any comments about the former.

Mouni Sadhu's failing health made his last years a bit of a struggle. He retired and committed himself to putting together his vast notes about The Path and the methods of sadhana. As I was told, he passed away in the toilet. Natasha, a Russian nurse taking care of him, upon hearing a sudden sound, tried to enter the toilet, but Mouni Sadhu said firmly, **"No need to help! It's time for me to go"**. Upon his sudden death, probably from heart arrest, all his notes, together with the almost finished manuscript of a book about the 'influence of diet and health on a Quest', were with his personal attendant. In spite of my persistent attempts, I couldn't locate this Russian nurse, as already more than eleven years had passed since his samadhi.

Vera Rundus also told me that Bhagavan's devotees from Brazil were frequently visiting Mouni Sadhu as he was for them a guide and living link to their Guru, Ramana Maharshi. On one occasion Mouni

Sadhu crashed his VW van while driving back (in order to get some forgotten necessity—either salt or sugar) to the local shop from a picnic with Brazilians. The van, rolling down the serpentine road on the slopes of the Dandenongs in the East neighborhood of Melbourne, hit a eucalyptus tree. The impact threw Mouni Sadhu out of the van. A doctor present during this accident confirmed his death. A test with a mirror kept close to his mouth did not show even the slightest sign of breathing. His heartbeat had stopped. Twenty minutes passed. The fellow Brazilians started to chant some Sanskrit shlokas. Suddenly Mouni Sadhu sat up as if nothing had happened and said, "The van is OK. It is drivable. Let us move on . . ."

A few years later I was in a crash myself. Around the curve of a suburban street, I met head on with another driver who cut the bend too sharply. He was also driving as fast and as carelessly as me. The impact was tremendous. Our individual speeds of 70 km/h added to 140. My huge Toyota Crown Station Wagon flew into the air landing on its side some seven meters further on. Wrenched off the car, its front wheel guard propelled away making a terrifying humming sound. Fortunately, no people were around to be decapitated. After the sounds and movements of the collided vehicles had come to a standstill, I found myself in shock performing a rather meaningless action of kneeling on the asphalt and sweeping with my bare hands the glass and metal debris from the road. Suddenly someone with very gentle voice said from behind:

"Nothing really bad happened! We are both still alive. There is no need to worry." Then he touched my back . . . and a charge of lightning passed through my body. I was stunned. Turning back I saw an old Greek man looking at me with a friendly smile.

"Who are you?", I asked. For some time he kept smiling while looking at me with his warm and soft eyes. After a while he answered,

"It doesn't really matter who people believe I am. You better try to find who YOU are!!!" Ramana Maharshi's ATMA VICHARA!!! were the magic words that flashed through my mind. I wondered if I had been dreaming. But no, he had just appeared on The Path as 'a sign on my Road'. Much later, I was to write to this man and I found out that he was a disciple of Mouni Sadhu! I also found that, just to make living, he had been running a Fish-and-Chip shop in the Melbourne suburb of Huntingdale. After the accident we never talked or met. A year or so later I noticed that his shop was nicely renovated and hanging on the window was the sign 'For Sale'. So he too had merged in Ramana-Arunachala.

I continued with my business alongside my sadhana on The Path. For all sixteen years of my stay in Australia, I went at least once a week to Necropolis to meditate on Mouni Sadhu's grave. On every Easter, Christmas, Guru Purnima or Onam, I burned incense and offered him my prayers. He was guiding me. This was always evident. In times of difficulties and confusion, he even entered my dreams and granted support by advising. Many years passed. I met and stayed in close association with many spiritual teachers and gurus: Swami Chinmayananda, Swami Damodarananda of the Fiji Branch of the Ramakrishna Mission, Ammachi and a few others. I learned some lessons and failed probably in many. With time, my sadhana intensified and my disillusion with mundane life grew to the point of leaving Australia. Renouncing worldly life, I became an inmate of a well known Math in Kerala and dedicated myself to work in their newly started, declared as charitable, hospital in Cochin. Impelled by circumstances, I took my first long break and left for a twenty-one day retreat to Tiruvannamalai. Is it not strange? So many years of dreaming about it, such long diversions . . . and then, finally, bathing in The Presence, listening attentively to His thundering—in Timeless Silence—words of Wisdom of The Only Truth. Finally, my unforgettable teacher Mouni Sadhu led me to The Master! How lucky am I!

Sri Ramana Maharshi

I realized that Tiruvannamalai Ashram was aware of the fact that Mouni Sadhu's real name was M. Sudonski. But it is widely and perhaps wrongly believed that he was Polish. Mrs. Vera Rundus was confident that he was Russian. This error regarding his nationality is understandable since Polish and Russian names have strong similarities. In Russian (Cyrillic) his name would spell as **Сугонский,** which is usually transliterated into English as M. Sudonsky (or M. Sudonski). The initial 'M' is quite probably **Михаил** (Phon. Michail), which is the Russian equivalent of English Michael and Polish Michał.

I hear some people say that there is no living Guru in this ashram. They are very, very wrong! Bhagavan Sri Ramana is now unlimited and even more alive than ever! I may briefly mention here that Ramana Maharshi told me this Himself in a vivid dream in which I went down into the depths of His Maha samadhi with a small Indian boy. Now that Bhagavan has drawn me here, I experience His palpable Presence with every cell of my body, with every breath.

Is all of this a mere coincidence? The first person, with whom I spoke, an inmate of Ramanashram, asked me—on seeing me borrow from the Ashram library a copy of Mouni Sadhu's translation of Sédir's 'Initiations'—if I happened to know anything about Mouni Sadhu and if so to share something more about the name and life of this one of few mysterious disciples of Ramana Maharshi. Such were the beginnings of my article, which was published later as a shorter version in Ramanashramam monthly magazine 'Mountain Path'.

I noticed some significant symbolism in this renewal of the memory of my Teacher Mouni Sadhu, after a gap of several years of flurried involvement in *sadhana* oriented towards social work, and so I started to ponder on these questions:

"What is the lot which my destiny has now for me? Is my karma nearing its conclusion now that I have reached the Feet of The Master? Should I spend my last days near my Spiritual Father's home? Should I take the view that I ought to accept this as his prasad? Whatever it was that had to happen, should I simply let it happen?"

So I asked Bhagavan in meditation. The Silence lovingly enveloped me and I understood without any doubt. All has been preset from the beginning of time. I have chosen, before incarnating, this adventurous life, so I must simply drift with The Current trying to make right choices. That is all. But He who dwells in my heart as Self, knowing that clarification would still be appreciated, sent me a spectacular messenger. Around 11 PM on the Full Moon night of April 6, 2001, a huge meteor crossed horizontally the dark sky over Arunachala (in Tamil: சிவப்பு ஹறில் Aruna = Red, Chala = Hill—sacred mountain in Tiruvannamalai where is Ramanashram and where I live now) and burst into sparks over the Great Arunachaleswara Temple. It 'whispered' to me in Silence,

"There is nothing to worry, *tombi* (in Tamil—young brother). Yes, come! Here you will dissolve in My Totality . . ."

The huge circle in time is closing now!

A MISTAKE IN ADDRESSING REQUEST

Travelers' clan came to Poland from Crimea some 400 years back. As recorded in historical annals, the ancestor of the family lineage was a Muslim from the Crimean Tatars. During the Moguls' invasion of Poland he chose to defeat Genghis Khan's army, where he held the position of general. So the connection to this culture, although mostly unknown to him consciously, was encoded in Traveler's sub-conscious mind, genes and blood. He was raised in a family affiliated with the Christian tradition where Christmas and Easter were celebrated but his parents were not followers of any church—they just observed festivals because, in those days, in Poland everybody did this, including high ranking members of the Communist Party. Traveler himself was always a rebel and persistently denied everything related to religion. He thought the idea of a Supreme God or His 'only chosen son' as not the truth but an idiotic concept lacking logic. His 'god' was Nature; mountains, forests and wild animals.

Now, after receiving a sign from Arunachala, Traveler started to think about which direction to go and how to make the next step. In his memory echoed words of Mouni Sadhu which he had written down after his only visit to Ramana Maharshi in his diary 'In The Days Of Great Peace', where he mentioned the miraculous help of the deceased Muslim Saint Haji. This was a situation seemingly impossible to solve, being in India, and he needed to solve it in order to depart this country. Traveler decided to read this book again to gain some clarity. In the Ramanashram Library he met Mr. Jey-Jey, an inmate of the ashram. After a long conversation, it was decided that he would write down everything he knew which was related to Mouni Sadhu and his path; leading him to the place of Ramana Maharshi Samadhi and the ashram surrounding it. And so it was that a story in this collection was created and subsequently, after editing to make it shorter, it was published in the ashram's monthly magazine: '*Mountain Path*'. But Mr. Jey-Jey did not know where Hajis' grave was. Traveler asked many other people but no-one knew.

After a few days, an auto-rickshaw driver said that he knew where Haji's Samadhi was and promised Traveler to take him there the next day. The ride to town cost in those days only Rs 20 so Traveler decided to accept his guidance. Driving through the crowded Market Road was an experience which required nerves 'of steel'. Every few seconds, a deadly collision was averted by the rapid maneuver of the driver: a bus pulling out of a dense crowd and approaching his tiny vehicle head on; a bullock cart suddenly crossing the road; a sacred cow making an unexpected turn toward a fruit stall; an absentminded villager zigzagging his bicycle in a semi-coma of the euphoria of being in such a big town. After miraculously surviving all possible threats, the auto-rickshaw stopped in front of a wide gate where two policeman, their bellies hanging down over their uniform belts, were chatting. The driver pointed to a tall slim building on the opposite side of the road. It was a mosque. The place was in a most unsuitable location for a saint to have a grave: in a small mosque on the busiest road in town and, on top of all that, just opposite the Police Station, with a stall selling cheap cloth attached to its front. Traveler paid the driver and told him there was no need to wait for him as he wanted to walk back. After leaving his sandals under the side of the cloth seller's stall, which was on the left side of the entrance, he proceeded to enter. As a white man, and not a Muslim, going into a Mosque for the first time was a bit stressful and challenging. How would he be treated? Tension between West and East was already high, with all the American's and their allies' hysteria about terrorism. 'Possibly they will kick me out or even beat me, believing that I am a spy'— thought Traveler. But the desire to convey his request for help directly at a saints' Samadhi was stronger than the fear of an unknown fate in the hands of Tamil Muslims.

Darghar (Samadhi) of Muslim Saint Syedini Bibi.

He timidly entered the narrow corridor. Soon, after his eyes adapted to the darker place, Traveler realized that the Samadhi was on his left and that the corridor was separated from the Samadhi area only by a low brick balustrade and led to the mosque's main building at the far end. Traveler noticed an old lady who was on her way with a bucket of water and tried to avoid her, but she stopped him firmly. Traveler got a shock when the old lady knelt in front of him and washed both his feet with her own hands. After she finished, she made a gesture inviting him to go inside. He had never expected this. With eyes full of tears, he entered a small room where, on the street side was the Samadhi. It was a coffin shaped structure made of green painted dry clay covered with an ornamental green cloth with the shapes of stars and a new moon embodied on it and garlands of white jasmine flowers laying on its top. On the left was attached to the wall a small tin for offerings and, on the right wall, many small triangular niches with olive lamps inside. The walls of the room were painted with the same green color as the Samadhi but with only half of its color intensity. From the top of the wall hung improperly attached electric wires, fuse boxes and some very old electric gadgets. The place was very simple but clean with a floor neatly tiled with brown ceramic tiles. There, on the opposite wall to the entrance, was a Fakir, perhaps over ninety years old, meditating. He had a long beard and fluffy white hair, covered by the traditional Tamil Muslims' white cap. He immediately got up with energy of a young man and, after spreading a rice straw mat for Traveler, left the room; leaving him alone.

Traveler, after prostrating to the Samadhi, sat cross-legged on the mat and tried to meditate. But his experiences with the old lady and the Fakir were so strong, so unexpected and so unconventional for the XXI century, that even basic concentration did not come. He just sat with closed eyes and slowly, coordinating syllables with the rhythm of his breathing, repeated silently, in his mind, his mantra. That was the only thing in this situation that he could do.

After a few minutes, Traveler started to feel a warm light beaming on him, as if from a spotlight such as those used on performing actors during the making of a movie. This was bad! Now they were filming him and would, for sure, use it for some propaganda. Big trouble! But the whole area was silent. No one was given commands. It is impossible for Tamil people to perform any task in silence. So what was it? He decided to open his eyes. Another shock. There was not a single person in the room—only the Samadhi, which was radiating a warm golden light. After a while, he realized that the floor, wall and ceiling were also radiating this friendly and loving light. The entire place was filled with Presence. A shocked Traveler stretched his hands toward the Samadhi as if in a gesture of begging for an explanation and asked, in the silence of his mind:

'What is all this about? Are YOU, Haji, trying to tell me something?'

Another shock: he noticed that even his own palms were radiating an identical golden light. This was almost too much for him!

139

'Haji, Older Brother, tell me please, are we ONE?' Traveler asked in a trance-like state of amazement. The light subsided immediately. He noticed a stream of incense smoke from the shelve close to Samadhi stretching straight toward him as if confirming: 'a connection was made and the message was understood correctly'.

Traveler calmed down, explained his need of guidance and, after inserting Rs 10 into a small donation tin, left the place. That night sleep did not come. He spent the whole night on the roof terrace—meditating.

Days passed but nothing significant happened. In the case of Mouni Sadhu, the problem was resolved in three days. Doubts started to drill Traveler's mind. Maybe all this was only a dream? He started to doubt his memory. A few days later he was walking in the neighborhood of Ramanashram, just to become familiar with the surroundings. Passing a big mango tree growing on the side of the road leading from the main Chengam Road to Nanagaru Ashramam, an old Muslim sitting on a plastic chair in its shade called to him:

'Com here *thombi*! What is your name?' he asked, commandingly but softly.

'Sir, people have given me different names but now I use the name Andrew.' answered Traveler.

The old Muslim said nothing but looked at him a long time, scanning his entire body. After a few minutes, when Traveler made a move to go away, the man suddenly said:

'Andrew, I have a feeling that you are going to be living here permanently. So I am offering to sell you a plot of land with a coconut hut on it.'

'Thank you Sir, I appreciate your offer as it sounds like a good idea but land here must cost a lot of money.'

'Do you have any money?' asked the old Muslim.

'Yes Sir, but only Rs 500 and a return ticket to the ashram in Kerala where I am now staying.

'Listen *thombi*, I will accept Rs 500 as a deposit for the land. The price is Rs 80 per square foot and the plot is 2,640 square feet. You calculate. Tomorrow we will meet here at 3 pm and will go together to a lawyer to make a contract. Do not worry. I will pay for the auto-rickshaw and the lawyer. The balance for the land you will pay me after you recover financially and, in the meantime, we will complete all the formalities necessary to register it in your name.'

This turned out to be the same lawyer who advised all the old disciples of Ramana Maharshi: Paul Brunton, Arthur Osborne and a few others. The lawyer's 'office' was a front room in his ancient residence less than a hundred meters from the Big Temple. In a corner of it was a pile of folders with documents, books and loose sheets of paper. It was obvious that no essential document could be located without at least a month of sorting out this mess. Under the window was a row of metal and wooden chairs, each different and all showing signs of having once been painted in various colors. On the lawyer's monumental desk was another pile of documents reaching a height of no less than eighty centimeters. There was no room for processing anything new. The lawyer was approaching retirement.

The lawyer had already prepared a draft of the document. He only needed to fill in the missing details of names, the amount of the contract and the deposit. After he succeeded in writing, with correct spelling, Traveler's very foreign name, he asked about the deposit. Traveler said, as was agreed with the old Muslim: Rs 500. The lawyer almost choked:

'Are you mad or are you joking? This is an office of the oldest lawyer in town and here jokes are not permitted. Respect this place and me! A deposit for purchasing land is usually ten percent of the price.'

'Sir, I did not ask you to make comments. I only hired you to help with the legal formalities.' said the old Muslim. 'Please write an agreement, that is all. The deal is between me and Andrew. There is a higher authority who has requested and who will supervise this transaction.'

The document was signed by both parties. Traveler handed over to the old Muslim his last bank note and the lawyer, because the poor buyer had no more money, added from his purse one rupee as required by local custom. This was the only monetary donation ever accepted by Traveler in his life. The old Muslim went back home in an auto-rickshaw, Traveler walked back to the ashram. Before they departed Traveler asked the old man what is this higher authority he mentioned in the lawyer's office. There was no reply. The old Muslim only looked in a very strange way at Traveler and in no time was gone.

For the next three days of his stay in Tiruvannamalai and on the entire journey to Kerala Traveler was on a strict water only diet as he had not even one rupee to buy food. From the railway station he also walked 8 kilometers to his ashram as buses are not free even for monastic renunciates.

Soon Traveler left the ashram, went to Western countries, earned some money and paid the old Muslim the balance for the land. More than ten years passed. He gradually upgraded his coconut hut to a solid brick house and permanently settled there, as was predicted by the old Muslim.

One day he told this story to a visitor from his fatherland—Poland. The visitor also had something serious to ask for and so was very interested in visiting Haji's Samadhi. Traveler explained how to find it.

Two weeks later the visitor called him and said that he had some important information to pass on to him. But he wanted to do it personally. So they met the same day. The visitor's revelation was: this is not the Samadhi of Haji. Haji's Samadhi is on Bavani's Nagar Dharghars Compound close to the Government Hospital. This Samadhi, which Traveler believed to be Haji's Samadhi was actually a Darghar (Samadhi) of the lady Muslim saint Syedini Bibi who passed way in 2. 10. 1888.

Niches for olive laps at Darghar of Syedini Bibi.

She, knowing Traveler's heart and intentions, conveyed his request to Haji and gave him the experience with the clear message: WE ALL ARE ONE, SEPARATNESS IS ONLY ILLUSION. So in fact there was not a mistake.

Traveler visited the REAL Darghar of Mohan Sarat—Haji fourteen years after being granted his help.

Darghar (Samadhi) of Muslim Saint Mohan Sarat known as Haji.
On a back wall hand prints of visiting his grave contemporary saints.

BLUFF OR RUN

The letter from home awakened him from the meaningless pastime of exploring the new dimensions of adolescent life. His father was seriously ill and had been admitted to a hospital close to the capital city, a few hundred kilometers from home. The possibility of a major operation was so high that it seemed almost certain. He went straight to the Technical College principal and asked for a few days of leave. It was granted and he immediately departed. He loved his father so much. Only with him he felt secure and in a deep, relaxed mood. There was never a need for long talks between them. The peace radiating from his parent said much more than the warmest declarations of love. His patience and gentleness were well known in his work place and among the family members. Just by his mere existence his father helped him, even from a distance, much more than any other person in his whole life.

The journey to the town where the hospital was had not been an easy one. First he walked four kilometers through the swamps to the little town nearby, and then came the ride on the old smoky bus to the bigger town, squeezed for a few hours between the farmers and factory workers. From there he took a train and for seven hours was engulfed in dense clouds of cigarette smoke from co-travelers, until finally he reached his destination—a capital city. There he had some food at the railway station fast food bar, then changed to the suburban train, which took him the twenty kilometers to the little resort where his father's hospital was.

Absorbed in thought, he didn't realize that when he arrived at the hospital it would already be after visiting hours. He woke up at the very gate of the hospital, where he read, 'No admittance after such and such time,' and 'No exceptions.' Not there. Not having much money, he returned to the railway station and decided to spend the night there. It was a small suburban station, with two tracks going in opposite directions and a concrete platform with a full roof over it. A small booking office was already closed for the night. He walked along the platform, as it was late autumn and not warm enough to sit for a long time on a bench. After one a.m. a drunken man staggered onto the platform and collapsed on the bench, immediately drifting off into an intoxicated sleep. He wore a long, warm overcoat and his shoes were covered with cement. He was probably one of the petty farmers, getting extra work at one of the big building project sites in or near the capital city. He had probably done some work on the side and afterwards, having some extra money, got drunk and missed his train home.

Sometime later a group of six scamps came along. Their leader was a tall man with a huge torso, dressed in tight American made blue jeans and a green ex-army camouflage winter parka. They woke up the drunken man and asked him for a cigarette. He muttered that he had none left. The leader of the band told one of his boys,

"Fix him up for the exercise." The boy, in his twenties, slowly put a knuckle-buster on his right fist and started punching the face of the drunken man, breaking his nose, tooth and cutting open his cheeks. The scene looked like an American made film about adventures of the famous gangster Al Capone and his band of Mafioso's in Chicago in the thirties. But in fact it was the sad reality of a post war Eastern European country under the leadership of the communists. The blood splashed on the man's overcoat and the bench. After a few hits the poor man fell on the ground unconscious. The leader kicked his face. No reaction. The band, disappointed, walked away spitting in disgust. Now the leader spotted him. Another target! More fun! "Neatly dressed" they thought, "he must have full pockets."

"Hey you! Come here!"—Called the leader.

The game started. He walked towards them slowly, relaxed, the way only the conqueror on the battlefield can walk after defeating his opponents. He walked with his hands in the pockets of his Chicago style overcoat and stopped some seven meters away, with the light from the platform lamp behind him.

"Hey boys, don't be shy! Please feel free to meet Pale Andy from Silesia! Hurry! Or should I introduce myself?" He talked slowly, with power and irony, lisping like someone who has no respect for the inferior amateurs, and finding in his overcoat pocket a short pencil, he held it in his hand and pushed it through the fabric, imitating a gun pointed at them. They were just rowdies, hooligans, and not real bandits or elite gangsters like the Silesian underground. The leader lost his self-assurance and stammered.

"No, Sir, we're just passing by. We're in fact in a hurry. Maybe some other time, Sir." So saying he and the rest of the boys backed up, trembling from fear, and soon disappeared behind the closest corner.

He sighed with relief. It was a close confrontation on unknown territory, and he wasn't armed. Not even a flick knife. He didn't like to travel with his gun, as it was too big a risk. The police checked travelers often and walking on the street of an unknown town it was difficult to 'evaporate' in case of a police check. He already knew from experience how they can mess up everything, and what it means to be in their hands. It was not an easy life in this country. Hit or they hit you was the motto. He preferred not to hit, only if it was really unavoidable. Till now he had won more times by bluffing than by fighting.

He changed the station on the same line towards the capital town and again walked along the platform. The night was not to be a boring one. After three a.m. another gang came along, and this time they surrounded him unexpectedly. He was already tired and didn't hear them walk up silently on their basketball type, rubber sole runners. Again the same question:

"Do you have cigarettes?"

"No, I don't smoke", He lied.

"Come on, don't be so avaricious! Share your supplies with the 'suburban community flowers'."

"I really have no cigarettes!" He retorted. One of the suburban flowers ironically said:

"Make him a hole in his overcoat, (meaning stab him)." Suggested one of the gang. But the leader, a tall, slim man with extensive scars on his face replied.

"No, we'll have better fun. He's going to have a surprise!" He took out of his pocket a flick knife with a deer carved on its bone clad handle, opened it with a click, and touching the overcoat button on his stomach said:

"We're not such bad boys. We want to make you our friend and will give you a chance to be polite. I want you to offer us a smoke from my supplies." He took from his pocket a packet of 'Sports,' the cheapest and most abominable cigarettes of those leading the world to the 'luminous future' working class smocks.

"You can treat us with these! We're simple boys. We don't mind that it's not the 'Marlboro' brand." Saying so he threw the packet on the train line.

"Bring it back!" He shouted sharply, pushing him towards the edge of the platform. The leader laughed and lifted the point of the knife towards his throat. The train had just entered the station. This was not the best time to bluff again, and not the best location for it. He balanced on the edge of the platform, watching the shiny blade of the leader's flick knife. The train was only five meters away. The leader of the gang was obviously waiting for the best moment to push him under the train. He decided to jump down, fast and without hesitation. One second of uncertainty, or one false step, and the game would be over. He leaped down as if shot from a middle ages catapult, and ran across the lines like the fastest African gazelle. The engine bumper bar gently stroked his overcoat, missing him by only a few millimeters. Now he was separated from his would-be friends by the train. He started to run fast along it to find a spoiled open door, as he was on the opposite side of the platform. One door was open and in no time he climbed into the carriage. When the train moved he was already seated on a bench with his overcoat collar turned up. He looked through the window, checking to see if the band had boarded the train. If they had he would jump out of the moving train to avoid another confrontation inside. But they still stood on the platform, amazed at how cleverly he had slipped out of their hands.

The next morning he went to the hospital and finally met his father-friend. The doctor's prognosis was not the best. He had cancer of the kidney and was going to be operated on the following day. A suburban railway station was not the best place to spend the night, as he'd found out, so he took the train back to the capital city. There he could even sleep sitting in the crowded waiting room of the Central Railway Station. The police woke him up a few times to check his identity card and ask countless questions: why he was traveling, where he was going, from where he'd come, what he was doing here, what he was doing every other day, what he had done yesterday, what he was going to do tomorrow, and what his name was at least three times while trying to read it from his identity card. He was cynically cooperative and asked them if they were interested in knowing his grandmother's maiden name and name of his dog, but they had no sense of humor and only scolded him. Anyway he survived all of it and had another chance to see his father the next afternoon. The operation was finished when he arrived. It had been very successful and enabled his father to live at least four years longer. Father, in spite of being weak after a long and difficult operation for someone at the age of sixty two, gave him so much energy and so much attention that it looked as if instead of the son visiting the ill father to uplift him, the father was recharging his son's life batteries.

A few years passed. He finished college and graduated from the university. His best friend-father passed away. He went through some good and bad experiences. He learned some lessons in addition to the university curriculum, but he still wanted to serve his country, to do whatever was possible to do under those abnormal conditions of a totalitarian communist regime. He learned to swim in the absurdity of inertia of the administration and arrogance of an ignorant, communist, red aristocracy. He was climbing the career ladder fast, starting from the position of assistant to the professor at the University, to the post of director of the planning department in one of the provincial governments, to the appointment of adviser to the minister. He was in charge of drawing legislative documents for the country as well as being in control of international trade. The deals with the Soviet Union, their best friend and Big Brother, were not at all beneficial for his nation, and he tried his best to straighten it out. It was a very risky game as the Red Empire secretly controlled the country.

In line with his character, he acted openly in front of hundreds of participants at the central conferences, using arguments of high patriotic value and weight, and unquestionable language, or rather, jargon, of communist propaganda. He knew well how to juggle words and use logic to prove, without saying it straight out, that it was in the best interest of the nation (meaning the proletariat-working class) to disobey the directives of the Working Class Political Party (just a misleading name for the Communist Party) and not to allow the Soviet Union to milk the country's economy. In this way he managed to prevent many costly arrangements of calculated, international rip-offs. But he knew that he was dancing on the sharp edge of a razor.

At any time he could disappear deep, deep underground in a UB 'physiotherapy clinic'. Being aware of it he never moved alone. He always had as a companion—someone loyal to the Communist Party, its Secretary, Trade Union leader or any of his Ministry Directors of Departments. His driver was well armed, and even though a UB man, he felt that he was loyal. He himself always kept a small Belgian gun behind his belt. This was more psychologically beneficial then a real protection. His best protection was provided by his ability to bluff. Being constantly followed by the secret agents of the UB, having his office and residence phone tapped and all correspondence checked, he publicly laughed and joked that none of his colleagues were as secure as him. It was causing consternation between those who sent agents to spy on him and the silent appreciation of the others. Amazed colleagues from the government offices sometimes asked him with respect.

"Who is behind you?"

"You would be very, very surprised! The best if you never ask!" He laughed. This and similar statements planted in their minds a fear of the All Powerful Unknown. He had nobody behind him to support his games and position. He was just bluffing, but skillfully. Maybe God was on his side, but he didn't believe in Him. Not yet. He was educated in communist controlled institutions and programmed to reject even the possibility of a Higher Existence. He didn't know that he had an appointment to meet a Guru who had already incarnated and was waiting for him to come, to wake up from this torpor, and in the meantime was protecting him from the dangers of his very risky games.

By bluffing he survived a few years, swimming in the dull waters between the Communist Party and the UB 'sharks'. But it started to get too hot. The system tried to work out what his real power was. One day he would surely end up behind the bars on the window of a very special train on his way for an indefinite vacation in the very healthy and immense woods, to recover after a month of torture by skillful 'physiotherapy' in the gray concrete 'clinic', or after disappointing his 'massage' specialist he would rest in a shallow grave under the green grass in one of the ghostly, secret cemeteries on the outskirts of the famous health resort Otwock.

His relationship with his wife had been a bumpy one. They lived separately but still under one roof, as in this country to get separate apartments, or even a single room was next to impossible. Often even formally divorced couples shared the same apartment for a long time. He decided to run, but on his own. There was a possibility to go to Holland where his aunt had some friendly connections through her work in one of the foreign embassies.

He was still incurably naive and applied for a passport and lodged an application for a six-month unpaid leave through the Personnel Department of his Ministry. No reply. After more than a month he went to his boss, a minister, and straightforwardly asked what had happened to his application. The minister smiled sourly, coughed a few times and said,

"How is it possible that you are still so childish? Do you think that after so many years here, knowing the strategic military secrets and our country's plans for the future; you can just go to our enemies from a NATO country for six months and work there earning dirty imperialist money? Why do you want to mingle with the spies and agents of the capitalists? Your application created a big concern in the security circles as your family connections with an illegal immigrant to the USA, your uncle, is well remembered. Be reasonable and just forget all about Holland and pray, I mean hope, that those who are the guardians of our safety will forget it all. We have been forced to prevent your attempt to go without our permission, as we are aware that you are capable of doing such a silly thing. Now you are listed in a special book and can't cross the country's border even to our brother communist neighbors. You will be able to travel only with official delegations and on a government group passport. Now go, and I don't want to hear about this affair again.

He got up to leave, then froze. No! His rebelling mind said, and he bluffed again.

"Very well comrade Minister. You know how interested I am in the healing of our economy. I will stay here with pleasure." This was truth. He was preparing the drawing for the Parliament of the new legislation, giving a chance for the small individual farms to prosper. But his rebellious mind couldn't hold quiet any longer and said: But in one-year time, when I am really ready, we will return to this subject!" Saying this he didn't know that he was predicting his departure to the West without talks, permission, or his boss's knowledge.

The game started to be more exciting. His 'guardian angels' sometimes even proved to be useful. He didn't need to light himself a cigarette. He simply showed it to one of those complacent guys and the UB lighter served him in an instant. His wife, when shopping, would ask them to tell her the time and she would even give them the shopping bag to hold when looking for change in her purse. He had some friendly unexpected visits, some strange interruptions in telephone conversations (the recording tape would end and they had to reverse it manually, as the personal touch was always better then the revolting technology of the stinking imperialists), the car was miraculously found opened in the morning (a compulsory detailed personal check of the car was then necessary, as the skillful help of a mysterious night mechanic to cause a road accident was quite possible), and many other attractions. He increased his security as much as he could, but now he decided to run away at any cost. Time was working against him. The game started to be too serious to try gentle methods for too long.

In those days for some reason the passport's validity was good for a maximum of one year in case of travel to Asia, America (except the USA) and Africa. He went to the Personnel Department with a blank application for a passport, asked the Department Director's secretary to ask the Director if he had time for a short chat, and when she went to her boss's office, opened her desk drawer and stamped his application with a Department of Ministry seal, his signature stamp, and then closed the drawer. When she returned he had already folded the document and put it in his jacket's internal pocket. The head of this Department was a gloomy UB officer who kept a watchful eye on the Ministry and the ideological health of all its employees, as well as the nominee's morals. Nobody would have ever dreamt that he would do it, and in such James Bond style. The application was filled; he granted himself a full one-month leave and lodged it in one of the small provincial towns. In those days there were no computers to possibly crosscheck the information. He stated that he was going for a trip to India, to validate his passport for one year, and that he was going alone. His wife lodged her application for the passport in the town where her parents lived, stating the same: India, alone.

They didn't know why they were going together. His wife didn't believe that he was seriously going to leave behind everything: the house, furniture, collections of stamps and coins which his mother had started long ago and which he had continued, investing substantial funds, his beloved mountains, friends, family, his dedicated and loving dog and, on top of it all, his job. There was a strong possibility that he would be nominated soon as one of the deputy ministers. The future showed them why they went together. There was a hidden reason. Far away someone was on his way towards Earth, for whose safe landing both of them were necessary.

Officially they had one week of leave and said that they were going on a trip to the mountains. Nobody was surprised. He was always going there when he could, even with a severe flu, skillfully stimulated in order to get a medical certificate. But the mountains were on the South and they traveled to the North and boarded the ferry going across the sea to Sweden. On the border the emigration officer would never have imagined that this relaxed and playful, joking couple could be listed in the Black Book—a list of those individuals who can't leave the country even with a valid passport and current visa, because the system loved them so much. He neglected to make a routine check. Poor fellow! He probably lost his well-paid job for his carelessness while being on guard of one of the leading communist country borders, and possibly had also some 'invigorating physiotherapy' sessions. Maybe he is still on vacation, forgotten by now, working in the pure, unspoiled forest of Siberia, chopping wood for the paper industry to print propaganda.

But in our couple's case the system woke up too late. They were already in the West. For two months all their correspondence was intercepted, even to colleagues from high school that he wrote asking to notify his family that they were in reasonable safety in one of the Western countries. He sent a letter to his old boss and reminded him that one-year had just passed since their conversation about Holland. He apologized that he couldn't discuss the matter personally with him but he had already left. He felt a bit sorry for his boss as he too could have some trouble. Their conversation about Holland was surely recorded on the tape-recorder serviced earnestly by the curious UB operative. The boss, on the other hand, was sad and felt a bit sorry because he liked this unpredictable rebel and didn't want to know what could accidentally happen to him, we should say, in one of those Western countries. Obviously a meeting with a dedicated, foreign appointed agent would be totally by chance . . . ?

He didn't feel safe. Poland was too close. He could almost smell the dinners cooked from the meager choices available. After a while they decided to go further across the dangerous waters of the Northern Sea to another imperialist country—England. Their ferry passed a furious storm. It was very close to the end of their wanderings on the forbidden, foreign lands and seas. A few passengers were injured, but they survived unharmed.

In the new country he started to master English by drawing pictures on paper and trying to communicate with shopkeepers, neighbors and new bosses. Being a born handyman he in no time learned carpentry, plumbing, plastering, tiling and painting and started to renovate houses. He again demonstrated his childish naiveté. Writing letters to his old country he gave his real address on the back. Really stupid! A few months later and secret agents were in his home. Obviously they missed him, but being too busy to come again, helped themselves and dug through his personal things, showing great interest in any paper with writing. In those days he didn't write poetry or short stories. Instead he had some applications to immigrate to the USA and Canada. They left everything in a mess. In those days they must have been well paid because they refused to take as a souvenir, £200.00 lying loose on the side table.

But the system was agitated. He had done something unforgivable. He had been trusted by the system, he belonged to the nomenclature (those who are given jobs by the Communist Party by nomination and not hired; from whom are chosen the top leaders; ministers, secretaries of provinces and ambassadors to other countries.) The system decided to punish him, not because he was really so important, but because they wanted to frighten others so as not to follow in his steps.

Soon the Polish Secret Service—UB—made an attempt to silently assassinate him. One sunny morning, on a busy street in a crowd in downtown Balham, a suburb of London someone shot an air rifle in his direction with a bullet filled with poison, which causes kidney malfunction in a few days, even if the bullet is quickly removed by surgery. Maybe an attractive girl was passing at the time, but for some reason the well-trained operative hit the roll of aluminum and tar tape he was carrying and not his leg. Some mysterious power was protecting this insubordinate fellow. Because he instinctively made a movement to check what hit the tape, it looked as if he had been shot, they didn't check the next week to see if he was already dead. They were fully confident. Western medicine didn't know the antitoxin for this secret poison. Hundreds of escapers from the Soviet Block like him were killed this way.

One month later his country started to boil. Mass uprisings against the hopeless totalitarianism shook the foundations of the system. The possibility of a civil war hung on the end of a hair from the bald head of the First Secretary of the Central Committee of the Communist Party General Jaruzelski. The Red Aristocracy, to protect their privileged position, announced marshal law, a state of emergency, where they had the power to act without any legal restrictions. The tanks entered the streets of the towns. The UB became extremely busy with internal affairs. After some long tremors and palpitations, the 'luminous' Communist system shamelessly collapsed. All had forgotten him, friends and the UB. In the meantime he immigrated to another continent as a political refugee and in multicultural society became ethnically anonymous.

His life proved his technique as a good one: "Bluff as long as you can, and if you can't, don't wait; run, run fast as you can."

BEYOND THE BORDER

The sunset announced the arrival of the sparrows, flying high in zigzags, having dinner in the clouds of seasonal insects. Above them hung a dome of intensely blue sky. It looked unreal, like a motionless picture of total immobility. The clouds also seemed not from this planet; disk-like, similar, unnaturally regular in shape, with horizontal stripes of different shades and colors, like the atmosphere of Saturn seen through a telescope. The total immobility resembled the crazy paintings of Arthur Dale, which have successfully uglified Australian art galleries, and are admired for their free market monetary value by the brainless but rich homo-ignoramus upper snob class.

The man seated on the flat concrete roof of a large building watched it, fascinated. He felt like a visitor from a different dimension being allowed a glimpse of the Changeless World of Symbols. After a few minutes he realized that the swallows didn't fit into this picture. Only they moved, performing acrobatic dances in the air, in the background of this deadly stillness and immobility. He tried to guess what the message was that this presentation was carrying. What was the meaning of this mixture of two different realms: the apparently one dimensional sky, clouds, sun and the three dimensional sparrows. Does it mean we can do what we want, in as much as we are able to perform acrobatic attempts to change our fate, but nothing will happen? In vain will be our struggle. All is prefixed from the beginning of time; all is unveiled gradually according to the master script of this Divine Drama, authored by the Creator Himself. He had memorized the statement the late Ramana Maharshi of Tiruvanamalai had made when His mother, after discovering Him on the slopes of the hill Arunachala, had tried to take him back home:

"What has to happen will happen, try to prevent it if you wish."

The man facing the nearby sea looked down towards the horizon. The horizon was not clearly definable. The sky was gradually becoming the sea. There was supposed to be a horizon, a border. Yet both the air and the water had exactly the same color. Was it really important where the border was? Are all borders important? We like so much to divide everything, to label the parts and units and store them safely in the separate drawers of our memory. When a new situation, object or experience comes, it's so handy to open the drawer, and without thinking, take out the old, faded label. If it resembles even slightly our model, we stick the label on it and fit it into the systematized classification. We love to create all sorts of artificial borders. Already there are so many borders: the borders between countries, between nations, races, castes, sexes, and people of different status; the borders between good and bad, pain and pleasure, health and sickness, death and life. Let us look, for example, at the reality of that last one. Is it very clear when the body of a person is dead? We say that after anatomical death, life can't return to the body. The heart is not beating; the breathing stops and the body temperature drops down, but still many tissues grow and function, for example the fingernails and the hair. Don't yogis' hearts and breathing stop in samadhi and the body temperature also decrease? Do we consider them dead? How many people in graves, excavated after many years, were found lying in a position showing that they had struggled trying to free themselves from the coffin. They were certified dead and hastily buried to get at the inheritance.

The borders are very often flexible and only depend on the geographical locality, culture, or its lack, and obviously time. For example, those brave warriors from Papua, New Guinea, 200 years back, were admired and worshiped by their tribes after killing, roasting well over the fire and then eating the catholic missionaries who were trying to eradicate their beliefs and who made fun of their gods. In those happy days it was a sign of bravery, real manhood and proof of real warrior-hood. Now, in the 20th century (it was year 1998), the same act in the same country would be considered a crime, and the well-fed warrior would be proclaimed a savage cannibal and sentenced to a long term of hard labor, if not capital punishment, as still the ancient law is in operation—an eye for an eye, a tooth for a tooth. In reality, sharp borders do not exist in Nature. All is overlapping itself on different levels and in many aspects of manifestation of Reality. We don't always see it because of the limitations of our senses.

On the stage of the landscape entered a few big, fat, heavy birds flying slowly towards the sea, almost touching the tops of the coconut palms. They didn't act; they only appeared like the narrator who comes before the spectacle unsuccessfully trying to explain to the deaf audience the hidden teaching of the drama. Saying nothing they said,

"All is passing by. Those who enter the stage of life in heavy material bodies have one day to abandon this splendid world too, just as we are leaving for the sea . . ."

The sun was already resting, but its rays suddenly painted the immobile clouds in a last attempt to get the stage ready for the final act of the Grand Performance. It was silent. Even the sea was calm and the waves didn't chant their usual mantra—OM . . . OM . . . OM . . .

Suddenly the silence was broken by the rattle of a motor boat rushing along the backwaters, which separated the long, narrow peninsula, on which stood the massive building with the flat roof on which he was sitting, from the mainland. It sounded like a silly joke. The boat, built without the use of nails or screws, was made from the planks of teak wood stitched together with coconut strings, and coated with tar to waterproof it. It had a shape just as the boats have had here since the times of Sri Rama and Sri Krishna. The huge vessel had a coconut palm leaf roof from which a few semi-naked (for Indian standards) western tourists waved and shouted loudly, probably intoxicated by some substance. The rattling motor propelling the boat and the boat itself were like hopeless misfits in the placid surroundings.

The man on the roof noticed that across the sky moved another object. It was unlike the clouds, being much smaller. It was, compared to them, a tiny thing. But in reality it only looked tiny because of the distance. It moved horizontally, being itself on a 35-degree angle to the horizon. It produced no sound, only reflected the light of the sun. What was it? There is no plane with such a shape. It had no wings, no visible engine or jets. What? What? Meteor? No. It was not even a 20th century object. It seemed rather like something which had accidentally manifested from the future, or else something visiting us from outer space. It flew high above and was unaffected by the apparent conflict below between the all-pervading silence of Nature and the brutal rattle of the boat's motor. Maybe the crew of this mysterious craft was uninterested in what the inhabitants of this planet Earth, who proudly called themselves humans, thought or felt. The people continued their activities, totally unaware that above their heads was flying an object, probably from a different world, speeding towards its destination to perform some work or investigations.

They were also unaware of the Truth and Wisdom the heavy birds were silently teaching. Most of them believe they are above the law of passing time, the law of the food chain, the cycles in which matter is entering the bodies of different forms of life, then soon returning to the primordial elements for a rest just to mix a little bit, and after a while assume another form. They think, in their intellectual ignorance, that there is almost nothing more on this world left for them to discover, that nothing can amaze them. But those self assured scientists, thinkers who use only 10% of the human brain's capacity, never even try to discover who they really are, to reach beyond the border of cognition where sophisticated instruments cannot reach and measure. How often, going home after a busy day spent implanting partial knowledge into trusty students' heads, have they passed by a man with matted hair and eyes calmly radiating Peace, seated on the roadside? He was not trying to teach what he knew. All that he knew came from his own experiences, which cannot be described in the human language. Who would listen to him anyway? He doesn't have a Ph.D., or even a diploma. He hasn't accumulated encyclopedic data in his memory, which people call knowledge. Instead, he is full of the Wisdom, which has come to him in the form of revelations during his glides into the giddy heights of the transcendental realm beyond the borders. All he has learned is a result of spontaneous illumination. He knows who he is, and it's all that's worth knowing.

The Earth, rotating slowly on its axis, passed the point of another border, after which the light of the Sun could not be reflected by the planet's atmosphere. The landscape veiled the darkness of the night. Now the sky decorated the billions of distant stars, like in a huge planetarium. All the stars blinked in a friendly way at the seated man, and through the medium of the light said:

"Nothing is final, our brother, nothing ever ends. We are everywhere. We are life, but not life which you people experience. This we call an unstable form of organic matter. We are living different lives than yours, but we are not less aware of our existence than people like you. We are filling the Infinity. Life on your planet is not something special. It exists everywhere, even where your imagination can't reach. Everywhere is the same life only in different forms. It is only one life, and it is eternal. We all live the same life in the heterogeneity forming The Oneness. But the universe is only an illusion. The distances and time too. All energy is interconnected and communicates instantly. We are mighty stars, many times larger then your Sun, but from afar we look so small, like the dust of gold on the black velvet of space. Close your eyes. Forget the illusion and us. Do not watch this Grand Performance. It is beautiful, it is fascinating, but it is also a part of illusion. Try to be, but not as such and such, just exist."

The seated man listened attentively and, following the advice, closed his eyes. He calmed the mind and watched how manifestations created by him dissolved and ceased to pretend to be Reality. Some of his creation was not bad at all, even charming, but after closer examination proved to be no better than other shadows. When he reached the void of non-existence, the shadows disappeared completely, along with the borders. It was the Realm Beyond the Borders.

What remained was only the Awareness of pure existence, where there are no expectations. It happened in the totality of things, but it transcended the manifestation of objects and time projected on the medium of space. Where could he aim to return? To whom to tell the story? Who can listen to it if there is no one else? He kept quiet, as it was better to simply be Silent. Only the language of Silence could say the word from which it all emerged, the only word with a complete meaning. All Creation repeats this Word, the Word Seed—"Om." Can we say anything that contains a more significant message? Is there any word with a more pregnant meaning than Om?

BEER AND SANSKRIT CHANTS

The full moon was very bright. Jim could see his full glass of beer quite clearly. It was close to eleven. Hiding from his wife Sophie, behind the garden shed, he filled the glass for the last time.

"It's late; it's time to go to bed. Even if sleep won't come, I have to go," he thought. Suddenly, his eyes noticed the light coming from the dwelling across his fence.

"Who is there?" He wondered. The previous tenant, Anastasia, moved away a few days ago. Ah! It must be Alex painting. The unit was sold to a man returning from doing contract work in Kuwait. Jim knew Alex well: busy as always, he took the job, and having no time during the day worked through the night.

"He must be hungry and tired," he thought. Jim left the beer bottle and limped home.

"Sophie!" He asked his wife. "Can you make some coffee for Alex? He's still painting; he must be hungry and tired. And give him some food too."

Next door to the unit where Alex was working a meeting of a spiritual group was being held, led by an Indian man, a Scholar, educated in Vedantic Scriptures. Now the meeting was ending. The Sanskrit slokas still sounded fresh in the air. The Scholar was happy and feeling great. He was proud, he did it well, and not even one mistake in reading; Vidya—Knowledge, Brahman—Supreme Existence and Bhakti—Divine Love were the topics discussed. So many people had attended the meeting. They finished with prayers, chanting "OM SHANTI" at the end, and rushed to the kitchen where drinks were waiting, as well as some food as prasad. Slowly, one by one they left, going home. Passing by the unit next door, where the light was still on, they thought:

"Someone is working; there are ladders. It's silly. It's night. It's very late."

Jim's hands were swollen. He was sick from many years of heavy work for the railway, but he was firmly holding a coffee mug and a paper bag with snacks. He called on Alex. When Alex opened the door, Jim said:

"You must be tired; you must be hungry. Have something to eat." Their eyes met in silence. The softness in Jim's eyes told Alex much more than the Sanskrit chants he'd heard. Jim went back home to try to have a little sleep.

The next morning, happy and proud of himself after a successful meeting the night before, the scholar was kind enough to come to Alex, whom he'd known for years, and say:

"You have been working all night. What kind of person are you? My guests were asking if you are not demon! It's incredible! You must be mad!" He laughed.

A few weeks later the man from Kuwait arrived. Alex received a letter from him with a bill for the electricity he had used during his painting job. It was too much for the unit's new owner to pay, although the work was done at his urgent request. Due to lack of time in the day, Alex had worked in the night to meet the deadline.

The man from Kuwait, being very spiritual, soon joined the group chanting Sanskrit *slokas*. He too was Indian. He didn't know that just behind his fence lived Jim, the Greek, from whom he could learn equally as much about the taste of decent beer and how to practice love towards his fellow men; Jim, from whom he could learn much more than from chanting Sanskrit verses with a dry heart.

AMBROSIA

The evening heat was very mild. After a sunny, brilliant day, Mother Nature was resting in the gentle breeze from the nearby Arabian Sea. In the silver greenish light of the Moon, the tops of the coconut palms looked like bunches of feathers from gigantic birds, perhaps living in the higher worlds or dimensions.

Sitting in the shadows, a man was also resting after a busy day. He, who had accomplished his worldly tasks and who had settled in this remote heaven, was now living in his Guru's presence. Guru was his world, his beloved mountains, vast oceans and plains. He was now his only real relative. Guru was his way, as well as a river and a boat to travel in, and his Ultimate Destination. Serving His children—as He called all creatures equally, both human and animals—was now the only purpose of his existence. The man seated under the tree served Him by serving them—all beings of Earth. He did not expect anything for it, nor did he ever ask Him for anything. What could he want? In Him was contained everything! The fact that he was given the opportunity to serve Him and his vast family of spiritual brothers and sisters was more then enough. He was lucky. From the multitudes of those who strive for happiness, he was one who drank of it daily, Ambrosia—the nectar of immortality—thanks to His grace. What was it? Something very strange, much unexpected! Even if he openly told what it was, very few would believe that it was the truth. He had discovered its most secret recipe before he had come here. It was a mixture of the tears of unconditional, pure love, and sweat from the labor of serving those who are in need or in trouble. Now he was living, drinking as much of it as he wanted. He was drunk. He was intoxicated.

His eyes fell onto the window of a small building in the complex. A light was still on there. He was there, his Guru being everywhere, all-pervading, He had chosen, in His great mercy, to descend to this low plane of existence for the sake of beings ignorant of their True Nature, beings that are potentially free, but because of their confused state of mind, they are bound by a powerful Maya, the genial sorceress of Maha illusion. How he had earned such grace, he would never know. But he did not want to know anything. He was as he was, now, here, gliding in a void, ignorant but knowing that he was fulfilled, satisfied, complete, drunk from Ambrosia. He was happy beyond any means of expression. He was in a delirium of Bliss.

A RIVER—NO RIVER

I t is most likely a very old, extensively eroded volcano. The top of the mountain consists of a crown, two kilometers in diameter, of rocks, forged like steel, almost black in color, sticking up as twenty or more meter-high towers amongst the stony debris surrounding them.

In the center of the crown is a crater, which time has converted into a swampy meadow with a lake on one side. The slopes of stony debris, rising some one hundred meters up towards the gigantic monoliths at the crown, are covered with dead, ghostly looking dwarf bushes with brownish silver bark and high-altitude trees twisted by the wind. Through the meadow runs a clear, rapid stream with a waterfall in the gap, at the edge of the crown, cascading a few hundred meters down. Near the lake lies a bivouac site for mountaineers.

They walked along the tarred road towards their car.

"Listen," she said, "It's so silent. There's no wind, and there are no animals and no birds. Look, not even one bird! I feel that it's an evil domain. Something terrible hangs in the air; maybe death! This must be a place of meetings for condemned souls. It's better if we go back." But . . . they went against their destiny—to meet the Unknown.

They had come to the village at the foot of the mountain for a few days of rest. Their destiny started to pull them apart, showing the many differences in their way of thinking, attitudes and expectations.

She was a Scorpio with fluctuating moods, dreaming about financial security and material stability. He—The Traveler was a Pisces, impractical in thinking; a daydreamer with a strong repugnance for the material aspects of life, unable to keep hold of money or things, ready to give his last shirt to anyone in need. They were already exhausted. After two years together they were feeling they'd lived together at least eight years karmically, in an incredibly intense and in many ways rewarding and fascinating but also irritating relationship. Still bound together by the adhesion of strong attachments, they threw themselves from one extreme to another in a fruitless attempt to find equilibrium, without compromising their highest values, and still surviving as a couple.

She, as a Scorpio, hardly liked to admit defeat. Now she felt that her dream world was close to a major earthquake, and was growing more and more restless looking for changes, going to different places, doing different things. He, although not fascinated by this, kept her company. In the beginning they had fantastic trips to the mountains lying to the west of the Big Town. There they did some spectacular rock climbing. They would camp in an old deserted quarry, meditate, tell stories sitting at night around the campfire and do many, many other things. In her subconscious, she felt that it was only an episode and that he would have to go one day. Gradually more and more 'candles' were being blown out. The direction of their relationship became obvious, but they still tried to patch it up.

He stopped their car under a huge gum tree. In the nearby car park was another vehicle and in its open door stood a man in his twenties. The Traveler detected his disturbed state of mind. Something heavy was hanging in the air. The most logical thing was to drive away immediately. But he thought,

"What has to happen will happen. Let destiny take care of us." He wanted also to expose her to fear in this clearly dangerous situation, just for a test. He was curious to see how brave she was. They started walking towards the lake. The Traveler heard from behind a well-known from the past sound, the 'clang' of a reloaded pistol. During this time of the year there was nobody nearer than some five kilometers away, where there was a chalet. The Traveler was unarmed. Since immigrating to this peaceful country he never carried a gun. He knew how to disable an armed man, but it was possible to do so only from a short distance. Now he had the gunman at about ten meters behind his back. They continued to walk. Being very sensitive, she felt danger and kept quiet, holding his left hand tightly. He tried to tune into the stranger's mind to read it. They reached the lake. He decided to turn back and confront the gunman. He knew that to take the initiative into his own hands would give him an extra advantage. He perceived indecision and a shade of fear in the gunman. That meant that the gunman was not into killing them; he was in trouble himself, but if his fear turned into panic and if he perceived his security as being at risk, the gunman would use his gun.

From five meters away, the Traveler smiled toward the stranger and said in a relaxed way, "Don't you think, mate, that it's too cold for camping?" The gunman's tension and concentration were broken. He answered with astonishment,

"Absolutely! At night it must be well below zero." They passed one another, checking their intentions by looking into each others' eyes. The Traveler decided to take the risk of not hitting him. He felt that the danger was high and would be increased with distance, but now it had most likely been dispelled. Nothing happened. Half an hour later they met this man again near the chalet. He stood on the very edge of a few hundred meters high cliff, where the waterfall from a stream started its long drop. The Traveler, now well in tune with the gunman's mind, felt that he was a man in real trouble; lost in his insecurity, in a paralyzing panic. Maybe, in a rage, he had committed a grave crime and now didn't know how to get out of a tightly closed, blind circle. He looked miserable, lonely, depressed and devastated by the seriousness of his position. He had no place to turn to, no future to live in dignity, no courage to render himself to the police or even to jump down the cliff and put an end to his spoiled life.

Driving down to the caravan park where they rented a cabin, she was at the steering wheel while he read the book they always read when they were driving: "Towards the Goal Supreme" They descended from the height of the evil domain, its possible residence, to the valley of humans to face the next event of their destiny.

After dinner they had some local red wine and were again restless in their minds, arguing about petty things. They went for a walk in the darkness of the night. It was a strange walk. At first, he felt in oneness with the Infinity of Existence painted on the high, black sky by the millions of sparkling stars so visible in the countryside, and he made a statement, which badly agitated her. She was still carrying a lot of tension because of the emotions experienced with the gunman. In an explosion of anger she retorted,

"How can you, a beginner, say such a thing? What do you know?" They withdrew themselves into their shells, like snails powdered with lime, and continued their walk in silence. The moon was their torch, and the stars were lamps on their path.

They entered the very dense jungle of slim and young, six to eight meters tall trees. Their branches grew higher than their heads; no undergrowth. They had difficulty in keeping their direction. There was nothing to use as a focal point of reference. The long walk in this jungle was like a dream; unreal. It was as if they were going from nowhere to nowhere, from never to never. In the moonlight, the light gray trunks of the trees looked like theatrical decorations made of artificial, indistinguishable, smooth bamboo logs. After a few hundred meters they entered a fog. Now the surroundings became even more surreal, like being in a fantasy film entering Hades, the Greek netherworld of condemned and lost souls of murderers, rapists and, of course, of communist leaders.

After a while, small, hard stones were felt under their feet; the river—fast flowing and cold—murmuring something in a language known only to water. The fog veiled everything. The opposite bank of the river was invisible. There was only fog. Maybe there was no 'other' bank. In the dense silence, there was only the gentle sound of the splash of water touching the small stones. Billions of round stones appeared to be artificially made, regular shaped like gigantic sweet 'Smarties' from Safeway's Supermarket, clean polished by the river and kept in Nature for millions of years. No talk; silence. Are we dreaming? Where are we? Are we really us?

He rested on the river stones, facing the milky fog above, drifting into a strange dream, a non-dream state. It was more like an experience of nonexistence, a sort of suspended beingness. She kept quiet, insecure in her restless mind in this unreal scenery. Maybe, she was wondering why she went for this walk with this unpredictable man, maybe, she was counting the remaining 'candles', or maybe, she was only chanting her mantra.

Time passed, but for the Traveler time ceased to exist. Maybe one hour passed, measured in Earthly time, maybe eternity. For him it was as if a second and Eternity were one. Suddenly he sat upright, looked around and realized that he had become somebody else. He was not the same man who had lain down on the stones near the river. What had exactly happened, nobody knows. Maybe this river was not a river but the flow of ethereal Time, the Magician. Maybe the dense, almost unending bamboo-like jungle of slim trees didn't exist; maybe the fog was not the fog but a form manifestation of his Guru—who had come to rescue him, again. Anyway, he was no longer his old self. The attachment to the young lady sitting next to him, pretty and fifteen years younger than himself left him, as if touched by a Sorcerer's wand. Now he saw through her personality like an X-ray machine. It was not a very impressive picture. They returned home in silence. What more was left to say? She felt the unavoidable approaching and calculated new strategies. Scorpios never give up! It looked as if not many 'candles' were left for them to blow. It was the beginning of the end. He remembered what had happened once to Lahiri Mahasaya after drinking special oil given to him by his mysterious Guru Babaji; he lay all night on the bank of an icy cold Himalayan river and went through a purification procedure. The Traveler thought,

"Maybe the wine from the local vineyard was not ordinary 'wine' but some Siddha tonic of freedom."

She soon found a way out of the dead-end road and made a last desperate attempt to firmly bind him. He, being loyal and naive, agreed to marry her under the condition that his Guru gave them His blessing. It appeared that the powerful Maya had happily grabbed him at the end by her many strong arms. But it was not so. It was only a bluff and, this time, not his. In spite of his destiny, maybe pre-set in millions of sparkling stars in the Southern sky to marry again, his Guru, in His immense mercy, altered his fate once more and set him on the road to Freedom.

"No more diversions from the Path." he promised himself, knowing that he always kept his promises. "From now on, I must behave as Guru's 'grown-up' son."

A GLIMPSE

Traveler who had never visited India had a dream: the heat of summer in its fullness in Tiruvannamalai was almost unbearable. The dry air, vibrating on the rocky slopes of Arunachala could not satisfy the thirst for oxygen. Nature suffocated in dizziness, and all the creatures withdrew themselves into lethargy, just to survive the worst hours of the heat. The evening would bring some relief and the black sky would sooth the eyes burned by the blazing sun.

Arunachala

Traveler walked with a small Indian boy under the shade of the trees. They both wanted to go inside and underneath of Ramana Maharshi's Samadhi. No one had gone there before them. Thinking about it so intensely, they hardly noticed the inhospitable climatic conditions.

They soon crossed the entrance gate. The gray granite staircase led them down six or seven meters under the surface of the courtyard. It was pleasantly cool there and silent, very silent. The noise from the external world didn't penetrate through the stones. The boy held the hand of the Traveler. He was a little bit afraid, feeling strange, like in a different dimension of existence accessible only for departed souls. The total silence made the place even more uncanny. When they reached the bottom of the stairs, they noticed massive, square paneled, forged ironwork doors, skillfully decorated with different aspects of Indian Gods. The door's portal was in contrast plain, made of three solid pieces of stone. The top section formed a shelf, possibly destined for accommodating a bronze idol or an oil lamp. On it stood not an idol, but a live, large, very black, glittering scorpion. It was the most dangerous species of its kind. Both the Traveler and the boy felt the scorpion's personality was like that of a negatively minded, jealous, Ravana-like, demonic human trying to frighten them, who had assumed this body only for the purpose of misleading them. The scorpion moved with grace, confident of his deadly power, his abdomen dancing anxiously on the edge of the door's portal. In body language he was saying:

"Don't try to cross the doors. I will jump on your neck and sting you to death. This is a door mortals can't cross!" The Traveler held more firmly the boy's hand and said:

"Don't worry tombi (Tamil: younger brother). He's only pretending. Just ignore him and see for yourself that he is powerless." They opened the heavy doors and crossed inside. The scorpion, disappointed, shrank and gradually disappeared.

Inside it was even more silent than on the staircase. Ramana Maharshi's Samadhi room was small and almost empty. Close to the entrance, to the left stood the famous couch, and on it . . . Ramana Maharshi himself, reclining on his right side, supporting his head with his hand as the Traveler remembered from the many photographs. The Traveler and the boy stopped, amazed, stunned at this sight. Ramana Maharshi, smiling lovingly made a gesture encouraging them to come closer, and said:

"You, Andrew, think that I am dead? How can I die? I am not what you now see here. I am more alive than ever. They all think that I am gone. Where can I go? Now, give me something to eat!" The Traveler was stunned that Master knew his name. He had some tapioca chips in his pocket and handed the packet to Ramana Maharshi. They watched Him eat slowly. Ramana Maharshi took only two or three pieces and gave the bag with the rest of the chips back to the Traveler.

"It is enough", he said, and gently rubbed the right arm of the Traveler. "Go now, go back to the World. You will be taken care of. The *darshan* is over. Go; you can't stay

Samadhi of Sri Ramana Maharshi

here any longer and, remember son, please find your own Path, do not follow others." They prostrated and left looking secretly back. Ramana Maharshi lay on the couch in the same position as before, but now he was totally motionless. There was not even the slightest trace of a breathing movement on his chest.

Traveler woke up from the dream very elevated. From his *puja* table, smiling straight at him was a likeness of Ramana standing next to the picture of his Guru. Both, Ramana Maharshi and the Guru were his spiritual Parents, being in fact only different aspects of the same, The Oneness.

Traveler started his *sadhana* following the teachings of Ramana Maharshi, this great contemporary Rishi and, after a few years, he met his personal Guru and became His disciple. Time was passing by. Traveler forgot the dream.

Once, a Sri Lankan family, who had lost their three year-old girl, organized a satsang in their home, inviting people from amongst the

Guru's followers. Even though they lived in a remote suburb, several of the members of their group were willing to come. The Traveler and his son joined the company.

After *satsang* everyone dispersed around the house chatting together with the hosts and the local Indians invited for this occasion. The Traveler's son, who had a very sensitive nature, took care of one of the members, a drummer, who was blind. They walked around the house and he explained to the blind man how everything looked, giving him some objects to touch and painting with words the pictures of the images imperceptible to him. The Traveler thought,

"How much I can learn from my son. He is so young but by his actions he is teaching me the very principles of spirituality; he is showing me how we should live, how we should care for our fellow men."

Traveler had a cup of chai with his friend Rama, a Malaysian Indian. They talked about their first meeting some six years back, when Rama had come to the Traveler's house with the intention of seeing a car which the Traveler had advertised for sale in the weekly paper, The Trading Post. At first they talked in the living-room. After a while, Rama noticed hanging on a wall a photo of Ramana Maharshi, a famous photo showing a light behind His head and His smiling eyes. Rama was somehow moved seeing it and asked anxiously,

"Who is that?!!" The Traveler explained it in detail, as well as he was able to in his limited English. The conversation ended with Rama borrowing a book about Ramana Maharshi, In Days of Great Peace by Mouni Sadhu; then, opening his wallet he asked,

"How much should I pay for the car?"

"You didn't even look at it!" replied the Traveler.

"Never mind, I'm buying it." Rama said confidently.

A few years later Rama met The Guru through the Traveler.

173

Now after this *satsang* they talked also about the Traveler's plans to go for good to The Guru's ashram, and about all the aspects of this complicated 'operation' of cutting off all worldly bonds. Suddenly a small Indian boy came up and, standing in front of them, with a look of great seriousness on his face, he pointed a finger at the Traveler and said:

"You will become a swami." Then, turning the direction of his index finger towards Rama, said:

"And you will die of a heart attack." They were struck dumb. The Traveler recognized, without the slightest doubt, the small boy from his past forgotten dream, and now was not sure if he was still dreaming or if this was a waking reality. The Traveler didn't have any desire for kavi cloth (a swami's red/orange attire). He just wanted to surrender to his Guru's Lotus Feet and serve Him in any way possible. Rama, on the other hand, realized that being an extremely busy entrepreneur, often working long hours under tension, was in fact at a high risk of experiencing what the boy had said. The small boy ran away and joined the other children in play. The conversation lost its flow. Something had separated them. Rama felt very sad, and the Traveler drifted into a meditative mood and lost interest in everything that was happening around him.

A few months later the Traveler left for India with the intention of staying there. He didn't have the right visa, only a six-month tourist one, but he hoped that everything could be straightened out.

His arrival at the Guru's ashram seemed as if arranged by someone invisible but in charge of whatever was happening. On the train he met a friendly Ayurvedic doctor from the town close to the ashram who offered him a lift in his car to the ferry through backwaters. On the way they stopped at the doctor's office. There, the doctor offered him a small glass of some herbal mixture saying that it was a tonic, which would make him feel better. The Traveler drank it without thinking. A wave of heat overpowered him, and the doctor's surgery room in which he now was started to swirl. His first thought was that he had swallowed poison. Now, too late, he remembered that his Guru had not only dedicated admirers but also ardent opponents who, in the past, had made attempts to kill Him. The Traveler didn't die; and, after a few minutes, all his tiredness caused by the long travel was removed as if magically washed away. He felt fit and refreshed, like after a long and invigorating sleep.

Following this treatment the doctor drove him to the famous backwaters where a few boats were waiting for customers. Being unfamiliar with the local fees for the ride, he paid ten rupees (instead of two), which in Western standards was still very cheap; an equivalent of US $0.30. Everything was exotic: boats made without screws and nails, Chinese fishing nets on wooden cranes, coconut palms, dark-skinned people, but at the same time he felt that he was coming back home! This feeling didn't leave him for many days. He walked slowly along the footpath from the ferry to the ashram's gate. He walked looking through the thicket of coconut palms at the impressive ashram temple-building.

Suddenly cold water splashed over his feet. While walking he had inadvertently knocked over a brass water-vessel that was standing on stones near the village's water-tap. "This is very auspicious," he thought, remembering Ramana Maharshi's first rain-bath in Tiruvannamalai right after He arrived there, on his way to becoming a renunciate.

"What's ahead of me?" he thought, feeling that the worldly dust from his feet was washed off, and that now he belonged to his Guru and The Guru only. This feeling never left him for the next six years. It became a part of his innate nature.

On entering the ashram compound, the first person he met was one of his Older Sisters, who was well known from The Guru's tours to his adopted country. She helped him with registration and accommodation.

Two days later he was already running errands around the ashram, repairing electrical fans, doing some carpentry work, and 'resting' by folding the ashram's monthly spiritual magazine, printed in a few languages. While working in one of the rooms where he was installing a new fan, he had another mysterious meeting. This happened—we should remember—during the first week of his stay in the ashram. He knew only a few people, those who accompanied The Guru on His foreign tours. Just before lunch, one of the senior disciples, whom he had never met before, popped into the room and without any reason said:

"Don't worry; you'll only do this work for a while. Later we'll work together." Saying so, he smiled and in no time was gone.

"Who is he? What did he mean? How can he make a statement about the future with such confidence? Is he mad?" he thought.

The Traveler was dwelling on those questions for some time. It had happened a few times before to him, that people, or his dreams, foretold future happenings. Sometimes it sounded absolutely crazy, but it came to fulfillment at the right time. For example, once, when working in a high position in the Central Administration of his country of origin, and, while building a house for himself in one of the health resorts close to the capital city, a plumber who hadn't finished the job disappeared for a few weeks. When the plumber returned he was drunk and angrily demanded money even when his job was unfinished. The Traveler refused to pay, as he knew from experience that the job would then never be completed. The plumber, upset and having no means to force him to pay said in fury:

"Now you are a top man, working in government and don't understand me, but soon you will know from your own experience how it is to be a tradesman." The Traveler thought that the plumber was totally crazy! Why should he become a tradesman? But, the future very soon proved that what the drunken plumber had foretold was to become real. The Traveler soon and unexpectedly immigrated to the West and started to earn his living renovating heritage period houses. Many times he had to negotiate with his clients, persuading them to pay him in advance so that he could continue his work. But he never left a job unfinished even when being paid fully in advance.

Now The Traveler arrived at the conclusion that everybody has, from time to time and only for a short time, an open gate to future events, recorded from the beginning of time in the so called Akashic Records. Generally people are absentminded and unaware of it. The children, with their pure minds, perhaps have this gate open more often, but it happens to all of us. Obviously our Older Brothers and Sisters, those whose third eye is permanently open, are able to scan the past and the future as they wish. What can we, the beginners, say? Are we not like the blind in a labyrinth looking for a way out while standing at the very gate? But if we calm our restless minds and listen attentively to what others say, we can sometimes pick up some hints; some glimpses indicating unavoidable events, which are going to happen.

Few years later: In 2002 Rama died in a light-airplane plane crash, which he was piloting. He had a heart attack during the flight, lost control of the airplane and went straight down vertically, hitting the airfield.

Traveler, while staying at the ashram, was called by many: "Andrew Swami" thought he was not formally initiated into *sannyasa*.

A few months after arriving at the ashram Andrew-Traveler had a dream:

He was a very old bearded *sannyasi* staying in a mud-brick hut with a coconut-leaf roof in his Guru's ashram, on a narrow land divided from the mainland by backwaters. His name was Swami Avakaranikara (which in Sanskrit means 'dust'). He shared his hut with very venomous black snakes. He often felt them crawling over his body while immersed in deep sleep. It was during the time of the Rama Empire.

One afternoon, as the monsoon rains had subdued, his Guru prearranged a homa, to be performed in front of an antique small stone-carved Devi figure, for his Guru-Guru-Guru's disciple from Shambala. Before the *homa* started, the Guru called Swami Avakaranikara and embraced him like before taking a long journey.

The Swami was surprised, as the Guru had never before taught him. He prostrated before the Guru's Feet and took his place next to the Guru, by the side of the bricks arranged for the *homa*-fire. The smoke of burned wood, ghee and herbs enveloped Guruji as well as the disciples seated around the *homa*-fire. Swami Avakaranikara entered into *samadhi*. Twenty-one days passed as he sat in lotus-posture, like a monument without the slightest sign of breathing. On the twenty-second day, the Guru ordered a grave to be dug for him and to be placed there together with the stone *devi*. He said that He will meet him (Swami Avakaranikara) again in the same place but only after twelve thousand years.

Traveler was sent away to do some work for his Guru. Before leaving he visited for the first time the old Kalari Temple located on the ashram premises. Even in the beginning, after joining the ashram, he feared to go close to this dark and small room. He never understood why. Today, suddenly overpowered by bravery, he sat for meditation there, cross-legged, in a corner near the doors; with closed eyes. He took three deep breaths and tried to concentrate on the natural flow of his breathing. But, from the beginning, he was somewhat distracted as he felt that someone was staring at him, in spite of no one else being there. So he opened his eyes. Lightning passed through his body! From the back of the shrine a small figure of a Devi made of gray stone was staring at him. He knew that he knew Her. How? He had never seen this figure before. Devi's eyes were saying, in silence:

"Welcome back. You will stay with me for a while but your *sadhana* will require that you go back to the world. Do not be attached to anyone, not even to me. Be open, but never trust anyone blindly. Practise discrimination between the Real and Maya. Never compromise your integrity. You are from a family of great sages. Maintain the family's standard.

Later, the Traveler learned that the Devi made out of stone was excavated from the earth grounds during the construction of the ashram building, as the Guru demanded to dig deeper than needed for its foundation, saying:

"She wants to go out." *Vedic* scholars could not identify this stone carving of Devi nor could they establish her age. They said that it came from a remote and completely unknown past from which only legends remain.

When the Traveler returned from his assignment, the ashram inmates told him that, when removing some boxes with tiles from his hut, which had been temporarily stored there, they found a nest of the most dangerous black snakes in this region called Five-Steppers, because when bitten by them a person can at most make five steps before dropping dead. He then did remember that in the past something had crawled over his body while immersed in sleep, tired after many hours of *seva*, but had thought that was only a dream.

TAIPAN WALL—PREFACE

Believe me or not but this is not a true story. In fact it does not much matter. It can only help a little in broadening our understanding and initiating wonder over the marvels of unending existence. If we find ourselves capable of performing the miracle of opening our own minds we would be able to contemplate for a while the false reality of this supposedly well-known phenomenal world. By doing it honestly we can easily end up with a correct but surprising conclusion that in fact nothing of what we see or experience is real as everything fluctuates, changes, has a beginning and is heading toward an unavoidable end. All which is changeable can't be real. Everything is like Plato's pictures but in this case not on cave walls but on a screen of space-time. Because it is totally irrelevant, if we believe in this revelation or not, let us better relax and look at this story, presented in the following pages, as a piece of literature more symbolic than real; as a composition provocative, but at the same time helpful, to evaluate our attitudes and views on life on this planet, on relationships with other humans and to try to develop a vision of our ultimate destination.

The birth of this story was not the most peaceful. However, although there was not, at this time, in this country a major earthquake, war or deadly pestilence, but instead dedicated reformers of the world were making fanatically dogged but unsuccessful attempts to destroy these few words. It was fascinating to watch the growing development of feelings in people of authority to correct those who see life from a different angle, and are trying to communicate it openly with their fellow humans. Such menials, dreaming to be moral guardians of mendacious spiritual mediocrity, are ever ready to use any means to enforce their own point of view. In the recorded history of mankind are many instances of unlimited suppression of thought executed by those who found themselves with the power to enforce their will, simultaneously strongly believing that they are the only ones who are right. To mention a few: the Catholic Church in medieval times with their witch hunters from the Holy Office; the Gestapo with True Aryan Race human 'breeding farms' and Auschwitz as its extension to terminate unwanted low category humans; the KGB with its famous chain of 'GULAG' hard labor 'reeducation' camps; and most recently Chinese 'LAOGAI' concentration camps, perfected by 'prosperous' communist 21st Century, cross-breeding free slave workers, and using high-tech equipment, materials and know-how imported from the West. But the truth is that the Real Truth has many faces and none of them is the only real one. The Truth manifests Itself in a myriad of kaleidoscopic forms, feelings and concepts which are sometimes contrasting in nature. In our case the attempt to eclipse the story was made even without fully knowing it, and assassins based their assessment of affairs only on a few hints spoken casually by the trusting and chronically naive writer himself. At the time when this camouflaged, secret combat took place the story was not even one fourth on its way to being recorded on the memory of a hard drive of its author's computer and its original title was 'Initiation'.

Probably, one source of this action was fear to hear called by the very name things, which self-imposed missionaries of 'chastity' were most probably doing in the past, or learned what they sadly missed. Probably for them, we can guess, a relationship between man and woman can only be considered as sinful, creating the feeling of guilt as manifested by a discharge of lust, but never as a divine mystery and a very much spiritual experience. I as author, who happened to transmit the story on the medium of paper do not support so puritanical a philosophy but at the same time do not allow ourselves to vulgarize any human activities, as they are all, in our understanding, divine by nature. To find hidden teachings in life we should be brave and believe in and put in practice an ancient Greek motto: 'Τίποτα το τι είναι ανθρώπινο θα πρέπει να είναι για εμάς ξένους'. (From Greek: **'Nothing which is human should be for us foreign.'** To destroy illusion is the best to experience it consciously with wide open eyes and by doing it realize the emptiness of pleasures. Hiding one's head in the sand, Australian ostrich way, and contemplating at the same time controversial fantasies and prankish possibilities murmuring "Maya, Maya" when the safety valve of the mind is endangered, will lead nowhere. This is in fact pure hypocrisy or at least duplicity. Obviously this story is not intended for reading by monks and nuns as they are trying to transcend the natural-to-all-creation sex drive. It is also not intended to stimulate desires for making love in those who are committed to normal worldly lives. This story is only a channel for showing the existence of continuity of life, its higher possibilities and dimensions not even perceivable by the general public.

Those who still have an urgency to classify this story, but also have a doubt how to go about it, are advised to read it first, but entirely. The best thing will be, we believe, before expressing any comments, to become familiar with at least a selection of poetry from the famous classic "Mathnawi" of the 13 th Century Sufi mystic Jelaluddin Rumi (1207—1273). It is available to the non-Arabic speaking world in a recently published English version by Mypop Books (ISBN: 0-9618916-1-0, Library of Congress Cat. Nr: 89-092396) 196 Westview Drive, Athens, GA 30606 USA (404) 543-2148 under the title "Delicious Laughter".

Many times throughout human history books have been burned. This is nothing new under the, still blue, sky of Earth, despite chemtrails. We can even expect further hostile activities and are ready in defense as we have mastered some skills in the past when we were dealing with the mighty forces of suppression. Nowadays words can be easily deleted from a computer's memory if a hasty-trusty author gives a password to access his machine to his impudent associate with the mind of a Middle Ages Inquisition type. But to delete anything from

Akashic Records is impossible, as there, everything exists in the master form of *clichés from* the beginning of time. Even if the mind, which was used to transmit something, were to be destroyed together with a rebellious, impertinent individual, so called author, the story would pop up sooner or later through another medium.

But let us abandon for a while our dear privacy rapists to breed happily as the times for any form of violent activities are favorable in the present stage of Kali Yuga in its delirium. Maybe they are now busy setting off in a hurry on a worldwide cleansing mission to chisel off from the walls of the famous Khajuraho Temple, built during the Chandella dynasty which reached its apogee between 950 and 1050—unique sandstone 'porno' carvings of *"Kama Sutra"* 108 sex positions; or to burn to ashes the 13th Century Indian paintings on silk preserved in the British Museum showing Brindavan Gopis playing in the waters of Kaveri River with Lord Krishna, pride of masculinity; or applying for jobs as digital spies at NSA or other constitutional privacy rights-violating organizations. Let us better think for a while what is our ultimate destination which to the majority of us is an enigmatic mystery or, if totally misunderstood, an excuse for an entirely animalistic existence with a dash of 'try to become rich' clever attitude. Is it only a path towards the grave and the return of a body to the elements? Certainly not! It is something splendid, incredible, something so magnificent that it is completely inexpressible in words. It can't be explained. It has to be lived. We can have glimpses, almost touch it, almost smell it but never fully comprehend.

We are, generally, spiritually blind dummies. No-one likes to admit it openly but we really are. Not knowing where to go; not knowing where this so desired everlasting happiness is. We are limping step by step on a dusty road, unconsciously heading back home to HIM whom we used to call God and in whose reality many of us do not believe at all. We in this story will adopt another name for this intelligent, invisible but most powerful creative energy which both sustains and destroys. Our lives are happening on many different levels and even simultaneously in different dimensions. How then can we see HIM who is above and beyond all Dimensions? Can a drop of ocean water comprehend the majesty of the entire ocean? We are such drops! We are not even aware of most of the processes going on automatically in our own body, not to mention in our minds or spirits. Nothing in our lives is simple; nothing is, as it apparently looks, plain. Most of us believe that there is no higher purpose in life. Even some 'gurus' declare that we are meant just 'to be'. There is a higher purpose! In fact this is the only factor, which gives us an excuse for eating our 'daily bread' and obstinately making the same mistakes. Life never begins in the moment of birth and ends in the hour of death. Life has in fact no beginning and no end. Our roots live in a past so remote that it is unknown even to modern history and archeology. Uncountable lives which we have already completed are nothing more than a continuing process of learning and rediscovering our own divinity. We are interconnected with the entire Universe, with every atom of it, but there is a particularly strong bond between so-called 'twin flames': souls very closely connected for eternity. Some may say that it is not true, that it is another illusion, another New Age theory. We can say: Yes and no. Both approaches are equally correct. From the perspective of totality all is illusion, but don't we live in this *maha*-illusion up to our necks? Those who have met their twin-flame/soul mate in this life have no doubt that there is something in it—at least symbolic. We know too little about ourselves to say categorically: 'no' to anything.

So, let us presume that this story which began more than fifty thousand years ago has ended very recently; just one year after the First Gulf war. In fact it still continues and never will end. Two people about whom it is all about were never born, so there is no need to guess who they are. Now, as you read these words, they are both already dwelling in the astral world and are immortal.

This, what follows, is a reconstructed story. A French lady, resident of one of South Indian ashrams named Varenia, deleted the original story from the author's computer. Only the preface survived and later was accordingly edited to vent the author's frustration. Merci beaucoup 'spirituel' soeur! (French: Thank you very much 'spiritual' sister!)

TAIPAN WALL—A STORY

It was a happy time more than fifty thousand years before the Common Era, when everything was in a pristine state and people lived in tune with Nature. In the Murinmanindji Tribe of Real People a boy was born on the banks of Rua-Vaã River in the North of Agu-Bã, a continent millennia later known as Australia. From early childhood he was very restless. As a teen he started to participate in hunting and fishing expeditions of the adults and demonstrated high intelligence and bravery. Rarely did he play with his peers; rather he listened to stories told by the Elder. When he turned sixteen he left his tribe with the permission of the Elder—the spiritual guide of all the North Agu-Bã communities. His intention was to explore the Southern parts of the continent where no-one from his tribe had ever traveled. He became a traveler. We will call him Traveler as he never adopted another name. In his clan culture a name was always associated with a talent, interest or occupation. So he was called Traveler because of his inborn tendency to wander around. No-one knew about the shape or size of Agu-Bã except Record Keeper. Before Traveler left for his trip the Elder and Record Kipper took him to the Cave of Records, which was hidden in canyon a week's walk away. There was a map of the continent of Agu-Bã engraved on a shiny metal plate. It was an artifact left for the Real People by the visitors who came from the sky in a humming metal bird. Record Keeper taught him how to understand the graphics of the map. The Elder showed him also a few pictures of those strange, wise and non-earthly visitors. They were very tall, slim and all wore a sort of space suit with a helmet covering their heads. Their faces were not visible through the helmet's opaque front membrane. The Elder explained that they came from another planet, which was in the orbit of another sun and they were called by the ancestors 'Vedaaavas 'those who knew'. They stayed with the Real People only a few months. Communication was telepathic. The visitors communicated between themselves also only telepathically. Many mysteries of life and death were passed on by them to those who deserved to be initiated into the mystery of existence. The Elder also told Traveler that some of the original teachings of the 'Sky People' were encoded in the tribe's songs and legends of this remote past, which is now commonly called Dream Time. Legends explain the illusion of material existence and the vortex of intelligent energy from which all what we see has emerged. This was intended by the Great Spirit, who in this way, being one, became many. They explained to the ancestors that people's brains decode frequencies of energy vibrations and, in their minds a holographic picture is created and this, in their ignorance, is taken for real.

Traveler, though young, was already trained to be a fully-fledged warrior and hunter, able to survive in the most severe climatic conditions, and to find food and water where only rocks and sand were. He crossed the vast desert without any serious difficulties and after fourteen months of walkabout arrived at the shore of the ocean. It was a nice sandy beach where a small river entered the immensity of the Southern ocean. He contacted telepathically the local tribe's Elder and, after being granted permission, joined them in a camp under a cliff of volcanic rocks. The tribe was harvesting delicious, black molasses from the shallow waters of a small bay which were later baked on campfires. This occupation looked idyllic but in fact it was much more dangerous than hunting in the bush. In the ocean gigantic sharks—man eaters were swimming in plenty, waiting only for the opportunity to have a decent meal of one bite. Almost every month one of the swimmers was eaten by sharks and a few more got badly hurt, some losing legs or arms. After a year staying with this tribe he moved again, directing himself South-West toward mountains whose location he remembered from the metal map. In the future these Gariwerd Mountains, rising from the surrounding plains, would be called by white skinned invaders and colonizers – Grampians. After a month he arrived at the Northern end of the range. It was a fascinating place. Huge cliffs, some of spectacular orange color, a massive flat area of smote lava flow, unknown plants and birds. After catching and roasting a few blue tong lizards he spent his first night in the 'fortress' of Lah-arum known later as Hollow Mountain. This unusual accommodation was created millions of years back by furiously strong winds blowing sand from the continent's interior. This monumental hill carved out of soft sandstone, a lump of golden colored rock once separated during a massive earthquake from a nearby cliff, with caves on many levels, windows, balconies and passages offers a dream-like residential complex.

Traveler again contacted telepathically the local tribal Elder and after getting permission joined them. This tribe was constantly on the move, changing hunting grounds, staying in caves or under balconies formed by the rock, protecting themselves from cold winds by erecting temporary fences covered with kangaroo skins. This location, full of mountains of quartz sandstone rock, amplifies the spiritual vibrations of ancient Elders. There is an almost tangible presence of the Great Spirit pervading all Creation. The canyons and cliffs of immense beauty and the lack of a permanent dwelling place of this tribe suited his soul and his restless character. Also one young lady was always on his mind. She seemed to be reacting favorably to his looks and whenever the opportunity arose she served him more intimately than the other males, giving him the best parts of baked kangaroo meat, the fattest blue tong lizards and the best *sura param* berries.

One evening after dinner, the Elder called him to his place under the rock balcony. The boy saluted him and waited with respect. The Elder smiled first with his eyes only and then with his entire face. After a few minutes of scanning the youth, the Elder asked if he liked Bun-Go, a young girl who was his great-great-granddaughter. Traveler burst into happy laughter.

'Yes, Pa-Pa, she is my favorite girl but, but . . . Bun-Go rarely looks at me, only sometime she serves me the best pieces of food!

'Nothing to worry about, my boy! Yesterday, as it is in our tradition, she requested my permission to be your spouse if you, of course, as a man of free will, have no objection.' Young Traveler fell to the Elder's feet and, by embracing them, and kissing them, he expressed in this way his immense happiness. The decision was made—after the evening session of singing hymns to the Great Spirit and Ancestors, the Elder announced this news to the entire tribe. Because unions of the free-willed Real People were based those days on a mutual commitment and integrity was a way of life, no big ceremony was needed to seal such agreement. Bun-Go's and Traveler's bodies were painted with ash mixed in water in festive designs and led by the tribe to a big boulder under the slopes of Woogaroonda (later called Iskra Craig) and seated on top of it. The whole tribe encircled them singing and dancing. Two men played the didgeridoo and one the bull-roarer, an instrument used only for initiation ceremonies. After half an hour of this simple ritual of requesting blessings from the all pervading the Oneness, the newly—weds were left there for their first night together.

Next day Traveler, to honor his new life, was given the leadership of the hunt. Now he was a family man. Going towards the plains the hunters bid farewell to their ladies. This time among them was also his wife Bun-Go. They were very successful. Two kangaroos and one emu were killed and twenty five blue tong lizards. Traveler decided to go back to the camp over Imeerawanyee (later known as Stapylton) because he wanted to perform a prayer for his happy future with Bun-Go on its summit. After the hunt he collected special herbs for making an offering to the Ancestors, God Sun and Great Spirit. All the hunters went over the step on the end of Southern Ramp. Traveler was last. He lifted himself up holding by his right hand by a stone used for ages as a hold and lifted his left arm to grab the next hold. Suddenly 'the sky fell on his face'. The hold broke and he fell backward, hit a sloping platform with his back and head, made a somersault straight over the cliff and, unconscious, and 'flew' down. A couple of wallabies grazing nearby, hearing the sudden sound of his body hitting the rocks, got frightened and ran away in a panic. His smashed body was recovered later that night, using torches to light a path through the dense bush to the boulders where it lay.

It was close to sunset. The ladies cooking dinner were looking for the men coming back from the hunt. Bun-Go was looking even more intensively than the others. She wanted to be again with her new husband. When they saw the line of hunters something painful in her heart announced bad news. Traveler was not among the returning men. All the men had faces painted with red clay—a sign of mourning. She never remarried and in time became the Medicine Woman of her clan. Her name was changed to Hearts and Wounds Healer.

It was the end of the twentieth century. A man in his early forties walked along Elizabeth Street in the City of Melbourne. He was a foreigner who had emigrated to Australia because in his country freedom was suppressed, and he felt like he was in a mental prison where he was not permitted to have different opinions to those officially declared by the ruling Party. He left his fatherland and became a Traveler. Moving through a few European countries did not satisfy his need to be far away from Communism and to feel he was in the right place. So he moved to the Southern Hemisphere and there in Australia in its multinational society tried to settle. His marriage ended in divorce. Now he was single, living in one of his past clients' garden shed. He was earning his living renovating period houses, restoring them to their past glory—Australian heritage. Living in the Eastern suburb he rarely traveled to the City feeling there almost like an Aborigine from the Outback. The bells of a clock on the Central Post Office Tower announced one o'clock—lunch time for office workers. Hundreds of executives, clerks and intern staff started filling the streets creating a dense crowd. All were in a hurry to their favorite Greek, Lebanese or Italian bistros, cafeterias or restaurants. Some who were faster adjusting to, rapidly Americanizing culture of Victorian capitol, were heading toward McDonalds, Pizza Hut or Hungry Jacks.

They bumped unexpectedly into each other on the pavement at a crossing with Little Collin Street. Traveler walking straight lost his concentration looking sideways at one of shop window displays where a collection of hiking boots was on show. She was standing, waiting for a green light to cross the street. Traveler apologized as much as his limited English permitted, looking at her with curiosity. Long, very long ago, when he was a young boy an Old Traveler told him that nothing happens without a reason. He told him that mysterious synchronicity arranges the most unexpected events, which are needed at a particular stage of life to learn something important. She had short blond hair but a rather coppery tone to her skin. She was a sporty-looking young lady in her middle twenties, wearing a very short skirt, like tennis players do. They smiled at each other and the lady said:

'Never mind. It happens. We both were not concentrating. I should also watch out for people walking 'in a trance'—like you. This traffic is so distractive. All those people are in some sort of trance. Aren't they?' Traveler, not knowing why, asked:

'Can we go for a coffee? It is lunch-break time. I hope you are not in a hurry! Our accident probably happened not without a reason.' She smiled, relaxed and responded:

'Yes. I have time. We can have a coffee. Perhaps there is a reason. Let us find out why we met in such a strange way.'

They went to a small café in the mall of Little Burke Street. Traveler knew its owner, an Italian man, Dominico, as he was Traveler's neighbor. He was cultivating a vacant block across the fence of 'his' garden in his spare time, and never missed an opportunity to teach him a little of his native language of which he was proud. Dominico was happy to see Traveler. He immediately enquired:

"Benvenuto amico mio! Dove avete trovato la bella signora?" (Ital.: Welcome my friend! Where did you find such a nice lady?)

"Il mio buon amico, vi dirò in seguito. In questo momento è puro mistero che non riesco a capire me stesso." (Ital.: My good friend, I will tell you later. At this moment it is a pure mystery which I can't understand myself.) Dominico seated them in a corner, close to the front window. Traveler ordered two spinach quiches and two cappuccino coffees.

Traveler introduced himself to the lady and she explained that she was on a short vacation from her job as a helicopter pilot in the US Army. She had been stationed permanently, together with her squadron, in Kuwait since Sadam Hussain's Iraq invasion of this country. She told Traveler that she was visiting her uncle who had immigrated to Australia when she was a small girl and she had never seen him since. She told him that she was born in the Standing Rock Indian Reservation where her mother was serving her people. She told him that her father was second generation American—Irish and that her mother was a pure American Indian of a Siouan tribe, known commonly as the Sioux of North Dakota. Both her parents were medical doctors but her mother was also an energy healer, shaman and a 'wise woman' sort of spiritual guide for the people of her tribe. Her parents named her Shauna and her mother secretly gave her a tribal name which she couldn't tell to a stranger. She explained that the natural color of her hair was black and for fun she bleached it for the first time in her life to surprise her uncle.

In their one hour chat they developed a very strong and deep friendship and felt like they had known each other for ages. The decision to go for a weekend to the Grampians was as unexpected as the entire meeting had been since bumping into each other. Traveler had only an old, red, ex-Post Office van full of tools and materials, which he was using for his business, so he rented a nice, white Lexus sedan. They met the next day at five a.m. in front of the National Gallery as Shauna was staying in a hotel nearby. Traveler booked two rooms in South Grampians 'Log Lodge'. On the way they had breakfast in 'Gold Rush Tavern' in Bacchus Marsh, and visited an old gold mine in Balarat. At eleven a.m. they arrived at Mount Zero parking lot which was close to Hollow Mountain. Traveler proposed to trek immediately towards the summit of Stapylton, a mountain dominating the Northern Grampians, as it was already late. Shauna, not being familiar with the area, agreed to go wherever Traveler suggested. She unpacked her bag, put on classic blue Levi jeans and a tight gray t-shirt. She then packed some chocolate, dates, bottled spring water and a 'Megalite' torch/flashlight in a small backpack just in case. Traveler carried it with his Pentax camera. They changed sandals for runners and set out on the path to their destination. In Hollow Mountain they explored all the 'rooms', 'passages' and looked through all the 'windows'. Shauna was silent. She later made the comment that it felt like being in a temple, in a very sacred place. After this exploration they ate some dates, some dark Swiss chocolate, drank half of their water and then walked towards Taipan Wall passing the cliff on their left. After passing the cliff they stood for a while startled by the glory and immensity of this cliff. They were on a hill opposite, which was only half its height, looking directly over the valley which was overgrown with eucalyptus. It was a spectacular cliff of orange, yellow and greenish color sandstone rock – over one hundred meters high, partly overhanging. It looked solid and appeared to lack cracks or steps, but in fact there were many climbing routes for advanced rock climbers. Above Taipan Wall was the stony dome of Stapylton—their destination. They made a photo of themselves with a background of Taipan Wall using the self-timer of Traveler's camera and started to descend to the valley. Traveler, knowing the area from his many rock climbing visits, led them to a ramp on the right side of the mountain. It was as broad as a country road and embraced, in a semicircle, a hill from its South, and ended on the very top of a cliff to the far right. After twenty minutes of scaling the ramp they were at its end. There is a two and half meter step which has to be climbed straight up. Below it is a small platform with a slope towards the cliff edge. Traveler had passed it in both directions many times. It is easy but can also be a risky place. On the step are a few secure holds and one or two horizontal chips to stand on when climbing over it. Advanced tourists, who did not have any fear of exposure, could pass it easily and without belaying. But still it was a risk. If anyone lost their balance they could end up flying down the Taipan Wall cliff.

Traveler asks Shauna if she'd like to go up first. She looked around, suddenly, in a strange mood like waking up from a long sleep. She raised her head and moved it around in the air like a wild animal does when intuitively detecting danger. In her face manifested a grimace of alertness mixed with fear. She said, turning to a confused Traveler,

'Let us sit here for a while. Something is going to happen. I do not understand what but I'm sure that we must wait. I feel a presence of spirit of death here. 'Traveler was surprised. What was wrong? The weather was good, the rock dry and they were not so tired as to need to rest now, and both were more than fit to climb this step easily. But following her suggestion he nestled himself close to the rock and to her, some three meters right of the step. Not even five minutes passed when a bunch of stones rolled down the slope over their step, jumped over and flew down the cliff with a humming sound. Soon, there reached them loud talk in a strange language from a group of careless tourists going down the same way as Traveler and

Shauna intended to go up. When they passed without exchanging greetings contrary to the normally accepted practice on mountain tracks, Shawna commented:

'Israelis!—self proclaimed rulers of the Earth. If we hadn't taken a break we could have ended up flying together with those stones which they carelessly set loose.'

They climbed the step and continued along the Stapylton ridge towards its other end where, a few hundred meters down is Hollow Mountain which they had visited that morning. They jumped over a twenty meter deep, two meter wide crack on the ridge and started to ascend. At Hollow Mountain Shauna suggested having a short break. Traveler went to the Western side windows and she lay down on the floor of the biggest cave. Being a bit tired she quickly drifted into a semi-conscious state and started to day-dream of past events. She was a young girl scrubbing a kangaroo skin on a flat rock. Ladies were cooking food on an open fire and singing a monotonous song in a tribute to the life-giving Sun. The men were still hunting. It was close to sunset. The orange disk of the Sun was sinking behind Mount Arapiles, visible in the distance, Her mother called her. The Elder wanted to talk with her. Her voice and language was very different from what she knew, but somehow understandable. She was gliding between realities in entirely different lives in times so very different. Traveler, finding Shauna sleeping, sat close by and waited for her to come back to present reality. When she woke up they continued to descend. By five they were at the car.

They had not had a proper lunch, only chocolates and dates, so Traveler proposed to drive to a good restaurant for dinner fifteen kilometers away to the South: Halls Gap. It was a small tourism-oriented village with many restaurants, lodges and guest-houses. Traveler usually, when in the Grampians for rock climbing visits, ate self cooked or ready-made food from cans. He never visited any of the local restaurants. Not knowing where to go, they asked for advice in a small grocery shop. The owner suggested they go to 'Emu Tavern'. It was an upper class BYO (meaning: bring your own wine or beer) restaurant in a building imitating the times of the Australian Gold

Rush. Its walls were built from rustic eucalyptus logs and unprocessed huge stones. Tables were made from Jarra—a burgundy-reddish gum tree wood which was as hard as stone, common in Northern Grampians, and the floor was tiled with black Indian slate with brownish-gold patches and veins. Traveler and Shauna went first to a nearby liquor shop and purchased a bottle of famous, special reserve, black label 'Wolf Blass' Cabernet Sauvignon—well over ten years old. Each bottle had a number as this batch was limited to only three thousand bottles, as it said in the attached leaflet. Traveler got goose bumps after realizing that the chosen bottle had No. 1944. Very, very strange—his year of birth. The waitress, dressed in Gold rush period clothes, recommended them real emu meat steak grilled on charcoal, a tavern super specialty. After tasting it Shauna commented that it was the most delicious meal she ever had since she left her family to live on her own. It reminded her of the wild turkey which her father hunted during their camping trips in Dakota's wilderness. Her mother wrapped it in clay and some leaves, then cooked it in hot ashes.

They talked, trying to get to know each other better. Shauna avoided the subject of her work in the army but told Traveler a lot about the spiritual heritage of her mother's tribe. He told her about his experiences in Eastern Europe and his 'vacation' in Siberia, his now simple life which was only occasionally sweetened by rock climbing trips mostly to the Grampians.

Driving to their lodge was like watching a movie with a landscape from a different planet, when being in it. It was the clear night of a Full Moon and all Southern Grampians' rocky formations and huge eucalyptus trees, stretching thick, silvery bark-less branches over the country road, looked like mythological giants frozen in immobility of an unavoidable fate. It was well after ten when they reached 'Log Lodge'. They said to each other 'Good night' and went to rest in their rooms. Traveler took a quick, hot shower and immediately went to bed. Some noise coming from the open window caught his attention. The window had an insect screen so no animal could get in easily. He walked to the window and, when his eyes adapted to the darkness of the night, spotted a possum dining on some flowers of a nearby tree. The possum's eyes were glowing greenish like phosphorus on wrist watches from the fifties. After watching the possum for a few minutes, which was unconcerned about his presence, Traveler went back to his bed.

It was probably after two a.m. when the door of his room opened. Shauna, wearing a night gown walked to his bed and sat on its edge. She touched Traveler's hand and whispered: 'Wake up please!' and gently shook it. Traveler opened his eyes and asked:

'What is happening? Is something wrong?'

'Listen! I think it must be very important. I had a very strange dream. In it I was told by an old man, looking like Aborigine Elder from the book 'Mutant Message Down Under' which I read last year in Iraq, that we must go NOW to a certain place. The man showed me the way. I can't explain more. Please come!' Traveler became fully awake. He believed that sometimes in dreams people receive important messages. He himself had in the past a few such experiences. The night was warm, no other people were around so they did not change clothes—only took a couple of blankets to wear over their shoulders. Shauna led him toward a narrow path weaving through bush-land under the Iskra Craig, a not very big mountain, and the last one of the North Grampians area. Both of them took their 'Megalite' flashlights but, because of the bright moonlight, there was no need to use them. A few hundred meters from the road they noticed a cliff. It was not tall but had distinctive overhanging rock balconies. Access to the area under them was blocked by a mesh fence stretched on galvanized pipes. Shauna asked Traveler what it was. He was familiar with the area and explained that the fence protected an Aborigine site with famous rock paintings, over fifty thousand years old; mostly reddish hand imprints and inventory marks of killed animals. Using their flashlights they explored the ancient art. The red pigment made of some plants and clay had not faded much. The contours of the palms were clear, most being smaller than those of contemporary man.

They continued walking, passing by tree-ferns looking in the darkness like unmoving, standing people. Shauna, who was in a dream, was being instructed by Aborigine Elder and she knew, despite never beings there before, when exactly to turn right and enter the dense bush. After a few hundred meters they entered a small glade. It was not far from the Western slopes of Iskra Craig. In the middle of it was a huge boulder with a flat top overgrown by moss. Shauna took Traveler's hand and led him to it. Supporting her body on the boulder she turned towards a somewhat confused Traveler. 'Do you know that we were husband and wife in the remote past? We were Aborigines! The Elder showed me a fragment of our past life as young members of a clan dwelling in these mountains. You had an accident after our first night together and fell down the cliff. Do you remember the step on our path yesterday toward the summit of Stapylton when the Israelis dislodged some stones? On this relatively easy step the hold you tried to use to lift yourself up got separated from the main rock and you slipped on the ledge, lost your balance and fell down the cliff. You died so young! I never remarried!' She embraced Traveler's waist and gently pulled him toward herself. 'Look around! They, our past relatives, have gathered here to meet us once more!' Traveler looked around. It was difficult to distinguish if the out-of-focus shapes were actual people or just ordinary bushes. She pulled him closer looking into his eyes. In the full moon-light she looked like a goddess made of pure silver. Their lips met gently. A long—very long—kiss took their breath away. Intoxicated by a growing desire to possess her Traveler started to explore her body. She was not idle and was also touching him and fondling. One more long kiss and Traveler lifted up Shauna's nightgown, with her help. She undid his pajama top buttons and took it off and then she pulled down his pajamas' pants. Holding each other tightly they started kissing again and tenderly caressing each other's erotically sensitive areas. Shauna's breasts were well formed and firm. She responded to his caresses by increasing the intensity of her breathing; getting more and more aroused. Soon, their tongues found each other and were twisting and vibrating, passing back and forth energy charges. They lost themselves in the ecstasy of a rapidly rising sexual charge. Shauna embraced Traveler's neck and lifted herself up. He held her in this position supporting her buttocks. Slowly she lowered herself and helped him with one hand to enter her. They froze for a while, only gazing into each other's eyes and feeling energy flowing powerfully without the slightest movement.

They were experiencing a union similar to Indian Tantra when sexual energy flows without any movement. Behind them something made a humming sound like bees 'singing' together. Traveler looked in this direction and spotted a wombat watching them in appreciation, making sounds only known to him which probably meant wise advice not to hurry. Traveler laid back against a rock and Shauna started rhythmically to pull herself away supporting her legs on it, still strongly hanging from his neck. She was pinned on his member and, by moving her body, controlled the speed and depth of penetration. Traveler was motionless, slowing his breath as much as he could to control his excitement. They stayed in this standing position for quite a long time. When Shauna got tired Traveler lowered her to the ground and then lifted her up and put her on the boulder. She helped him to climb it. They spread the blankets, brought from the lodge on the moss and lay on them facing the sky to rest. Neither of them wanted to break the silence nor disturb the spectacular view of the Milky Way. Here there was no pollution, there were no town lights and the Universe looked pulsating with life and its vastness clearly felt like an extension of their own being. After a while, Traveler touched Shauna's hand. She in return took his hand and put it on her breast. Realizing that she wanted more foreplay he started again to explore her body. She immediately joined him in doing similar things to him. After being again aroused they started to make love, first slowly and gently then, after a while, more vigorously with a passion. She was actively cooperating and suggesting changing positions, experimenting with all possible ways of lovemaking. After twenty minutes they orgasmed simultaneously. Afterward, Shauna lay on her back and Traveler continued caressing her. Gradually they drifted to sleep. But it was not a long sleep. Shauna woke up first and kneeled over Traveler. She kissed him when he was still sleeping and started to press secret acupressure points, activating sexual passion, whose location she had learned from her shaman mother. Traveler opened his eyes and watched her, allowing her to do what she wanted. When his penis hardened again she sat on him like a Sioux warrior sits on a horse and directed his member inside her. Slowly, slowly she started to 'ride' this 'horse' moving sometimes slightly to one side or the other, sometimes rotating, going shallowly or deeper. Being in total control she gradually increased the intensity and tightened the muscles of her vagina.

Suddenly the Earth trembled in a quake, the Universe exploded with light. There were no objects only energy as blazing light and as all body mega-orgasm pulsating with pure delight of unity. They rolled to the side and holding tight their bodies, melted in union, ceasing to feel any trace of separateness. Both their minds stopped but they understood on a different level of existence that they were not individuals, that they were eternal energy, that what they initiated thousands of years ago was still as valid as it was when they were members of a hunting tribe. They were those mountains, those stars in a dark Southern sky . . . and all of this was them, all formed from energy, pretending only that they are solid things.

Driving back to Melbourne was not as pleasant as driving towards the unknown waiting for them in the Grampians. They both knew that from now on they must go different ways, at least for sometime. This was unavoidable. Shauna had only four days left from her official leave and one more year to serve on her 'tour of duty'. Traveler was driving and Shauna was taking about the book she mentioned before; 'Mutant Message Down Under.'

'Do you believe in reincarnation?' asked Shauna. 'I think so. I had a few opportunities to have this proved. Once I saw myself in a different time with my son. We both looked very different but without the slightest doubt I knew that it was him.'

'Do you think that we really were married as a young Aborigine couple, as this Elder told me in a dream? I did not make it up! I find you attractive as a man but I feel that there is between us a much stronger connection than between two young people tempted to have casual sex.'

'Most definitely! On many occasions I have dreamed of being an Aborigine. When we met in Melbourne City I, from the first look at you, thought that somehow I knew you.'

Next day Shauna met her uncle, who got a shock seeing her blonde, and afterward went with Traveler for a three days' camp to The Cathedrals; mountains which were close to Melbourne. There they picked agaric mushroom with orange-red caps, growing abundantly in a pine forest; grilled trout purchased in a nearby farm; made love in a tent, on Sugar Loaf Hill, on North Jawbone Peak and under wattle bushes full of honey sweet yellow-gold blossom. Time almost stopped for them and they nearly forgot who they were and where they were.

At Tullamarine International Airport in Melbourne the operator announced that Emirates flight to Dubai would be delayed for one hour due to a technical problem. Shauna, after checking in, proposed to go to a café and have their last talk. They sat in a corner, sipped coffee and exchanged their contact details. Then Shauna asked how Traveler saw their future: 'Would you like to settle with me after I complete my army contract? We are well attuned as a couple and have a lot more to do which has been left from the past.' 'Definitely! We can organize ourselves here in Australia or in America if you prefer. I do not have any strings here and do not mind to change again my country of residence. My son stays with his mother and is not much interested in meeting me for any reason except, occasionally, for entertainment. We go skiing, ice skating on artificial ice or rock climbing.' Shauna and Traveler decided to wait with their decision where to settle until the time when she would be free from her present work commitment.

Three months passed and Traveler moved from his garden shed to a rented bachelor flat in Caulfield. Now he was renovating the Victorian weather-board residence of a high school teacher. The place was not far from his new dwelling. It was a huge house in South Caulfield with lead-light windows—so popular at that time, wooden decorations and details. Being in need of a helper, not necessarily experienced in painting and carpentry, just to move ladders, sand repairs and mix paint, he employed a Polish engineer Mark. Mark was an alcoholic and once, when drunk at work, fell from scaffolding erected around a submarine, whose construction he was supervising. Now he was on a small Workers' Compensation pension, officially unable to work but wanting to have some extra income. He had no skills in Traveler's job but was willing to do anything. He was also a talented bridge player and three times won the Australian tournament. Traveler warned him that, on this job, being intoxicated would not be tolerated. Mark had married a Polish lady in Australia, who somehow was not afraid to share life with such a hopeless addict. One day Mark did not turn up for work so Traveler drove to his flat. Mark was drunk, very drunk. His wife was upset and almost crying. There was no point talking. Probably Mark's refrigerator would be more receptive than him. Mark started to babble something inarticulate but a few words alerted Traveler. He was talking about some explosion in the air and a big helicopter falling on the ground in flames. Mark, when asked, could not explain what it was all about and turned again to his almost empty bottle of 'Johnny Walker'. Traveler went home with a bad feeling like a very bad, black and slimy energy had stuck to him.

Mark went on a drinking binge, a mad drinking carousel and never returned to work for Traveler. He forgot even to collect his wages for two days. Three weeks later Traveler's old landlady called on a Wednesday, telling him that a letter for him had arrived and it looked like it was an official letter from the USA. Traveler, very anxious, immediately went there. His uncle from Chicago had passed away a few years back. He had no friends or relatives in America and no official business with any company or authorities. The letter was from the Defense Department. He opened it with shaking hands. It was a formal notice that Lieutenant of the US Air Force, Shauna H . . . was killed when on a mission of her Tour of Duty and her command is greatly indebted to her for this ultimate sacrifice. In the letter was also stated that she had been awarded the Medal of Honor, the highest American military medal for bravery. The letter was signed by two star General B . . . . t. Below the official section was a note that in her personal things had been found a list of people who should be informed if something fatal happened to her. Traveler's name and his old address were on this list.

For two nights Traveler did not sleep at all and on the next Friday, after knocking off work after lunch, went to the Grampians, but this time without any intention of rock climbing. He wanted to meditate on the very spot where he had made love with Shauna. This was an unforgettable spiritual experience, a glimpse of the Totality of Existence, and since then he has always remembered what he learned firsthand about, as she called it, the Oneness. First he went to Hals Gap and looked in a liquor store for the same wine he drank with Shauna in 'Emu Tavern'. On a shelf where before had been a few bottles now were none. He asked the salesman and, with his help, located behind a display cabinet a carton box with two bottles of this vintage. His hair stood up on his head when the first bottle which he took from a box had the number: 1963 – the year of Shauna's birth. Again a coincidence. It can't be! It is impossible! This kind of coincidence has no right to happen! It must be a message from her! What does she want to communicate? Traveler went outside; sat on a bench under the roof of the grocery store on the pavement, the same one where they once asked for a restaurant recommendation, and started to sob. His sobbing turned to uncontrollable weeping. It lasted long. People passing by thought that he was probably badly drunk. Now he had lost his partner who had waited for him for thousands of years. What is in this life left worth to continue? Painting rich Australian executives' and lawyers' houses? Any idiot could learn to do this! What is the point in earning money and having no goal in life? Traveler had no goal. He was drifting from day to day, from a check for his service to another check, paying taxes, talking to other tradesmen as unhappy as he was or trying to pretend that they were not. Is it not better to jump from the Taipan Wall and end this misery, this life without any substance and maybe, if an afterlife really exists, meet with her wherever she is? Someone sat on the bench close to him spreading around an odor of the cheapest of cheap tobacco.

'Do not be sad, my boy!' said the stranger. 'Everything is happening according to the master plan of the Great Spirit. Abolish stupid thoughts. You have a different destiny from spending the rest of your life in America, or Australia, or killing yourself jumping from a cliff. Here in Australia you are also only temporarily. You can't stay here too long. Aren't you a Traveler? Go now, drink your wine and afterward meditate. Everything will be fine!' Traveler wiped his tears away and looked at the stranger. The man, smoking an abominable

200

cigarette, was an Aborigine in his late sixties wearing holey jeans, checkered flannel shirt and 'A Men From Snowy River' movie type of hat.

'How do you know?' Traveler asked.

'I do not know anything, boy!' replied the stranger. 'Go now. Stay all night in the bush!' The man got up and limped away.

Traveler drove his red Ford Transit van to Mt. Zero car park, and, after parking there, immediately left for his destination taking a blanket, a bottle of wine, a bottle opener, a glass tumbler, his trustworthy Hungarian combat knife, a Megalite flashlight and a box of matches. The glade looked different in daylight. When he was there with Shauna all the bushes surrounding the glade looked, in the Moonlight, like transparent mist, like a theatrical decoration, utterly surreal. Now they looked more real, solid and green. Bottle-brush trees were blossoming in a deep red color. The boulder was as before: overgrown on the top by a slimy moss. The sun was just starting to touch the horizon in the direction of Mt. Arapiles. From this low position Mt. Arapiles was not visible. Traveler decided to climb half way up Iskra Craig and watch the sunset from there. He thought: 'Shauna would like to be here and watch the setting sun together with me.' But she was not there, not even in Kuwait, not in America, not even on Earth any more. Had she ceased to exist or was she still alive but in another realm?

After sunset he climbed down to 'his' boulder, spread a double-folded blanket on the moss, and after climbing on top of it opened his wine. He drank the first tumbler fast, like water. The second, rather more slowly savoring its excellent gourmand flavor. It was a deep red wine with intense blackcurrant fruit, layered with dash of coffee, chocolate, plums and obviously smoky oak barrel, velvety tannins and even, as if confirming it to be Australian, eucalyptus. He started thinking about Shauna. How strange the way they met, how strange that their relationship had spanned thousands of years. How delightful was the body contact with her when the powerful energy flowed between them from in and out. He drank more wine. After the third tumbler he started to sing in Russian. Somehow he liked Russian songs much more than the songs of any other country and in any other language.

Девушка плачет,	Girl is crying,
Девушке сегодня грустно,	Girl is sad today,
Милый на войну уехал,	Her Darling went to war,
Эх, да милый в армию уехал!	Oh, he went to join the army!

Traveled started to sob again. Now here is not even one 'Девушка' who 'плачует. No 'Милый' who 'на войну уехал . . .' Now he was crying because Shauna was killed in a war and they will never meet again. How had her sacrifice helped humanity? Was America endangered by the Middle East conflict? Why must people always have military confrontations? What business do the Americans have in the Middle East? Perhaps they only want to control the Arabs' vast oil reserves. Has there been any example in human history that has showed that peace, freedom and happiness was gained by war? Traveler finished his wine and laid down on a blanket putting the flashlight and his combat knife on either side of his bed. He drifted off to sleep and immediately had a dream. He was sitting cross-legged on top of this boulder. All around was only a dense glowing white light fog. From the fog came a man. He was not Caucasian, not Negro and not Aborigine. His skin was brown and he was wearing a beard. The man stopped two meters from the boulder and smiled warmly. After a few minutes of silence he started to speak in a melodious voice, 'My son, it is good that you have come here. This is your very own sacred spot. Here you were initiated into the basic knowledge of the Oneness. More initiations will follow but in a distant land. Do not forget that sex is a sacred Union of two manifestations of the Great Spirit. To prevent experience of the Oneness Dark Forces long ago implanted in humans' psyche the association of sex with fear and shame, and a feeling that it is a dirty act. It is wrong, as this union is liberating when properly understood and free from prejudices. It results, as was originally designed, in experiencing glimpses of the Oneness.

Shauna, who as Bun-Go, was in the past your wife, was also your life partner a few times before playing different roles but she is not your Twin Flame. You will meet in this life the person who is. The relationship with Shauna is completed to the satisfaction of both of you, and there is nothing more that you both can learn together. You should never think about committing suicide. This does not make sense. There is no escape from life as life is eternal and no need for trying to check by this stupid way if this is true. In one of your past lives you did commit suicide but then circumstances were very special and it was justified. You were offered, in this present life, difficult experiences to learn; making choices based on moral priorities and not on conveniences. This helped you to grow in strength. More experiences and obstacles will be coming as you are not yet completely prepared for your life's mission. Your and Shauna's paths are not parallel. She can't keep you company in the second half of your life or even in the after-life and that is why she was removed with her consent from a time before incarnation. You two will meet after your physical death but only very briefly. Do not forget that you two also are one and will live forever. You are everything and everything is you. Learn to be detached. This splendid world is only a holographic illusion; a result of the imagination of the Great Spirit. When the opportunity presents itself, leave Australia for good. You are going to be guided to the place where you will be able to fulfill your assignment. But you must be alert that you won't miss again. Never ignore even odd looking people. The messenger will not arrive in a limousine! Now have a rest. Do not get stuck on this encounter with Shauna. This was a very important experience but not the ultimate one. Do not forget it but concentrate from now on, on moving forward. Be well my son! Let peace dwell in your heart.'

Next month Traveler found in a garage of his client, the Chinmaya Mission, an old calendar on which was printed a contact number for a Melbourne meditation and discussion group. The leader and coordinator of the group was a retired medical doctor; the widow of an Indian colonel. A picture of the Swami, who looked like an ancient *rishi,* aroused in him curiosity. He called this number and soon become involved in *Advaita Vedanta* classes and actively participated in Swami Chinmayananda's lectures and retreats, arranging venues and recording Swami's talks. Four years later Traveler got involved with another Indian guru to whom Swami sent him and unexpectedly moved to India. Despite terminating, after six years, all connections with ashrams and gurus, Traveler settled there permanently; waiting for the 'master plan' to unfold as was predicted by the mysterious man from the dream in the Grampians' bush.

A DREAM

The Transformation had begun. Vibrations were subtly manifesting everywhere, penetrating deeply into the core of things. The ice-like coat glazing all creation was gradually starting to crack, melt, and fall away like the anti-heat protection plates on a space shuttle entering denser parts of the atmosphere at unimaginably high speed. The Real Shape of things was becoming visible.

Now everything looked so different! Everything was so new, so fresh! Things and beings looked as they really are. The fragrance of life awakening to the Reality was filling the entire atmosphere. The bees, happier than ever before, were dancing on Real Flowers and collecting Real Honey. The Witness was seated under a tree, a Real Tree. He was submerged in Peace, inhaling to the fullness of his lungs the fragrance of this Real World. All he was witnessing was so different from the world he was used to living in, but at the same time it was not strange at all. It seemed very familiar; like his very own. It was so joyful to share the happiness of life, Real Life in Total Oneness, with all the manifestations of The Oneness.

Listening to the tingling Sound of the vibration of the Awakened World, he was drifting gradually into an even deeper and deeper peacefulness. Sound was coming from everywhere. Whatever his eyes looked upon was a source of Sound. The tone of the Sound was high-pitched, but also gentle and naturally pleasant to the ear. It somehow resembled the sound produced by crickets, Australian cicadas. It seemed strange, but at the same time, the Sound was also experienced as radiation of crystal clear bluish Light. This Sound-Light was emanating from stones, trees, humans, and animals. The

Witness of the Awakened World, the Witness of Free beings and Real things, the Witness of The Oneness noticed that he himself was also producing the Sound. Every cell of his body was a source of the Sound. Only the Sound-Light existed as Real. All forms bearing different names were the modification of the Sound. All forms were but a temporary distortion of the Real Sound that was permeating space. All was made from the Sound-Light. The Witness was witnessing his state of peacefulness. He was not thinking, evaluating or comparing, but he was fully aware of his awareness of the peacefulness, and of his own awareness of the awareness.

Suddenly his eyes met the eyes of Him who was a full manifestation of The Oneness, Him who voluntarily appeared on the surface of this dreamlike, ice-frozen, unconscious world for the sake of beings sleeping in ignorance. He came to lift the veil of ice, to melt the glaze distorting the Reality hidden in the manifested world of things. He smiled as only a parent could smile at the sight of a son returning home after a long, long journey. His eyes were saying:

"How pleased I am that you have found the way. You see how simple it is to be in Peace? How easy it is to be, just to be? You are the Sound, you are the Light and you are the Primordial Energy and you deserve to live in Peace. Do not drift back into an unconscious sleep. Stay awakened! There is no need to wander again. Here you are home."

The sweet feeling of love that was arising spontaneously in his heart overwhelmed the Witness. He did not know that so much love could be lying dormant inside of him, waiting to flow towards Him whom he had been searching for all these years. He could not believe that it was really happening. He met Him! He found Him! He existed and He was Real! There was nothing more to look for now. He was the guide towards fulfillment of his life long journey.

The Witness realized he was witnessing the secret alchemy of the illusion. The Real Sound-Light, the Love Waves, as It can be called, being curved and swirled by the Real Force of The Oneness on a non-real medium of space and time, was manifesting itself as separate existences. In fact, it looked like foam in which each bubble was a hologram with its center simultaneously everywhere and, at the same time, not existing at all. In Reality, The Oneness was not limited by space and time as those phenomena were contained within It. The Oneness was playfully appearing as a multitude of things and beings. It was incredible how he could not have seen it before. It was so evident! How could he so blindly have believed in the reality of the unreal?

The Real Bees continued their dance under the Real Sun, collecting Real Honey from Real Flowers. The Witness closed his eyes. He had enjoyed seeing the Real World long enough. Now he wanted to Be, just to Be. Gradually he lost the feeling of his body. Time ceased to exist and his mind stopped functioning. He was suspended in absolute concentration on his beingness. He was floating on the Ocean of Reality with Real Sound and Real Light reflecting in ripples only as temporary distortions on the surface of It, and then appearing and disappearing as transitory things and beings. He was delightfully playing in the Eternity of Existence.

Suddenly, the worst imaginable tragedy happened. He opened his eyes and awoke from his dream about Awakening. He was sitting on the roadside facing west. An enormously large red sun was just touching the horizon, about to rest for the night. Some of his companions were busy making a tea in a large vessel. After a while, he gradually started to recognize the shapes of his brothers and sisters, the silhouettes of: Lion Brother, Squirrel Brother, Puma Brother, Brother Owl, the First Sister, the Older Sister, Tiger Sister, countless Mouse Sisters, and many other still nameless Brothers and Sisters.

His eyes again met Guru's eyes. He was Real! He existed! Here in the unconscious sleeping world He was exactly the same as He was in the Real World. What a relief! The softness of Guru's glance was saying:

"Son, where are you going again? Come back . . . come . . . come . . . come back Home." Then He smiled tenderly and lovingly with encouragement. The others who were seated around Him continued to gaze unconsciously at the phenomenon of the Real Being, the Incarnation of The Oneness in the guise of a limited and ordinary person, the Unlimited dressed in a human body. He was like an iceberg showing only an insignificantly small fraction of Himself.

The Witness did not totally lose his peacefulness. He had brought back a fair share of it from his pilgrimage to the Real World. It remained in him as his assurance that the World of Real Sound-Light, the World of The Oneness, truly existed. He knew it would be only a matter of time when he would be permitted to return there and stay permanently. This was his birthright. He was born to become Free! He belonged to the Real World, the World of the Oneness. It was his Real Home. Here in this labyrinth, this hologram of illusion was only to learn how to find his way back home.

One of the Mouse Sisters put a glass of chaya into his hands. He closed his eyes patiently, and with total confidence, knowing that one day he would be fully awakened to the Reality of The Oneness, immersed again in the unconsciousness of the phenomenal world. But now he knew that he was not hopelessly on his own. He, his Guru, was in both worlds, and he could still hear Him lovingly calling him:

"Come back come, come back Home son . . ."

A BOAT

The Ganges River was magnificent here; more than one kilometer wide, flowing fast and carrying downstream the karma of those who in full faith took a bath in its sacred waters. She was also carrying away the ashes of those who had finished their Earthly existence and had arrived at the time to merge once and for all in Nature. Its rapid flow reminded those with an analytical mind of the slow but constant changes in their lives, of invisibly passing uncompromising time, and of the death approaching them closer and closer every hour, every minute and with every breath. The Traveler was resting with another man at the junction of a country road. They sat under an old neem tree, watching in a retrospective mood the Mother of Rivers visible through the trees. A couple of monkeys were happily playing, unconcerned with the Ganges Divinity like most local passers-by. He was reflecting on why he was traveling again, why he was in India with this man he knew for some time and who he knew was mentally unstable, a doubting individual, always skeptical and cynically self-assured, suffering an advanced schizophrenia. Why wasn't he staying where he belonged, in the place where his Guru lived? What more was he searching for? What was he doing right now, here, on this dusty road in India, which he had never even visited? But all appeared so vividly that he believed it was really happening!

The Traveler's dreaming eyes registered some distant movement. It was a group of young ladies and girls walking in their direction. All of them were dressed in white clothes. Some of them were Indians; some Westerners. In the middle of the group of around fifteen was a tall blond haired lady in her late thirties. She walked with difficulty. Her eyes were almost closed. She was either drunk or intoxicated by Divine Bliss. The others had been guiding her steps and supporting her unsteady body. When the group came close to the seated men, the tall lady shook off those holding her and, regaining some of her external consciousness, walked straight to the Traveler and sat on the dry grass on his right side bumping against his body. They sat in silence. There was no conversation between them. The Traveler could not see her face clearly as the reflection of the sun on the Ganges waters was in the background. The Traveler felt from her a powerful source of very positive vibrations of love and calmness. He could not even think in her presence. He was simply relaxing, absorbing the energy radiating from her. After a few minutes the tall lady turned towards him and softly said,

"Lead me to the temple. Please." They got up. The Traveler offered her his bent right arm. In Europe this is a traditional act for a gentleman accompanying a lady. The lady accepted his help, and they started to walk slowly toward the temple. The Traveler did not have an easy task, as she was still not completely sure footed. Somehow he managed to prevent her from falling. He wondered how he knew where to go, as He had never in his dream gone this way before. After a few meters the tall lady turned towards him and asked,

"Whom do you follow?" For the first time their eyes met, and the Traveler noticed with surprise how intensely deep blue they were. Never before in all his life had he met a person with such eyes. They reminded him of the blue bottle-flowers (in Polish called— habry) from Eastern European rye fields. He told her his Guru's name. She held her arm closer as if in appreciation of this, and they started simultaneously singing one of his Guru's famous bhajans: "Om Namah Shivaya . . ."

So singing they reached the temple. It was a fairly old, small temple, not in good shape; in need of general repair. Surrounded by a high brick and stone compound wall was a large, open square paved with sandstone slabs in which joints some weeds and grasses were growing. Not less than a couple thousand people, mostly men filled the area. They all rose upon seeing the approaching party. In the middle of the compound, the Traveler noticed a stone pedestal called peetam; a seat for the person speaking. It was covered with a good woolen rug and an orange silk cloth embodied with green elephants. The tall lady sat on it cross-legged after first prostrating to all present. The Traveler was wondering what would happen next. She again turned her blue-blue eyes on him and said gently, but with the noticeable shade of a command,

"Now you go back to the river and take care of the boat." In the Traveler's mind there was a strong resistance. He didn't want to go anywhere. He wanted to be with her and to listen to what she would say. Why should he bother about some boat? He didn't intend to use a boat anyway. What was she talking about? The tall lady immediately detected his desire not to go and said firmly with an accent of anger in her voice,

"You have to go! It is your duty and destiny. Go, Go!"

The Traveler woke up on his bed, in his apartment, in the western country, far away from India. For a long time he couldn't distinguish whether it was a dream or a waking reality. The experience with the tall lady was so vivid, so real, that the room in which he was sleeping appeared to be misty, off focus, like in a dream. Somehow he managed to get up, take a bath, drink a large mug of coffee and drive to work. But all day he felt that he was living partly in a different realm, on another plane of existence; that he was still talking to her and walking on a dusty Indian road, close to the sacred Ganges River. It was amazing that he, having never been to India, saw everything in his dream so clearly, so real. The future proved that all he saw then was just right, exactly as it turned out to be.

After his work and evening meal, he again started to read his Guru's biography. He liked it the most. The stories, recorded with such detail, always stimulated him spiritually. The phone rang. On the line was one of his spiritual sisters, a retired Czech lady, 'Davina'. They used to talk from time to time about their experiences and share books. She told the Traveler that recently, in the Theosophical Society Bookshop, she found on the floor a pamphlet about a Greek lady, called 'Swami Shivamurti Saraswati', who was going to visit Melbourne for the first time in the near future. The pamphlet gave a full itinerary of her few satsangs: date, time, location and the topic. His 'sister' felt that he might be interested. The Traveler said,

"No. Thank you. I have my Guru, and I am not into seeing any other 'Swaminis'." He didn't want to go anywhere else. He thought that his searching for a Path and Guru had ended. Now he had his Guru, so why should he be interested in seeing any other Gurus, pandits or Swamis visiting town? But in spite of all of this, his spiritual sister said she would mail the pamphlet to him, as she still thought it might be of interest to him.

The next day the letter with the pamphlet came. We can't even imagine the Traveler's surprise when, on the cover page, he recognized, without the slightest doubt, the tall lady of his dream. The photograph was in brownish ink as was the rest of the brochure. He immediately developed a desire to check her height and the color of her eyes. He felt that they would be, as in his dream, intensely blue-blue.

As booking was necessary for attending, so he rang and scheduled for the first satsang. The Traveler was not particularly interested in the topics of the talks. He thought he'd heard all of it many times before;

from Swami Damodarananda of the Fiji Ramakrishna Mission, Swami Chinmayananda, his great teacher of Advita Vedanta, as well as in his readings of the Bhagavad Gita, Atma Bodha, Viveka Choodamani (sacred Hindu writings: Divine Song—part of Mahabharata, Self /Soul/ Knowledge, Power of Discrimination) and many other scriptures and spiritual books. It would all be the same, only presented from a slightly different angle with the stress on different details.

The first *satsang* was hosted at 'Geeta International', a school of Yoga in Melbourne. He learned from the organizers before the program started that the Swamini, some twenty years back, had lived in this town and, as a girl, was a student of this school. Afterwards she had been married for a short time. From there she went on a short organized tour to India, to Swami Satyananda Sarasvati School of Yoga in Bihar. She never returned to the West. After twelve years of strict training under Swami Satyananda and his senior disciples, she was initiated into sannyasa and, almost immediately, was sent to Greece to start an ashram to teach yoga and meditation. Then, having been born in a western country and educated in an English school, she didn't speak Greek, her parent's native language. The first years of her stay in Athens were very difficult. She worked as a painter at various places; in taverns, shops and private homes. Evenings she was secretly conducting classes for a few curious young Greeks. In those days, yoga and meditation were not publicly acceptable in this Hellenistic culture. There was even a risk factor involved in it, since Greeks can be impulsive and hot tempered. Now, after eight years, she runs a large and well-established ashram near Athens, and is herself a Guru to many spiritual seekers from all over Southern Europe. The shape of her ashram and its location were visualized long, long ago by her Guru, Swami Satyananda Sarasvati. It fits the description given to her in the past perfectly. The Swamini has regular TV programs on spirituality and meditation in Greece, Yugoslavia and Italy.

The satsang started. Swamini Shivamurti had come. She radiated peace, calmness and serenity. Her manner was humble, simple but confident, and at the same time full of dignity. The Traveler had the impression that she was struggling hard to be in touch with

Swami Shivamurti Saraswati

the objective reality surrounding her. She prostrated to all present slowly, like in a slow motion picture. Then she sat cross-legged on the couch prepared for her. Above her hung a large color photograph of her Guruji, His Holiness Swami Satyanandaji.

Smiling gently she scanned the gathering, and when her eyes met the eyes of the Traveler she smiled and nodded her head in recognition and silent welcome,

"Oh, I am pleased you have come!" The Traveler was sitting as if in a dream, shocked by seeing her intensely blue-blue eyes. It was her—the tall lady from his dream! The only difference was her dress. Now she was wearing not a white sari, as in the dream, but a *kavi*. On her head was a colorful turban. In fact, she was really very tall, much taller than any man present at the *satsang*. After the session the Traveler booked a few other sessions. There was not the slightest doubt about the Swamini's identity. There are not many ladies around as tall as her, and probably no one with those blue-blue eyes as hers.

The Traveler felt that there definitely had to be a purpose for him having had such a dream predicting her arrival.

At the next satsang, conducted in the private house of an Indian family, he sat much closer to her. The Swamini was explaining many spiritual techniques of *sadhana*, such as *U-jaya, Yoga Nidra* and *Hatha Yoga*, with a special emphasis on pranayama, and explained variations of practices in meditation. When she came to *Japa Mantra*, she asked the gathered people for a mala to demonstrate the counting technique. Nobody had one, so the Traveler offered his *rudraksha*. The Swamini looked at his Guru's picture found in a locket attached to it, and smiled at the Traveler. It was like an echo of the dream-question and his answer: "Whom do you follow?"

He was enjoying her talks. Many doubts had been cleared. Her gentle approach and straightforwardness suited him. In her explanations there was a minimum of Sanskrit terminology. Everything was presented in purely Western style, in perfect English, with total confidence in the subject.

Before the next session, the Traveler decided to ask a few questions about a few points he was still unclear about. He wrote them at home and had the list ready in his pocket before attending the next session. When the question and answer session started, he took a little piece of paper out of his pocket and waited for the right moment to ask. His surprise was complete when Swamini started answering his questions one by one, casting glances at him from time to time. This awoke in him a desire to have such a Guru with whom he could communicate verbally, and who would clear his doubts even without being asked. He started timidly to imagine that it wouldn't be such a bad thing to go to Greece, which was culturally closer to him than India, and undergo a spiritual training there. He loved his Guru more than himself, more than anybody else on the entire Earth. He didn't want to betray his Guru, but still, deep down in his heart, he felt left aside, and not taken proper care of because Guru rarely spoke to him. The language barrier was a major difficulty. From three or four sentences uttered by his Guru, the translator sometimes interpreted only three or four words, and even these not always in precise English.

At the end of this satsang, Swamini turned her blue-blue eyes once more towards him, and said gently but with a tone of reprimand,

"Some people sometimes entertain unreasonable ideas about swapping Gurus. It is not possible. We are not the ones who choose the Guru, but it is He who chooses us. The communication between the Guru and his disciple is on a more subtle level than speech. Even if the Guru never gives any verbal instructions, this doesn't mean that the Guru is not guiding a disciple. This is His duty. His only purpose for incarnating on this planet is for guiding those who were appointed to Him to be lead towards the final emancipation. Most disciples have already spent a long time with the Guru, often many lifetimes on this or other planets. The instructions and the verbal teachings were perhaps already given in the remote past, and because they are imprinted in the disciple's sub—consciousness, there is no need to repeat them. On the other hand, the disciple's only duty is to serve his Guru and do his sadhana in earnest. The Guru is **the boat** with which the disciple crosses the river of transmigration, transcending his body, mind and intellect, good and bad qualities, likes and dislikes. The disciple's only duty is to take care of this 'Boat', even if this should cost him his life. Guru and God are one, but it is the Guru who should be considered as the more important one by the disciple. Never ever should we think, after being called, about changing our own Guru. If we do, it will slow down our progress of unveiling our own identity for many, many lifetimes. It is true that all Gurus are one in their true nature, but we belong to a particular one only. Every true Guru knows each and every single thought of his disciple, and in fact, of everyone. He very rarely discloses this to people, but we can be sure that He is constantly watching us."

The Traveler felt very ashamed, like he was publicly reprimanded. Now he fully understood the meaning of the command he heard in his vivid dream:

"Go back to the river and take care of the boat." It meant: "Do not wander any more. You have been called. Go to your Guru and serve Him with all the strength of your body, mind and intellect. Do not ask for anything. Don't feel bad because of an apparent lack of communication. Dive deep into the Silence, and there you will understand the constant whispers of your Guru's Wisdom."

Soon thereafter, the Swamini left the Big Town going back to her ashram in Greece, and the Traveler too left for India to join his Guru's ashram, to serve, or if we prefer this expression, 'to take care of the boat'. His relationship with the Guru has now been reinforced by the conviction that there is no need for one to make decisions as the Guru decides everything.

WHO COULD GUESS

Ivan Sergeyevitch Kupawov was released from the GULAG's labor camp and advised by the KGB authorities to settle for two years in Novosybirsk before he would be allowed to return to his beloved St Petersburg. Being a qualified and experienced geologist, he was given orders to work in the Far East Siberian Search Company for Mineral Deposits. It was interesting work and also good money. There was nothing to spend it on however, as they worked in a total wilderness. Now he was semi-free but the environment around him hadn't changed since he left the GULAG camp: taiga, taiga, taiga (spruce forest) only. The company was well equipped with modern, technologically advanced instruments for scanning the interior of the Earth to a depth of three kilometers in search of deposits of coal, iron ore, uranium and other raw materials—necessary for building up the strength of the country, making it a progressive leader in the World, and ensuring it a glorious future.

They only worked eight hours a day and thirty-eight hours a week, strictly following the Soviet Trade Union's prescribed regulations; but, where to go and what to do the rest of the time? Most often they drank vodka and sang uplifting army and gypsy ballads. In the GULAG camp only the guards drank, but here everybody did. Drinking vodka was normal in this country for all engineers, doctors, scientists, army officers and teachers, so why should the geologists be different? Even high school students were not abstinent! There were no exceptions!

"Whoever doesn't drink is spying for the KGB." the Russian people would say. Nobody wanted to be suspected, so everyone tried hard to get as drunk as possible.

Once during the spring, Ivan developed a desire to have a break from these abusing body and mind sessions, and decided to go alone into the taiga for a walk, and eventually for a hunt. After getting permission to take an expedition rifle with him as protection from the bears and wolves, he collected some food from the kitchen: dark rye bread, onions, smoked pork fat and some sauerkraut, wrapped in rapeseed oil greased newspaper 'Правда' (Truth), the official newspaper of the Communist Party. In fact the truth was that this newspaper was only good for such things as wrappings, toilet paper substitute, and for starting campfires.

Since it was springtime the whole taiga was full of flowers, predominately the white bells of the wild garlic—a miracle plant, a blessing from the non-existent God, as the Communists would say. Thanks to this plant, rich in healthy properties, thousands of prisoners, in hundreds of 're-education' hard labor concentration camps, were able to survive for years on the other monotonous, nutrition-less food. It now looked as if all of Nature was trying to hurry and live as intensely as possible through the short warm weather period. In a few months everything again would rest in suspended animation under the white thick cover of snow.

Ivan loved to be on his own in the taiga. The years of his enforced labor as a wood-chopper created invisible but permanent and strong bonds in him with the taiga's Nature. He understood every single sound of the taiga. He even felt his oneness with everything living there. It was incredible that being alone he never felt lonely. He could not understand this phenomenon, but it was so obvious that he noticed it and enjoyed it very much. He looked up and saw the round silver disk of the Full Moon in a blue, blue sky. How many things the Moon saw; how much suffering in this vast country, ruled in usurped representation of the working class, by the red aristocracy: the KGB and the Communist Party. He was the silent Witness to the long nights spent by unlucky people locked up in cages called 'dog kennels,' waiting to freeze to death in temperatures close to—40 degrees C. and exposed to the strong northern winds. He saw the mass murders of thousands of Polish officers, doctors, teachers and engineers, taken as prisoners of war when the Soviet Union invaded Poland from the East and Hitler's Germany from the West, as was agreed in the Ribentrop-Molotov treaty at the beginning of World War II. He saw executions of GULAG camp inmates after the smallest offense or after attempting to demand that their basic human rights should not be violated. He also saw the unhappiness of those whose reunion with their families, after their exile from Siberia, was suspended or canceled due to the successive changes at the top of the Communist Party leadership.

Ivan walked towards the Tunguska River. He remembered the mystery: how at the beginning of this century, in the Tunguska Region, something exploded a couple of hundred meters above ground. Never before in modern history had such an explosion occurred. It had a power of 40 megatons—many times stronger than the American bombs which exploded on the populated civilian towns in Japan: Hiroshima and Nagasaki—just to show to the Soviet Union how powerful a weapon they had developed. The tectonic shock wave from the Tunguska explosion even registered on the seismographs in London, New York and Melbourne. The villagers from nearby Tunguska, some forty kilometers away, saw early one night a shining object, like a meteor, crossing the sky, rapidly changing direction twice and exploding in midair. The sound of the explosion was heard as a loud thunder in Novosybirsk, two hundred kilometers away, and the Earth trembled in the wake of the hit. Much later hunters found that the trees of the taiga in this area lay broken like matchsticks in a circle over fifteen kilometers in diameter, showing by the direction of their fall the epicenter of the mysterious explosion. Years later, already after the Second World War, scientists tried to investigate the phenomenon. There was no crater at the sight, since the explosion had happened fairly high in the air, but they detected very high radioactivity, and there were heat scars on the fallen trees, as well as those still growing at some distance. We still don't know what happened there. Nuclear and thermonuclear bombs were not yet invented. The huge meteor theory has been excluded as no particles of foreign material were ever found and meteors never change direction rapidly. Maybe it was a space ship intending to land on our planet on a mission from the remote sectors of our Galaxy. Or perhaps our own expedition, sent by an advanced civilization of an earlier Wave of Life on Earth to investigate the mysteries of Infinity, lost control of their thermonuclear reactor at the last moment and exploded. Who could guess?

Ivan spent the first night camping on the bank of the Tunguska River, so called because the small village bearing this name is on its bank. He started a campfire and grilled his smoked pork fat on a stick from a spruce tree. He added some juniper berries from the unlimited taiga supplies for taste, and ate it with dark rye bread and sauerkraut, followed by an onion. Being an experienced Siberian, he prepared a luxurious and fragrant bed for himself from young spruce tree branches and moss. Soon he drifted into a refreshing sleep. He felt strange because for the first time in a long time, he wasn't under the influence of vodka.

The next morning after breakfast, with the same delicious menu as last night's supper, he crossed the river on a log from a fallen tree, which had grown on the bank of the river. Due to rising waters from melted snow at the beginning of spring, the bank had eroded, causing the tree to fall. Being aware that the Tunguska Village was more than forty kilometers away, he didn't expect to meet anyone. This was too remote an area even for the silver fox hunters. He himself didn't want to hunt. What for? Why kill?

Ahead he noticed a clearing. He was surprised and directed his steps there. Who had cut down the trees here? Was it a forest fire? No. There were no black marks on the trees. Maybe it was another GULAG camp? He came out of the woods and . . . what he saw was a real shock. A modern village! Who lived here? Who had built a modern village in the middle of the World's Greatest Nothingness? He pinched himself to check if he was dreaming. No. The village still existed right in front of his eyes. The houses stood in a row just like one of the displays at the Sovhoz (cooperatives) community in the Ukraine and Belarus; built to show foreign visitors how comfortably

Russian peasants live. He guessed the building at one end was a community hall. The other few were probably non-residential buildings: a kitchen and common dining hall, something resembling a small hospital, and a huge incinerator like the Nazis used to burn Poles, Russians and Jews in the Auschwitz concentration camp.

Suddenly, another shock. He almost had a heart attack. From the closest unit came a creature with a human-shaped body but with long brownish hair all over the torso, like the East European bear and . . . a pig-like head, in the likeness of the Communist Party's Secretary, Comrade Pushkov. The creature carried a galvanized iron container, similar to those that farmers use for transporting milk, moving behind buildings. Ivan stood paralyzed. Is it just a crazy dream? In his University curriculum he had studied zoology and anthropology. He knew for certain that such creatures did not exist on planet Earth, and nobody from outer space had officially landed here at least in recent times. The UFO stories were probably just daydreams of Westerners spoiled by their high standard of living and drug abuse. But he could not dwell on this question for long. The creature had come back from behind its dwelling. It noticed Ivan and froze. It sniffed the air like animals do when they want to catch the scent of their deadly enemy. Its assessment was probably against him because the creature started to run in his direction as fast as top world athletes in the Olympic Games can. The distance was no greater than two hundred meters. It would take about twenty seconds for a gold medalist, he thought. Realizing this, he understood that it was time for a retreat, and started to run like a Canadian prairie trapper, holding the loaded rifle in his right hand, not the Winchester brand but an old ex-army Russian one. After one hundred meters he looked back, and terrified, noticed that the creature was not more than eighty meters away. It showed no sign of tiring. Ivan felt an incredible fear of the monster. There was no other choice but to use the rifle. He stopped; the creature was now around fifty meters away. He unlocked the safety lever, and aiming without much concentration and . . . no shot! The ammunition was old and moist—useless! The game now became very serious. A few seconds more and it would get him; it was better not to imagine what could happen. Its hands were probably stronger than an alligator's jaw. He stopped, took a few deep breaths

219

and hid behind a spruce tree. When the creature passed the tree he hit it with his rifle using it like Neanderthals' cudgel. The monster fell with an open head and its brain splashed on the ground. Ivan, still holding the rifle ready for use as a club, slowly moved closer to it to check if it was really dead. From up close he saw all the details of its body. It was like an American made film about some creatures from another planet, made up by the film director to scare teen-agers. He could not believe his eyes. He spotted a metal collar on the neck, in a clear plastic protection shield. He knelt and read: Советская Станция Мутантов. Экземпляр № 675 (Soviet base of mutants. Specimen No. 675)

"Oh! Bloody demons! They were breeding here in the secrecy of the taiga a race of devils, mutants born after a nuclear disaster, from women who were exposed to the strong radiation during the early stages of pregnancy." He remembered the accident in the Ural Mountains, which had been kept in great secrecy, so that even Western enemies know nothing about it. In the beginning of the sixties a nuclear reactor or nuclear bomb, which was assembled there had exploded and over a hundred thousand people were killed in a few seconds and the town became a radioactive desert. For many years this region, forty kilometers in diameter, would remain inaccessible to people.

Ivan also remembered well the story told to him in the GULAG camp by one student from another communist country, who was there on a 'vacation' for 're-education' and whose name was David. After completing his college studies, David had been placed at a Government Farm called Garbno to work for a year. It was located near the town of Kętrzyń, four kilometers from Gierłoż, and Hitler's secret headquarters during WWII. This town in the forest had no houses, instead there were enormous bunkers camouflaged with trees growing on top, and with masking nets stretching from their walls to the trees growing between the bunkers. On the grounds of the Garbno farm were the ruins of a very special project. Hitler was trying to breed there a super-race of pure Aryans. In the luxurious barracks lived charming, young, beautiful ladies, carefully selected from all the countries conquered by his forces. They all fit the scientific formula of the typical Aryan race: blonde hair, light complexion, blue eyes, square jaws. There, those most dedicated to the fascist ideology, and also typical Aryans in their physical characteristics: officers from the Wehrmacht, Luftwaffe and Gestapo, spent short holidays and weekends enjoying the luxurious conditions, excellent food, French wine and the ladies. The ladies who got pregnant were sent to another luxurious complex in the Bavarian mountains where the delivery took place. In this 'heaven in hell' the ladies and their blue-blue eyed babies spent one year. Then the ladies were sent back to the 'breeding farm' in Garbno, or killed in one of the concentration camps if the child didn't meet the expectations of the Nazi anthropologists. After one year with the mothers, the children were distributed to Gestapo-, Wehrmacht-, Luftwaffe—and Navy-officer families, as well as to high ranking National Party members to be adopted as their own and brought up in the best possible ideological Nazi environment. The project had been very successful. The supervising experiment scientist kept a close watch on those children; their health, school progress and morale. But Hitler didn't manage to replace the degenerated European population with his super-race. He himself ended as a half-burnt corpse on the front of his last bastion, a bunker in Berlin. Many of those who had been born through the project survived the bloody war and the heavy bombing of the Third Reich by the Western allies, and have started their own families by now. Possibly none of those blue-blue eyed Germans is aware of the fact that he or she is a creation of an experiment initiated and ordered by one of the Incarnations of the Devil himself, Adolf Hitler.

In the GULAG camp, David introduced Ivan to the man with the shining eyes, whom David called a Free Man but others Fox. They talked together about Hitler's experiment. The Free Man only laughed. He said that changing the body and programming the mind doesn't lead to anything worthwhile. What has to be achieved in our lives, he said, is to rediscover our own identity, our oneness with The Oneness. He said that all creation is only a temporary manifestation of the Highest—God. Only He is real and eternal Existence. He told them that on this planet and on all the other inhabited worlds live many Light Bearers, who neutralize the negativity of those with a demonic nature, and guide those who want to tread the Path towards the Light Divine. There are also, from time to time, Super Light Bearers, Incarnations of the Highest who descend to the material plane to uplift declining human morals. But now Ivan, looking on the dead body of the monster-like creature thought,

"The demonic fantasy of Hitler and other Devil Incarnations like Lenin, Stalin, and the latest one, Breżniev, have no limits. Where in the World is now an Incarnation of Love to balance the evil? Does it exist? I will never know. Maybe the Free Man in the GULAG camp was just fantasizing. Even if not, our country leaders will filter the news as contradictory to the official Marxist Ideology." How could poor Ivan guess that in somewhat less than thirty years, an Incarnation of the Highest would personally visit the Soviet Union and counsel hundreds of people in his beloved Moscow? How could he know that this would happen at the beginning of the collapse of the 'undefeated, most humanitarian', communist empire? Who could guess that the impossible would happen?

Ivan returned as fast as he could to the geologist's camp. Badly shaken by the experience, he was crying out,

"God, my God! Do you hear me? If You exist please visit this country and see for yourself what they are doing with Your children." Just before sunset he reached the tents. His colleagues, already quite drunk, were singing loudly,

"Девушка плачет, девушке сегодня грустно . . ." (Rus.:The girl is crying, today she feels longing and sad . . .) Ivan was very hungry but first he drank a full glass of vodka, fast, greedily in the desperation of a person who wants to forget. After a while, when his blood had distributed the alcohol and his nerves relaxed under its toxin, he told his revelation,

"Comrades, do you know that some twenty kilometers from here is a village of mutants? I killed one of them!" There was no end to the laughter. The *politruk* of the expedition, after a few minutes of restraint, couldn't hold it any longer and burst into uncontrollable laughter and murmured. "Mutants, hybrid babies . . . Ha, ha, ha. He killed a hybrid infant. Ha, ha, ha."

The following day Ivan continued his claim. Everyone was irritable and had badly hurting heads. They weren't in the mood for such jokes. They were getting ready for their next carousal to eliminate these bad feelings, and didn't want to listen to his crazy revelations again. But when this craziness was repeated the next, and the next day, the political officer suggested to the director to send him back to Novosybirsk for psychiatric treatment, as his revelations were the result of a mental illness and were negatively influencing the other workers, who were dedicated to the Communist Party ideology. Ivan was locked in an underground room for a few days, which was built for the occasion with great dedication by his colleagues. They assessed him as possibly dangerous. Soon he was taken back to Novosybirsk, skillfully tied up in the helicopter which brought them their once a fortnight fresh supplies of food and indispensable vodka, which was needed to keep the morale of those specialists dedicated to the progress of communism in this vast country, high and in good shape.

Unpredictable are the ways of Him whose existence is so earnestly questioned by the communists. Ivan, after scrupulous medical examinations, was assessed as fully normal. This brave assessment was authorized by a Dr. Kunya, who as a hobby specialized in 'Indigo Children', UFO abductions and . . . in mutations after exposure to radiation. Ivan resumed his employment. Many years passed. Ivan, having a lot of savings from his wages from working for the Geological Company for fifteen or more years, managed to bribe whoever was to be bribed, and bought false Jewish papers. He then migrated as one of the officially-approved-for-repatriation Jews to Israel. There he met a Russian lady who liked him, and who had also migrated from the Soviet Union. She was living in Melbourne, Australia and was only visiting her family in Jaffa. They both had a lot in common and both wanted to finally settle down. After the marriage ceremony in the synagogue, Ivan, sponsored by his wife, migrated to Australia. There he soon became a successful stallholder, selling sheepskin seat covers for cars on Melbourne's' 'Victoria Market'.

A few years later on a sunny Australian spring day in the middle of November, walking down the street of the Melbourne Jewish suburb Balaclava, he met . . . David. Incredible! He hadn't changed much. He looked a bit older and there was some gray hair, but the same slim body, the same energy and the same smile. He was wearing overalls. Now he was a tradesman running his own business. They arranged a meeting for the next day to talk things over. Who could guess that through Siberia and Israel their roads would meet again in Australia's Down Under, on the other side of the World.

They spent the whole afternoon in one of the Balaclava cafes talking about what had happened after . . . When they finished, David, changing the subject said:

"Listen Ivan. I would like for you to meet someone who is coming to Melbourne in two weeks. You know me. It's not a fishy business. I'll pick you up from your place on the 28th at 6 p.m. Now I won't tell you who it is but it's important that you meet Him." Ivan asked with interest,

"Him? Have you turned gay? Is he going to be soon your 'wife'?"

"No, Ivan, it's not what you think." laughed David. "You have to find out yourself who He is.—They exchanged phone numbers.

The Melbourne Masonic Conference Center was full of waiting people. All were dressed neatly. The air was fragrant from the smoke of something they burned everywhere. It was in the form of long thin sticks. In the entrance on the floor lay a red and green silk cloth, and on it lay a large brass tray, a bowl with fresh roses and a jar of water. Between the crowds white dressed people moved about. Some of them stood at the entrance and chanted a mantra, "OM AMRITESHVARYAI NAMAHA." Others were silent. Everyone was anxiously waiting for Him.

"Who is He?" Ivan asked David.

"Wait! Don't talk now. See for yourself." The intensity of the chant increased and . . . after a while, He entered the hall, and stepping on the silk cloth placed His feet in the brass tray. He was very tall, dark skinned with dark hair, strongly built, and dressed in white. Probably Indian, Ivan guessed. He stood motionless, with closed eyes, holding His head slightly bent down and His palms in a praying mode or in the Indian greeting mode for 'Namaskar'. The white dressed people, kneeling on the floor in front of Him, washed His feet with the water, dried them with a snow-white towel, and placed the roses from the bowl on them. One of the white clothed people placed around His neck a colorful garland made of white and red carnation flowers, like those used on the first May parade in Moscow. They lit the camphor on a sort of large brass spoon and started to wave it in a clockwise direction in front of Him. Something Divine hung in the air, a feeling Ivan had never before experienced.

Then He walked to the stage and prostrated to all those gathered before Him, then sat cross-legged on a small platform covered with a rug. Some people returned the salute, prostrating toward Him themselves. The Man in white smiled. What was this smile? How could He smile this way? All of Him was smiling; His face, hands, body, and mostly His eyes. Then there was a short talk. One huge man wearing a red robe translated it into English. Ivan didn't understand much. His English was not yet so good and strange accents were even more difficult to understand. Afterwards they sang. It was a very interesting performance, but quite foreign and exotic for his Slavic taste. Still, Ivan liked it. He felt in it some indefinable charm, like devotion to Nature or God. After singing, darshan started, as David called it. Ivan sat as close as possible to see Him. He welcomed every single person as the most loved child. Only a mother can welcome one in this way. Later he learned that they all call Him Appa (Father). He was cuddling people, rubbing their backs and hands, applying something on their foreheads, and whispering something straight into their ears. Ivan was inspired. It was the first time in his life that he saw such love. He Himself, and the people around Him, were submerged in the Golden Light of Love. Everyone's faces beamed with some Divinity. After two hours of watching and crying for no reason, except from great happiness, he decided to go himself for darshan.

When He held him, he understood that it was not a person touching him. It was pure Love Incarnated in human form, which He had assumed in order to allow humans to experience Him in such an intimate way. Ivan understood the importance of this meeting. He now met face-to-face an Incarnation of the Highest about whom long, long ago the Free Man had talked. He understood that the unlimited power of Love at His disposal was more than enough to balance thousands of evil beings like Hitler, Stalin, or other old country leaders. There was nothing to be afraid of. He existed; He was real, more real than all this around him. Then He pulled him up and touched his forehead. Ivan felt a warm current of energy passing through his body. He smiled towards him and whispered:

«Мой сынок не смутится, всё будет хорошо.» (My son, do not be sad, everything will be well.) He thought,

"Me, His son? Is He joking? And how did He know my language? How did He know that I'm Russian. Then it was the truth, what the Free Man had said when talking while hiding behind The GULAG camp latrines; the most important thing is to rediscover our oneness with The Oneness—the Highest of All. Then, if I am His son, then I am of the same nature as the Golden Light of Love as He is, only not in an awakened state." He patted his shoulder in the typical Russian bear style and smiled again, as if in confirmation of his thoughts.

Ivan walked back to his corner in the hall as one would when drunk. He was drunker than he had ever been in Siberia, but now not from vodka but from love. Everything swirled in front of him like on the carousel in Moscow's Park of Freedom. He wanted to shout to the entire World, louder than the thunder over the Siberian Great Nothingness, louder than Tunguska's mysterious explosion, so loud that even the Moon the Silent Witness—and even the stars in the black sky would hear:

"He loves all of you!!! Brothers and Sisters, whose daily experience was an unbelievable suffering in Siberia's hard labor concentration camps in the GULAG; you who lost faith in yourselves and in other people, wake up!!! God exists, He is real!! He has become A Man in White for the comfort of us. Our communist leaders were lying when they said that it is only a myth and that religion is the opium for the weak minded. We are not hopelessly alone. Brother wake up! You are, in your inner nature, the Golden Light; you are Divine Love. Forgive them your pain. They are our brothers too, only right now they are more ignorant and more arrogant, but it is certain that their time will come too. Don't believe the communist propaganda that God was invented to more easily manipulate people. They denied His existence to more easily manipulate all of us!" Ivan almost collapsed from emotion. This was something worth going through all the past hardships and sufferings, in order to experience it even for a minute before death.

David sat next to him. They didn't talk, being united by the past and now united in the Love awakening in them. What could words express? Who could believe that they were floating on the Infinite Ocean of Bliss? Ivan was silently crying and repeating:

"Who could guess?" and slowly shaking his head.

Who could imagine that He, The Highest, had heard Ivan's words, when frightened at the sight of the nuclear mutant, devastated after killing him, and rushing back to the geological camp calling God? Who could guess that the Man in White—Love In Love—*Satguru*, would go the next year to Ivan's beloved St. Petesburg and console hundreds of his brothers and sisters, some of them ex-GULAG camp veterans, and lift from their hearts the heavy load of hatred, showing them the Path to the Golden Light. Who could guess? But the impossible did happen, as nothing is impossible for Him!!!

WHERE ALL ROADS MEET

Two Friends

C lose to Poland's southern border in the broad valley of the rapid River Raba, halfway between Krakow, its first capital, and the Tatra Mountains, there is a small town called Myślenice. Its name means: 'Thinking Ladies.' Perhaps in ancient times a unique and now extinct tribe of women lived there, like the famous Amazons, whose members used their brains for thinking instead of the hormonal cocktail flowing in their veins, controlling both body and mind; which is the case of the normal female variety of the human species today.

Spring was at its height and it was close to Easter time. The teenagers and youths were becoming restless. Jack, Andrew's friend, was sixteen years old and very restless too. School vacation had started and he traveled back to his hometown of Myślenice from the boarding high school he attended, located some distance away. The school occupied a gloomy old building, full of mysterious nooks. It was an ex-court building and a relic of the Austrian-Hungarian Empire. There, he spent an exquisite time doing all sorts of crazy things. There he also met his best friend Andrew, also in exile from his hometown for being very naughty. During the long midday break, they used to go the karczma, an Eastern European variation of a western pub located in the town's central plaza. There they enjoyed a huge mug of cold Żywiec beer mixed with raspberry syrup. It was a delightful invention of those genius Slovaks living across the Tatra Mountains.

After finishing their boring classes in mathematics, Latin and history, they would go exploring the mysteries of the court building: the torture chamber with chains on the walls and a fireplace to heat the pincers and rods (which were now missing) which were used for bringing back the memory of transgressors, and the small cells deep under street level used to lock up those who fell into the hands of the guardians. The walls of the cells were full of inscriptions in Polish,

Czech, Hungarian and German. The dungeons were the best place for smoking cigarettes. They would smoke in silence, imagining the time when the walls reflected the screams and swearing of the tortured and imprisoned High Country rebels and robbers.

One day they unintentionally made a pogrom of rats. Andrew had brought from home a cylindrical aluminum container left over from the Havana cigars his uncle, who was visiting Poland, coming from Chicago, USA, had been smoking. The friends immediately found a perfect use for it. They filled the container with everything they could find that would burn rapidly: Old, now banned, celluloid based cinema film, sulfur, charcoal, potassium permanganate and the heads of matches. They lit it in the hall of the court prison, having fixed the phial firmly in a gap in the wall. After a few seconds the flame of the burning mixture became long, narrow and bluish, and it hummed like a real space rocket. The aluminum phial melted in no time, and all of its still furiously burning contents fell into an open metal barrel, in which chlorinated lime was kept for disinfecting the school latrines. The heat of the flame caused a release of free chlorine, a yellow gas, heavier than air and extremely poisonous. It spread all over the halls and narrow corridors of this place of past suffering, and made its way into the sewage pipes. The pair of pyromaniacs left as soon as they realized what was happening. The next day when the teacher in charge of the boarding house went to bring some potatoes from one of the cells, he found dozens of huge, dead rats.

They loved this particular teacher. Himself a heavy smoker, he never tried to punish the boys for smoking in the bathrooms or prison cellar. Being hooked himself on this terrible habit, he felt rather sorry for them because of their growing addiction. He was a mathematical genius. They tested him. He really was! On top of that he was an advanced alcoholic. He had a much older and abominable, fat wife. Maybe because of this he had started to drink. They called her 'Toad.' She often shouted at him loudly. His apartment was at the end of one of the first floor corridors of the school boarding house. Once, during such a dispute, she pushed this unfortunate, talented man onto a red hot, single plate electric stove standing on a pile of bricks in the corner of their kitchen. Heartless monster that she was, she probably did it on purpose. Now the teacher ran across the halls and corridors of the boarding house screaming in terrible pain. He had an imprint of the stove spirals on his bottom, melted and grilled together with his best synthetic polymer pants. He left behind him a trail of white smoke from his still burning pants. After seeing this incident all the boys swore never to get married. Why risk having such a miserable life? It is impossible to guess what can change a once charming and pretty girl. In their teacher's wedding photo, hanging on the wall of his bedroom, his wife looked like an angel: sweet, attractive, and slender as a squirrel. But passing time veiled the memory of this terrifying incident. Most of them later did marry, Andrew too, but not Jack. His destiny was much different. For now, they both played according to the demands of their age, knowing nothing about their destinies.

Now Jack was back in his family home. Andy was not around. Boring! He decided to go to the river and poach a salmon. It was the best time. Those huge fish were swimming upstream of the rivers from the Baltic Sea to the High Country for spawning. In Myślenice the milldam was the best place to catch them. There the salmon had to jump to cross over a three-meter high artificial waterfall. Jack was very experienced. After a while, he had a salmon over forty centimeters long hidden in his trousers. It was still alive and its movements created excitement among the few girls enjoying a sunbath on blankets spread on the grass. He smiled mischievously. Then he noticed the 'Nature Guard' approaching the area with a shotgun. Jack started to walk fast so he could hide behind the dense alder grove. This only increased the already strong suspicion of the guard. He shouted,

"Stop! Don't move or I'll shoot!" Jack 'unfolded his wings and flattened his horns.' Holding the poor salmon in one hand he ran, at the speed of a top class athlete during the international sports games. The shot sounded loudly and Jack moaned from pain felt in both his legs.

"He shot me with salt crystals, skurwysyn," (Polish swearword meaning: 'son of a prostitute) muttered Jack. Another thought immediately followed,

"I have to run faster so he can't get me." Jack was tough on himself and was determined to escape certain harsh prosecution. What he had just done was considered illegal. In those days only the 'red aristocrats' from the top hierarchy of the Communist Party could eat salmon legally.

The next day Andrew arrived on a light German-made moped called 'Simson.' His town was boring; there was no suitable company to do silly things with. There was Jack, and a girl who was somehow special to Andrew. Andrew found his friend in a bathtub soaking his wounds in cold water with some cider vinegar added. He was singing loudly his song of pain. Its words were not the most decent in the Polish language, but they were internationally acclaimed as the best swearing words, since they contained many strong 'Rs' in their spelling. Andrew well understood the benefits of this swearing therapy. He had read in a magazine that American psychologists found that intense pronunciation of words with strong 'Rs' causes relaxation, even in highly stressful situations. In fact, any word will do. It doesn't have to be a rude word of the street. For example, 'kurrrrrczak,' which in Polish means 'chicken', is as good as 'kurrrrrwa,' (Pol.: a prostitute), one of the most popular and strongest swearwords.

Some years later, in the extreme Northeast of Poland, far away from the small town of Myślenice, a new technical college graduate— Andrew—worked on a huge government farm called Garbano. He had continued his studies at the University, but because of too many tempting distractions failed the first semester exams. Now he was waiting for the new academic year to start, and this time he'd probably be more serious.

Unishevsky's Trip to Germany

It was a warm Autumn evening. The sky was covered with clouds; it was probably going to rain. He and a few fellows from the farm staff were sitting on a bench near the entrance to the office building. They were silently smoking cigarettes and listening to a story told by the oldest worker, whose name was Unishevsky. He was a strong man. He was a laborer on the farm cultivation fields. In the beginning of WWII, after the German invasion of Poland, he was arrested by the police for selling meat from an illegal slaughterhouse. By decree of martial law, all animals belonged to the German forces, and Poles were not permitted to slaughter any pigs, cows, sheep, goats, or even chickens, ducks, or geese. Unishevsky was lashed at the police station and sent to one of the concentration camps for an indefinite hard labor, called 're-education.' There he quickly learned the enemy's language, and when the German 'Landwirt—Bauern' (farmers) were selecting slaves for work on their farms, he was one of the first sent from the concentration camp.

He was as strong as a bull. Work on a farm was nothing for such an athlete. The food he received now was the same that the farmer's family ate. The farmer was humanitarian in nature, and felt uneasy using slaves. After his visit to the concentration camp he felt ashamed at what the Germans were doing. After a while the farmer's older daughter Greta, a seventeen year old, tall, with blue eyes, blonde hair and long slim legs, started to stare at him during meals and tried to find any opportunity to be around him when he was working alone in the fields. It did not take long for them to find mutual pleasure in making love on the green grass of the meadows, or in the golden fields of wheat. Unishevsky was lascivious, and Greta was hot-blooded like the Spanish whilst sophisticated like the French.

The girl was free of complexes and had a lively imagination. She skillfully secured the deepening of their eventful and piquant relationship. Such idyll lasted until winter. When the cold came and the snow covered the meadows, they started to meet in the barn. There, the old farmer, the girl's father, discovered them together. He was more furious than ever in life, and beat both of them with a spade, almost killing the unfortunate lovers. Unishevsky, covered in blood, was chained and handed over to the police. Soon he returned to the previous concentration camp. But his destiny was to work again handling meat. He joined a team of laborers at the Wermachts' slaughterhouse. Every morning, well before sunrise, the trucks drove them to work and returned them to the camp late at night. They ate at work.

Unishevsky recovered fast from his injuries by eating German army meat, and his strength increased. After a while he found a way of smuggling fresh meat into the camp for his starving comrades. Christmas was approaching. Unishevsky wanted to prepare a feast at the camp. One evening, just before the end of his shift, he unhooked half a large pig from a transporter and threw it onto his camp's truck parked nearby. Unfortunately the guard, standing on the upper floor of the meat processing plant, saw it. Unishevsky was taken at gunpoint to the guard's house. There he was chained and beaten with another iron chain. When he regained consciousness, he was covered with blood, lying on the floor of a moving army jeep. The gloomy guard was seated on the bench. The silent trip lasted not more than four hours. When they crossed the gate of another camp Unishevsky noticed no name, only a sign over its entrance: "ARBEIT MACHT FREI" (Work creates /makes freedom).

"Where am I?" he wondered. The guard kicked him off the jeep and climbed down. From the camp's office building a Gestapo officer walked towards them. He was tall, with blonde hair and blue eyes. He was clean-shaven and smelled of good quality cologne water. His black uniform looked like new. Unishevsky's guard, standing at attention, handed him a delivery letter. The Gestapo officer opened it and smiled while reading. He looked with curiosity at Unishewsky and said:

"Welcome, 'Sir', to your last home. You are a very notorious criminal. This is a special camp for individuals like you. Up until now the survival record here is seven months. You will die in less than six. You obviously are most welcome to try to beat the record and live a few days or a few weeks longer. Our motto is, as you see on the gate, 'Arbeit macht frei.' Do you know what it means? Work makes freedom! We will help you more than you can imagine. We are very skillful. You can be sure that here you have no chance." But

Unishevski was determined to survive. He looked straight into the Gestapo officer's eyes and said.

"Jawohl, Herr Kommandant. Wir werden ja sehen." (German: Yes, Mister Commanding Officer. We will see.) It was really a hell. The days were spent in exhausting work at the blue-stone quarry in the Schwartz Wald (Black Forest), and the nights were often spent standing in the open for assembly. Once, in a fortnight, he was flogged with a riding whip, which had small lead balls on the end of its straps. His whole body became one big sore. But he did not give up as so many others did, who, desperate to avoid more suffering committed suicide by hanging themselves or by jumping onto the electric fence which surrounded the camp. Every day he repeated a few thousand times to himself,

"I will survive! I will get out of here alive! I have to be free!"

The time was passing fast. The deadline of six months went by. Soon it was already more than seven months, but Unishevsky was no less alive than on the first day of his arrival. One early afternoon Herr Kommandant called him to the office.

"Are you still alive? Congratulations Sir! Now you are the record holder. Now you are a hero. But I am very sorry. We can't tolerate Slave heroes. It would uplift the morals of others. You have to die. Tonight you will be caned to death in front of the camp inmates to boost their morale." Unishewsky took a long breath and mentally repeated,

"No! I will survive! I will come out of here alive!"

"We are your enemies but we are civilized people. We respect the last wishes of those who are sentenced to death. Take a cigarette from the box on my desk and think of what you want to ask me for. It will be granted. I can even provide you a fried salmon for your last supper if you request. You have my word on it." said the Officer. Unishevsky lit a cigarette, lifted his face and puffed a perfect smoke ring towards the ceiling. Blinking his eyes he said,

"You said, Herr Kommandant, that you will grant me what I ask. I want to survive and get out of here!! Give me a chance!"

Total silence filled the camp's office. All the staff member's eyes were on Uniszevsky. Above him hung still the ring of smoke, like an aureole above the head of a saint on a church painting of the middle ages. Herr Kommandant was from a good, old, aristocratic family with traditions. His surname started with a 'von,' which means he was a count. He could not break his word given publicly, even if it was done hastily to a Polish slave.

"Well, you are as clever as you are strong, my friend. You will have a chance! Look over there, on the side table are two half liter bottles of Vodka. If you can drink it all and manage to leave this room on your own feet, your life will be spared. If not, being drunk, you won't feel the pain." Unishevsky nodded his head in agreement, and walking towards the side table thought:

"I've never drunk that much vodka! I can't—for sure, I will die from alcohol poisoning." but quickly in his mind he repeated his magic formula,

"I will survive! I will get out of here alive!"

He filled to the rim a large glass of it and drank it like water. The Germans, full of wonder, watched him in silence. He filled a second glass. Herr Kommandant said:

"Take from the table whatever you like to follow it up with."

"I never follow it up with anything after the first glass", replied Unishevsky, drinking a second glass at a draught. The Germans moaned with admiration. After he finished the first bottle, the room where he stood appeared to be nice. The faces of the officers staring at him were almost friendly. He looked at the portrait of their 'Führer'—Adolf Hitler, hanging above Herr Kommandant's desk. He too looked funny, rather than hated.

"They must retouch his devil's horns." he thought. The officers noticed his ironic smile and one of seniors suggested.

"You should propose a toast to honor our Führer."

"It was not a condition in our agreement, but I don't mind to do it, if this will make you happy." said Unishevski. Swallowing the next full glass of vodka he shouted loudly,

"Heil Hitler!"

After he finished the last glass, the floor of the room danced in furious convulsions. He walked slowly toward the door, stepping widely on his legs and using his arms to keep his balance. The office was silent, like at the grave of Marshal Wilhelm II. When he opened the door and crossed it, consciousness left him like the dove, the harbinger of freedom that had left Noah's ark after the Big Flood. He fell down the steps onto his face like one dead. The Germans in the office shouted,

"Hurrah! He won! We knew that he was not a human but the devil himself." In the euphoria of their excitement they had forgotten that they were of the 'Überman' (superhuman) race, and he a subhuman slave from the country they had just conquered. The Herr Kommandant himself, having great respect for Unishevsky for his bravery, cleverness and determination, ordered his subordinates to carry him carefully to the barracks where they let him sleep.

Six more months passed after this experience of drinking away his death sentence. It was the beginning of March, 1945. One day, early morning, U.S. Marines freed the camp. Most German officers were taken prisoners, some were shot. Only Herr Kommandant, the aristocrat, committed suicide. For, as he expressed himself while reloading for the last time his spotlessly clean pistol 'Parabellum', it was a dishonor, worse than death, to be captured by those 'Yankee cowboys'.

U.S. army doctors checked Unishevsky, and then sent him to the detention camp supervised by the United Western Forces. He was now free to leave any time and able to settle in any European country. As long as he stayed in the camp, he would have to return there for the night. There were other restrictions as well: Alcohol wasn't permitted at the camp, and ladies were not allowed to stay on its premises overnight. They had to leave no later than six in the evening.

The time for Unishevsky's revenge came. He found, without much difficulty, a few former slaves, similar to him and organized a gang. They had two pistols, ammunition and a few grenades. These weren't difficult to find in those days. Arms, explosives, and all sorts of post-war junk lay everywhere and could be purchased from any local street kid for a mere few packets of American cigarettes. Unishevsky divided his gang into two three-man teams. They were dressed in woolen jackets and long ex-army overcoats. They cut off the right pockets of the jackets to be able to handle the pistols comfortably. The gang walked in a relaxed way around the town, and, in the middle of the day, amidst a crowd of pedestrians, shot German Police patrols. They were full of terrible hate and rage, and, stimulated by it, had no fear.

After killing the policemen they walked slowly and cold-blooded from the stage. No one suspected them to be assassins, for their clothes muffled the sound of the pistol shots. Now, Unishevsky can't remember how many Germans he killed himself, but knows to have been many. After one year the camp was closed down and they were given UN refugee passports. Because Poland ended up in the grip of communist suppression after the war, they were advised not to return there. U.S. intelligence services already had many reports about the ill fate of those who had returned to their homeland.

Robbery in Baden—Baden

Unishevsky and his gang decided to earn their living at the expense of their former oppressors. Their choice fell on the health resort of Baden-Baden. It was a favorite place for German financiers and industrial magnates to meet. The gang secretly observed one of the chalets for more than a month. One of them even got a job as a bread deliveryman to be able to see it from the inside. Unishewsky decided to strike at dusk during the Easter Day banquet. The gang consisting of six men cut off the telephone wires just before sunset and two of the gang were left outside to guard the chalet, armed with Wermachts' forces standard 'Schmeissers'—machine guns. The rest of them entered the hall holding pistols in their hands and grenades hanging on strings across their torsos.

"Hände hoch!" (German: hands up) "Everyone down on the floor! Don't move. We won't ask a second time." Unishevsky went to the kitchen and brought back everyone who was working there. He and one of his fellow bandits watched the high society party stretched out on the floor. Most of them had gotten really rich on highly profitable deals with the Nazi army. For them the war was an excellent opportunity to increase their business.

Suddenly a single shot broke the silence. Unishewsky had shot one restless fellow who had tried to be a hero. He had tried to make use of the small caliber silver plated pistol hidden behind his belt. After killing this one German, all crazy and suicidal attempts to resist the robbery stopped. In the meantime the other two emptied most of the pockets of the men, and removed most of the diamond rings, necklaces, diadems and watches from the ladies. All the valuables were left in a pile in the reception hall, and the party, shivering from fear, was locked in the well-built, fully stocked wine cellar. The gang started to select the booty. There was too much gold to carry. They picked only the most valuable pieces, assessing them by the number and size of diamonds. They also took the money and some gold 'Patek' and 'Longines' wristwatches. The rest they left on the floor with a note that it was a premium for German's discipline and good behavior.

The gang left on heavy, 'Sahara' army motorbikes with sidecars, which they found there. Their escape was full of excitement, as German police soon blocked all roads and patrolled the trains. A few times they were almost captured but somehow managed to stay free. After almost one week of travel on foot, by car, motorbike, train and boat, they reached Munich. There, Unishewsky decided to dissolve his gang. They divided the money and jewels into approximately equal parts, and wishing each other good luck disappeared into the crowds of post war Europe. One of them married a Dutch girl, and using his share from the robbery, bought a large petrol station near Amsterdam. He lived there and worked in the adjoining garage. After forty years he retired and his son took over the family business. The others disappeared in post war Europe like stones falling into a lake.

Unishevsky wandered around Germany. He was not very happy at all. His treasure made him very wealthy, but it did not make his mind calm and peaceful. He was extremely restless. A few times he made attempts at settling down, but couldn't stay anywhere longer than a few weeks. One day he unexpectedly met Greta. She looked muffled, dejected and was in low spirits. All her dash, loftiness and charm were gone. Neither of them was delighted by this event. She was married and had a child, a baby girl. When Unishevsky politely asked about her daughter's age, Greta was embarrassed and flushed. He nevertheless calculated that it must be his daughter. The farmer had arranged for Greta's marriage very soon after they had parted, but the girl was born less than six months after. Uniszevsky offered her a very precious pendant with a multi-carat stone set in platinum in the shape of a rose. He did not remember the industrialist's wife who previously wore it, but she was surely huge, fat and unhappy in her too abundant life. They parted without another word. What could they say?

Return to Poland

After two years of aimless wandering, a few jobs, and one other robbery committed single-handedly, where he robbed a suburban post office at gunpoint to get a fresh supply of cash, Unishewsky decided to return to Poland. He took only a little money and hid the rest of his treasure in an easily recognizable spot in the Bavarian Alps. He was arrested at the Okęcie International Airport in Warsaw. Polish UB officers (equivalent to the Russian KGB), laughed seeing his UN refugee passport. Unishewsky spent his first night on Polish soil being interrogated by a half drunk, uneducated UB officer. It wasn't too bad because the officer often drifted off to sleep, and upon awakening didn't remember what he had asked before. He obviously wasn't able to make any notes as writing was beyond his abilities. In the morning the situation became worse. The half-drunk ignoramus went home after finishing his shift. A new officer, being sober, started business energetically. First he called two professional brainless clubmen. Unishewsky received a skillful beating. They used the rubber batons with such mastery and expertise that, in the beginning when he was still fully conscious, he couldn't see their movements. Being aware that beating an unconscious man was a waste of their energy, they revived him by pouring cold water from galvanized iron buckets on his head. After this treatment, when he still wasn't ready to answer their questions about his involvement in Western intelligent services, the target of his spying mission, and contact names and addresses, they started to pull out his fingernails and burn his chest with a kerosene torch. Unishewsky woke up in terrible pain deep under the surface of the Polish capital.

After realizing his stupidity, he cried like only a lost soul can cry. He became fully aware of the perplexity and powerlessness of his irredeemable situation. How could he have jumped from the 'frying pan' of Nazi concentration camp torture, into the 'fire' of these degenerated, sadistically cruel communist UB officers? But there was no returning, and it was not a dream. Unishewsky started again to repeat his tested and proven magic formula:

"I will survive! I will get out of here alive!" He did survive! He didn't end up smelling the grass roots, shallowly covered by the soil of his beloved fatherland, as many unfortunate 'guests' of this underground 'clinic' did.

A few years later, at the top of the Communist Party's hierarchy, some changes happened. They were only cosmetic changes, but still it gave relative freedom to a few like Unishevsky, and a false hope to the nation. Polish President Bolesław Beirut had died from the 'Russian flu' (meaning: he was assassinated by an injection of poison given by a KGB doctor when visiting Moscow to receive instructions). The reason is still unknown and is kept strictly secret. Maybe Stalin suffered a migraine? We will never know! His splendid funeral was followed by naming Comrade Ochab as the next 'ruler of the country' (meaning, supervising the Soviet Union's Empire Politburo orders to exploit Poland's economy). Ochab's leadership didn't last long. It was like a one-day butterfly, leaving the space to a post-war communist hero, Wladysław Gomułka, who had opposed the Russian Red Army's plundering of the Western provinces of Poland on the way back to the Soviet Union after conquering the Third Reich. Gomułka spent a few 'restful' years in a political prison in Sztum, and from there went straight to the post of President of Poland and First Secretary of its Communist Party Central Committee. Strange, but very true!

The system freed Unishewsky, gave him a bright new Polish Identity Card and an average of one week's wages for his immediate living expenses. He was directed to the Northeast district to settle on a large government farm, Garbno. There he worked in the fields from the first day of his arrival until the day of his retirement. He earned very little, but it was just enough for a simple life. He married a very peaceful and quiet lady and they had two children, a boy and a girl. Now his life looked very untroubled, tranquil and stable. He had a loving, gentle wife and intelligent children. He could steam a full bucket of potatoes for himself, as he had often dreamt of when being hungry in the German Concentration Camp. But now there was no need to do it. His pigs ate steamed potatoes. His wife was very skillful and he ate well-done beefsteaks and pork chops or sauerkraut stew. Regardless of this, deep in his soul lived a nagging feeling of guilt.

For a while Uniszewsky drowned this guilt every few months by buying a carton full of bottles of cheap fruit wine from the cooperative, and after informing his bosses and wife that he would return in a few days, he would disappear into the ruins of Hitler's Super-race Breeding Farm, still standing on the green meadows, and surrounded by old linden trees. There, he drank to the point of unconsciousness. The memory of the blue-eyed German policeman he had shot was not as easy to kill as the memories of the massacred men. In a delirium of drunkenness he would talk to them, trying to explain his motives, trying to excuse himself for what he'd done. Showing them his extensive scars, he told them about his suffering, how it had created so much hate and rage in him which then led to the merciless killings. Once, just before such a retreat, he met Andrew and told him,

"I have found the formula to survive extreme difficulties, but I can't find the formula to gain peace of mind. After the war I made the worst mistake in my life, taking into my hands the revenge for my suffering. I killed many young and innocent men. Now I realize that I will never find peace. The remorse of those killings erodes all enjoyment in this life. Having done that, I've put myself on an equal level with those who killed and tortured us. Now I understand what Jesus Christ meant when he said: 'I am saying unto you, forgive your oppressors' sins and you will be forgiven yours.'

"If ever I can go back to Bavaria, I will dig up my treasure and give it to a charity in Germany. I do not want those diamonds and gold." Saying so, Unishewsky shuffled along like one who is going for a meeting with the devil himself, or one going to his own unavoidable execution. He was carrying on his shoulder a bag full of bottles of cheap wine, and an unbearably heavy load of guilt. He would return a few days later, pale as a cadaver, with terrible hiccups.

After some time, the party, again seated late one evening on the bench near the farm's office building, was talking about their past experiences, smoking strong cigarettes to repel the annoying mosquitoes. They were all excited. Last week a Trade Union excursion from another government farm had accidentally discovered a treasure hidden close to the nearby town of Kętrzyń. In the Kętrzyń forest, Hitler's secret fortress, Gierłoż (now a great tourist attraction), had a hidden cellar full of the best French wine, cognac and English whiskey and gin, overgrown by bushes. The workers taking part in this trip, the driver of the bus, the director of the farm and the agronomists, all got so drunk that the next day, when another group discovered them, it was not clear if they were dead or alive. But the doctors from Kętrzyń District Hospital, being experienced in such cases, managed to save their lives. The pumping of their stomachs was not the most pleasurable experience, but the memory of the exquisite liquors would stay vividly with them for life. All Garbno workers were jealous!

'Czech Spring' Intervention

Suddenly a humming noise filled the air. What was it? At first they thought it was a few combine harvesters passing by on their way to the workshop for repair. But the noise was increasing and soon became almost unbearable. Everyone sat silently, and not knowing what was happening they nervously smoked their cigarettes and looked up into the sky from where the sound was coming. The sky was covered with clouds. In the darkness, only the glowing ends of their cigarettes could be seen dancing up and down like the dots of light dancing on the screen of the electronic heart scanning instrument used during operations. Now the entire land rocked from the mighty sound. Unishevsky broke the silence first,

"My friends, the war has started again! The sound is coming from hundreds of Russian planes flying over us from the Latvian capital city of Kaliningrad." The store man, who on the farm was the first Secretary of the Communist Party Committee, left without saying a word. Now feeling reasonably safe, the director of the farm proposed,

"We should try to listen to Radio Free Europe." They tried, but Russian jamming was stronger than ever. What was happening? What would tomorrow bring? These questions hung in the air, expecting no answers. Waves of countless heavy cargo planes passed over the Garbno farm in two-hour intervals for a full two days and three nights. The extensive noise caused a rapid drop in the cows' milk production, as even the animals became stressed. Nobody would have guessed that the Russian Red Empire had so many airplanes, and this was only an infinitely small part of their full force.

The morning brought them the Red Army. Military convoys moved day and night along the tar sealed roads. On the intersections appeared new signposts in Russian Cyrillic alphabet and soldiers wearing field uniforms directed the traffic. Those poor fellows were sometimes left without water and food for a day or two as nobody thought of their needs. Their superiors cared only about political priorities. Obviously these soldiers could not get anything from the local people, as everyone treated them as the representatives of enemy forces. The massive movements of the Red Army were reported by arriving travelers. They had covered all of the Eastern part of Poland.

Three days after this 'till now peaceful invasion, official mass media announced that in Czechoslovakia imperialists had started an anti-Communist revolt, and the united forces of the Soviet Union and other countries belonging to the Warsaw Treaty were invited by the Czechoslovakian Communist Party's Politburo (Central Committee) to help overthrow this illegal government formed by the usurpers. This started the so-called Prague Spring Massacre. In fact, the imperialists were not involved at all.

What had happened before the invasion was an unsuccessful attempt by the Czechoslovakian Communist Party's leader, comrade Dubcek and his fellow idealists, to introduce a 'real humanitarian version' of Communism. Who could believe that, amongst the top rank communists, there still were naive idealists trying to make 'white from black'? Obviously this could not be tolerated by the 'Big Brother' who supervised his Red Empire colonies. Humanitarianism and real communism? It sounded like imperialist propaganda, like a cheap joke! The tanks had to roll across the towns and be located at strategic points. Daydreamers had to be thrown on their knees to beg the working class for their pardon. The result was a huge wave of refugees pouring towards the Austrian border. There were not only the guilty idealists, but also the workers themselves, who didn't want to throw anybody on their knees. They were all fed up with communism, and were trying to reach the free world and seek political asylum.

A Trip to a Country of Southern Neighbors

Andrew received a military summons one week later. He was a trained leader of a tank platoon, and belonged to the army reserve in the first line Garrison of Ożec on the southeast border with the

Soviet Union. There, on the banks of the deep, slow moving Bug River, flowing majestically over the dark and fertile land of Western Ukraine stood an old army barracks. His father, many years back, had served a two-year term in the army there as a cavalryman.

The echelon (a Russian term used for an army convoy train) was formed in one night. Two tanks from his platoon broke down before they reached the train station's loading ramp. Everything was done in a hurry and with a lot of shouting and frayed nerves. The loud swearing, with many words containing strong 'Rs' once again proved very helpful.

Andrew remembered his training time spent with others like him in this peaceful base, already as an officer in the reserve. It was a really happy time. They forgot the world and its problems. It had been a time of relaxation, a time to forget for a while the gray reality under the Communists. The Garrison Commandant, fed up with their nonchalance and lack of discipline, called a meeting and bitterly told them,

"You all look like a bunch of Palestinian commandos. The uniforms' black berets are made to be worn, boys, on the head; even if it is totally empty like is yours! The beret should not be stuck under the uniforms' jacket epaulettes. We will soon have an important inspection from the Ministry of Defense. I would prefer it if you would not show yourselves in the barracks during the day. You will all have to spend tomorrow in town, or wherever you wish except at the base. You will get some money for food from the quartermaster. Remember, do not cause any trouble! I can be hard on you if necessary!"

The next day they wandered around dating local girls, drinking wine and singing. In the afternoon they celebrated Andrew's birthday. He bought a good supply of wine and excellent smoked sausages. They reveled on the bank of the Bug River. On the other side was the Soviet Union. The border from the Russian side was more strictly guarded than any other border on Earth. They started a small campfire and grilled the sausages, holding them on long sticks over the flames. The wine started to circulate through their blood, adding energy and fantasy. One of the 'Palestinian Commandos,' who had his beret folded properly and stuck under his uniform jacket epaulettes, proposed that a huge heap of dried willow twigs be put on the fire. The twigs were kept there for preventing land erosion on the riverbanks. It was obvious to all of them that this particular individual's head was not completely empty, and having some brains left he was still thinking. It was the biggest campfire Andrew had ever seen. But not everyone who saw it appreciated its evident charm. The Russian border guards telephoned the Polish Garrison and the military police arrived on the scene. But it was too late. They found only some empty wine bottles and a still furiously burning fire. There was no trace of the offenders.

The next day was the inspection. The dry grass on the barracks' central plaza was painted with green oil paint making it look very nice and 'fresh.' The tanks stood in a row, nicely polished with diesel oil. The 'Palestinian Commandos' were locked up to avoid further trouble in the barrack's day-room, and watched with disgust the uplifting political speeches on the TV.

Orders to join forces invading Czechoslovakia came next day. So, now, Polish armored troops from the Ożec Garrison embarked on the train after sunrise. Everyone received war emergency rations of food and cigarettes: Three tins of pork luncheon meat, a few packets of hard, stone-like tack with cumin seeds, butter in a small flat tin, sugar in cubes, and dark chocolate. They immediately ate all of it, as the future was uncertain. The cattle carriages in which they traveled were at the end of the train. Due to the weight of the tanks, ammunition and engineering machines, there were two diesel engines. One pulled the train from the front, and the other pushed it from behind. They were all tired after packing, and even the caffeinated dark chocolate didn't prevent them from falling asleep.

The train rumbled down the lines, passing by villages and small towns with little houses and gardens full of apple trees in blossom. Andrew was sent by the major in charge of security to the very front of the echelon for watch-duty. The first shift was four hours, and then the relief would come. He went from carriage to carriage, carefully crossing the metal footbridges over the joining hooks and bumper bars. He tried to be very alert. In the past he had not had the best experiences with moving trains. His machine gun, a 'Kalashnikov,' caused some problems as it caught onto the metal bolts, which stuck out, and also on the steel ropes, which secured the war machines to the platforms. He stopped at the huge mobile segment of a bridge, which was installed on a chassis similar to the tanks, and lit a cigarette.

On the very first platform, just behind the engine, he found a watchman's cabin and rested there. Time passed slowly. Three hours. One more hour and the change of guard would come. The train entered the Beskidy's sub-mountain district and neared a town called Dębica; its name means 'the forest of the oak trees.' His mother was born there when it was still under the Austrian Empire. Andrew felt sleepy and took a new packet of the soldier's allowance of cigarettes from his pocket and lit another one, hanging his machine-gun on a hook. There were no visible imperialist spies or saboteurs to shoot. Smoking, he got lost in sad thoughts,

"Why are we forced to get involved in this military intervention? Stupid! This is a war with friends! Let them decide what kind of communism they want, if they want it at all! Poland never was involved in any aggressive war, and never made any attempt to conquer its neighbor's lands. It has only fought wars with aggressors: Russians, Tartars, Swedes and Germans. Because of this damned communism we are now facing this terrible dishonor. God, if God exists, will not easily forgive us."

The train approached a bridge, which was built when times were not so good but probably still better than the present. It was built during the life of the Austrian-Hungarian Empire of Franz-Joseph. The bridge was built of huge solid steel arches riveted together with thousands of one-inch thick rivets. It was built over a small river and stood on tall pillars made of red bricks. The steel construction of the bridge resonated with the rattling sound of the train.

Suddenly, a powerful jerk shook the train. Andrew almost lost his balance. From the back of the echelon he heard loud, terrifying clangs, clashes, rasping and grating sounds. The train vibrated like prey helplessly caught in the steel-like clasp of a strangler-killer, but it moved at almost the same speed as before. After a few long minutes, the engine machinist realized that something was terribly wrong and put his engine on idle. Later, when it was all over, they reconstructed the tragic happenings: the large, improperly secured digging machine had moved its shovel sideways and got stuck on the steel construction of the bridge. It was soon joined by a section of the mobile bridge. Because there were two powerful engines, all the other carriages were pushed and pulled under this obstacle and entirely smashed; the tanks lost their towers and big guns; then the trucks fell down to the river like children's tin toys. The ammunition miraculously didn't explode but was scattered over a large area. The passenger carriages filled with the sleeping soldiers were completely smashed. The bodies of over six hundred soldiers were minced into pieces and fell into the river, whose waters became red like the famous Hungarian wine called 'Bika vére' (In Hungarian—Bull's Blood) because of its deep burgundy color.

Andrew's friend from Myślenice, Jack, ended up in a Division of the Krakow based 'Red Berets' airborne commandos. He was trained in judo, karate, rock climbing, parachuting, and fighting with knives, and all sorts of skills in sabotage, assassination, and so on. When the trouble with Polish Southern neighbor started he was also called to the reserves and took part in taking over the airfields of Czechoslovakia. He jumped from the transport plane 'Anushin' carrying a small machine-gun, a 'Sten,' originally designed by Polish engineers during WWII for the Warsaw uprising, and later modernized and adopted by the communist gunsmiths for missions by the Warsaw Treaty Special Forces. He and his fellow commandos took over Prague's International Airport without even one shot, and without even one brother Czech killed. They were supported by the sabotage team, which had secretly been sent there earlier.

A year later Andrew, who learned from this Czechoslovakian adventure, that for some reason it is easier to convince people of one's owns point of view when holding a machine-gun in one's hands, was back at the university, struggling with books to master organic chemistry, ecology, microbiology, botany, meteorology, and many other subjects. Now, in his private, illegal arsenal there was only one WWII Russian-made most primitive machine-gun, 'Pepesza,' and a Russian barrel pistol, a well-made copy of the American 'Colt.' Collecting such things was his hobby, cultivated from early childhood. He liked to clean and polish cold metal and to touch the gun. Just a toy for a grown up boy! Easter was approaching so he went to his family, who lived in a small town in the High Country in the southern end of Poland. It was a long journey on the train. Nine hours of standing in the overcrowded, cigarette-smoke filled train.

At home, revelation! One month back, Jack had visited Andrew's family. He was hungry so Andrew's mother had fed him well. Jack was still in army action pants and boots, but wore a civilian's gray jumper. In a bundle made of a woolen blanket, he had his winter army parka, uniform belt with a bayonet in the sheath, and the newest type of Russian AK 47 machine-gun, a 'Kalashnikov' with three fully loaded magazines. He told them honestly that he had deserted the army. He had had enough of it. They had extended his army service indefinitely after the Czechoslovakian intervention. He confessed that he was intending to go to Austria and live there. Why Austria? He didn't know himself, but was confident that he wanted to go there. Andrew's mother had given him a warm, water-resistant navy blue overcoat, which she had made from Andrew's uncle's British navy officer overcoat. She also gave him woolen pants, a sheepskin fur hat and some money. Jack departed on a lorry going to Zakopane in the Tatra Mountains, close to the Czechoslovakian border.

In Andrew's family town Jack turned for help to an old tuberculosis sanitarium central heating stoker. His son, Stach, worked in Zakopane as a member of the Mountaineer Rescue Team (GOPR). In his spare time Stach smuggled Austrian—made machine-guns across the borders of the two countries through the high ranges of the Tatra Mountains. Business was extremely risky, but also extremely profitable. Because of this, he never thought about for whom those instruments of killing were destined (as none were ever used in Poland).

Jack Crossing Border

Fog was crawling along the bottomless valley like tongues of a glacier on the Himalayan heights. It was cold and humid. The rigid, steep cliffs of the surrounding valley ranges still wore patches of snow, colored pinkish by the morning sun. Spruce trees were scattered over the lower part of the slopes. Many of them were lying broken by the furious 'Halny,' a wind so rapid and powerful that even large roofs of houses could be lifted and smashed a few hundred meters away. It comes in early Spring when the warm air, moving north from the Hungarian plains called 'pushta', is rapidly cooled on the heights of the Tatra Mountains and then comes down its northern slopes.

From under the granite moss-covered boulders came three men. Two of them talked in a mountaineer's dialect. They wore down parkas with the GOPR blue cross at the back. One of them commented, "Videem panotzku hteete snadano" (In Slovak Tatra mountaineer's dialect: I see you Sir want a breakfast.) The third man was Jack. He confirmed that he was hungry, so they opened their backpacks and took out dark rye bread, well smoked bacon, onion and dill cucumbers. One of the three men—Stach—even had good imported wine from Hungary, the famous 'Tokay.' Now he could afford to buy good drinks and not spoil his stomach with sulfuric acid, which was commonly added to cheap fruit wines to prevent it from turning into vinegar. All three of them ate silently. The day found them climbing up the gully of the massive range towards the country's boundary. They spent the afternoon in a cave, sleeping on a pallet used in the wintertime by the bears sleeping there through the cold weather. Being refreshed by the rest, they crossed the border that night.

The night was clear. In the sky blinked countless stars and the moon was full. The landscape, in the silvery-greenish light, looked like a different planet. The ranges appeared to be higher than in the daytime, and the walls even steeper. They rested on a small pass between two peaks, and then started to descend towards Stary Smokovetz, Slovak's nearest High Country town. Jack's descent was difficult as he was carrying a bulky bundle of a queer shape. They passed Drace Pleso (In Slovak: Frogs' Lake) with waters of an intense green color in the daytime and also deadly poisonous because of the high sulfuric salts content. They were already close to the chalet where one Slovak, belonging to the arms smuggling gang, was going to store their GOPR parkas and supply food and Czechoslovakian money for the train ride towards the Austrian border.

Suddenly, from under a dwarfish pine bush, called a kosóvka, a command in the Slovak dialect, came: "Stop! Who is passing? Border Patrol!" The three Poles started to run. Shots sounded: "Ta, ta, ta, ta . . . ."; the well-known rattle of the Russian-made machine gun AK 47—'Kalashnikov'. Pain rushed through Jack's right calf. He swore, hissing,

"They got me, sons of a bitch". They hid under the kosóvka. Jack unpacked his bundle and removed the bayonet from its sheath. It looked like a miniature ancient Roman Empire sword. Dark from oxidation and sharpened on two sides, the blade didn't reflect the moon's light. He crawled to the other side of a tourist track and put the deadly weapon in his mouth. He was a professional in these matters. The Slovak soldiers slunk silently along the track looking for them, holding their machine guns ready. When they passed him, Jack jumped on them from behind. He hit the first soldier's neck with the edge of his hard, steel-like, straightened right palm. This perfect karate blow knocked Brother Slovak down unconscious. The second Slovak brother, before he managed to pull the trigger of his 'Kalashnikov', received first a kick in his abdomen, and when he bent over in pain, another kick hit his face. Jack, as an extra security measure, hit the men's heads together, inducing a deep amnesia. They unloaded the Slovak's machine-guns, took their torches and bayonets, and to slow down any eventual chase, removed their army pants, underwear and boots. They threw all of it far into the kosóvka. Jack was pleased that it had not been necessary to use his bayonet. He had had enough bloodshed after the Prague Spring Intervention. Jack was in a lot of pain from his calf. He found the hole made by the bullet and pushed an 'ironed cotton' into it, an efficient army remedy to stop bleeding which he had fortunately found in the personal injury kit of one of his 'sleeping brothers.'

Morning found them already in Stary Smokovec, where a gang member gave them shelter. Jack stayed there to heal his wounded leg while the rest of them left for Vienna to collect their contraband. They were in a hurry as Stach had to be back on duty in GOPR in Zakopane in a few days. There was no way to operate on Jack's calf. To report his injury to the medical authorities was equal to confessing their encounter with the Slovak border guards and volunteering for a 'physiotherapy session' in the Czechoslovakian KGB gray concrete bunker. This, as a rule, would be followed by a long 'vacation' in Siberia or by a 'rest' in the shallow grave of one of the secret cemeteries in the small ghostly groves. He took his chance and left the bullet where it was. The wound healed itself unexpectedly fast. It was probably the Czech 'Pilsner Beer' which had such a miraculous influence on his body's system.

Two months later he had stolen an identity card with a visa to all Eastern Bloc countries from a Polish tourist (meaning a smuggler of goods and Western currency), who looked similar to him and boarded a train through Hungary to the Bulgarian capital city of Sofia. He still had his odd bundle and put it on a shelf in the carriage next to his. Somehow it didn't attract the attention of the custom officers, and his 'Kalashnikov', bayonet, ammunition, and even the winter army parka safely reached Bulgarian soil. He traveled immediately to a small town near the Greek border—close to the town of Kurtzhali. There, his first experience was to enjoy a bottle of good local grape wine, and then to purchase a pair of electrician's insulated cutting pliers. He felt sorry that he wasn't able to go the short way to Austria with Stach and join his friends' smugglers. But he felt that waiting indefinitely in Stary Smokoviec for their next expedition would be too risky as local secret police could have easily spotted him. A report of their encounter with a Slovak border patrol was definitely known to all law enforcement personnel.

He now started preparations for crossing the Greek border. Around the border were fifteen kilometers of no-man's land. Even local people were forbidden to enter this wilderness, which lay too close to the Free World. Jack rented a room on the ground floor of an old Turkish styled house and wandered around the town with a difficult decision to make: where, how, and when to make the attempt to cross the border. There were too many unknown factors. He ran out of money, so he started to work in a local car body repair shop which earned him cash for Bulgarian white bread, smoked Black Sea fish, goat's cheese, and magnificent grape wine, which he found too tempting to resist. Enjoying such luxuries, he almost ignored his safety.

He was on the verge of calamity when he realized that the local police were becoming curious as to why this Polish tourist was staying there so long, and had even taken a job. It was late afternoon; Jack had just returned from work and was resting and sipping red wine. From inside the house he heard the voices of policemen and his landlady, who replied loudly in order to warn him. She said,

"He is still at work; I haven't seen him returning home." Jack jumped through the window, managing to take his precious bundle and electrical pliers. Now he had no option but to cross the Greek border immediately. He bought a bottle of wine, two loaves of bread, two rings of donkey meat sausages and some smoked goat cheese. It was already dusk when he entered no-man's land. First he walked along the unsealed road, but he then turned to the unknown hills, valleys, and high limestone cliffs, when he was almost intercepted by an army jeep driving towards the border with soldiers in exchange for those on duty. Jack tried to move only at night in the moonlight, because during the day Bulgarian air force helicopters flying at low altitude often patrolled the area.

The first day he spent in a dense forest. There were many edible mushrooms but because of safety reasons he couldn't start a campfire to cook them. The second day he spent under the cliffs of a narrow valley with a small creek flowing along it. He discovered strange, almost identical openings in the rocks of the cliff several meters up from the ground. Having nothing to do, Jack climbed to one of those openings. There was no formal path leading there, and the climb proved to be extremely difficult. Inside, he found with amazement an artificially made cave with a bench carved from solid rock, and walls covered with symbols and inscriptions in a strange script of an unknown language. Who had lived here, long ago? Was it a Neanderthal caveman? No! They didn't know any script to write. Who, then? What did these hieroglyphics mean? Perhaps it was the secret of a life, long forgotten, which he had read of once in a magazine in the army base canteen. Jack spent the entire day there, sleeping on someone's ancient bed, dreaming that he himself was living in this cave and knew the secret of the life written on the walls in the form of a poem. In his dream, some people dressed in sheepskins brought him food, which he pulled up in a basket using a rope. He woke up hungry and was disappointed when there was no basket of food. Because the distance was unclear he had already started to ration his limited food supply.

After five days and six nights he reached the border. Once walking at night he almost fell to his death from a cliff. It was so dark that he had not realized that the next step was going deep into non-existence. But as usual he was lucky. He fell only about three meters down onto a dense bush growing on a narrow ledge. He lost only one of his machine-gun magazines, which fell to the very bottom of the abyss.

The border was very well organized. Watch towers stood every five hundred meters. The border itself was double fenced. First there was an electric fence with a bare wire on ceramic isolators. Next there was a cleared area about five meters wide. Maybe mines also? Those obstacles were followed by another fence with some strange, round metal-like pipe containers attached to it. Jack decided to cross the border in daytime, as there was a greater chance of making a serious mistake at night due to limited visibility.

He unpacked his 'Kalashnikov,' checked the mechanism of the lock, inserted one magazine and reloaded. He put the spare magazine behind his army belt along with his bayonet, and the pliers in the right side pocket of his pants. Now he was ready. He ate the rest of his food and finished the wine. Suddenly he knelt on the moss and not knowing why, he prayed,

"O God, if You exist, please help me to safely reach the free world. I want only to work like a normal human. Oh, kurwa, I have had

enough of this communism!" It was a strange prayer—not very holy
words, but sincere ones. What else could he say? This was his first
prayer since childhood, when he used to pray with his mother before
going to bed.

Jack crawled toward a spruce tree whose branches touched the grass,
and which grew at equal distances from both watchtowers. It was
on the edge of the forest and not more than fifteen meters to the
electric fence. On his right he noticed a stack of thin, long pine logs
prepared for some renovation work on the watchtowers. He broke off
some small branches and covered himself. Everything was ready. He
made the sign of the cross on his forehead, and supporting himself on
his elbows, unlocked his machine-gun, setting it on single fire. The
soldier on the right tower was sitting on a stool dozing. Jack aimed
at him, but he was so nervous that the barrel of his weapon danced
too much to shoot. Laying down the machine-gun, he closed his eyes
and took a few deep and very slow breaths. Then he realized that the
back sight of the machine-gun was not set properly for a distance of
two hundred and fifty meters. When he corrected it and aimed again
he was much calmer. The sound of a shot split the air. The Bulgarian
soldier dropped to the floor like a drunkard falling under the table
after reaching his limit. The other soldier on the left watchtower got
up and looked with curiosity and surprise through his binoculars
in the direction of the shot. The second shot ended his curiosity.
He hung dead on the platform rail, looking from a distance more
like a sick person than a dead one. Jack jumped up from his hiding
place and ran towards the fence. He was well trained in how to force
electric fences. He spread his army parka under the fence to ensure a
proper insulation, as he didn't trust the Bulgarian made pliers. Then
he slung his machine-gun across his chest, and using the electrical
pliers, cut a gap in the fence over one meter wide. When the passage
was made, he dragged one of the pine logs over and lifting it to a
vertical position, pushed it towards the clearing, and then fell flat on
the green grass as fast as he could. The loud explosion of two mines
sounded more like the bang heard when a jet fighter crosses the sound
barrier then a blast. The path to freedom was almost open. He ran
along a freshly scarred path. At the end of it was another fence, but it
was not an electric one. Jack cut the wire as if in a trance. He was in a

hurry. Any moment something unexpected could happen. He ignored the signaling rockets, which automatically fired from the pipeline metal boxes attached to the wire after he disturbed the fence. Their red stars burning in the blue Bulgarian sky acknowledged his debut in the Free World. But Jack was still not sure of his safety and ran without stopping for breath for a long, long time. From behind came a few rounds of 'Kalashnikov' machine-guns fired by the Bulgarian border guards who arrived by jeep after seeing the signal rockets. He knew that they must pretend they were trying to do their duty. After an eternally long run, totally exhausted, Jack found a sealed road, and on its side an empty cigarette box with Greek writing on it. We can easily imagine how immense was the surprise of the school teacher driving his car along this road when he spotted a man holding a Russian-made machine-gun with a spare magazine and a bayonet behind his belt, gesturing for a lift.

Unishevsky's Trip to Germany

Poland was the first Eastern Bloc country which shook off this malignant communist system. Russian soldiers from the Red Army garrisons started returning to the Soviet Union for an uncertain lot. Polish citizens could now travel freely abroad. The free economy created an incredible opportunity for those with initiative and self-assurance. Old professional smugglers, supplying cosmetics and cotton underwear to Bulgarians, technical equipment to Hungarians, and anything useable to Russians, became almost overnight respected international trade dealers, making millions on full truckloads. Many government farms were sold to previous directors or communist party secretaries. Almost overnight in Poland new opportunities and new ways of life were created. Many workers from the farms and factories were sacked, as they were often over-staffed. Those who had reached retirement age received old age government pensions, too large to die from starvation, but too small to live like human beings.

Unishewsky was now seventy years old and already a few years on pension. His wife had died of breast cancer soon after he had retired, and his children had their own families. He applied for a passport, and when he got it, flew to Munich in Germany.

The Munich jewelers looked at him with hesitation when he presented his collection for sale. Unishewsky wasn't asking for too high a price though, so they quickly reached a mutual agreement. The greed of the jewelers helped them to close their eyes when they saw the splendid gold watches of the famous Swiss manufacturers in pristine condition: Pateks, Longines and Tissots, with engravings on the back; 'For my best friend, always loving . . . Gëring,', 'In respect of your loyalty . . . Führer.' The diamond jewelry was not a problem at all; its quality automatically sealed the deal.

The next day nobody noticed an old man, neatly but modestly dressed, leaving the offices of the Red Cross. In his pocket, folded carefully, was a receipt for an anonymous donation of 364,075 DM. He walked along the streets. There was no reason to hurry. He had managed to do the last thing he wanted to finalize in this life. Having known the town very well from the past he registered the changes. The old man entered a small café and ordered a cup of black coffee and a glass of French cognac, 'Courvoisier.' Slowly drinking the coffee and sipping the cognac he drifted into a meditative state. He remembered his suffering in the concentration camp, shooting the young policemen, the robbery. What a terrible and stupid life! Only pain, hard work, and then killings! Now, he suffered from pangs of conscience, even in retirement.

Looking up he noticed on the other side of the street a group of white dressed people greeting with humble respect a man, also in white, who had just arrived in a Mercedes Benz. He was not tall, though strongly built and with a dark face. Between the people in white who had come with him were two wearing bright red dresses; one of them was a blond lady and the other was a huge man with fluffy hair and a beard. He also had a dark face. Unishewsky left the café, leaving money on the table for his order and a tip for the waiter, and walked across the street to satisfy his growing curiosity. Why were they dressed in such a strange way? Nobody in Europe wore red clothes from head to foot! Only Russian athletes wear this color on tracksuits when taking part in the Olympic Games.

The strangers disappeared into the modern massive community hall building. A young athletic German lady stood on the pavement, near to the entrance. Her eyes were blue and her red hair was made into a long braid, like maidens in the eighteenth century used to wear. She was also dressed in white. Her face was beaming externally, manifesting her internal state of extreme happiness. She smiled towards Unishewsky and said,

"Sir, are you going for the Guru's darshan?" He stopped and surprised asked, "What is darshan?"

"Darshan, Sir, is a personal meeting with a Mahatma like our Guru."

"What is a Mahatma and who is this Guru?—asked Unishevski again.

"He, the Guru is . . . but better Sir if you go and see for yourself. Do you have time? Please feel free to go inside and watch Him for a while." Unishevsky had nothing else to do, nothing to lose, so he entered.

Inside, by the sliding paneled doors leading to the ample hall, stood a couple of white dressed young people. They directed him to the shoe room where his shoes were put in a plastic bag with a number on it, and was given a token with the same number. Now, even more surprised and curious and wearing only socks, he entered the hall. The air was strangely fragrant. There was a crowd, but on seeing his gray hair, people made space on a bench for him, very close to the stage where the mysterious Guru dressed in white sat cross-legged and motionless with closed eyes. He looked like a statue. He tried to see if He was breathing but could not see well enough to tell. The Guru meditated for a few minutes, and then the huge man dressed in red which he had seen before entered the stage and saluted the Guru by lying flat on the floor and sat behind Him. Unishevsky's curiosity was growing. Why did these people behave so strangely? What was it all about? Another man, also dressed in white, entered the stage and after prostrating fully on the floor, also sat cross-legged close to the Guru.

The Man in White—The Guru—opened His eyes and smiled looking around at the gathering. Unishevsky thought that His look was like a gentle touch, and His smile as a beautiful, fragrant flower. Who is He? The Man in White, the Guru, started to speak in a strange language. After a few sentences He stopped, and the man in red translated this to English and the man in white into German. The Guru was speaking about love, saying that love, which is not expressed externally, is as useless as the sweet candy left in the wrapper. A person having a candy can look at it as long as he wants, but will not be able to experience its sweetness. The Guru also said that all humans have gone through some bad experiences, have all committed serious mistakes in the past, but now should not dwell on them. The past is dead. What has happened has happened and one need only learn the hidden lesson, and avoid repeating the same mistakes. Each human should not dwell on the memories and nourish the guilt in their hearts, but concentrate on living in the present in accordance with moral rules. One should not even be concerned about the future. It will take its own course. One's duty is not to miss the present. Guru said that each living person is actually pre-programming their own future, which is a direct result of choices and actions taken in the present—now. Unishewsky listened attentively. It was a long awaited answer to his inner doubts and burning questions, clarifying his doubts, pacifying the fire of his guilt. Tears of gratitude rolled down his wrinkled face.

The Guru finished His short address and more people entered the stage. They all sat cross-legged around strange musical instruments. The Guru started to sing in His native language. He was leading and the others repeated His words. He looked like a person not completely conscious of his surroundings, of what was happening; with closed eyes, hands held up, unsteady. He occasionally laughed and shouted like one intoxicated: Shiva, Shiva . . . Krishna, Krishna . . . Unishewsky liked the songs. They were very different from what he'd ever heard, but rhythmical, melodious and full of devotion. The singers repeated the stanzas many times, increasing the intensity of their voices. The songs were charged with something he could not define.

After the singing ended, darshan started. This was what the lady with the long braid at the entrance to the building had meant. The Guru was seated on a big chair. Most people approaching Him had blissful expressions on their faces. Many held their hands as if to pray. He was cuddling all who came for a personal meeting with Him. Sometimes people were crying, and then He dried their faces with a white cloth and comforted them until they calmed down. From time to time the people wearing white were bringing other people in wheelchairs or helping those who walked on crutches to make their way to Him through the crowd. Many people were crying from emotion, not only during darshan but also afterwards when sitting at their seat.

Unishevsky spotted an old man. He looked like a retired ex-Vermacht, high ranking officer; straight, muscular body, neatly combed grey hair, dressed in top quality casual clothes. He probably remembered well the terror of the Stalingrad Battle, or the extermination of the Warsaw Ghetto. Maybe he had medals from the Eastern Front hidden in a private collection, or maybe even the highest Nazi medal of honor for bravery on the battlefield—The Iron Cross. He could even be one of those officers who became one of his admirers during the vodka-drinking ordeal in the Concentration Camp's office, when trying to save his life. This man's face was glowing with love, and was expressing through every pore of his skin total admiration and utter wonder on seeing the dark faced Man in White. Now he knelt in front of the Guru with palms folded as in prayer. The Guru in turn pulled the old man onto His lap and rubbed his back smiling mysteriously, as if seeing the film of his life's events.

Many hours passed. Unishevsky watched all, hungry for more and more. He realized that the Guru was refilling the hearts of these people with the sweetness of love. Unishevsky didn't feel like a stranger at all. He felt at home. He did not know anyone, but felt an unexplainable closeness to all present, especially to the people wearing white clothes.

Someone touched his shoulder. He woke up from a trance-like state. At his side the lady with the red braid was squatting.

"Are you not going for darshan, Sir?" she asked with concern in her voice. Unishevsky surprised, asked back, "Me? Can I also go?"

"Certainly you can. Anyone can. You even should! We are all His children," replied the young lady, who smiled as if to her own grandfather; who knows, maybe she really was his granddaughter— Greta's daughter. But Unishevsky would never know. He was excited and he readily joined the queue of people waiting for darshan. He could not remember how long he waited. He could bet it was only a minute or two. In almost no time he found himself on the lap of the Guru who cuddled him like only a mother or father cuddles her own child. He gently rubbed his back full of terrible scars, touched his fingernail-less hands like something very precious, and put His hand on his chest in the very spot where the heart is. Unishevsky felt relieved, relaxed and happy, just as one would upon receiving freedom after a long life in chains.

The Guru said something to the interpreter, who, nodding towards him said,

"The Divine Guru says that what you have done in the past should not occupy your mind. The Guru is very pleased that you realized your mistake, and out of your free will gave to charity what was not yours."

"How does He know?" he thought. He looked at the Guru's face with this question in mind. For a fraction of a second their eyes met. Unishevsky could not explain this, but he experienced a flash of understanding that He knew everything; that there is not even a single fact in the entire creation of which He was not aware of. Then, in his mind, the revelation exploded:

"He Is God Manifested!" He couldn't think anymore, he only fell in front of Him, on the floor, sobbing like a child, and embraced His Holy Feet. All the memories of the past, all his incredibly intense suffering appeared now like an insignificant dream, like unreal hallucinations. What was important, what was real, was just happening to him now. Unishevsky walked back to his bench in a state of blissful drunkenness from the nectar of love, which the Guru had given him. He passed a tall man around fifty sitting on the floor. He too was crying after his darshan, and with folded palms whispered in Polish some rather indecent but exalted words:

"O, kurwa. He is perhaps God. He has forgiven me. O, kurwa, He loves me. I will kill myself."

"Are you a Pole?" asked Uniszewski.

"Did you think, kurwa, that I'm Szkop?" (szkop—very contemptuous and used only in offensive Polish slang name for Germans) It was none other than Jack—red berets' ex-commando himself! Jack was able to express himself so precisely only by using this vulgar language. He did not know a better way to express his extreme excitement on meeting an Avatar, an Incarnation of the Highest, and he was doing his best. We can only guess that those not so decent swear words were spoken with unbelievable devotion, and were not only pardoned but even appreciated, as the Highest, whom the Guru—the Man in White—is and Who knows both our limitations and our hearts.

Jack, after a life full of adventures, had finally settled in his dream-town Vienna and was working there as a bus driver. He learned about The Guru from a magazine he had found in a bus, and traveled to Munich personally to check if what people said in the article about Him was true.

After the program they bought some books in German about the Guru. The lady from the bookstall, wearing red clothes and with a pale serene face was helped by a solidly built, bearded Indian man. They were already covering up the display of books, photographs, incense and other exotic Eastern things connected with the Guru for the night, but she happily stopped to serve them.

It was very late, already after three in the morning when Unishevsky and Jack walked together out of the hall. Unishevsky proposed,

"Let's go for a beer." They found a pub still open and ordered tankards of the famous 'DAB.' The beer was magnificent. They drank it in silence. What more was there to say? They were both still experiencing blissful happiness. Until now they were strangers, living in their own worlds with memories so entirely different. Now they had rediscovered that they always were brothers—two of the 'Man in White'—the Guru's—wandering children.

"We met where all roads meet." said Unishevski. They continued to contemplate the experience, watching the bubbles of the foam on the surface of their beer. The foam bubbles disappear just as individuals disappear from the surface of this world, but the substratum of their existence, the beer, was never affected by it. They both felt that they had reached the end of their paths, their destination, not even suspecting for a moment that in fact the real Path starts just from the very point where they were now.

Andrew and Jack meet in India

The crowds of devotees who had arrived at The Guru's ashram to celebrate His forty-third birthday were incredible. In the last moment, a huge auditorium to host more than ten-thousand people had been erected, but only one third of the crowd found room under its aluminum roof. Through the ocean of the international mixture of the Guru's children, dazed by the situation, walked a visitor from Austria. He had just arrived and felt hot and dizzy in this crowd. His whole body was sweating because of the humidity and the temperature in this tropical climate. Suddenly the Austrian/Polish visitor's eyes fell on a man dressed in white carrying two buckets of hot boiled drinking water. The visitor from Austria could not believe his eyes. The man in white looked like his best friend from the happy past, from times together at high school. The man with the buckets wore a beard and seemed to be living there, so he wasn't sure. He asked timidly,

"Is that you, Andrew? It is impossible!" The man put his buckets down and looked at Jack as he would if a visitor from outer space had landed just in front of him in a UFO.

"Jack!!!" he shouted. "You look the same. What are you doing here? You see, all roads lead here. How small this world is! To meet you in India, after so many years, is incredible!"

Jack started to cry. His old best friend had unknowingly repeated almost the same words said by Unishewski that night after the Guru's darshan in Munich when they were having a beer in a German pub. They fell into each other's arms. From the stage of the new auditorium sounded the Guru's vibrant voice singing a *bhajan*:

"O Guru, Your son is weeping in a pain—seeking Your help. Do not live him alone in this world of confusion . . . ."

"The next day the old friends told each other their stories. Jack had tried to encourage Unishevsky to come to India and spend some time in the Guru's ashram, but there was no reply to his letters to Poland. Maybe the old man had finished his life of intense rambling on Earth, and was now invisibly hovering in the ether and listening from the astral to the Guru singing. Who knows?

Jack changed. During his three weeks in the ashram he didn't swear even once, he didn't have a cigarette, and he even forgot that beer existed. He started to experience strange but pleasant warmth in his heart. What it was he didn't know, but he liked it much more than the warmth in the body from wine or beer. He told his best friend,

"I'm a driver. Here in the ashram I feel like after entering the sweet highway leading to the place where all roads meet, where all driving stops, my heavenly Home, the place where there are no more distances, where the past is not separated from the future, where time does not rule, where only the eternally long Now exists."

Jack returned to his beloved Vienna to resume his driving duties, and Andrew went to another town, where the Guru sent him to do some work. Traveling on an ashram lorry he was thinking,

"How strange are the ways that lead so many entirely different people to the Guru; how many coincidences and synchronicity happen around Him. Here on His lap they all become unified as His children, His Golden Sons and Daughters, my Brothers and Sisters. How great it is that the Guru can travel to so many countries and create opportunities for thousands to meet Him, who otherwise could not travel to India. Maybe one day He will decide to visit Poland. There are so many who are internally injured by the years of communism, who need His love really badly. Let us pray for it."

Exactly one year passed since Jack's visit to the Guru' ashram, when the Guru personally expressed His intention to visit Poland. It was in response to the invitation of some Polish devotees who had traveled to Sweden, had met Him and attended His programs in Stockholm. One of them in a letter to Andrew, written in great excitement straight after his return from Sweden, described his experience of watching people receiving the Guru's *darshan*. He wrote: "It is incredible to watch people reflect their inner feelings. Most of the people walk away after *darshan* with an expression of such Bliss, as only humans can be in the second after meeting face-to-face with God Himself . . ."

We can't even imagine how many such Unishevskys or Jacks will be there to see a light at the end of the long and dark tunnel of their life-long suffering and disappointments and an existence where most of the higher values have been negated and their emotions suppressed.

WATCHING THE CLOUDS

It was already after sunrise. From the window of his apartment on the 44th floor of Freedom Tower he saw the storm approaching—it was about fifty kilometers away. The navy blue clouds moved quickly across the remains of a volcano that was now a large bay. Millions of years ago the volcano erupted with such violence that it left no trace of its existence, only a large crater fifty kilometers in diameter. Over time, the ocean filled the crater with its water and created the picturesque bay.

"There must be a fantastic snow-cover in the High Country", he thought. Feeling very well, he decided to take a day-trip to the mountains and do some skiing. Skiing was one of the ways he kept his body fit.

Breakfast was ordered on his personal computer, and within minutes was delivered on the small, soundless lift from the underground community kitchen. After eating, he began to pack his personal necessities for the trip. He would travel on the super-fast train, which connects his town with a larger one, passing by his beloved mountains. While packing, he remembered his grandfather's book about his first steps on this continent more than one-hundred years ago. He, too, had a deep love for the mountains; but to get there the poor old fellow had to travel almost six long hours in a slow vehicle emitting poisonous fumes, risking his life with the possibility that, at any moment, there could be a collision with another vehicle controlled by a drunkard, with absent-minded pedestrians or with stray animals. In those days even the best drivers often died because of one common problem: drunk drivers. But, now for him, the trip will be a comfortable and safe journey taking only one hour and five minutes.

Suddenly, his personal computer started to print something. In a few seconds a blue form with red stripes on the edges lay in his mail tray. Urgent! He usually attended to his correspondence once a week, but this time he intuitively felt that it was something very important. And, it was indeed, exactly as he felt. The Central Computer of the planet was advising him that, according to the scientifically calculated data of his astrological life span, he was due to die seven days from today. He was being asked to dispose of his personal belongings, return his PSU-t (Personal Unit—a communication device providing coverage for the entire planet—enabling people to communicate with each other; instantly providing arrival and departure schedules of trains, local and intercontinental supersonic planes and interplanetary spaceships; the planet's weather conditions, as well as weather conditions of all the other planets under his planet's supervision) to the local Community Office, and to terminate his apartment as well as his magnetic access card. He was also asked to personally go to the 'Departure Place' at a specified date and time where the dematerialization of his body would be done with dignity, and in a brief and painless session.

"Well, then, my life is almost over. Only seven days to go." He wasn't sad or anxious. It was the way everybody finished their material existence in the mid twenty-second century. He was even pleased because he felt that his mission had been finished, and he would again be with his Guru, his Eternal Guide. In light of the information he just received, he decided to extend his trip to at least five days. The two remaining days would be sufficient to finalize his worldly affairs. Anyway, it was his last trip to his beloved High Country. For him, the mountains always were the best place to meditate. There he felt the Presence of The Oneness more intensely than in any other place.

Ready to go, he called by PSU-t for a 'cabsly' the fastest, safest means of fully automated urban travel of his times, and took the lift down to the underground cabsly stop. A short time later his cabsly arrived. He put his luggage inside and then climbed in. The cabsly's interior was ample enough to comfortably accommodate six passengers plus luggage in a separate compartment. A computer panel and access card check-point was located on the interior wall of the cabsly. On it he programmed his destination: Central Railway Station, and after inserting his access card in the sensor he pressed the green button 'Ready-to-Go.' The Plexiglas doors closed and automatically locked. The automated pilot announced: "Please remain seated during your travel." Traveling through the underground tunnels did not last long—it only took seven minutes to travel twenty-five kilometers.

The cabsly, suspended on a magnetic field created by a super-conductive coil around the tunnel, seemed to glide through the air, touching nothing. Travel was in total silence. There was no sound, no noisily propelled engines nor machinery. Powerful air-pumps situated along the tunnel created a vacuum at the front of the vehicle that propelled the cabsly's movement. He listened to a super-digital recording of late twentieth century Indian classical flute music, "Full Moon", on the cabsly's quadraphonic sound system. This music was the only thing he had from his grandfather apart from the book.

Changing from the cabsly to the super-fast train was almost as fast as the train itself. He went deeper underground, three levels down on the escalator, and boarded the train after a brief wait.

In spite of it being the peak skiing season, not many were going to the mountains. Most of the train passengers were headed toward another big town. "Maybe the snow is not deep enough?" he thought. After placing his travel bag in the overhead locker he programmed his PSU-t to give him a full report of the weather conditions in the High Country area. Reclining comfortably on the air-cushioned chair he watched, rolling slowly across the PSU-t's liquid crystal screen, the weather data presented in three-dimensional life pictures. A downy layer of snow more than two meters thick covered the slopes. The conditions were, in fact, more than magnificent: sunny weather, very gentle winds, and spectacular single stratocumulus shaped clouds rolling across the highest peaks. He was pleased. He loved clouds. He loved low clouds, and these clouds were riding on the low air-currents.

It was a strange hobby watching the performance of unending and unlimited fantasy in the sky. By watching the clouds he was imitating his father who had become famous for this very unusual pastime. His father could tell great stories just by looking at the clouds. He painted the stage and the action by using skillfully chosen words. His father was always saying, "The wonder is not what you see but how you see it and interpret it." His 'old man' liked it most, just to be suspended in the density of the whiteness on the white snowy slopes, or on the peak of some mountain. It was his own experience, an imitation of the separation from the unreality of this by Maha Maya created material manifestation. Long, long ago when he was a boy, he and his father had skied on the slopes of this same mountain. Once, they even continued skiing in the milky, dense clouds, not being fully aware of the closeness of the cliff. Nothing happened to them because they were protected by The Oneness whose Incarnation was his father's Guru.

When the train stopped at its destination in the underground station, he called the resort cabsly and went to his favorite 'Tatra Lodge', where he always stayed when skiing. The lodge was fairly full, but he had previously booked a single room on the 20th floor before he left town. The room's window faced east. The view from there was spectacular. All he could see was the mountain range extending all the way to the horizon, and clouds on the blue sky like a mirror's reflection of the mountains. It was all he wanted. He unpacked his few belongings, and after having a cup of traditional, twentieth century style coffee, left for the skiing equipment station.

Soon he was dressed in a silver coated, leather-like orange garment worn for warmth and visibility in fog. The clothing was also an advanced magneto-aerodynamic skiing suit. He had taken boots and a pair of polymer coated skis made of a titanium graphite composition. The skis were ideal for his height and his level of skiing proficiency, plus they were equipped with a plasma jet for safety in case of emergency. The ski lifts, surprisingly, had changed very little from the days when he and his father took skiing trips to the very summit of the highest mountain.

The view was incredible! Far, far, maybe seventy kilometers away, he could see the major continental commodore, a field of landing and departing spaceships, with its interplanetary passenger and cargo rocket cylinders ready for take-off. In a separate section visiting ships from other galactic civilizations were visible. Some were pyramidal in shape, some like huge ping-pong balls. The air on the mountain was more than crystal clear. It was pleasantly cool. The temperature was probably not much lower than—10°C. He remembered that his grandfather had mentioned in his book that in his time, the air was a dark brownish color from pollution created by vehicles, industry and households that burned wood and organic fossil matter such as oil and coal. It was very sad that for so long humans had had no respect for their Mother Planet, but there were some benefits too. In those days, the pollution made the orange and red tones in the sunsets and sunrises more colorful and vibrant.

Now, about seven kilometers in the distance on the south side, he saw a massive mountain range made of rock that the ancient sea had built from sedimentation. The mountain range was a few hundred meters high and snow powdered its steep cliffs. The winds and water had eroded the rock over many millions of years making it resemble a gigantic Easter cake, the kind that can now be read about only in ancient nineteenth and twentieth century books.

He decided to meditate before skiing, and entered one of the vacant privacy cabins. It had a clear Plexiglas dome, measuring approximately four meters in diameter, and was air-conditioned and soundproof. He changed his skiing suit for a cellulose, disposable kimono, similar to the kind used long ago in judo contests, and activated the dome's polarity shade filters. He left open a one-way view of the south side of the huge range.

First he did some yoga exercises—a modified, ancient *Surya-Namaskar* = Sun Salutation—and then sat on the futon cushion in an orthodox, yogic, lotus posture. He quickly entered the state of Silence. This was not difficult for him because he had been living most of his life in that Silence, slightly modified to accommodate the mundane activities. Going into Silence was as easy as plunging into the calm, cool waters of the mountain lakes, or walking down the steps of the Golden Canyon, so well known from one of his past lives.

In *samadhi* he once more penetrated the most significant experiences of his previous incarnations. He saw himself in the Oligocene Period as a sea mollusk living in the shallow brownish waters of the warm inland sea. He saw his shell cemented into the sedimentary layers of rock in the huge mountain range opposite his privacy cabin. He saw many of his past lives on different continents, in different countries. He saw himself as a monk living in a cave carved from rock, and as a Ukrainian peasant killed on the potato fields by an enraged Stalinist guard. Then he saw himself as the rich owner of a precious gemstone mine in Brazil, living a surprisingly detached, happy and peaceful life. He saw himself as a miserable landlord in England, who, out of jealousy, murdered his wife and her lover, and was then executed for the crime. He also saw himself as a disciple of the Incarnation of The Oneness, the Highest, dressed in human form.

He was able to see the logic between the successive lives, and he understood all his experiences as having been necessary in order to eliminate and exhaust dormant vasanas, to purify the mind, to sublimate it, and to achieve a state of desirelessness. How wonderful it was to grow slowly, being constantly but most of the time invisibly, guided by his Guru. How delightful it was to later be under His direct, personal care. How fascinating was this game of forgetting his identity, his sovereignty, and going through the unreal dreamlike enjoyments and sufferings. Now, being only a Witness, he felt gracious for all that had ever happened to him. The memory of the loving and smiling face of his *Satguru*, and how He assumed different garbs in many of his incarnations, was always giving him his highest sense of Bliss.

As he remembered His shining eyes, he was again experiencing the Divine Love in the purest form possible for mortals to experience. He always experienced Him as having form, being formless, and as all pervading, so he smiled lovingly to the Golden Light of Love filling infinity. The Light was again showing him his Guru's oneness with his own Self.

"I am so pleased that you have finished your work on the Planet Earth and are coming back Home for a rest. Hurry! I have a new job for you. I know, son, that you do not mind doing more work. You will go to a different solar system and work on one of the planets there. You always liked changes and challenges. This is going to be a really special one. You will live in the ocean of ammonia as a huge electric silica amoeba, and help other intelligent life forms to evolve, to expand their consciousness, to experience their oneness with Me. Come, son, come!" He was so happy. His Guru spoke to him again. He happily accepted the promised mission. He felt so free that he could accept anything and everything that He would ask him to do.

He had no personal desires, no wishes, and no goals. Everything he was doing was based on the performance of service to Him.

The weather continued to be favorable, and he spent a few invigorating days on the sunny slopes of the mountains skiing, walking along the cliffs, meditating, and enjoying his last days on this temporary home called Planet Earth. Behind him was a long list of very interesting lives: advancement from the most primitive life forms of viruses, to human lives. He had grown slowly through millions of years on this planet into the shape presented to him by The Oneness at the beginning of Time. Now fully grown, he worked from his free will to help his younger brothers and sisters to safely walk the path he once walked.

Two days after returning to town, he sent his PSU-t to the Communal Office and sent the notification through his computer to cancel his access card on a certain date, then he vacated his residential cubical. On the day of his final appointment, he went on the cabsly to the Departure Place, arriving a quarter of an hour before his appointment, and registered by inserting, for the last time, his access card in the entrance sensor. Then he waited. Punctually, at 3:00 p.m., as was stated on the note from the Central Computer, the nurse called him to the changing room. There he was asked to dispose of his clothes, put on a cellulose kimono, and wait in the adjoining room. The nurse was pleasant. She wore a blue dress fashioned from twentieth century uniforms.

In the waiting room he met a few other people also waiting for their bodies to be dematerialized. There was a very old interplanetary rocket pilot, a teenage girl, and a sixty-year old man, an artist and watercolorist specializing in painting astral light. In a few minutes the nurse called all of them to the departure hall. There were six to eight beds with tops made of glass, approximately one inch thick. The beds were standing between tastefully arranged tropical plants growing in hydroponics tanks, some with magnificent and very fragrant flowers.

The nurse asked him if he was ready. He confirmed that he was by nodding his head and lay down on the bed she indicated. The glass top was pleasantly warm. Inside the glass he noticed some very fine, brownish-gold wires forming a mesh. The nurse excused herself from him and went to the next bed where the old pilot was laying. She asked the pilot if she could activate the annihilating generator. The old captain, with typical Australian accent said:

"Yes, mum, please go ahead." He watched with interest how the old captain's body disappeared. There was a moment when it was semitransparent like a jellyfish. This lasted about one second, and then . . . nothing. The pilot disappeared, his body disintegrated and converted into pure formless energy. The nurse returned to him and politely asked the same question. He said

"Yes, I am ready." First, he had a brief thought about the feeling.

"How is it? Is there any sensation when dematerialization happens?" But he consciously switched his mind to the Golden Light of Divine Love, in his Guru's eyes. His thoughts were always focused on Him. The nurse smiled and switched on the system. He noticed that his body disappeared; yet there was not even the slightest change in feeling or consciousness. The only difference was that he no longer had his old and well known warmed up body. Looking around he thought,

"Well, what will I do now? How will I move having no legs?" He saw everything as clearly as before. He stopped for a moment at the sight of a beautiful bunch of orchids. Many times he saw them growing in the tropical jungle of Borneo where he had worked for a few years. After a while he realized that he could move just by using his will.

He went through the wall to the waiting room. The wall was neither an obstacle nor an obstruction. The people could not see him, but he saw them as before. Then he moved through the ceiling, through the roof, higher and higher, farther and farther, like an airplane, faster and faster. He liked it! After a while he noticed that all light was condensing and forming a tunnel. It was a strange tunnel. It was in the form of a funnel or a long cone, and the walls appeared to be made of light that had been woven into a fine mesh like the thread in a silkworm's cocoon. At the end of the tunnel, a visible source of Light was shining. It was The Light of Lights. He felt It as a Presence. How could he not recognize It? It was Him—his Guru in formless manifestation. He flew into the tunnel, relieved and happy, pulled by the sheer gravity of the Golden Light; closer and closer until he merged into IT, in Him, finally losing any remaining traces of individuality that he had preserved in order to enjoy the Bliss of Love. He became Divine Love and Love only.

He woke up in his van, parked on the beach where he had been camping all weekend. The waves of the ocean roared some ten meters away on the volcanic rock cliffs of the peninsula that divided the large bay from the ocean. The feeling of relief, of freedom, had not left him completely, but he felt sorry for himself that it had all been just a dream. Being only half awake, he almost believed that he really was a Free Man, that he had given his old, used up body away and merged into his Guru. He almost believed that he would soon incarnate on a remote planet to serve his brothers as an electric silica amoeba floating in an orange-colored ammonia sea.

He started his van's engine. The cloud of bluish-white smoke veiled the area, and dimmed the disk of the rising sun. He had to hurry as it was already late. It was Monday morning, another working day. It would take at least an hour-and-a-half to drive the seventy kilometers of highway from the peninsula to his Big Town. The traffic was as heavy as always after the weekend. A few times he barely avoided a collision with other vehicles driven by young surfers still drunk from an all-night party. While driving, he watched a small flock of miserable birds flapping their wings in the dense urban smog, desperately flying towards the huge, deep red disk of the sun. The sun was also struggling to illuminate the streets of this twentieth century town through the polluted air. He smiled, looking at the sticker of his Guru—attached to the steering wheel.

"It's only a bad dream." He joked bitterly,

"I will wake up soon. He is only playing with me." He looked at the clouds, orange in the morning sunlight.

It was his son not his father, as in the dream, who found it a fascinating hobby to watch the clouds, imagining the unimaginable. One thing at least was positive and uplifting: he had his Guru, and it was the same Guru in this quasi civilized contaminated world as in his dream, and he was getting ready to go to His ashram to live under His direct care and guidance. He asked himself:

"In the end, what is a dream and what is not? Everything is relative, dreamlike; is it not? Why worry? Why be sad?"

VOID

A Nothingness of a void is enveloping us. Unfamiliarity. No one to communicate with. A feeling of insecurity. No one to love and no one to fight with. Is it time to learn to be on our own—suspended, to depend on no one and expect nothing? There is nothing and there is no one.

What is the use of making peace with the past? The past is dead. It was a dream only. There is also no need to try to understand a vision of the future. It will take care of itself. Maybe there is no future for us.

All disappears in formless non-existence. Is this what we were aiming for? It can't be! Looking face-to-face with Truth. In IT's eyes is a Nothingness, that's us. Dissolution. We want to feel again The Presence. Where are YOU? We want again to feel the warmth of Love. Our eyes are open wide, but dry. We can't even cry. Emptiness. There is no other presence than ours. Was it all then just a stepping stone, a concept only created to comfort our restless mind? Only our existence is Real and It is not separate from us.

Fullness of void, luminescence of The Darkness, voice of Silence . . .

A Nothingness . . .

VISIT

This morning the Traveler started as usual with a cold-water bath, followed by a routine of ashram activities. Today was his turn to make the morning chaya. He managed to find some dry ginger and a few cardamom seeds in a kitchen cabinet. It was not much, but sufficient to add a special taste to the chaya. He did not feel very well. He had come to Chennai, previously known as Madras, a few nights before and he hadn't gotten much sleep. He'd made a nest for himself on the balcony of this over-crowded branch ashram. The brother mosquitoes in Chennai are very lively and aggressive. He now became a target of their nightly raids.

It was Sunday in the middle of November. His Guru was in Down Under, in the country he'd come from a few years ago. He'd met Him there for the first time. Coming to Down Under as a Traveler in transit, he had spent sixteen years there. The year he met Guru was a real turning point in his life. Meeting Him was indeed one of those rare, unforgettable experiences of one's life. In his memory, it was as fresh as if it had happened yesterday. He had just returned to Melbourne from Perth, where he had attended a ten day spiritual retreat with a great Vedantist scholar, Swami Chinmayananda. He could not follow Swamiji to Sydney, as his business commitments forced him to stay in his town.

Two days later he received a message from one of his spiritual sisters that Swamiji had rung from Sydney and advised them to go and meet a great Indian saint, who was visiting Down <u>Under</u> for the first time. His name was very long and difficult to remember. He was not very enthusiastic about it. Why should he meet this person from India? He was highly charged by the long retreat and Swamiji's discourses on the Bhagavad Gita, Viveka Chudamani, and Upanishads. He could almost feel the timeless Truth circulating in his veins. The Sanskrit shlokas still sounded fresh in his ears. Nevertheless, he thought it would be impolite to ignore Swamiji's request and not go.

The following day he went with his family to the hall where the Indian saint was giving darshan. It was not too crowded, maybe fifty people at the most. Those accompanying the saint were all wearing white clothes. They told him that they call Him Guru. He sat on the floor, as the others, and watched for some time the spectacular projection of love, compassion, and deep concern, which He was giving to the approaching people. When his turn came, he dove into His arms, warm and pulsating with Love. He forgot himself entirely. It was an eternally long moment of thoughtlessness. He experienced perhaps a glimpse of Pure Existence, his attribute of less beingness. Later he could not recall anything. There was no memory of the experience, only deep calmness and some sort of amazing fulfillment, a state of total security where there was nothing more to search for, nothing more to want. Somehow he managed to drive home safely. That night he slept with an unceasing memory of His dark, soft, warm eyes, looking at him with love. Nobody had ever looked at him like that before.

The first thing he felt the following morning was an immense desire to go and see Him again. There was an invisible pull, like a powerful magnet, forcing him to cancel his business arrangements for the day and go, go, go back to Him.

Again he queued up, seated on the floor, awaiting his turn to have *darshan*. Again he watched Him and the people. Again he saw the unbelievable massive flood of Love. He was instantaneously developing close relationships with seemingly total strangers, with people who were from such a different culture than His own. For Him there were no boundaries, no distinctions; cultural or national, no distances of the mental make ups or gaps of age to cross. He was accepting all, and in return He was accepted by all, as their own very intimate friend and relative. Again He cuddled him, as He is always doing with those who are receiving His *darshan*, regardless of age, health, social status or sex.

This time he was more conscious and managed, kneeling in front of Him, to raise himself up and look with curiosity straight into His dark eyes. In that moment his mind again stopped, and his consciousness traveled far, deep into Guru's sparkling eyes. He did not feel strange there. On the contrary, he felt at home, secure and welcome! There, in the apparent darkness of infinite space, he recognized the all-pervading Golden Light of Divine Love—the Real Him. This light was filling all of creation, which was contained in Him, and appeared to be the substratum of all that had ever existed.

When he returned from this brief trip to Infinity, he became conscious that in fact he too was made of this primordial substance, only in him it was not yet activated. He understood that what he always considered as himself was unreal, perishable, changing with passing time. The Real him was of the nature of this very Golden Light of Love; eternal and indestructible. He was gazing with thoughtless wonder at His face. In this look was the expression of a long expected recognition and acceptance of something approaching, but not yet definable. There was a spontaneous surrender to Him and the Unknown awaiting him in the future.

In his present state he had no conscious control over his body and mind. He could not explain how it happened, but he whispered automatically to the Golden Light in Guru's eyes: "I love you." This was the only thing his mind registered, and he was utterly surprised. He had been trained by all of his life experiences not to demonstrate or express his feelings. Why was he now saying to a stranger from exotic India such words as he had never before said to another human? It was too early for him to realize that he was face-to-face not with another human, but with the Highest. He smiled in understanding of his state and its limitations, and replied very naturally and softly, "You are my son." Those simple words spoken in perfect English clicked in his mind like an electrical switch turned "ON", opening the small door of understanding, showing him their real meaning. He admitted to himself that he was in fact His son. Obviously he could not explain it, as it was not rationally explicable. But he felt that he was exactly as He said, that it was the only truth he had been waiting for, for so long. The only recognition he ever really wanted. It sounded like total craziness, but the future showed that it was not craziness at all.

Those few words re-established between Guru and him the bond of Guru—disciple relationship, existing from past incarnations but veiled by the curtain of time. Saying those words were essential for him in order to re-enter the path of a spiritual quest under Guru's direct guidance. It was like saying a password in the army base to cross the gate.

The future years and the unfolding events in his life showed how skillful He is as a Guide. He went through accelerated karmic experiences, rapidly burning off dormant and active *vasanas*, and gradually freeing himself from worldly attachments. It took him over four years of literally bloody, merciless war with *Maha Maya* to get free. But thanks to Guru's grace he managed. As he settled in His ashram he ceased to be a Traveler. He became a Dweller.

Years later he was working at various ashram posts, happily doing whatever presented itself. A recent unexpected trip to Chennai for a month was another opportunity to break an invisibly developing attachment to place and work. Now, before breakfast, he had a bit of time for himself. He decided to go to the ground floor temple hall and meditate in one corner, which was separated from the rest of the hall by partition walls. He sat there facing east and drifted into His Presence in the Silence of the introverted mind. From the very beginning of this day he felt His Presence much more intensely than he had during the past few weeks. In the Silence he talked to Him, telling about his love, his determination to face his destiny, his occasional problems with the mind wandering in undesirable domains of sense enjoyments and memories of the past; which sometimes raised the level of adrenaline in his blood. He found in this internal conversation all the necessary support, counseling, and advice he needed. Guru, as always, responded instantaneously to both, his physical and mental needs, desires and wishes. After a few incidents, when quite ridiculous desires for chocolate or coffee were fulfilled in most unlikely circumstances, he thought to himself, "Be careful boy, Guru can readily give you all those objects you sometimes think of and the biggest trouble could start. I have to be more careful of what I am thinking, and not allow any mental dissipation. I have been told so many times that I am born to be a Free Man, and I have to do everything possible to fulfill my destiny."

Slowly he came back to external consciousness. He gently moved his head, hands, and legs. After a while he was able to get up. When he prostrated toward the rising sun, the feeling of being watched hit him strongly. Someone was watching him from the right side. There was a clearly perceivable Presence. He turned his head in that direction. On the wall was hanging his favorite photo of his Guru, which he hadn't noticed before. His face was very alive and He smiled lovingly. He even smelled His famous rose oil. He had come! He had visited him to uplift and give him strength and peace of mind. He obviously knew how badly his heart was aching when, a few days after Guru's group left, Swamini Prana rang from Singapore and told one of his spiritual sisters, who once shared with him Guru's *prasad*, to pack in a hurry and join the group in Down Under. Guru knew that for the first time since he'd settled in the ashram, he was jealous about something. This experience also had a beneficial side, as he realized that in his heart there was still an attachment to be annihilated. Guru's unconventional visit brought him back a most desired peace. Tears of gratitude and love for All Knowing Guru rolled slowly down his face, colored by the rising sun. How can he be sad being constantly in His Presence?

People say that Guru is gone. They are wrong! They are very wrong!! Where could He go? How can He leave if He dwells in our hearts as our own Self? Leaving He is not going; going He is not leaving! Is there any place where He is not? Who will believe that it is so easy to meet Him when we want? He is always waiting in the Silence, in the dark infinite space full of Golden Light; on the front of our closed-in meditation eyes. He is always ready to console us, to give advice, to guide and serve. He is the Greatest, most humble servant of all. He watches us constantly from inside, and is whispering patient advice, giving hints where to go, what to do, how to act. If we could plunge into Silence more often, switching off our restless minds, we would be able to understand His silent talk, to follow the intuition, to tap into the river of His mighty wisdom. Why shouldn't we try?

It was already half past ten. Time for breakfast! Babu Swami had probably finished cooking some delicious *cangee* and a simple vegetable curry. He got up from his meditation seat and walked up the stairs. On the balcony he met Rayana Swami. He patted him and said,

"Feeling Guru?" Did he know? Maybe just a few uplifting words? Maybe he met Him too. Who knows? Only him, who knows, knows that he knows!

UNDELIVERED LETTER. 1

My Darling Sister in The Oneness,

This letter will never reach you. It was written long before a small statue of Devi had been carved from a stone, and should be still on its way when the mighty waters subside after the transformation ends. There is no such dimension as time in this Post Office I use. So . . . do not wait for it. Just Be. This is the only way to be happy.

My steps are wobbly. My eyes can't see well. Too much Light! It is burning my face. Where can I hide? And why should I? It is coming from everywhere. It fills the space, it pours from the eyes of people passing by; it falls down from behind the clouds. I am drunk! I am drowning!

Step by step; from nowhere to nowhere. No starting point and no destination. What can I want for? Here, where we are, we are now, how can we want to be more?

Their faces are smiling, but I smile and cry. What do they know? Do they too feel The Oneness? Perhaps some do.

The symphony of Existence is so loud. It makes the Silence most eloquent and enjoyable and the peace serene in the midst of action. Resting in sweat; sweating at rest. Don't say anything. Listen! Do you hear It? Do you know what I know, not knowing? You should!

There will be no need to pay anything back. There is no one to collect a debt. Dust only; which does not care. There is also no debt. Who owns anything, and to whom to give? Me? You? Are we two? I know it was only a joke, but you may really return here. If you will, that's only out of free will, to serve. So . . . we will meet again.

I am gone. They say that I am not here anymore. But where did I go? Only this body that I wear moves. If they believe this lie, please tell them to listen and hear. Who is then singing the praises of our Divine Parents, who plays the melody of Love Divine on the tops of the coconut palms?

Step by step; from nowhere to nowhere. What is the distance? Is there any? Walking or standing, which is faster? BEING!! Is there any limit for the grace of the Unlimited? How can nothingness absorb so much of It? Nothingness is not even a sponge as a sponge is already a thing. How can it function drunk, submerged in this blazing Golden Light? . . . How?

My Darling Sister, you must finish this letter yourself because I can't. It doesn't matter who writes to whom. It doesn't even matter what's written. Can words say anything? Better just to live it as it is. It would be silly to try to finish what has no end . . .

UNDELIVERED LETTER. 2

Another letter; and to whom? I don't know. I also don't know why.

I am sorry. I have forgotten what I wanted to say and to whom. Even if I could memorize it, it won't change anything. Even if I don't ask anything or say anything, all will come by itself when needed. So . . . there is no need to waste our time. Even a single second can't be regained if once lost. In fact, time does not exist, but here, where we are now, it flows in only one direction.

Ultimately there is also no space. All is contained in an infinite point Here and Now. Why then, would someone suggest that I should come there more often? Do I go anywhere? Am I ever away? How can I leave? From where can I go and to where? You still don't believe? Well. Close your eyes and see! And . . . , who is smiling at you from the nonexistent space of your own mind? Is it not me? In all pervasiveness of Guru's mystery, distances do not exist. I am bound to Him for eternity, to His sacred dwelling spot of everywhere. You too! So . . . we are there—here, together as Golden Light, as Timeless Love.

Every game has its own rules. If it must be that way let me travel through the illusionary space propelled by the mighty jets of Love Divine, staying still where I always was. Let all happen that has to happen in the fullness of its time, in a moment of climax, in the pregnancy of our destiny.

White, stained with blood, or red in pure whiteness? My national colors; my unearned offering and honor. It doesn't matter! Probably, less contrast might not frighten onlookers so much. Let sacrifice happen according to the preset scenario. Pain of existence; Bliss of nothingness. What was first? When a development reaches the beginning of the final act of this spectacular, dramatic performance, Guru will decide when and how. I'm ready.

Don't you even dare to think that it will be the end! No! On the contrary! It will be the beginning of an ultimate adventure, which will never end! Only Mr. Wind, doing his duty, will take care of the worthless ashes, and the sacred land will accept them as welcome food for the plants.

Work. More work. Rest at work. Slowly gaining the speed of immobility. By being far, closeness is increased. He is so sweet! For what is this game of losing one's sight, searching in the darkness and finding, when all hope is lost? It, what was so incredibly near that was always impossible to feel, that it was so difficult to see.

Even if all of it has no meaning, it is a delightful pastime to drink His superior 'wine', to sing, to laugh in madness and to cry in ecstasy. It is like watching in utter wonder a grand movie. All has already happened on a different plane, in dimensions hidden from mortals, where our Real Home is. So, we are only dreaming it again. Let it be. Close your eyes to the world, nest yourself comfortably on the lap of our Divine Guru, secured by His unique, godly arms and dream this Sweet Dream of The Reality while fully awake in illusion! If you like, cry loudly in an ecstasy of Bliss or be Silent.

Do not say anything! I know . . .

UNDELIVERED LETTER. 3

Letter of a madman to . . . . who (perhaps only) understands.

Monotonous ripples of rain. Uncounted little drops of water fall from clouds sparkling lights like flawless diamonds. Water runs down from the trees, from the roofs and from the drenched clothes of people. Our tears too flow down and wash from us the dust of our memories of the past. We are singing Your Name so loudly that nothing else can be heard. Is it not enough to remember Your smile, Your eyes, Your Name? What more is worth remembering? Has this long dream any real value? Only experiences to help recognize the right direction. Where have the well-known shadows—cast by our vivid imaginations—gone? Where are the once so dear phantoms created by our potent desires? Where are the echoes of the loud words of anger and soft, warm whispers of their fervent assurances? Where are supposed to be the tasty fruits of their sworn promises, which never were meant to be kept, which were nothing but empty phrases and empty sounds helping only to make one more step, to win one more petty enjoyment or one more thing? We would like very much to remember you only, you very small bee who proved through good and bad to be credible in your selfless love. We can't describe how grateful we are for your pains and toils of making for us the golden honey when we were deathly ill. Whatever will happen to us, we will always try hard to remember your teachings, which were never said.

We have listened long and attentively to this grand symphony of Existence, learning from unending mistakes; preliminary lessons from our great teacher the beetle and from the competent master caterpillar. A dog showed us what faithfulness is. We tested our strength and tried to find if ultimate limits do exist. The earth trembled under us in a euphoric dance of immense pleasure. Cosmic vastness accepted our loud cry in the hopelessness of unbearable pain. What once was dear and near is now gone, like dry Autumn leaves which are blown away by good Mr. Wind.

We have become addicted to Your 'wine'. We don't want anything else. But, who can fully enjoy drinking, when drinking to a mirror? We would like to share this sweet ambrosia; but with whom? Who would appreciate this strange drink and be ready to pay its price? Who would like to listen to the words uttered in madness by the drunken dirty dust, less important even than pure Nothingness? So . . . we wrote to You this letter. Only You will not laugh, not ridicule us. You were always kind to us. You talked to us with such love that we melted entirely in its warmth and disappeared in Infinity when gazing deep into Your dark eyes. You, who knowing everything, care to know how we feel and ask if we are happy! How could we answer? Thanks to Your Grace we have become Emptiness full of happiness, we are now Happiness Itself. Something is changing though still as it was, but we are very aware of this state of our happiness which is self propelling and will never end.

The Silence is loud! The Essence is so filling! You have given us the largest family that ever existed; an indefinable Totality. All is ours and all are our Dear Ones. Where should we send this letter? Where are You now? Aren't You everywhere? How? Where? Why?

They make unnecessary noise. Do they really know something or are they just pretending and guessing? Or maybe it is You who said a word? Never mind. We can't know anything and don't even want to know. Not caring for any changes we accept readily whatever comes as we believe and feel strongly that all comes only from You.

We know that you will have to send away this neophyte. So what? He will go far, very far, where clouds move very low, almost touching the tops of the trees and where snow covers all high, very high. So . . .

What should we say? It is almost time to return there from where once-upon-a-time it all began . . .

But do not worry! We will visit You every night. We will come down from the sky as the light of a distant star, as the Silence from the infinite space out of which we were born. We will kneel in front of Your dark, loving eyes. But it must be our secret! Those who sleep should not be allowed to see this magic of ours!

Our love for You has no limits. The illusionary distance will only increase this, which is already infinite. The impossible will happen! For us, You are always The First, You are in front of all others. You are even ahead of The Only One, as You are Him who has come to us—who are so shamelessly low, to show us how to bow, how to prostrate to big and small, to Nature, to all. We are now bound to each other and we will keep our strong hold onto You. You will not be able to stay behind. Oh, No! You will have to go with us wherever we go! So . . . we will stay together forever. We will talk to You, the You in trees, in mountain ranges, in humans and in animals. We will listen to You too, always eager to know what You say. It is true that all that has to be said has been said, but still it will be an immense delight to listen to Your silent, soundless speech, to have all this once more confirmed by YOU.

It all has been predicted by a visionary whilst dying on Turkish soil, when greedy neighbors divided our country. He saw it happening long, long before we entered the stage: "The lucky number will be divided by two and after forming a Whole, Complete Symbol—a Voice, will become identical with a year of a twice-born free son of a humble slave. Being only a symbol he will be Real and will return from afar to this land, which lacks hope so much. He will know The Word and will show to the people how to walk The Path to The Light." So we have to go . . .

But there is still a little bit time to play around. We can still enjoy our old ways for a while. We still can, as small plants, hide in a crowd. We can still have joy doing small things, growing steadily in Your shade, becoming trees, getting ready to give fruit to those who are hungry, getting ready to quench the thirst of those wanting to drink this secret wine of Yours—ambrosia. Now we ourselves will start to tirelessly collect the golden honey for those of our brothers who are deathly ill. We will try to imitate you, our dear little bee, from the times of our great test. You have shown us The Way, how to make the impossible happen, how to do, not doing and how to be, not being, how to Be. We owe you almost as much as Him who was second after you, still being The First. Our humble *pranams* to you two, to both of You who are in fact only a different form of Him, the One—Undivided.

TWO LOVE GENES

The Commander of the Program sponsored under a grant from the Commonwealth of Galaxy 'F' was going for the third time through data supplied by the central super computer 'Ramcom' regarding the beings from one of many planets included in the Program and called by her inhabitants 'Earth'. On this planet many primitive species lived in perpetual conflict and were predating each other. One of these species had a partly activated intelligence, and by its use could occasionally make right choices between good and bad. They were mostly interested in pursuing pleasures and avoiding pain so, in fact, rarely used this inborn faculty. They called themselves humans, and were divided into five races: black, brown, yellow, red and white. They spoke many languages, which had evolved from a universal one given to them in the beginning of creation by their Father. The separating and the mixing of the languages, and the confusion that followed, had happened after the third wave of life on this planet was almost totally destroyed by the arrogant humans who had used, for their selfish ends, forces which were usually inaccessible to life forms at such an early stage of their civilization. Unfortunately, those mighty powers were given to them by Lucifer, one of Satan's senior deputies—a Leader of rebels in this Galaxy against the Father—The Eternal One.

The Commander was a little bit confused. Among three-hundred-and-eighty individuals nominated by the computer for participation in the Program was one mortal whose character did not match the strict criteria established by the Supervising Panel in The Department of Progress in The Government of Free Beings in Galaxy 'F'. His name was coded A.M.B. 238765321, as it was necessary to keep everything in strict secrecy. Satan's spies had already managed to penetrate even this Department, taping computer data for their destructive work. The key to the code was in his and his deputy's possession only.

Raya, a female officer, was educated on the largest moon of the planet called by the humans, Saturn. She was a sort of challenge hunter. After many years spent in various posts on different planets and interplanetary stations, she decided now to settle down a bit and work only on the New Race Program in the Department of Progress. She didn't know that the Father actually was the isotropic line parallel to itself, and vibrating without movement of itself at multiple right-angles. He was also similar to the axis system of energy strings, in which the points of intersection of lines are simultaneously everywhere at the same time. He is one, but manifests Himself as many. This apparent modification doesn't change Him because He is Real, which means unchangeable. All dimensions are contained in Him, and He controls everything in creation, which is only His play-game of a hologram created from Himself.

The Father had recently become particularly interested in the work of this Department. This fact was stimulating Raya very much, as she, deep down, always wanted to serve Him more directly. She was even dreaming that maybe one day, after she had paid off most of her karmic debts, she would return to her favorite place, Saturn, and stay there on one of its satellites for the rest of her life in one of the communities living in the desert caves, meditating on the Father. Maybe even one day, if He wished it so, she would attain a State of Awakening in this lifetime, merging in Him for Eternity. On the expedition she was one of the deputies of the spaceship Commander.

But now the Commander was in a dilemma. He knew that a mistake on this computer was impossible. Many safety systems had been installed, the highest intelligence devices and advanced truth filters had been developed on the basis of the experience of over two-and-a-half billion years of existence of the recent galactic civilization, enriched by knowledge brought from a few inter-galactic expeditions. "Probably", he thought, "there is a reason, hidden even from me, that this naughty rascal was nominated." But the most shocking thing for him was the incredible coincidence. From millions of females from so many planets, Raya, his deputy, was selected as the Rascal's partner in this Program. Ridiculous, unthinkable! The commander didn't feel very comfortable about this. Not at all! He felt, after ten years with Raya in the Program, a bit, or maybe even more than a bit, attached to her. He was, which surprised him, obviously jealous! But he was disciplined and loyal to the Father. Not even the slightest desire not to obey entered his mind.

It was late autumn; a year after the Rascal had finished his five-year University course. Following others, like sheep, he had married a female human, called on Earth 'woman'. Such contracts are made between individuals of the opposite sex with the aim to procreate, and by this maintain the planet's population. There is no genetic check or an approval of perspective partners. Everything is a sort of lottery. They call such a nucleus community a 'family'. There is another motive for these unions. The individuals are afraid to be lonely and at the same time have a strong desire to enjoy sex by making love, as they call it. By doing it humans try hopelessly to find lasting happiness.

Rascal loved the mountains. Despite drinking alcoholic beverages and smoking the dried leaves of tobacco, called cigarettes, both being very harmful, he still had a reasonably well functioning intuition. In the mountains he perceived The Presence. He didn't know whose, but he was sure that something subtle but very powerful was present there. In the mountains, far away from the crowds of contaminated towns and other humans in their trance-like lives, hurriedly pursuing their endless and, most of the time, ridiculous desires, he was more in tune with something he didn't yet know how to name, how to call it. In the mountains he probably perceived the Father's Presence, but he was not aware of it. Not yet. In fact he didn't believe in the Father's reality or in His existence. He was educated not to believe in Him, even to reject the very possibility of a chance of His reality. But deep down in his soul, the existence of which he also was programmed to negate, he felt Him as the substratum of everything, as the Life of his own life, and the life in surrounding him: Nature.

Rascal had just arrived in Zakopane, a town set in a large valley under the footsteps of the Tatra Mountains, the highest mountains in Eastern Europe. He had come by train; a very primitive and slow means of transport humans use on Earth. This vehicle is limited to metal tracks and often uses as fuel fossilized plants called coal. In this way the humans, traveling slowly, pollute the atmosphere of the entire planet, as well as rapidly converting the coal, which is one of the most valuable organic raw materials and extremely rare in Galaxy 'F,' to ashes.

In Zakopane he got onto a bus. This vehicle moved on pumped up wheels along passages reserved for it called 'roads', emitting clouds of white and black smoke consisting of even more toxic chemicals, and terribly polluting the air in the human colonies called 'towns'. Its engine used a liquid fuel, oil, another scarce and precious raw material existing on this planet and commonly misused. Its reserves are limited but humans rarely think about future generations. Its smoke caused the deterioration of buildings, the poisoning of plants, as well as causing many sicknesses in the human populations such as asthma, lung cancer and heart malfunctions—the sicknesses known only on planets during their early stages of industrial development, in the times when there was no balance between the production of consumables and the protection of natural resources, including geological deposits, water and the atmosphere of the planet.

Within twenty minutes, he was at the door of his Aunt's house, and rang the bell. She was expecting him, and with a smile invited him inside. Her dwelling was simple as she was a low-income widow, but the feeling was great. Aunty had a good heart and a positive outlook on life. It created strong positive vibrations around her.

Rascal was tired after traveling seven hours on the train. It was already dark. They ate supper, then had cake for dessert and drank tea, one of the many narcotic beverages humans use. It's made of the leaves of a plant consisting of a drug called theine, an alkaloid that stimulates the nervous system.

The Aunt offered him a book to read before sleeping. Rascal, after having a short shower, went to bed. The book was small and slim. Its title was rather strange: 'Humans Yesterday, Today and Tomorrow.' Someone who was not a native speaker of his language translated this text into Polish, originally published in English nearly one-hundred years ago in London, the capital of a country on a large island near the continent on which Rascal was living.

He didn't want to read anything. He was very tired. He only wanted to drift into a deep refreshing sleep. Tomorrow he would have to trek the hills and valleys on the way towards his beloved mountains. He saw them through the window. Their peaks in the distance glowed in the silvery green light reflected from the Sun by Earth's only natural satellite, what humans call the Moon. But he opened the book. He opened it not at the beginning but on page 21, for good luck – a human superstition. Maybe he was influenced by his Aunt's intention; she had smiled so strangely when giving him the book; or maybe someone else whom he didn't know was guiding his hands. Who knows? The first sentences he read electrified him. They were as follows: **"All the humans on Earth are continuously watched by the beings of the White Brotherhood, beings who are eternally free; but out of the compassion they feel toward their spiritually younger brothers and sisters living in the darkness of ignorance, decide to incarnate voluntarily on Earth. Some dwell in astral dimension but work on Earth affairs. They supervise the planet's spiritual evolution and help those who like to accelerate their progress, those who want to free themselves, those who are ready to shake off ignorance and start to live in knowledge of their oneness with Him our Father, those who are ready to break the cage of their personality, transcend their mortal existence, give up old habits, forget desires, resign from attachments. They will not be forgotten! They will be called! Not even a single one will be left undetected. The beings of the White Brotherhood are responsible for picking up such souls and guiding them. They all**

have appointed souls. They know in advance who will become ripe fruit on the tree of life."

Rascal was deeply moved by those words. He felt like he was rediscovering what he once already knew. It was like a confirmation of a truth so obvious that it should be commonly known. It was like finding what he was subconsciously expecting all his life. He understood that he was on the track towards the Father and that He was real. Life was not as hopeless as it appeared to be at first glance. Now Rascal was confident that his intuition was right, and his teachers and learned professors were very wrong.

He hardly got any sleep. He read the entire book twice. Many ideas in it were for him too foreign, too mystical, too strange and apparently impossible to accept straight away, but it opened for him a totally new, more complex and wider vision of existence. He realized that the picture was much more intricate then had been presented to him during his study of Dialectic Materialism, the official philosophy of his country's ruling political party, and controlled by its totalitarian government. Now he was at the gate of Advaita Vedanta, the philosophy of Sanatana Dharma—the eternal religion given to this planet as well as to all the others in existence by the Father Himself. It was preserved and passed down by the sages of the lore, advanced beings that voluntarily incarnate on planets to help their inhabitants grow spiritually according to the Eternal Law of Love set for eternity by the Father.

The next afternoon, Rascal was already organizing a camp near a small lake in the high part of the valley under the cathedral-like range of granite peaks. The sapphire colored water of the lake was of such clarity that it was impossible to estimate the depth of the stones and boulders lying near its bank submerged in water. Just before sunset his friend and rock-climbing partner joined him. He was also very tired after an even longer journey than Rascal's. Soon both of them went to sleep in a cave under a massive boulder.

The night was cold, only around five degrees centigrade. The light of the Full Moon was silver-plating the rigid landscape. After midnight, a low, very gentle tingling sound filled the valley. Slowly from behind the granite range, a dark triangle had appeared. It was gigantic. It was about fifty meters wide. On its corners were glowing dim red and blue lights, like whirls formed by gently dancing flames. It was moving slowly, majestically, and in nearly total silence. It had lowered itself and landed vertically not more than one-hundred-and-eighty meters from the boulder where Rascal and his friend were lying in deep sleep. A little door on the edge of the craft opened and a light platform automatically came down. On the platform stood two of its crew members wearing silver-gray, tight uniforms. They walked towards the boulder. They didn't need any light because they were able to perceive the infrared part of the light spectrum, making it possible for them to see well in darkness. One of them crawled under the boulder and touched Rascal's chest with a hypnotic induction projector, an instrument like a small mobile phone, a communication device that would be invented on Earth in thirty years' time. Rascal woke up, but he was hypnotized. They led him to the craft, and soon all three were lifted onto the platform and went inside.

One hour later, after the surgery, Rascal was still lying on the operating table. A few surgeons in sterile white clothes were packing sample containers and instruments and switching off assisting robots. He noticed in small cages sleeping hypnotized birds and animals. There were eagles, marmots, foxes and wolves. Their turn would come before sunrise. The sliding door opened silently and the Commander, followed by Raya, entered the operating theater. They both introduced themselves to Rascal, using an internal mind-to-mind communication system, and the Commander asked him to go with them to his office as something of great importance should be discussed. There, Rascal was told how he was selected by the computer of the Department of Progress to take part in the Program by having an experimental child with Raya who was already a first generation hybrid having an Earthly mother. It was explained how the Department was working on creating new intergalactic races of beings who would be strong genetically and faithful to the Father. He was told that the third millennium of the galactic civilization was approaching and a new race would have to cope with its future problems, and at the same time be more in tune with the Father, as

Satan's activities had recently intensified, causing a lot of trouble. It was decided that a means of resistance against the forces of darkness had to be, from now on, more radical. He was told that one planet from this solar system, called by humans Pluto, was scheduled to be pushed out of its orbit into the dark, cold space because its inhabitants had become very evil, technologically advanced, and totally loyal and dedicated to Satan. There was no other way but to eliminate them. He was asked to accept his participation in the work in progress. Rascal, being pleased that even he could be useful, accepted this offer. They told him that there was installed in his leg a mini transmitter, and through the automatic station of the Moon, his life would be monitored by the Department's computer. He was informed that for safety reasons, he would have a blockage of memory of everything he'd been told and that will happen to him for the next twenty-five years. Raya then led him back to his camping spot, under the boulder where his friend was all the time snoring soundly.

A week later, the spaceship was getting ready to take its course out of this Solar System and fly towards the constellation of Andromeda. All the members of the crew were busy. The spaceship computer was working at full speed processing data and summarizing this stage of The Program.

The day before the expedition left the gravity field of the solar system, Raya decided to do it while still in this universe. Astrological assessment of time and location were favorable for conceiving a child. By the late afternoon she was inseminated by the medical robot with the sperm taken earlier from Rascal. A new life was beginning to incubate in her body; a strange combination of genes, hers from Saturn's moon and his from Earth. The new member of a new galactic race started to slowly grow inside her. On Earth, according to the calendar used by the humans, it was the end of Autumn in 1971. The spaceship computer decided it would be a female, a girl. Raya gave her the name 'Samatha'. Only she would know it; and it was only for her own private use. Later, as is practiced, when the child was born, the computer would give her an official name. Tonight she was a bit introspective. It was a completely new experience for her. She would have a child! Such a miracle! A new life form! She already felt a strange, warm sensation. It was the love for her child germinating in her heart.

The Commander had just received the last printout from the computer. Work in this universe had been completed. Now the computer released the previously inaccessible data. He noticed a strange combination of genetic codes from samples of organic matter taken from some Earthly participants. Rascal was amongst them. Now he understood why they were nominated, despite not matching other criteria. In all of them a mutation occurred in the love genes. It could theoretically happen, but in fact it happened very rarely. All of them possessed Alpha and Beta love genes. Usually beings classified as mammals have only one of them, Alpha or Beta, to secure the instinct of reproduction. Their offspring never have both, regardless of their parents' setup. He became excited as he sensed the possibility of the continuation of the mutation in children born in The Program's experiment. All the sperm samples taken from Earth were going to be used on different planets according to The Program Master Plan, but all later; all except Rascal's. It was being given a chance to find out if the speculations were correct. The Commander called Raya on the intercom. After discussing the matter, she agreed to do some tests. She was carrying a fetus that was already two months old. The tests showed a revelation. Both love genes were retained, and the Alpha gene was doubled as a stabilizer. This combination gave a guarantee to continue the genes in future generations, regardless of the genetic set up of the other partners. It was a predominant genetic configuration copying itself in the progeny. Thanks to this, a new galactic race would have more direct internal contact with the Father. The language of Divine Love would be easily understood by them. This good news made Raya so happy that she even cried for the first time in her life, exactly as humans do when they are happy or in Bliss.

A few years later Rascal, tired and upset after an irritating conference in his office, was having a tub-bath. He sank into the hot water, almost completely suspending the functions of his mind. He was recharging, resting, totally relaxed. Suddenly, something inside of him asked loudly:

"Are you ready to enter the Path in search of the Truth? Are you ready to leave all of this and go towards the Unknown?" He jumped out of the bath, splashing water all over the floor.

"Who is it? Who asked those questions?" He checked the bathroom. Nobody was there. After a few seconds, the questions were repeated once more. Now he started to think about their meaning. He quickly evaluated the assets of his life, expectations, and chances for a happy future, and found nothing substantial, nothing worthwhile enough to live for. Then he answered, not knowing to whom or why, but with full consciousness and honesty:

"Yes. I would like to go. I don't care about all of this. I am actually fed up with the emptiness of my present life and foggy future. I feel that I have been born to become Free. Someone even told me this." He waited for the answer, but there was none. His declaration was accepted in Silence and Silence confirmed it as valid. No more communication.

Nothing was arranged, planned or secured. Unexpected to himself and his closest acquaintances, he left his country, his beloved mountains. He traveled with his wife, with only $20.00 in his purse, with no waiting friends or a list of helpful contacts. He 'burned all his bridges behind', leaving no chance to return. But he was confident that he would make no compromise, and that he was not alone. He was guided. This sometimes was so obvious that it was almost tangible. Two years later, he immigrated, officially now as a refugee, to another continent. This time he was not only with his wife, but also with his son who was born in exile. All the way, despite difficulties, he felt a strange, warm, loving and caring protection. He didn't know yet that the Father had already incarnated on this planet and by the power of his destiny he was on his way to meet Him as one of his Gurus.

For ten years he labored in this new country doing work he never expected that he could do. The language difficulties, customs dissimilar to his, the mentality of the native people, all of it made his life harder and quite challenging. It was Spring when He arrived. He was told by a friend about the Guru's coming. Their first meeting happened during the morning *darshan* He was giving to a small crowd of people. When He cuddled him, as He cuddled all who came to Him, he felt something strange happening to his mind. He stopped thinking. He just became . . . Existence. When he looked into His eyes, he saw something, which was impossible to describe with words, but something very familiar, something he had felt in the mountains and now immediately recognized.

"I love YOU!" He whispered automatically, gazing into the infinite depth of His eyes.

"You are my son." Replied Guru. The energy flowed through their eyes, and those few simple words were enough to create a bond, which would remain until his last breath.

Four more years passed. Rascal was working hard. He, under the care of Swami Chinmayananda, studied *Advaita Vedanta*—the Philosophy of Non-duality. Due to ego quarrels and his wife's hostility to meditation, which he started to practice, and his association with Indians, he divorced her. His old country regained its freedom and he flew there for a few days to meet his old mother. After a visit to Europe he spent a few months in the Ashram of his Guru, the Father in the form of a human being. There he was given the opportunity to see his and Raya's daughter. Guru took him one night for a trip to Titan, one of Saturn's moons. Samatha had just completed her studies on planets around Alfa Centauri and had come to a Saturn moon to get a treatment to enhance her intelligence and also to meet her mother, who had renounced mundane life, retired from work in the Department of Progress, and now lived in an underground cave meditating day and night on the Father. Rascal saw her from a distance standing with his Guru and His small group on the balcony of a huge, high hall decorated on the walls with Tiffany-styled glass panels and terracotta tiled floors. They just arrived after the Guru gave *dharshan* to a small, brown like melted chocolate moon. Samatha didn't know he was there, as they were in astral bodies not visible to her physical eyes. Maybe she didn't even know that behind the code identifying her father registered on the personal chip: AMB 238765321, a real individual still existed somewhere on the distant Earth. She was a very sporty girl, wearing clothes of twentieth century Europe on this Earth: a tight blouse and dark green checkered skirt. She was walking energetically and looked as if in deep concentration, like evaluating some serious issue on which she had to make the right choice.

Later, month by month, year by year, when he was walking in the nearby park in total darkness doing his evening *japa mantra*, he looked into the infinite sky spread with innumerable stars and thought, "She is there somewhere, my darling daughter." Sometimes he shed tears of love, sometimes only smiling towards the stars. He had seen her only once but loved her no less than his son Michael from planet Earth. He couldn't help it. Not knowing her closer was no obstacle for his love, because he had two love genes, and he knew that both of them, Raya and Samatha, were on the Father's team. His love genes were in good hands. She was ready to start her work for progress, for better attunement of our Galaxy 'F' with Him. Rascal soon joined his Guru, the Father Incarnate, and also started to work for the Light.

Everything happened very early on a foggy morning. Nobody expected it. The war had been going on for the last two months. People knew that such possibilities existed, but they were hoping it would never happen. Intercontinental strategic missiles had come straight down from space like lightening, detected by radar only a fraction of a second before the explosion. There was no time for warning and no defense possible. Towns were simply swept away by the mighty waves of fire, heat and radiation. All metal construction was melted. Tall, solid buildings fell like children's sand castles; penetrating gamma radiation annihilated all living creatures. It was sterile and deathly quiet, only the echo of falling brick walls occasionally broke the dense silence. The landscape of endless ruins looked like a different planet in the reddish light of the rising sun, struggling through the dense clouds of dust. Soooo . . . it had happened! Now everything was over. Flourishing civilizations of selfish, greedy people had been destroyed in an instant.

On the wreck of a tall building stood a man; a living man! He himself was astonished that he had survived. He was the Last Witness: the witness of the results of the incredible stupidity of his brothers. He was as calm as the corpses of those lying under many meters of concrete and bricks. For him too there was no future. He had also received a deadly dose of radiation. There was no doubt that he had only a maximum of a few hours of life left, more probably only a few minutes. Now he was a Witness, detached, unconcerned, and sphinx-like. All his family and friends were turned to ashes. He didn't know why he was spared. There wasn't even a second person to pass his testimony to.

It had not been long since he had come to this town where many years back his son was born. His Guru had sent him there to work for Him in His Center. *Kali Yuga* was in a delirium. Selfishness, crime, hatred and terrorism had reached their peak. When he had arrived here war was hanging on the hair-like thread of hope. Guru's children, as He called His disciples and devotees, had been instructed to repeat three times every day, morning and evening the mantra:

LOKAH SAMASTAH   LET ALL BEINGS IN THIS
SUKINO BHAVANTU . . .   WORLD
OM SHANTI, SHANTI,   AND OTHER WORLDS BE
SHANTI . . .   BLISSFUL . . .
           OM PEACE, PEACE, PEACE . . .

It purified the atmosphere on Earth from negative vibrations. It helped tremendously, but the forces of destruction were already in motion on the subtle level. According to the Laws set by the Father, hatred had to be followed by devastation and annihilation. Thoughts are forces, much more powerful than humans ever realized. Now it was too late. Too many negative thoughts had been projected. The Law was in action. The cycle of life had ended.

Today, on the interplanetary spaceship orbiting the Sun close to Mars' path, all were in a grave mood. They were very sad because the life on planet Earth had been destroyed for the fifth time in galactic history and second time due to human's mischief. Now the planet was badly radioactively polluted and would suffer a long nuclear winter due to the sun's rays being suspended in stratosphere dust. It could last up to three years. Temperatures on the surface would drop to minus sixty degrees centigrade, water would freeze up to thirty meters down, darkness, due to pollution in the stratosphere, would cover her. All plants, animals and humans who had survived direct destruction in country areas would gradually die off. The fifth wave of life on Earth had practically ended. The matter, which formed the bodies of all creatures, would return to the elements.

From space, Earth looked terribly sick. It had changed its color from a radiant blue to a gloomy grayish-brown. It looked dead, very dead. The Commander was devastated by the news. He had returned here, to the Solar System, after thirty years of work on planets of Andromeda. He liked Earth more than the other planets he had seen. He liked her succulent verdure so abundant in the tropics, her whiteness in the snowy mountains and her green oceans made of salty water. Now he was sent to monitor the sad happenings. He was instructed by the Department not to interfere. The events had to take a natural course. Destruction was not avoidable. It was the fulfillment of the collective karma of this planet's inhabitants. He knew it was not the end of life on Earth. The Father had preset for this planet seven waves of life before her final death. He was convinced that thanks to the results of the Program, just completed some ten years back, the new galactic race, which would be planted in the future on Earth, would have three love genes in their genetic code, which should permanently prevent it from a similar shameless destiny. It looked as though Satan had won this time; but in fact, in the long cosmic run, it was the beginning of his final defeat. The Father never lost control. He was just playing in Eternity on the medium of space and time, changing forms, pretending diversity, but abiding in The Oneness of Himself.

The Witness started to feel a strong itching in his leg. "Maybe my transmitter is damaged by the gamma radiation," he thought. Now it didn't matter. His life as Rascal was over. He became a Witness for a short time. He looked into the sky. There was no sky! Dust only, clouds of dust. From dust all this had emerged, lasted for a short while like the Cosmic Father's blink, flourished, got morally corrupted and into dust was again converted. He remembered a poem he had once written:

DUST I AM
I always was and I always will be.
The writings call me Eternal One.
From me the stars and galaxies were formed.
The wise do know and have respect—
the fool thinks himself as greater
They wash me off age by age,
From the prophets' and sages' feet.
From me the kings and the beggars are made.
The Bible called me clay.
You think you are different?
Not even an inch!
You are my child,
From me you were born,
And me you will become when gone.
Dust I am. Free Dust, Cosmic Dust.
Only I am who I am.
I take a million forms.
I can be whatever can be.
It's a game, it's a play,
Witnessing innumerable cycles of creation and dissolution
I last, changing forms, moving in space.
From me the sound OM comes and universes pop.
Dust I am. Free Dust, Cosmic dust.
But if you look well, look closely, you will find my secret:
I do not exist at all!
I am HIM who plays and HE is me,
We are not two, but one.
I ask you now: "Have fun,
Take part in the game,
Find who you are,
Join the team
Be in Peace, be well.

The Witness was at Peace, he was calm. He knew that in this form he would soon die, but his daughter Samata, his continuation, was there in the vastness of space—safe. She and other beings from the new race would create a better civilization where the Laws of the Father would be remembered and respected by all, where love would be as common as hatred is now. He felt dizzy, and an increasing heat in his body. His cells were dying due to the lethal radiation. He knelt on the broken bricks and concrete rubble facing the direction from where he had come—India. Then he chanted three times aloud for the last time: LOKAH SAMASTAH SUKINO BHAVANTHU . . . OM SHANTI, SHANTI, SHANTI and prostrating in the dust, died peacefully, merging for Eternity in his Guru – manifestation of the Father of creation, Preserver of life and Executor of Destruction in the Universe. His chant was for a peaceful start of the new Wave of Life. Only minutes after the destruction had taken place, he sowed the seeds of love and peace in the still warm ashes of life on the planet once proudly called by her inhabitants, Earth.

The Commander switched off the monitors on which the spaceship crew had been watching the last moments of human civilization on this small planet. The Witness' eyes had been used as a video camera, and through his transmitter at the base on the Moon, had been sending the pictures. Now the last witness had died. His mission was over.

THE TREE

The Witness was half way through packing his personal belongings, as well as the ashram tools, for his trip to the Big Town. He was going there to participate in the construction of another of Guru's monuments of compassion cast into concrete. The Witness felt a bit exhausted, and even agitated, because he had too much work to do these last few days. The demand for his service was very high— he was the only one present in the ashram that had access to the tools. The other people who usually did maintenance work had gone with Guru on the Tenth World Tour. Tonight, in spite of his fatigue, he had a good meditation on the roof of the temple building. He dove deep into Silent Peace, but came back spaced-out and withdrawn. *Bhajans* in the temple had already begun. This was not his favorite part of the daily routine, but he went to *bhajans* anyway, because he had decided to overcome his likes and dislikes.

At first, his experience was dry and artificial, but after a while he managed to tune into the *bhakti* vibration. He drifted into a meditative state and spontaneously started to experience, what may have been, one of his previous lives: he was an oak tree. All of this happened a few hundred years ago, probably in a forest of England or Scotland. A healthy, eight year old oak tree was growing some forty meters from a path. The forest around him was relatively dense but not very old. He could see travelers passing. He was experiencing everything that was happening in visible proximity of him as a tree, and he was also fully aware that he was a human-being, sitting in a temple in India, listening to *bhajans* sung by the ashram residents. The experience was very clear on both planes of existence. All was happening simultaneously.

He enjoyed his life in the body of an oak tree. He felt invigorating juices circulating through his trunk and branches, distributing the water and mineral salts delivered by his roots from the rich, brownish, fertile soil. His leaves were light green and very fresh. He guessed that it was probably late spring because fully developed oak leaves are usually a much darker green. The oak had full consciousness of being a tree, and the capacity to hear, see and feel. He could not understand the human language he heard from the travelers on the path, but having a well-developed intuition, he was able to feel the mental and emotional conditions of people as they passed.

Most of the people were wearing short red skirts and sandals that tied with strips of leather from their ankles, up the calves of the leg, nearly to the knees. He guessed that they may have been Roman soldiers. He knew that there must be a town or a castle near his forest, but he accepted the fact that he was not mobile. Despite this, he was very satisfied and even happy. A few times in the past he had tried to think of what he could eventually want, but he could not find anything worthwhile. The rich soil was giving him nourishment; frequent rains supplied water; fire was not a great risk since the forest was of a moist and cool nature. He was happy sharing his shade with the resting animals and, occasionally, the humans. He was giving shelter and protection to birds, squirrels, millions of insects, caterpillars and other creatures. One of his branches, which died and dried up several years ago, had become hollow, and a small colony of wild bees had made it their home. The humming noise the bees made was very pleasant and calming. All the neighboring trees were much younger than he. Some were elm trees, two from the road side, some were silver birch and many, many small oak trees that were his children. Every Autumn, the wild pigs that delighted in the seasonal feast spread his acorns far from the place where he was growing.

Today, the afternoon was sunny and pleasantly warm. He shifted his consciousness to an outstretched branch between the two small, silver birch trees toward the road. The ability to move his consciousness at will from one part of his body to another was compensating, somewhat, for his inability to move about freely. Just then he heard a horse galloping hurriedly toward town.

After a while he started to see the rider. It was a young man wearing dark green, nearly black clothes, and black, skillfully forged light armor. The man was armed. Hanging on his left side was a sheathed sword, and on his right calf, a dagger. Behind the man's belt was another dagger.

The Witness, as the oak tree, felt that the knight would rest under his shady branches. It happened exactly as he predicted. The knight got down from his horse and leaned against one of the oak's low branches, and his horse started grazing on the delicious rabbit cloves growing in the shade of the forest. While resting, the knight anxiously scanned the forest with his blue eyes. The Witness, in his human manifestation, sitting cross-legged in the South Indian temple, realized that the young knight was an earlier incarnation of one of the western residents present during *bhajans*. He did not know how he recognized it, but he was confident that it was Amer D., whom he had occasionally spoken with a few times during the past two months.

In the realm of the past he felt another person approaching: it was a girl or a very young lady wearing a long flowing dress. She looked sixteen years old, at most. She saluted the knight and knelt in front of him, but the knight immediately lifted her up and hugged her. After the short greeting he started to talk. The Witness, in his manifestation as an oak tree, could not understand the words but felt that the knight was trying to explain, and maybe convince the girl about something. Unfortunately, the girl did not listen at all. She was gazing at the knight's face with adoration and love, entertaining very worldly feelings, and probably the desire to be hugged more or even kissed. The oak tree felt her 'beingness' as something different than the other humans he had met before. He felt her to be more like a vegetable or a plant soul only wearing a human body. The meeting did not last long as the knight was in a great hurry.

The Witness saw the knight again after sunset. This time he met with a few similarly dressed men. They talked in great secrecy about some important matters, possibly political. It seemed to the oak tree that they were getting ready for a war, maybe to free the country from invaders, perhaps the Romans. The vibration of their minds was positive, and created a strong golden aura around all the participants of the meeting. After they finished the talks, they said some sort of a prayer together, and finished with a chant that sounded like a horn that's blown before a battle: ooommmuuuu . . . Accidentally, the chant happened at the same time the ashram residents in the Indian temple chanted: Om . . . Om . . . Om . . . after bhajans and the evening prayers. In the Witness' mind, both chants blended together creating a mixture of explosive power. Tears started to roll from his eyes, and he began to have trouble breathing. It culminated in a long. The Witness, who in this life was already living twenty-six years beyond his predestined life span, realized that time is only a conventional part of this Grand Illusion called Maya.

The happenings from the past happen right now, and all that will happen in the future has already happened long ago. Time was invented by the mind only to measure its own activities. In Reality, in the World of the Oneness, time does not exist. The film of Maya is completed by the Creator, the greatest master of illusion, and is stored throughout eternity on 'cliché', in the so called Akashic Records. Those who, thanks to the grace of the Oneness, have access to this library of happenings, can watch any sequence of this Divine Play, just like in a video library, and find hidden teachings and instruction in each act of the drama. For others, it can just happen from time-to-time, spontaneously, as it had just happened to the Witness.

THE ILLUSION

The Guru Bhava program in the ashram had just started a few hours ago. This evening the Guru was wearing green clothes. Not only the ashram, but also the atmosphere of the entire village was vibrating with mysterious Divine Energy. Most ashram residents and visitors participated in the program by just being present in the temple, singing bhajans, or doing some seva around the complex. Those lucky enough to be close to the Guru were experiencing His presence to the fullness of their being. The Guru, charming as always, had time to listen to the stories and the complaints of those receiving His *darshan*, and to counsel them; and at the same time, by His looks, words and gestures, guided, supported and corrected those sitting around contemplating Him.

It was after 11:30 p.m. Andy had already finished his work in the kitchen. He and six other ashramites had washed a huge pile of cooking vessels of different sizes and shapes. Some of the pots were made from aluminum, others from hand-beaten copper. A few pots were of such an enormous size that it was impossible to reach the other side of the pot without walking around it. The monster pots, designed for use on open fire stoves, are still very popular in India. These pots are ideal when cooking for the thousands of devotees who visit the ashram on Guru Bhava days, Christmas, New Year, and the Guru's birthday celebration.

Now, after having bathed and changed his clothes, Andrew was sitting on the porch of his hut. He was just beginning his late-night Guru Bhava meditation. On his left, hidden in the darkness of the night, was a pond pulsating with the life of frogs, fish and water birds. It was surrounded by a few coconut palms that seemed to bend toward the water as if in a salute to its life-giving power. In front of Andrew was a gravel road that stretched from the main entrance to the other side of the ashram where blocks of high-rise residential flats were under construction. Farther in front of him was a coconut grove and then a clearing, and in the distance another hut with another pond behind it. On the border of the coconut grove and the open space, stood a powerful lamp that had been installed a few months back. It was at least ten meters high. Its modern mercury light bulb gave ample light to the back of the ashram property. The light enabled people to walk safely at night from the cow shed to the main gate, or from under the Guru's house to the storeroom and the carpentry shop in the opposite corner.

Andrew was not able to concentrate very well. He was hearing *bhajans* being sung in the temple, the hum of the nearby sea, and most of all the sound of a mosquito trying to have its late night dinner on his blood. He opened his eyes, and what he saw first was a mosquito getting ready to land on his forehead. Andrew automatically speeded up the evolution of the mosquito's soul, which might, perhaps, return as an elephant in its next incarnation. Then, he noticed that behind a few coconut palms in front of him were two shining lamps.

The lamps were of the same height and not far from one another, maybe just two or three meters apart. He instantly realized that something was not as it should be. He was certain that there should be only one lamp. Andrew repositioned himself slightly, rubbed his eyes, and shook his head. Nothing changed. Two lamps were still in front of him! He stared with intensity and amazement at the phenomenon. He was aware that he was seeing an illusion and that in front of him there was only one lamp. However despite all his attempts to lose the vision of the second lamp, he still saw it very clearly. After a while, he noticed tiny particles around the lamps, maybe photons or elemental charges of energy vibrating, forming two individual, but intertwined, units. It looked similar to iron dust on a piece of paper when a double polarity "U" shaped magnet is located underneath. The particles were vibrating at a very high rate, obviously carrying a great deal of energy, but they were actually moving rather slowly. Especially interesting to watch was the interaction of the particles between the two lamps. The particles were accepting and, accordingly, adjusting to the presence of the second source of light without colliding into each other. The particles were accepting the appearance of a non-existing, illusionary lamp. Incredible!

Andrew was confident that there must be a reason for seeing all of this. He believed that the phenomenon must have been carrying a message containing a hidden teaching from his Guru. Nothing can happen without His intending for it to happen. What did He want to tell him, what should he be learning from this strange experience? Gazing at the second lamp, he thought the particles looked like 'well-trained bacteria parading under a microscope'.

Suddenly he understood that, through his physical senses, he always perceived only a distorted and fragmented picture of the world. He remembered what he had learned long ago: the human organs of perception cannot see the full spectrum of light; cannot hear the ultra and infra sounds so common and ever present in nature. He realized that even the first lamp was not real! Reality is permanent and the phenomenal world is transitory. It appears as real but its reality is as permanent as a reflection in a mirror.

He was seeing two lamps. One of them as part of the illusion called Maha Maya, the other as a second generation of Maya: illusion in an illusionary world. Andrew realized that his senses were only designed to protect his body from the basic dangers of the world. Even if he was exposed to radioactivity, his senses could not warn him. How then, can he expect his senses to perceive Reality? The senses belong to the unreal, the transitory world of things. Reality is beyond the perception of the senses. Andrew understood that he should look upon all material creation in the same way as he was looking at the second lamp, which did not really exist in spite of it being seen. He should see it; interact with it when necessary, but with the constant awareness of its unreality and inherent non-existence. This was the message! This was the hidden teaching presented in such an unusual way! The memory of the unreality of worldly objects would result in detachment from the world. It is impossible to be attached to, or desire something, when one is deeply convinced and constantly aware of its unreality. It is impossible to desire non-existing things!

After finishing his meditation, Andrew joined the others in the temple. Now he was watching another phenomenon: it was the phenomenon of the Guru. He looks like others; He wears a similar human body; He seems to be in a particular place performing some visible action; but at the same time, He is all-pervading and working intensely on many different levels of existence, simultaneously on many people, providing for everyone the experiences necessary to find the next step on their path to Freedom.

"What does this 'Freedom' actually mean?" Andy thought. It seems to be firmly established only in the conscious and subconscious levels of a mind convinced of the unreality of the manifested world. This will automatically result in total detachment. It is so simple that not many people will believe it, but this is exactly what gives us Freedom from the grasp of Maha Maya. This knowledge removes from us the identification with our body and mind, and annihilates petty desires and fears of the unknown. Who will tremble from fear watching a movie in the cinema while being aware of its unreality? The same can be applied to life in the world. What is left after eradicating wrong convictions is the same as the substratum of all—Reality, Consciousness, Love, Intelligence and God, our innermost Self. This knowledge opens the gate to an unimaginable, inexpressible and splendid world of unity in The Oneness.

The Guru *Bhava* program finished sometime after 3:00 a.m. At the end, the Guru, radiating Divine Love, showered everyone present with flower petals. This was the moment for which most had waited. Perhaps nobody understood the deep significance of this mysterious act, but all intuitively felt that something very great and very special was happening.

The following evening, when he sat in the same spot for meditation, Andrew was curious to see if the second lamp would still be visible. Only one lamp was in front of him. Then, he correctly understood the hidden teaching, and by doing so annihilated the illusion in the illusion, taking his next small step on the path to Freedom.

THE MINEFIELD

I n the air of the General's tent hung a deadly silence. Adjutants were packing old photographs, the memorabilia of the Colonel's promotion and the Captain's victory over his mind, the Lieutenants, Sergeants, Corporals and uncounted soldiers' souvenirs. The General, who was seated in a broad chair, was gazing on the greenery behind the window, seemingly showing no emotion on his face. He loved all of them; he was even attached to every single soldier, but he also knew that the destiny of his warriors had to be fulfilled according to their secret thoughts. The Army was afflicted by the mortal L.O.D. (lack of discrimination) virus. The disease was killing them one by one. There was no 'higher' in ranks or 'smaller' in status for it. The high rank uniforms meant nothing to this virus. The artillery of the enemy was, without a break, shelling bunkers of the General's warriors with ammunition of lethal doubts, fantastic desires, imaginations and aversions.

From the distant sandy path leading to the tent came the sound of someone's steps. All eyes turned towards the entrance. A soldier covered with dust and with a bleeding head rushed to the General. He fell onto the floor and staring at the face of the Commander-in-Chief, like trying to find an answer to "why?", whispered:

"Sir, Captain Ad-Too has left. He changed his uniform to peasant clothing and walked towards the jungle talking in a rave some nonsense about sex with one of your nun-nurses."

Through the sphinx-like face of the General a tear rolled down. One tear only but a very, very big one. The Adjutant's hands hung down. Immense heaviness overwhelmed their hearts. Who was going to be spared? Was there any vaccination available for this 'virus'?

All loved the Captain deeply. They believed that he was one without any blame; disciplined, hard working and positive-minded; ready to uplift others like a beaming lamp of love and compassion. He himself raised some, who in due time became officers in their own greatness. For years, the Captain looked after the finances of the General's army. The Captain, though seldom visible, was second in position after the General. He was in many ways unique; everyone ate rice, he chose to stick to chapattis. Now, even he was gone!

How many had left already? Colonel Maya was the first. He wanted to be a General himself. Long ago, he unsuccessfully demanded from Private Andrew to be promoted in Eastern Europe, where he was publishing a monthly magazine about the greatness of the General. After gathering sufficient funds he left to the North. There he was trying to create his own army. No one joined him, as his grand enemy was nowhere visible; it was hidden in his own mind and, as such, had to be fought by himself—alone. Next, the General's Personal Adjutant—Colonel left. He rightly decided that the General had no right to abuse him, and being tired of this war, which had been going on for over twenty-five years, he needed a permanent vacation. Because he was brave, left secretly like a thief, during the night, covered with a blanket; hiding on the floor of an associate's car. He later started his own business as a pearl dealer. His own adjutants and admirers followed him, which was a sign of loyalty and the ability to judge a situation correctly. All sneaked away secretly. Private Andrew also decided to leave. He did this, for a change, in the open. First, for his safety, he copied and secured on seven CD-ROMs some compromising evidence of the General's financial manipulations. He sent these to his lawyer on the Moon and later announced to each of the members of the General's army, that, 'this chapter in the book of life' had been completed and now he wants to go and 'read the next chapter' by himself. The General called him to obtain more information but the Private, being experienced in ducking from the KGB and CIA, said only a few nonsensical sentences. Seeing him so safely stupid, the General gifted him with a huge mango and wished all possible . . . in a hostile world without a war.

After those scandals, many lieutenants, sergeants, corporals and soldiers deserted their leader and left. Some joined another army, which did not fight any wars; some left for healing imagined wounds of indoctrination.

The General called the last four officers and said:

"Today we are going to attack our enemies. You, my dear ones, will lead my legions through the minefield. Whoever is afraid can leave now!" Immediately one of the officers left saying that he can't stand the noise of explosions. The remaining three (only three!!!), after having had a bath, changed their outfits for freshly washed ones, shaved their heads and went to the soldiers to give them last instructions. The General entered the state of 'No Perception'.

Heated by the sun, the morning fog disappeared. Through the fields rows of soldiers moved in silence. From time to time, the sound of explosions could be heard, like the fireworks in a Hindu temple during festival time. The vultures enthusiastically attended to tear to pieces the flesh of the bodies.

The General drifted to sleep. He noticed a demon hiding behind his tent door.

"What do you want here?" He asked. "I am ready to drag your soul to Hell! Did you imagine, stupid, that karma is not applicable to you? You misled so many innocent and naive people! Get ready!!! And one more thing: you can't take any of the wealth you collected!"

Suddenly a fear woke him up. He realized that he was lying under a coconut palm. Ants were biting his feet. There was no devil, if his wife couldn't be considered as one. She was standing over him, shouting loudly:

"Do you want us to become beggars? Go to work, you, you lazy dump . . . half-wit!" The dream was over. He realized that he was not a general but a carpenter, that there were no officers, no soldiers, only a few lethargic apprentices and sluggish laborers, and that there was no war, no minefield, no boxes filled with a treasure of gold and precious stones, only his ruined workshop, a backyard full of wood chips, four hungry kids, a fat angry wife, and a huge loan to pay back, taken from the local bank.

Thinking about cold beer, he had a lukewarm glass of coconut water and started to sand down the rawness on a door-frame; he was making it for the house, under construction, of a rich Muslim plumber who, after ten years working in Qatar and Dubai, had recently returned to India.

THE MAN FROM THE KGB DUNGEONS

All the men were playing cards, except David. He was lying on the floor of the carriage enjoying the warmth of the sun's rays entering through the bars of the window. It was the beginning of summer. The train, carrying prisoners in the last three carriages, was drumming on the lines, swallowing the kilometers of vast Siberian plains. The Ural Mountains had been left behind. David was already bored with looking out of the window. Nothingness. As far as one could see, nothingness! Slightly greenish nothingness! In his mind a story started to unfold.

He had gone to visit the town in Lithuania where he was born. One day he went to the market and bought some Georgian grapes. He was delighted. Never before in all his life had he eaten such heavenly sweet and juicy grapes. Unfortunately, the lady in the stall had packed them in a piece of the daily 'Pravda' (Truth), the official Soviet Communist Party newspaper. The slightly moist grapes quickly made the poor quality paper soggy and it started to fall apart. Some of the grapes fell onto the pavement. What a waste! David started murmuring his complaint,

"Idiots! How is it possible that in such a country, where people are flying to outer space, packing bags have not yet been invented?" He returned to the stall to ask for a more inspiring part of 'Pravda'. The lady became a bit nervous, but gave him a full front page with a photo of Rushchevin and U.S.A.'s President Onson. David remarked,

"Oh, the U.S. President; maybe with some Western help I will be able to get this home." He walked slowly towards a bus stop. He had not walked more than thirty meters when someone tapped him on the shoulder from behind.

"Hey, you! Where are you going in such a hurry?" David turned his head and saw a tall, young policeman and a short man in a gray overcoat.

"What's the matter?" he asked.

"You are under arrest for spreading dirty imperialist propaganda!" said the policeman. David was dumbfounded:

"What? Me? What are you talking about? I do not spread any propaganda! It's a mistake." Then, the man in the gray overcoat said:

"You, dirty servant of rotten capitalists, working for stinking dollars taken by force straight from the pockets of the American working class. You are Yankee rat. Shut up! You will tell your story at the right time." The young policeman looked a bit confused, but kept quiet only spitting on the ground in disgust.

David was handcuffed on the spot and the grapes, together with a picture of the very popular Secretary of the Soviet Union Communist Party, Comrade Rushchevin, ended up in the gutter. The policeman commanded David to follow them to the coffee bar Победа (Victory). He made a phone call from a rusty street booth with a window of tiny crystals of broken safety glass and in a few minutes an army type jeep arrived sounding an emergency siren. David was taken to the KGB's headquarters. There, both men led him to the officer on duty and, after checking his pockets and confiscating his wallet, David was immediately locked in a small cell. There was no possibility of explaining that he was innocent. Everything was done very fast and rough. He could not believe that it had really happened, and hoped that soon everything would be cleared up, and he would be released and allowed to go home. So he waited calm and relaxed, as only one can that is not guilty. After half an hour the metal door opened and two policemen threw a man onto the cell floor at David's feet. He was in an unbelievably miserable state. His mouth was dripping blood, his face was covered with bruises and scars, and his hands were covered in blood with some of his fingernails having been pulled out. He was rattling in an attempt to say something, but nothing articulate was coming out. To David it sounded like,

"Я не сказал" (in Russian: I did not tell.) David began to panic. He realized that this man had been terribly tortured.

"Are you all right?" he asked and then realized how silly his question must have sounded. Having nothing better, he took a handkerchief out of his pocket and started cleaning the man's face. The door opened again.

"Hey, you. Come!" The policeman in the doorway looked tired. His right hand was bandaged. David walked out of the cell trembling with fear.

"Go straight. Don't look sideways. Go! Move!" He walked as he was told. At the end of the hall was a door to the lift. They went down four or five floors. The underground part of the building was like an army's anti-nuclear bunker. Each room had a solid steel door. Everything was solid gray concrete. They entered one of the rooms. It had an area in the middle of about four square meters, which was tiled, and had a drain in it like a shower base. In the middle of the tiles stood a stool bolted to the floor, and in the corner of the room, a desk.

Behind the desk David noticed a man. He was hidden behind a huge reflector, a type of lamp used by military during night exercises. Another wave of fear passed through David. The man was wearing a brownish rubber mask on his head, which covered his entire face. He looked like a phantom from an American film David had seen a few years back. The door was closed from the outside. Only the two of them were left in the room. Silence. The phantom-like man was staring intensely at David.

"You stupid boy", he said slowly. "For what did you need all this?"

"I haven't done anything wrong. It's a mistake" David replied. The man continued:

"It doesn't matter if you are guilty or not. The fact is you ended up here. Our job is to prove your guilt. We cannot admit making mistakes! It would undermine our reputation. If you were arrested that means that you are guilty. Don't worry. We are experienced professionals in our trade. Now tell me, are you guilty or not?"

"Not at all, I am saying you arrested the wrong man", replied David.

"I already told you, it doesn't matter. You have to give evidence of all your crimes. You will speak, I know. No such heroes passed through our 'physiotherapy' rooms," said the rubber-masked phantom-like man.

"But I really have nothing to say. I have not committed any crime. I am a first year Polish student at the University of Mazury. I only came to visit the town where I was born. Please let me go home," pleaded David. The man in the rubber mask sighed, shook his head with disappointment and said,

"How silly it is to disagree with a senior KGB officer. When I say that you are guilty of conspiring with imperialists, undermining our revolutionary, unparalleled, humanitarian political system means you are guilty. I am going for a cup of coffee. On the desk are a few pieces of paper and a pen. Write down everything that you have done. Give names and addresses of all your friends and relatives. I will come back in fifteen minutes." The man in the rubber mask pressed a button on his desk and someone outside opened the door. David was left alone. First he tried to open the door. The solid steel door did not even make a sound. It was as if he was in a well—deep, deep under the streets of the town.

The minutes were passing fast. After twelve minutes he got up from the stool and walked towards the desk. He took the pen and paper. He wrote,

"I am innocent. I just want to go home. Next week I have exams. I have to return. I have not done anything wrong. I have had no association with American Imperialists. Please release me."

The door opened and the man walked inside, adjusting his mask. He asked,

"Have you finished your assignment, my student?" He took the paper, and reading it slowly shook his head with disbelief and disappointment.

"You really are an idiot my boy. Why do you ask for a session of physiotherapy? Why? We can make a wreck of you. We can make stones sing the 'Internationale' (a hymn of the international communist movement). You are young. Why waste your life? After a while you can return to a normal life, finish your university studies, get married and have children. I have a son, young like you but he understands that there is no point to oppose the 'system'. You are an idiot, an utter idiot. We are going to help you to become a hero!" He pressed the button on his desk. The door opened immediately and two men in blue overalls entered. Both carried long police rubber batons. The man in the mask said:

"Soften him a little bit. I am going for a walk. Don't be too hard on him. He is a debutante."

They chained David to the stool and laughingly said:

"We are very sensitive men. We don't like noise." And they put upon David's face an army gas mask with an absorber. The beating started on his back. He felt terrible blows on his shoulders, then on his neck, head, arms, chest and things. The men were very experienced. They were doing it systematically, with great skill and knowledge of the human anatomy. They knew the most painful points. David screamed, but the gas mask sealed his face. No sound came through it. The beating continued. After a while his consciousness somehow separated from his body. He heard the blows, saw his tormentors, but felt no pain. It was like witnessing a madman beating a silent drum.

The door opened. The man in the rubber mask, smoking a cigarette, entered and said,

"Enough! Give him a wash. He's bleeding. I told you, cretins, not to be too hard on him. Why can't you use your brains? One more such incident and I will send you for a 'vacation' to Siberia." The terrible pain returned after one of the men in blue overalls poured a bucket of cold water over his head. They took off the gas mask. The man in the rubber mask said,

"Now student, go and have some rest. Think the matter over. I will call you later. Now I have urgent work to do. Go!"

David found himself in a different cell. It was on the same level as the room with the desk and stool. He could not sleep. The whole upper part of his body was hurting. He could not even lie on his back because it was too painful. Even breathing was a torture. He was determined to ask to see someone higher than the man in the rubber mask and demand to be released. This was a tragic mistake. It was impossible and unacceptable to treat a foreigner in such a way. Four hours passed; then he was called to the same room. The man in the rubber mask was tired and sitting on the top of his desk. Without any words he showed David a stool, inviting him to sit.

"Did you, student, come to your senses? Would you now write your testimony, or do you need an extra session of physiotherapy?" David replied that it had gone far enough, and he demanded to be allowed to meet a superior in the KGB, immediately. The man in the rubber mask laughed sadly,

"You boy, are in the dungeons of the real rulers of this 'free country'. Here you have no rights to demand anything. Here you are nothing more than a reference number on a file. We decide what you can do and say. We can change you so much that you will even think, as we want." Again he pressed the button on his desk, and again the two men entered. The man in the rubber mask said,

"Take him for ten minutes to the electro-massage room, and then for one week to the wet apartment. Let him ripen."

When David regained consciousness, he found himself lying on the floor of a room, covered with damp green moss. He did not remember anything. Probably one of his tormentors had mercifully hit him on the head, knocking him unconscious before they started the 'electro-massage.' His hands and legs were burning, as if a red-hot iron rod had touched them. He realized that he had been burned by the use of electricity. He was so exhausted that he didn't even try to change his position to a more comfortable one. He just stretched his legs and closed his eyes again. He wanted to cease to exist. He had reached the end of his endurance. Suddenly he felt someone's hand gently touching his raw shoulder. He hissed with pain.

"Welcome home son. What have they done to you? Try to sit. Here is some food and water. You must eat and drink. You must survive! This is only a short bad dream. You are going to be free again. You have been born to be Free. Eat now." David opened his eyes. An old man was kneeling next to him. His face was covered with bruises and scars, but glowed and his eyes radiated warmth and something pleasant but so strange that David could not define.

"Who are you?", He asked the man.

"I am your older brother. I am 'resting' here too on the way to do my job in Siberia. They have their ways, we have ours. No need to try to change the system. It will collapse in due time because it is built on fake foundations. Guaranteed! Now sit and eat, my son." The old man said,

"You must realize, my boy, that from here you can come out alive only if you give them what they want. You must lie if you are innocent, making up the expected story for them. Otherwise you will suffer a lot and end up in the nearby forest where they store notorious heroes in a horizontal position, silenced forever. Be reasonable. It is not worth trying to prove that you have a strong will. They are trained to break heroes like you. Their teachers were the cruelest Gestapo sadists. It would be silly to die so young. You also have work to do. You have a life mission! You must come out of here alive. Don't stop, eat, its not old and moldy bread. It is the Highest, nourishing you and strengthening your body. Eat HIM. You body is built from Him!"

Later they had a few more talks. David did not understand many of the things the old man was talking about, but felt radiating from him a power of something very positive, very uplifting, something intuitively known but now forgotten.

The following week, after a partial recovery in the green, wet, moldy room, David again met the man in the rubber mask. He was greeted like an old friend.

"Oh! My student! How are you? How was the vacation? Did you come to your senses? What is your story now?" David bent his head down.

"I have no story to tell, but I want to get out of here. I want to live. Please make my story according to your needs, and I will confirm it as the truth. I have just had enough. Don't torture me again, please.", said David with entreaty in his voice.

"Bravo, bravissimo my boy. You learn ever so well. Well now, this is acceptable. We have great storywriters. I will take care of the technical side of this and you now have to recover fast. You are going to be a TV star next week." David was sent in an armored truck to a country retreat—a recovery prison. The food there was excellent and the beds were covered with white, lice-less bead sheets. He was even given fruit and milk every day. He also had to walk for two hours daily in the sun to regain his normal complexion. One week later he was driven back to the 'concrete palace.'

The man in the rubber mask, very proud of his work, presented him with a four page story of how he was drawn into propaganda and diversion work, how he was paid by the imperialists with a Casio wrist watch, a Sony walkman, and two pairs of Levi Strauss jeans— all smelling of rotten capitalism, how he was implanting doubts about his country in his fellow students' minds, how he wrote letters slandering communist leaders to his uncle in America and so on and so on. Luckily there were no names and addresses of his relatives or friends. David signed it without a word. The man in the rubber mask took him to the room opposite. There the barber neatly cut his hair and shaved him. David was then dressed in a new white shirt, tie, and surprisingly, the right sized jacket. After a small amount of make-up was applied to his face, somebody else took him to a TV studio on the sixth floor above ground. The interview was short. He was told to answer only 'Yes' and nod his head in confirmation of his treacherous crimes committed against glorious communism.

The next day, the Moscow evening TV news announced the shocking revelation: "Expert security forces of KGB had seized another well concealed spy who had been pretending to be a student from Poland. The dirty servant of imperialism was recognized and unmasked. The heroic working class of the Soviet Union can sleep soundly. The righteous hands of communist law are holding him. He will be punished according to his crimes. He obviously deserves to be sentenced to death, but the merciful administration is sending him for re-education to the labor camps, as only the sweat of hard labor can wash the dirt off of his hands."

The trans-Siberian express train was speeding along in a mad rush. David was still dwelling on the past. His co-travelers were now talking about Siberia. He opened his eyes. Someone experienced said:

"Comrades, we all have death sentences. We are going to Kolyma, to the uranium mines." Silence. Deadly silence. If this guess was correct, they were going to meet their end—death in the terrible 'arms' of leukemia and various cancers. David was shocked. Could it be true? Did such mines really exist? Was it right to have signed that absurd statement and disgrace himself only to die now in such an idiotic way?

Hours were passing. All were immersed in private and very sad thoughts. The train entered the taiga—the unending Siberian forest. Late in the afternoon the train stopped. Something was happening. Maybe food? Everyone was hungry. The guards unbolted the doors and ordered everyone out. Silence. Fear hung in the air. Maybe an execution? Shooting a few just for a fun? The guards were running around like crazy with their 'Kalashnikovs' AK-47 machine guns. Dogs were barking. It was a timber loading station. From here wood of murdered trees from 'безграничная,' the unending, boundary-less taiga, were carried by rail to the paper factory near Baikal Lake and there converted into the paper on which 'Pravda' (Truth) was printed; the newspaper, which mercilessly uncovers the Western conspiracy to undermine the 'freest country in the entire world', the glorious Soviet Union.

The prisoners waited in rows. On another line stood another train, and it also had the so-called 'slave carriers', carriages used to transport dissidents and community outcasts to the Siberian Gulag Camps. The guards talked with each other, and then they opened the sliding doors of the other carriages. There were women prisoners as well. The guards told them to get out and the announcement was made,

"You are all the enemies of the state, scoundrels and dirty sub-humans. You should all be killed, but due to our mercy, you can have some entertainment. Those women are criminals like you. Take them for one hour and make love as much as you want." The men went crazy. Many were there after years in prisons and working camps. They grabbed the nearest woman and ran to the closest hiding place. David did not know what to do. He was ashamed. He had never done it. He was a virgin and felt uncomfortable in this situation. Most of his companions were already trying their best. Suddenly someone touched his back. It was a young girl, no more then seventeen years old.

"My name is Natasha. Can we talk?" David woke from his shock and answered,

"Yes, if you like. I am David." They looked around as though to find how and where to run away.

"Let's go for a walk." she whispered with a trembling voice. Taking David's hand, she pulled him towards the pile of pine tree logs, stripped of bark and waiting for their turn to take part in raising the level of consciousness of the working class. They walked hand in hand like young people used to do on the boulevards of Paris, London, or even Moscow or Leningrad. David asked her why she was here and what she had done. She said,

"Nothing really bad. I just talked to a student, friend of mine, about Jesus of Nazareth. We found His picture in a book in the library. They arrested me for religiously influencing a healthy materialist, communist party member and son of the second Communist Party Secretary from the clothes factory «Красная Звезда» (Rus.: "Red Star"). They caught me and sentenced me to three years in Siberia. I'm afraid! I am very afraid." They sat on a heap of brown pine bark. The fragrance of the pine resin was overwhelming. Natasha started to talk in a soft calm, but sad voice,

"Why do we have to meet like this? Why can't we go to the cinema or theater? I would like to see a good play. Are we dreaming? I want to awaken from this dream! I'm tired of it. I don't like it at all. David, I have known you for only a few minutes, but I feel that you are going to be a free man. Don't laugh! I really feel it. Don't you know that women are more intuitive? I don't know about myself! They say that in Siberia no one respect ladies. Guards use them as they wish and they can't say a word, because, if they do they will be beaten and locked up for a freezing night in the so called 'dog-kennel boxes'. Do you know what they are? They are boxes made of wooden sticks with gaps between. They are less then eighty centimeters high and stand out in the open. Only few survive—most are frozen to death." Suddenly she turned towards David and said,

"I'm afraid. I don't want to go there. David, I have never made love. I don't want a drunken guard to be my first man. David I want you to be the first. Have you been with a woman before?" He shook his head.

"No? Then we are the same. Come on, they will try to destroy us but we will hang on to the memory." And they made love on a fragrant heap of brown pine bark like two lovers who had known each other for a long time. Their only guide was an instinct and a witness—the reddish disk of sun hanging low over horizon.

Afterwards, they lay on their backs and talked about their childhood, family and school. Natasha said,

"David, I am really grateful that we have met. With you I have forgotten my miserable destiny. With you I felt for a while that I am free. Don't say anything. We will never meet again. Siberia is vast, unbelievably vast. Only the strong can return from here. I am not so strong. Do you know the stories from the Bible? You have the name of the man who, with only a sling, killed the mighty armed Goliath. You too will conquer this totalitarian system. You will free yourself, and maybe even help others to do the same. Go, go now! I don't want to see your face anymore. I have imprinted your existence on my mind. In the higher dimensions we are one and ever free. Go, go, go, and going you will never go." Poor David did not understand much of her talk and was confused, but got up and looked at her once more. She was sitting calmly, gazing into space as though watching a film about something that is going to happen.

People say there are no such things as miracles, but a miracle happened. The last two carriages somehow separated from the rest of the train. But the prisoners' happiness soon changed to panic when they realized that they were rolling backward and steadily increasing speed as the railway line had been going slightly uphill. It was not noticeable through the window, as the whole countryside looked flat. There was no definite reference point, as the whole Siberian wilderness was overgrown with spruce trees. It was nothing else, only a ride towards certain death. Here, in this Great Nothingness, nobody would rescue them. They were locked inside. There was no escape. The guard in whose cabin the emergency brake was located had gone with the others to drink vodka.

Luckily, among them was a famous thief from Kiev, Ivan 'Golden Hand'. He was a genius at his trade. Somehow he had managed to smuggle a hacksaw blade through the prisons and 'physiotherapy clinics'. Now, without too much difficulty, he managed to cut through the steel bolt on the door. Looking out, they realized that at such a speed there was no chance to jump. David, the only one experienced in rock climbing, volunteered to try to cross the outside of carriage wall to the end where the guard's cabin was located with the hand brake. Any mistake would mean instant death. Somehow he was inspired by Natasha's words,

"You will be a free man. I feel it!", and was confident that he could even do the impossible. He did it with less difficulty then he had actually expected. He activated the brakes. The carriage slowed down and then stopped. For the moment they were all saved. The group waited for three hours for the next train. There was nowhere to go. For thousands of kilometers all around there was only taiga and nothingness. It was a prison with open, tempting gates, where death was waiting hidden between the trees. Later, the rescue train didn't manage to slow down completely. It hit the stationary carriages and derailed them. Due to this accident, all forty of them were taken back to the timber loading station, so memorable to all, instead of going to the Kołyma uranium mines.

After six months David was transferred closer to the civilized world, to the Kola Peninsula near Finland. There he joined the Gulag woodcutters. Winter had come. They were given 'vaciaki,' (thick cotton insulated parkas, pants, and hats), which covered their ears. It started to get colder and colder. The days were not so bad; they were short and most of the time sunny. But during the long nights the temperature often dropped to minus forty degrees Celsius. The snow cover was already more than one meter high. The guards introduced a new regulation. From now on, all the prisoners returning at sunset were obliged to bring back to the camp not less than twenty kilos of cut pieces of wood for the kitchen to use to cook their one meal a day, a soup made from horses which had died from starvation or sickness, potatoes, and cabbage, all with plenty of water from melted snow. The wood bundles were scrupulously weighed, and those who had not brought enough were sent straight to the tents without any food. One evening David was walking second from the end in a long line of prisoners returning from work. Behind him limped a handicapped banker of polish descent from Lvov who, during meeting, had inadvertently said that to discuss the financial strategy was a total waste of time as everything was in advance decided by Communist Politburo. He had forgotten that among his employees was the son of the local KGB chief. Close to the camp the banker lost his balance and stepped into deep, soft snow on the side of the track. He fell and lost some of his wood. He knelt down and tried to reach it, but the guard walking behind him impatiently shouted,

"Get up, hurry. Fast, fast, go, go, you son of a Polish bitch." The teacher tried to explain that it was his daily food. He was not well, and if he missed his dinner he might die. The guard did not want to listen. He shouted louder,

"Go, go, you bloody slave." When the banker, still kneeling, tried to gather his wood together, the impatient guard shot the poor man in the back, killing him, and then kicked him out of his way into the deep snow.

That night, David could not eat his meal and gave it to someone else. The next day while walking to the taiga and passing by the still fresh, red spots on the snow, someone from behind said,

"It's not the right way to escape. He's free now, but only from his body. Do you remember what I told you? Anybody can be FREE, we only have to rediscover who we really are." David looked back. Just a few steps in the rear, from a frost covered beard, were smiling the two radiant eyes of the Man from the dungeons in the KGB bunker 'physiotherapy clinic.' David recognized him instantly. Such eyes were impossible to forget, and on top of it he was still alive thanks to his advice.

"Who are you? Tell me! Are you God, to say such things?"

"Don't worry about me, boy. I have many names. Here they call me 'Fat Rat' because sometime I catch rats. Try first to find out what I have just told you. Find out who you are. It will take time but only then will you realize that in fact it is not you, me or them. All of it merges into The Oneness. Why be upset when one of the waves disappears as a separate manifestation, and merges, dissolving in the waters of the ocean? Will it affect the ocean? Think in terms of the totality and you will become one with entire creation! Afterwards, you will be Free, much freer than those guards or those who are not in the GULAG camps. Real freedom is not external but internal and as such cannot be taken away."

After a moth, just at the end of winter when all were weaken by poor food and cold weather another man was shut by the guard when tried to collect firewood he accidentally dropped.

A few months later another miracle happened. David was freed from the labor camp. How, without proper evidence or computers, and after so many changes the KGB headquarters order found him, only God knows. In the Red Empire the transitional political thaw had started. He was permitted to settle for sometime in Yakutsk, and after a year to return home.

The Free Man, the Man from the KGB dandeons, the man with shining eyes, had not been released. David met a few ex-prisoners who had remained longer than he in the camp. They had seen Him. He was still in Siberia, and from time to time was transferred from camp to camp. It didn't matter to Him. He was a FREE MAN. He didn't expect anything from anybody, but was ready to serve anyone, even a guard if ill or injured. He was doing the work the guards told Him to do, and when the opportunity came, he sowed the seeds of real Freedom into the ears of those who were fertile soil, who would grow and become beautiful flowers of TRUTH, and who were not interested in reading the 'Правда' (Truth) newspaper but in The TRUTH itself. Wouldn't he, being totally Free, be more Free somewhere else? He was the one who, amidst the snows of Siberia, and living in concentration camps, had grown to the peak of human possibilities. He himself had become one with The Oneness.

David returned home, finished his studies, and got married. He did some other stupid things, but he always remembered the words of THE FREE MAN. He remembered every single word of his teachings. He remembered it all, even in dreams. Sometimes he dreamt about Siberia, and talked in the dream to his great teacher, the Man from the dungeons of KGB.

After a few years he decided to find out what He was talking about, what is this 'The Truth', what is this 'The Oneness', and how does it feel to be really Free. He still didn't fully understand the depths of His message, but felt that there was something hidden between the words, something very great, something extremely magnificent. One day, he left behind the charms of 'the most humanitarian and noble' political system on Earth. He left the 'unparalleled country', ruled by the iron hand of the KGB in the name of the proletariat. He crossed the border of his safety zone. He entered the Unknown. He went on an unending quest. He became a Traveler.

He is still wandering around, still searching. We may meet him one day on the streets of Chicago or in Piccadilly in London, or sitting under an ancient neem tree on the banks of the Holy Ganges River in India. Maybe he is right now sitting on a bench just opposite you, wearing Levi Strauss jeans, and has a Casio wristwatch on his hand. He is determined to become as Free as the Man from the KGB dungeons, and he will succeed, because he believes in His words. The Man from the dungeons once told him,

"As a man thinks, so he becomes. What a man believes in becomes his reality." He may even go again to Siberia. In his mind, the hard work, the beatings and sleepless nights, the scratches from lice bites, the shouting of the guards and barks of their dogs, all hunger and cold, are overpowered by the memory of the beauty and purity of the Siberian vastness. In fact, he loves the air of the taiga; he loves the smell of the smoke from the wood fires made of Siberian spruce trees. He loves the gentle warmth of the Siberian sun during summer, and the crunch of the snow under his feet during the winter. He became a part of it and in this he made a small step towards merging with this mysterious 'The Oneness' the Free Man was talking about.

This is the end of a story, which is only a beginning of THE STORY.

THE CHRISTIAN BAJAN

The rainy season had ended more than a month before. The weather was now very pleasant; not too hot, not too dry, and even not too humid. South Indian nature was bathing in the greenery of tropical plants. Most of the evenings were clear. The sky looked like the open window to Infinity, sparkling with millions of stars. The moon, silent as always, watched the landscape.

He walked slowly, doing japa. The reddish clay sprang back under his feet. The clay had been shipped here in huge 'Ashok Leyland' lorries as landfill for the swamps. It was intended to become a housing area for the future staff of the adjacent hospital. The surface of the already filled section, where the truck wheels had polished the clay, shone like waxed plasticine under the light of the moon.

From the distance he heard the exalted voice of the mullah reading the prayers through the loudspeakers in one of the nearby mosques. It blended with the melodic but monotonous Sanskrit chanting of the priest from the Hindu temple, "Guru Brahma, Guru Vishnuhu, Guru Devo Maheshvaraha . . ."

A few kilometers to the south, on the other side of a large swampy lake, fireworks exploded in the air, like a handful of colorful sparks thrown to the sky as an offering to the Eternal One. Devotees of Jesus Christ were celebrating Christmas in their church. How wonderful was the unity in the diversity of the paths. All of it was happening in praise of The Oneness, that all-pervading unchangeable Reality! But the most eloquent, dominating of all, was the Silence, that dimensionless medium in which all sounds manifested. The Silence was whispering: I am who I am. All this is ME. Do not get entangled in the changing manifestations of ME. Find me in yourself! I live in you as Your own SELF."

He looked toward the buildings of the first two towers of his Guru's hospital. The monumental six storied lump of concrete and bricks stood on a swamp; as if in defiance of all the negative powers of the Kali Yuga civilization. It was really impressive. HIS unimaginable, infinite, mighty Love and Divine Compassion were assuming the finite form of the Institute of Medical Sciences and Super Specialty Hospital. The walls of the massive buildings echoed the distant sounds of the hymns in praise of God.

Suddenly, from the direction of the hospital project's vehicle workshop, the clear voice of Guru burst into the air. Brahmachari Ravindran was playing one of Guru's famous bhajans through the amplifier, "Jai Ambe Jagad Ambe . . . Mata Bhavani Jai Ambe . . ." Guru's vibrant voice, like a magic polarizing filter, segregated and put into one tune all other sounds. HE united all separate chants and songs into the one Grand Song of unanimous heartfelt worship of the Unmanifested and the Manifested.

On this night there was no fog over the swamps. He saw moving in the bushes, on the border of the hospital land, bluish sparks of fire-flies dancing to the sound of Guru's bhajan. All nature danced to His tune, even the bats flying low, catching the night insects.

What else could he want? Is there anything in the entire world worth desiring? How can he thank Him for all of his life's experiences? Will he ever be able to find the words to express his love, his feelings of oneness with Nature? It comes and goes, making it even more intense. He can cry in the joy of Bliss as much as he likes. How grateful he is that He thought of him to be a Witness and abide in Silence!

He wondered that if he, a beginner, is so intoxicated with the excess of Love overflowing in his heart, in what state must his Older Brothers and Sisters be? How unimaginable must be the heights in which they are gliding, how close they must feel Him in their hearts.

He walked slowly back towards the 'Mosquito Farm', as he called the project's guest house. The ground trembled and swayed in the shock of a sudden immense explosion. It was probably in this way that the Christians, celebrating Jesus' birthday in the church across the lake, accented the Elevation during the mass. Between the distant coconut palms glittered red lights made of paper; balloon-like Christmas stars hung from the houses of Kerala's Christians, or on nearby trees. It looked a little bit like the glass balls which decorated the Christmas trees in his old country in Poland, but here they spread all over the horizon.

In Eastern Europe, Christmas is in the wintertime. Here there is no snow and no bells on the horses pulling the sleds towards the valley hidden between the mountains, where lies a small wooden church with a Jesus on the cross, carved from a linden tree log made by the village's genius artist.

Here, all that was, all that is, and all that will happen are contained in HIM—his Satguru. All in All; God of Gods. One and only one True Reality. His Road and Destination. Living between us, the Incarnation of the HIGHEST.

SECRET CONVERSATION OF A SMALL PAGE

The Strength

My little ones, it is already time to go to bed. Lie down comfortably, relax and close your eyes, darling wags. Be serious for a while, please. I will narrate to you a strange story. But do not think of it as another old legend, or believe that it is all true. It does not really matter. Just listen, and absorb from it the essence or Real Truth spoken once by the gentlest creature ever seen by a human being.

This story happened long, long ago in a country called Aham Ayam, which was located on a big island in the middle of the cold and stormy Hearing Sea. But in fact it happened not so long ago, not at all. The fragrant wood smoke from the castle's kitchen stoves still tickle the nostrils of those who sometimes aimlessly wander among its ruins. And the fuss made by the cattle returning for the night from grazing in the fields still echoes there. In the days when all of this happened, the castle was in excellent repair, and not in ruins as it is nowadays. It all began one warm, late April night. It was already dark, but the enormous disk of the full moon glazed the landscape and the castle fortifications with its cold, silver-greenish light.

On the high tower built of gray stone, sat a small page. He was still a boy, more or less a dozen years old. He was alone, very, very alone. Dressed in red plus-fours and a green velvet jacket, he looked funny, like a mascot. On his knees he held an instrument resembling our contemporary mandolin. The small page was sad and love-sick. The entire world seemed for him a dark, merciless hell. Full of sorrow he sang the song of his broken heart and shed tears big as real pearls.

"O, pure plum tree

I love you, can you love me!"

Absorbed in the song coming from the depth of his aching soul, and being under the anesthesia of his immense pain, the small page did not notice that just a few steps away from him a stony flap covering the entrance to the internal, spiral staircase for warriors opened, and in it appeared a strange but not terrifying white head. It was huuuuge, much bigger than the heads of bulls or horses. It was covered with white hair and looked spotlessly clean. On both sides of it, sticking out like radar antennae, were big ears. They moved rhythmically, similar to the ears of an elephant fanning the air. From its face a pair of brownish, favorably disposed eyes, which were full of Wisdom yet still playful, looked at the small page. The creature murmured in a low voice and winked a few times, showing by this gesture a deep concern for the small page's miserable state, his broken heart and immense pain.

"Is anything the matter?" it asked gently.

"How cruel one 'of this world' must have been to drive you, my boy, to look for love among the trees. But it is good, from time to time, to be a little romantic. Don't cry! I am bringing you buoyant news. Cheer up! You will be told where to look for the infinite Ocean of Love. You will be guided step by step. Finally you will find it in the most unexpected place you can think of. Then you will rest there, fully satisfied forever. Shall I do that for you?" The small page jumped.

"What is it? Am I dreaming?" The white creature was still in the manhole. Seeing it he pinched himself painfully three times. Now it was even smiling and nodding its head as if saying,

"O yes, I do mean it". Trembling from fear, the small page fixed his eyes on it with wonder, but was preparing to die in its mouth at any moment. There was no escape! The creature was blocking the way to the staircase, and the tower dominating the surrounding castle wall over twenty meters away. To jump down from it to the shallow moat was unthinkable. The creature crawled out of the opening, and now the boy realized how enormous it was and how beautiful. It was longer than two horses but not so tall, as it had only six very short legs. It looked like a huge weasel, but its face resembled the faces of both a human and a Pekinese dog. On its sides were folded wings similar to those birds have. It smiled charmingly, squinted one of its eyes, and lying comfortably on the stony slabs of the floor said,

"Do not be afraid! I am Care Monster and will not harm you. I promise! I came only to help you because I know how badly distressed you are. Come closer, my boy. Sit with me for a while. Let us talk. You can even lie on my paw and be completely relaxed. Come! Be brave! You have to have strong nerves to be able to victoriously face your fate. You want to be happy, but happiness can only be attained by the strong ones. Those who are weak-minded are doomed to be always miserable and unhappy. They will always be victimized by others, and, what is even more dreadful, by their own fluctuating, mental states. They would live as slaves under the sway of external conditions. They will be incapable of even making the right judgment when presented with opportunities and possibilities. The mollusks, like molly-coddles, are good for nothing. They even tremble seeing their own shadow. A Traveler like you, on the quest of everlasting happiness, must be strong in body, staggering in mind, and firm in rightness of character. These qualities can only turn up in strong and heroic individuals as they are the offspring of strength. From strength is born fearlessness. So be strong, be fearless! Greatness is life. It expresses itself as harmless strength. Misery is decay and death. It expresses itself as destructive anger and aggression. Your state of greatness or misery depends entirely on your state of mind. 'As is your mind, so are you', say the brownies, and I, Care Monster, confirm it as the very truth. Think!"

The small page opened his mouth in utter amazement and walked, pulled by some invisible magnet of attraction, towards Care Monster, who by now was comfortably reclined holding only a little part of his fluffy tail in the opening to the staircase. The small page kneeled close to the mysterious visitor.

"Who are you? I've never heard about Care Monsters! How can you exist? No one ever saw you before!"

"Ha, ha, ha. You are a cleverer fellow than I expected, my boy. Later I will tell you the whole truth, but for now let us still be a small page and Care Monster. You are in distress and this makes you receptive to my words about happiness. What luck!

"Oh, I think that I have come just at the right time. If this heartless, plumpy courtier would have been more favorably inclined towards you, you would not listen to even a single word I say. I understand your feelings perfectly well, better than you can imagine. It all sounds terribly bad, but in the end it will give you much more good than a few thousand sinners like this one could.

"But now, my friend, let us get back to business. Listen to me carefully! The opportunity to hear what I am going to tell you will not be repeated in your life. In fact, only a very few of your 'brothers' and 'sisters' will ever have a chance to be exposed to such teachings, and even fewer will understand a small fraction of it. Perhaps one lucky one in many, many millions. But it is a rule that always when the prospective student is ripe, the teacher appears. So I am! If you will find enough patience to listen and make an effort, and to practice this what I say, you will be blessed forever. Are you ready? Are you seated comfortably? Let us begin then.

"All pleasures and pains, which we experience, my boy, come from our unreasonable, erroneous identification with the body, this fragile and easy to damage and spoil shell of flesh we are wearing. This faulty conviction is born from the ignorance of our True Nature. The goal of life is to transcend this body consciousness and regain understanding of who we really are. This is called Self-Realization. By being equipoised, steadfast and serene we can surpass the world with all its impermanence. Those who manage to develop such an attitude automatically convert all adversities to their advantage and use them as opportunities to grow in understanding of the Laws of Nature. We can even become unperturbed by the transmigration of our personalities from one body to another life after life; as happens to all of us. Death will stop terrifying us when we understand that it is nothing more than a preliminary and obligatory step to a new life. In such a way we can gradually train ourselves for the sunrise of Awakening to Reality, I mean for the swim in the Infinite Ocean of Love. By remaining unruffled by the turbulent happenings around us, we will gain clarity of vision, like a sharp-eyed hawk that watches the fields below from the giddy heights on which he glides motionlessly. We will understand that what is fluctuating, what is changeable, cannot be considered by the intelligent being as Real and as such has no right to actual existence and should not be taken seriously. It is only a temporary and quickly passing modification of elements. On the other hand the Real, as permanent and unchangeable, can never cease to exist, to be. Why then worry? Why think about this silly girl who is as changeable as the flag on the castle gate in a gusty wind. All that is needed to reach the top of perfection is a mastering of the use of the power of discrimination between the Real and the unreal, between right and wrong. Those who know this superior method can experience the Truth we call Reality. When they accept this Truth as their own and re-establish a relationship with it on all levels, their minds continue thereafter to exist as Pure Awareness. They are not affected, not touched by time, space and causation. This Pure Awareness is Absolute Reality. A perfectly fulfilled life can be led only by one who has succeeded in regaining this identification with the Absolute, Pure Awareness or if you prefer, Cosmic Consciousness. Small page, listen carefully; you are That!!! You are not this body clad to please a King in so funny a dress, not those legs that are thin as sticks, not this long faced head and not even your heart, brain or eyes. None of it! This is only your temporary costume. Do you stop existing when you change clothes? You, the Real You, are the Eternal Witness, the Infinite, Immutable, All-pervading Consciousness. This Awareness is a substratum of everything that exists. You were neither born nor will you die. From time to time you will cast off the worn out garments of your successive bodies, but you will stay unaffected by this process. In the entire Universe there does not exist a power which could destroy you or even cause you the smallest harm. This Awareness is Indestructible and Untouchable to all existing forces. The fear of death is based on the instinct of self-preservation of the body. It holds strongly only those ignorant ones in whom the body consciousness predominates. The Knowledge of our True Nature and its permanency automatically frees us from this misery.

"Remember this well; never grieve for the living nor for the dead, because neither are Real, and by their inborn nature they can't exist forever. Only Real remains the same. It is not affected by the modifications occurring in space and time. This is declared by all the ancient scriptures of the world preserved by Wise men. Nowadays rarely does anybody read them. But the meaning of their statements always remains current and topical, as it is universal. It does not advocate indifference towards the living or dead. Not at all! It means that what has a beginning has to come to an end, what was born must eventually die. This is the natural order of things.

"Our bodies manifest for a short, in the cosmic scale, time, and only for a certain purpose. Bodies are propelled by the force of their innate tendencies, which are expressed as desires. To fulfill desires action is necessary. This causes the movement of elements which science calls life. Where there is life there is motion, where there is inertia, death reigns mercilessly. I would like to repeat this once more. Existence cannot be lost. That which is going through constant changes is only the myriad of shapes and names. They don't last, just like soap bubbles made by the happy daughter of the castle washerwoman. The same entity in different stages of its ever-changing life will be called by different names. It can be in the beginning baby-child, darling son; some years later it will be a naughty teenager, then it could be a brave warrior, loving husband, father, until soon it will become an old grandfather, widower and at the very end a cold corpse. We are acquiring for each incarnation new bodies of varying sizes, shapes and models, but they are always perfectly suited for exhausting our accumulated urges. It is a chain reaction; veiled by ignorance, the intellect creates mundane ideas, feelings and desires; the mind entertains them as thoughts and all end as our actions. The actions are only a movement of energy in space between many levels. Always the beginning is on a subtler plane and the final result is on a grosser. The results of actions are fed back to the intellect and the mind which causes acceleration of our risings and fallings into material existence, our births and deaths and the repositioning of elements by changing its sequence and condensation. This is called reincarnation. So it manifests itself a lower aspect of existence, material form of life. This small 'i', our personality, I, Care Monster, infamously call "Oge". It is a most ugly entity. Unfortunately it is made by ourselves. It is touchy, selfish, arrogant, jealous, and lustful. It always demands attention, and is never satisfied. The more you, my little page, identify yourself with this monster, the more you suffer and the more you are confused when facing life's problems and challenges. It pretends, skillfully, that it is the Reality of our existence, but in fact it is only the distorted reflection of Awareness, conditioned and veiled by the many layers of the mind and the filters of the intellect. And what is this so powerful, mysterious mind? It is only a parade of thoughts, mostly silly ones I must say! Stop this parade and the mind disappears, as it has no independent existence. It is only a parasite living on the sap of thoughts. Just try! When you think of her, that heartless, selfish, greedy girl, you're in mental pain. Stop thinking or switch your mind with one-pointedness to the Absolute Reality and you will be in Bliss. To transcend the mind is exactly the same as to annihilate your deadliest enemy − your Oge. It is equal to regaining your Divine Sovereignty, with all its innumerable riches and powers.

"But possessing theoretical knowledge of the unreality of the material world does not sanctify your withdrawal from involvement. Not at all! You as an individual cannot renounce activities and stop performance in the game of life. It is a fact that you are this splendid Awareness and it is also true that creation is a super illusion. But . . . in this dimension in which you are now acting as an individual, you should perform your duties eagerly, as they are the means of fulfilling the very purpose of your life. If you are a warrior or a hangman you should kill without a second thought or the slightest blink of your eye, remembering what I said. Your appointed position sanctifies your actions. There will be no sin in those actions and they will not create demerits affecting your future. If you are not a warrior but a small page as you are now, you should sing for the King songs that are uplifting and mind calming. Do not feel sorry for yourself, rather feel obligated to be compassionate and helpful towards other beings; not only your brother humans but also the animals, plants and those beings which are present here, and also those who don't have material bodies like us, yet are very sensitive to humans' behavior and feelings. They can even suffer terribly if any negativity or falsehood is projected around them. You can help all of them; humans, animals, plants and bodiless spirits so much. Your songs can uplift them when depressed, and can open their eyes and make them understand and experience, at the very least, a slim, tiny glimpse of Truth. You would be surprised if you knew how well animals and plants understand our language, especially music. Plants also see!

"Tired? I am sorry but it is not the end. Listen! Despair is a gradual destruction, a sort of death in daily installments. It is self-annihilation, whenever it happens in one go, as in the case of suicide, or when it happens slowly by entertaining negative feelings or taking intoxicants, using drugs is a grave sin. But an even much greater sin than this is for man to fail to do his duty correctly and on time. Please understand when I say 'sin' I mean a serious mistake on the path of life. By doing such evil all that is in man called human is killed. On the other hand, a well-done job guarantees contentment. No one should have doubt. Nature may wink for a while, but in the end will see and punish the law-breaker through the law of karma. I will explain it later in detail as it is an important subject and needs a bit more time than we have tonight.

"Never fear difficulties. They will come from time to time and go after a while. It is guaranteed and it is a part of the game. The common reaction of cowards is to withdraw in the face of approaching trouble. By this they condemn their inborn right to be called humans. They also fruitlessly waste a great opportunity given them by birth in a human body equipped with the faculty of discrimination, an opportunity not accessible to animals, which must rely only on their instincts. Trouble? So what? Be glad! Do not complain! This is an excellent opportunity to grow, to make progress, to enter the unknown. One step forward on the way to the Goal Supreme is as important as a thousand steps. Don't you know that even the longest journeys start from making this most important first step?! Is it not great to overcome difficulties and solve problems? Those who are in the grip of paralyzing fear cannot achieve anything worthwhile. They are frozen in dread. Then be fearless! Dive deep into life! Don't look for supporting aids. Learn to swim in 'tempestuous waters' of events. Perform your duties as well as you can. Engage yourself in your small or big battles. Go and sing your song with pathos just a step or two from her, the worthless gadabout and tart. Ignore her! Let her do what she calls making love with this foul flatterer, that old and lustful King's Treasurer. Her greed and passion in due time will be punished. He will never give her the jewels and gold coins he promised as bait. He is not so crazy. If he does, his turn on the dais, kneeling in front of the well used stump to have his head cut off, would be as certain as tomorrow's sunrise. She pretends that she loves him only because of expectations, but later no-one will even be friendly with her. By then you will be swimming in the Ocean of Love. But when I think of your case I, Love Dragon, still assume that it is always better to have loved and relinquished than never to have loved at all. A firsthand experience of the selfishness and shallowness of worldly love is more valuable than any second hand ones. It can never be surpassed by the best discourses and lectures, not even mine.

"Do not imitate her in having expectations. Do your duty but do not claim the results. Renounce mentally the fruits of your work. If the old King pays you, accept it gracefully, but do not ask for money on every occasion or work only because eventually you will be paid. Work, because work has to be done and it happens that you were appointed to do this particular work.

"You, my boy, have already been told a secret about your real identity and general instructions on how to act in life. Believe me, Love Dragon never lies. The most important thing is that you put it all into practice and live accordingly, constantly keeping it in mind. Any knowledge without application has no value, just as forged gold coins. If you are eager and sincere in this life you can, if you wish, break the chains of your fate and become a Free Man. By being firm and determined in your mind you will see clearly the right and only sensible direction. Others will travel in circles endlessly, blind, anxious and uncertain on the 'thin ice of a lake', chasing the echo of their crying for help: ho, ho, hooo . . . . ho, ho, hooo . . . But you will stay perfectly tranquil. To operate any machinery we need the right tools and a basic knowledge of it. The mind is a sort of subtle machinery with its established ways of working. To be able to control it, it is necessary to posses the tool of concentration. This is forged in Silence, and we can gain it by the regular and consistent practice of meditation. To be able to meditate, it is vital to have at least a partly subtle mind. Preserve energy. Those who talk too much will never experience the Silence. For the mature, subtle mind to plunge into deep thoughtless meditation is as easy as for a duck to dive into the calm waters of a pond behind the castle orchards.

"The onward evolution is a gradual enveloping of Pure Consciousness in successive, increasingly heavy layers of identifications, ignorance and differentiations. There is an increase in the density of layers as they become grosser and grosser proportionally to immersion in the matter of the tangible world. We can call it also a conditioning. Meditation, if practiced correctly, is a total reversal of the process of such stupefying evolution. We can call it devolution. Under its impact all obstructing Reality layers get destroyed one-by-one.

"By examination of the mind we learn its rules, motives and patterns of behavior. Because knowing the nature of something is equal to having the power to control it, we will, through self-observation, become masters of the mind. By the power of discrimination we will direct its energy to those desirable and beneficial objects. From the fruits of such practice tranquility and detachment will emerge and this will send us a feeling of peace. Small page, do not be terrified when in the beginning of such practice instead of peace and tranquility, terrible negative ideas appear in your mind, pervasive desires and even hatred and rage. Just watch them. Do not be involved. Do not identify yourself with them. You cannot even imagine how much dirt we have accumulated in our subconscious through our many past lifetimes. This process of emergence of those abominable thoughts is necessary. It is a cleansing operation. Don't feel guilty. This is not you, only your stinking Oge is vomiting accumulated dirt.

"Human nature is constituted of three qualities: lethargy, activity and subtlety. By performing work selflessly you can sublimate yourself and become subtle. The more cleansed is man and the more selfless are his actions, the more potent he is in the mind and the more meaningful are his words and deeds! There are no shortcuts, believe me. And it is an indispensable prerequisite for successful meditation. Without mastering it the would-be adept will sleep soundly on the meditation seat or fidget restlessly as though placed on burning charcoal.

"But to become fully conscious of who we are, it is necessary to go even further and transcend completely this triad; body, mind and intellect and become established above the pairs of opposites; likes and dislikes, pain and pleasure and so on. We have to become effortlessly unconcerned, balanced and centered without distractions and deviations reflecting on our inner Self, which is this Awareness of Existence I already told you about, my small page. When living in such perfect harmony, in tune with ourselves, we will not need books, scriptures or teachers. We will become ourselves the mine of Wisdom about Life, Love and Awareness. It wouldn't be appropriate to go around begging for a glass of water while being immersed up to the neck in the ocean of sweet and refreshing nectar.

"If you will remember who you are, you will not be upset if the old King scolds you needlessly while in the throes of acute arthritic pain, nor will you think that the world is at your feet if he throws you a handful of gold coins. Be firmly fixed in equilibrium, experiencing both ups and downs with equanimity of mind. This will set you free from the fetters of birth in this low dimension. When you attain the state of utter subtleties and purity, those desires which seem all so meaningful now will drop by themselves as worthless, similar to dried up leaves in Autumn dropping from the trees. You will start to live satisfied in the ultimate fulfillment of yourself. This is what we call establishment in Wisdom. In that state it will be easy to withdraw the senses at will. The objects of the world will not draw your attention as they do now. You will be directed by intuition, and with the light of Wisdom you will remember the false reality of the world. Ignore its lures, and turn to the core of your beingness, to abide there in uninterrupted Bliss. But that is in the future. Before you get finally established in Wisdom, there is still a great danger that you can be unexpectedly carried away by the mind, poisoned by the excited senses. This can happen even if you are fairly advanced and feel confidently firm in your detachment from worldly charms. In the state of excitement of the senses the mind is automatically deprived of the ability to discriminate and at the end a fall is possible. But . . . if this tragedy happens, do not cry in desperation. Nothing is lost, as nothing is lost forever before the Final State. I, Love Dragon, always say that the greatness of the man is not in not falling but in the ability to rise higher after the fall. It is a human right to commit mistakes. This is called the process of learning through experience. But remember my boy, to repeat the same lapse, even once, is then a sin.

"The conquest of the senses is the most indispensable condition in the battle for perfection. The senses are controlled by the mind. Do not suppress the senses. It is not very good for mental and physical health. Learn to control the mind and direct its attention to something greater than those silly things. Watch the mind constantly! It is unbelievably deceiving. It can arrange such innocent situations that no one would suspect the hidden trap. But the seeds of attachment will be secretly planted and the mind, 'the master thief' will nurse it by creating a deeper familiarity with a person, than the seeming friendship to cover up subconsciously prompted cravings and in the end 'the dogs of war' will be released; I mean the desires will pop up to destroy the weak forces of Peace by projecting missiles of passionate thoughts and unavoidably an explosion of action will follow. From thoughts about sense objects grows the octopus of attachment to them. This sprouts when entertained as multitudinous desires. If desires get satisfied the attachment becomes well established and deeper rooted, producing more and more desires. Mind can never be permanently satisfied. If the desires are left ungratified, to starve slowly in the chains of will, they will unavoidably produce the malignant cancer of deadly, poisonous anger. The mind, under its influence, does not function properly. Affected by the toxin of anger, one enters a state of temporary delirium, a state of imbalance and almost madness. This obscures reason. Prolonged anger results in incurable insanity, which destroys the rest of reason, and with passing time gradually, step by step, the unfortunate individual himself. Anger, by changing the biochemistry of the body, induces psychosomatic illnesses. To be happy and healthy you have to be peaceful. As long as you are controlled and shattered by desires you, my poor small page, cannot be peaceful. Renounce then the desire for pleasures and the other things of this world as worthless, energy sucking leeches, and gain everlasting happiness in unsurpassed peace. To renounce desire you again have to have the right tool. For this you can use the sword of Wisdom, which can cut off the worldly bonds of attachment and expose the abominable inside of objects of temptation. Do not be afraid. You will not lose anything that is beneficial to you! Remember my boy, happiness is not the same as pleasure. Those two differ as completely as your King and his lowest servant, the castle garbage-man. It is not necessary that what is pleasant is good for us. One who follows a way of pleasure will become bound by attachments, and one who is after the everlasting happiness will get Liberated and will become Free. Be the latter one.

"Does it make sense? Yes. I think so, but one very important remark is missing. To build a castle we need a plan, and what is most important, the King's decision. Following the Path of self-remodeling, demands a commitment and a strenuous, determined effort with plenty of dedication and endurance. It is necessary to practice the prescribed exercises regularly and attentively. But when such an attempt is successful it leads us from the safety of the well known but limited realm of the senses to unlimited, splendorous realm of spirit not even expected by them. What is most frightening is that it is hidden in the uncertainty of being entirely unknown to the mind and intellect sphere. If we want to succeed we must possess knowledge of the psychology of the process and make a resolve to apply it and to be serious. There is in the beginning a doubt that with this we may lose or restrict our personal freedom. But when it is practiced with faith it becomes, on the contrary, an unimaginable source of freedom from all that which was previously hampering us as bondage and the delight of expansiveness. Even if we have knowledge and we make a resolve it is necessary to apply practice with self-commanded discipline. Imposed discipline is ineffective and naturally creates a negative counter-reaction and resistance. This leads to frustration by increasing our inner stress. Our powerful Oge is in the way and, being very touchy, it can't stand to be advised, or worse, directed by anybody. Obedience to the teacher guiding us on this difficult-to-tread Path, when it is executed with humility and reverence culminates as self-imposed discipline. So, the teacher has no other option than to shower the student with his grace, thus enabling him to proceed.

"But you must be tired by now, my boy. It is very late and I talk and talk. It is definitely enough for our first session. O yes! Are you surprised? We are going to have a few more instructive meetings! I feel that you do not understand much of what I am trying to explain to you. Never mind. In due time my words will bring a sweet and ripe fruit. Its taste will make you content as never before, as even you, little one, cannot now imagine. But let us finish our class. Give me a hug for good-bye. Now you are an apprentice in the art of bravery. Come on!" And c Care Monster uddled the small page. The boy almost entirely disappeared in the fluffy white fur of his new friend and teacher. The boy felt intoxicated. Care Monster's smell was stunning, and so many difficult, unknown words, such vast horizons and lofty ideas. His head swirled like after a triple long ride on a merry-go-round. Nevertheless he was elevated. He is, in Reality, not a small powerless page, feeling wrecked and jealous because of this girl's mischief. He is something unthinkably great. He is Awareness, which is the substratum of all! What does it mean? Substratum? All-pervading? Very strange terms!

"Does it mean that I am everywhere, even in the big town five days' journey South on horseback, even maybe on the foreign land across the Hearing Sea?" he wondered.

Care Monster told him to come back the next day at the same time to the castle library. It was going to rain all day and all night. The library was a very dusty place as no-one ever went there to dig in the old manuscripts handwritten on parchment made from donkey skin. Only rats and mice nestled comfortably between the ancient volumes. The people had forgotten long ago that books were their most faithful friends and instead looked for friendship between those who, like themselves, preferred to enjoy the pleasures of the senses at the splendid feasts organized frequently by the King, rich after his last victory over the Kingdom of Ventriloquists. The boy decided to go there in the morning and clean up a bit. Care Monster Care Monster was so clean. Small page never had any friends and because of this spontaneously felt very close to his so strange teacher. He thought that if Care Monster lay in the dust on the floor, unswept for a few centuries, it would be simply an insult. But now it is also late for us, my darling children. Sleep soundly and dream about Care Monster. Maybe he will appear in your dream and give you such a hug as you have never ever had before from anyone. I wouldn't wonder! He is a professional in the art of hugging. He is Care Monster and this is the highest status in the field of Love. Good night my darling children. Rest well. Tomorrow we will again hear what Care Monster has to say to our little page. Good night once more.

In the Library

Good evening jesters. Are you all warm and comfortable? It is important not to cause too much trouble to our bodies because they will pay back with the same currency. That is why it is better to start a spiritual quest at a young age, like our small page did, and not when old, for then the body's aches and pains disturb meditation or in acute cases totally prevent it. It is also not good to be too concerned about bodily comforts. The best is always the balanced, golden, middle way.

In our Aham Ayam it is now raining heavily, and our small page got wet running to the library to meet Love Dragon. Are you O.K.? No complaints? That's good! We can continue our story. Do not drift, darlings, to sleep. Stay wide-awake, as what Love Dragon is going to say is very important for your future too. It can change your lives by opening domains never expected to exist. The majority of people grow old and only a very few grow wise. We should take advantage of this story, as it is a rare opportunity to learn greatest secrets about ourselves. I hope Care Monster will not mind, he'll probably even be very pleased.

Soooo . . . . , all night small page dreamed about himself expanding to an enormous size. He covered with his body the entire castle, then the island on which his King's kingdom was located and then the entire planet. But he still kept expanding. After a while he was even bigger than the Universe, and still he did not stop expanding and expanding. He wondered how it was possible to expand more and more when he already had reached the furthest stars in the infinite sky. What is further? Is anything there? Suddenly he got a flash of spontaneous illumination. Obviously! He was there!! All was built from him. He was the substratum of everything. Didn't Care Monster tell him that he is Awareness? Small page woke up feeling invigorated. He knew that he was much greater than the King, who had only a small kingdom on an infertile island, and on top of that a bad hiccup and heartburn after last night's reception. He, small page, was not small at all! He was the greatest! Nobody would ever know this, as externally there was no change in him, but this would not reduce his greatness even one inch. He knew it and it was the most important thing. Care Monster knew it too!

Immediately after a light breakfast he ran to the library and swept the entire floor, mopped it three times with soapy water and made some order out of the mess on the tables. He even cleaned a well-established network of spider webs and threw the poor spiders outside into fresh air and rain. He thought that those ugly creatures were not worthy to listen to the next enlightening discourse of Care Monster. Small page was very curious as to what more Care Monster would tell him. How was it possible to know more?

Exactly at the appointed time the door of the oldest bookcase in the library opened with a squeaky noise and from behind it there came out none other then Care Monster himself. He smiled and cuddling the boy said,

"You are good, my page!! I am very proud of you. I am sure I do not waste my time talking to you and teaching you this most secret of the secrets. I watched you all morning, hidden in this bookcase. Nobody asked you to make preparations with such a great effort, but you cleaned the library by your own free will. Those people who can't do what they were are asked to do and also those who can only do what they were asked are not worth noting and are useless idlers. So this is your first successful step in the direction towards the shore of this Ocean of Love I told you about yesterday. Congratulations."

Small page blushed and asked timidly,

"Care Monster, I am an uneducated boy. I do not understand much of what you say. Yesterday you mentioned two paths: the path of work and the path of acquiring knowledge or rather Wisdom as you say. Which of these two, Sir, is the best for such a little person like me. Which is the fastest and easiest way to reach the Ocean of Love and to be permanently happy? I want to go there! I do not like life in this corrupted castle. I want to be happy! Can you explain it to me so that I will understand, please? It is all so confusing."

"O yes, yes small page. Clarify this? There now! Sure! A confused mind is like spoiled machinery. It is not capable of controlling the thought flow and the deadly enemy born from it—desire, which can charge at us. That is right! Yesterday I told you that there exists the path of work and the path of gaining Wisdom. They both are equally great and through the distant eons they have been followed by those rare, self-conscious individuals aimed at Liberation. We all have different physical, mental and intellectual constitutions. They form the nature of the individual and are determined by the proportions in us of the features which we talked about yesterday; lethargy, activity and subtlety or contemplation. It is obligatory to behave in conformity with our nature. Even those who have reached the peak of spiritual growth and are fully awakened also follow this rule. The varying types of temperament and predisposition can't be changed and definitely should not be. In tune with these, people choose their occupations. Can you imagine, for example, the hare dressed up and pretending that he is a turtle? The fox passes by. He smells the well-known fragrance of the best lunch and directs his steps promptly towards the actor. And what will happen? The hare will drop his costume, and propelled by his inborn nature run like lightening for his life. He can't help it. How to pretend that he is a turtle when his blood is boiling, heated by his inborn, active temperament. Each individual must be allowed, and even encouraged in, his endeavors to perform in tune with his inner and outer set-ups. If someone breaks this natural order of things he will unavoidably develop a neurosis. Do you follow me?

"Let us continue then. Vigorous, physical work is especially advised for those who are apathetic or energetic. A slack attitude is the greatest hindrance in one's spiritual progress towards the Ocean of Love. By hard work, first one will wash off with one's own sweat the lethargy hampering the free movement of energy and gradually become dynamic. The second group will burn off their excess energy and in turn become subtle and contemplative. Only those who are subtle can fully use the faculty of discrimination, and by this attain Wisdom. So, there are your two paths. One gradually evolves into the other. The first one is like the preparation of a junior student for a serious academic course, which is the second path.

"Man is predestined to be a generous giver and not a greedy acquirer and robber of Nature. Those who act against this rule meet unavoidably with misery, grief and degeneration. Others will enjoy prosperity and good cheer and will progress. Whatever is given with an open heart will be returned to the giver multiplied by ten. The more one gives, the bigger becomes his capacity to give. This applies not only to things but also to feelings like compassion and love. The man who offers himself entirely to Divine Awareness, which some call God, renouncing the world, relations, aspirations and desires receives a Divine reward; for he himself becomes Divinity. To evolve to Divinity is the goal of all creatures, but it culminates in the human race. Because it requires renunciation of desires, attachments and the fruits of actions, we cannot and even should not recommend it to those who are entangled in worldliness pursuing their petty goals and satisfying their desires. By making such a mistake we would cause more damage than good. It is much better for them to work for the fruits of their actions and gradually sublimate their character than to idle aimlessly, overcome by indolence in the name of renunciation. If you look around you, especially during the festivals, you will see how some monks carry themselves proudly but internally are almost unconscious and lifeless. They carry visible depression and disgust of trying to be a saint, sentenced to live among ordinary people. Also it is dangerous and extremely harmful to renounce action and suppress the external senses when one is still secretly playing in the mind with the pleasures of the sensuous world, imagining indulgence in forbidden pastimes. Public debauchery is less harmful than secretly entertaining persistent thoughts about it. Such disharmony between thoughts and lofty declarations is a characteristic of a hypocrite. It leads him to frustration, which can explode in a favorable situation as overindulgence in sense enjoyments and then, in great shame, to fall off the royal Path of self-rediscovery. Such a miserable hypocrite is over concerned with the outward expression of his attempts to look austere. He cares more for the impression he makes on others than for the inner results of his exercises. Such a falsetto, if not praised and appreciated, will quickly lose his enthusiasm and go openly back to the worldly business of sense gratification. Those who are sincere aspirants ignore the onlooker's comments and struggle to have a genuine inner experience, which is the only proof of their progress. So act and do not look sideways! Even for those who are inclined to follow exclusively the path of knowledge, there is no escape from activity. Anyone who is here on the material plane as a part of Nature is automatically bound to perform some actions, even if only to maintain his mortal frame. We progress on the path by being compliant with our prescribed duties. I, Love Dragon, call it by the beautiful term 'Amrad'. By following our 'amrad' with dispassion we will gain clarity of understanding of the secret laws governing Nature and the real relation between things and beings. It is a great mistake to abandon our amrad with the intention of performing somebody else's or that of one to whom we are attracted. Do not even try to follow anybody else's path. Find your own way and stick to it. Believe me; even if you feel that your amrad is faulty it is still a better haven for you then somebody else's foreign one. Amrad is always tailor-made for the person, like forged armor for the warrior.

"All living beings, especially man, act on different levels according to the intensity of their spiritual awakening. The most basic, lowest type, meets his needs in life by competing with others. This refers also to natural selection in Nature. Those who are strong, healthy and more self-assured win, and those who are handicapped or physically or mentally weak are annihilated. The weakling's share is consumed by the strong and thus the strong grow even stronger. There is no mercy in this as most of the actions are controlled by instinct and propelled by selfish desires. He takes what he wants from others believing that it is beneficial for him. In groups he does everything to prove his worthiness to be promoted. The self-centered type looks first for his own needs, always suspecting a shortage. This way Nature prevents degeneration of all species, including humans.

"A higher order is co-operation by individuals and communities between the different members for their mutual benefit. This enables proper growth and development of both single individuals and communities as a whole. Thanks to co-operation and the willingness to contribute labor and thoughts by individuals, the great civilizations on this and other planets were built and humans' science has already discovered some of the simpler laws governing creation.

"The highest grade of being can dedicate his abilities, thoughts and physical strength to the welfare of others. The highest grade is further divided into two categories. First, the lower of the two is dedicated to community, country, nation or King, while the higher offers all his actions to Almighty God. These are the most superior among men and only they are able to act desirelessly.

"Desire is the most harmful entity we meet and is of our own creation. It is our deadliest enemy. We are Awareness, but when desire pervades our intellect disturbing the mind and activating the senses, a veil is created preventing our inborn Wisdom to be tapped by intuition. That is why I, Care Monster, say that the most heroic possible act one can do is the self-conscious destruction of desires. If this is done successfully, our intuition will show us our Real Nature. This is called Self-Realization. By performing even the simplest work those blessed ones are divining themselves, their work and its fruits. So equally the giver and the receiver benefit and both are much uplifted. Since the beginning of time there has been in the universe a procession of beings who have risen to those heights. On Earth such giants of spirit are only found among man because only man has the capacity of discrimination. Animals use instinct as a guide in life. So you see, the selfless renunciates are not actionless at all but their attitude is very different to others. They first satisfy the needs of others and they themselves are content to live on what is left. It does not really matter if they live in religious communities, in seclusion or even being married, among people. It does not really matter what kind of clothes they wear and what kind of external stigmas mark their faces, if any. What counts is their attitude on non-attachment, and following it, tranquility of mind. The Path to Freedom is not the way of escaping from activities but of surrendering the fruits of actions as a sacrifice to Nature. Remember small page, this is the real and the highest stage of renunciation. Follow these steps my boy! Become a Real Man, rise above animalistic crowds!

"Listen! On the material plane life expresses itself as constant change, as we said yesterday. This can be disturbing to sensitive ones as nothing is permanent and impermanence creates a feeling of insecurity. Also, not all that comes our way suits us. If we want seriously to grow spiritually we should become equipoised towards the changeable world and also overcome aversion to one thing and attachment to another. Otherwise our mind and senses will become restless and start to cause a lot of trouble. Those likes and dislikes, cravings and repulsions are the product of our egoism. Freedom is not to be had for love or money so long as this egoism is not eliminated. If we change this pattern into choiceless and selfless, dedicated service and devotion towards Reality, the pairs of opposites will vanish and the demons of the senses become softened until they totally rest in Peace. Remember my boy; when one's life is entirely dedicated to the Ultimate, then the senses cease to be enemies and become but good servants, as they were originally only designed to protect the body from the basic dangers of the external world.

"Small page, I am teaching you the Truth which is Eternal, Timeless Wisdom. Listen to it attentively! If you attune to this Truth your mind will achieve equilibrium in proportion to the depth of your attunement. Identify yourself with this Truth! I, Care Monster, too wear this body of mine for that purpose only, but I am not this at all. I, Care Monster, am the Ancient Preceptor. I am the Highest Emperor. My empire has no boundaries. It covers Infinity. I am He who owns everything sentient and insentient. I am also this Wisdom itself. Those exceptional beings who imbibe my teachings will get permanent relief from the bondage of action. Surrender to the preceptor, and by obeying his instructions, with unwavering and permanent trust, you will open the gate to inexpressible heights of spiritual growth. This Truth can be understood intuitively and only by those rare, brave ones who, after surrendering to Me, can perform the same actions as before but selflessly, without a thought of doership and pride:

'I am doing it. I have done this great job. Marvelous I am indeed . . .' Detachment calms the mind, and the calm mind is sublimated and is able to listen to the voice of intuition singing internally the unending song about the Only Truth. Remember small page, you do not hold the world on your head, I do! Not they, not you, but I, Care Monster in my Real Nature, am the invisible doer of everything that is ever done. There is nothing in all the dimensions of existence that has not been done by Me and which I do not control and balance.

"There is bondage only when there is this identification with the work and attachment to its fruits. A spiritually enlightened person enjoys bliss even while being busy. The work does not affect him. He knows that it is Me who acts through him. Being in tune with the Real Him, being satisfied, content and centered in the core of his beingness, he has no more obligatory duties to perform. He has reached the state of actionlessness, but this is only on the mental level. Externally he works as before to set an example for his younger relatives.

"You, my small page, are worried that because you are uneducated you will not be able to follow my discourse. Do not trouble yourself. It is even better, my little friend. In your head there is some space for my teachings. You also have no calcified opinions to block the entrance for new ideas. In fact what I am telling you is only showing the right and most efficient way of travel on the path. The Wisdom can't be thought in any language as it is transcendental. In due time it is given to the aspirant as an illumination. For this is needed my grace and your effort, but it is not achieved by the effort. It only prepares you to be receptive and sensitive to absorb the Wisdom.

"Tomorrow I would like to meet you in the bower in the apple tree orchard. Let your mistress, pure apple tree, hear our talk and benefit too. She is a great performer of amrad. Always ready to give shade in Summer, and in Autumn offers sweet and succulent fruits. She never asks for a reward, being satisfied with what Nature has given her. Immobile, as a tree, she exercises patience in order to become a perfectly subtle human in her next incarnation. Your choice was not bad and not as foolish as it looked in the beginning. She is much, much greater and deserving of bigger respect than this egocentric, deluded girl, the old treasurer's lover. See you at the same time. Tonight I am in a hurry because I have another appointment with a few selected ocean creatures. They are interested in knowing the Real Nature of the ocean and are especially interested in the relationship between the waves and the ocean itself."

So saying, Care Monster cuddled small page briefly, placing his paw for a while on the boy's forehead, like in a blessing, and then disappeared in no time. The boy stood overwhelmed by the vastness of Care Monster's Wisdom. Never before had anyone talked to him so seriously and for so long. How had it happened that Care Monster entrusted him, who was so ordinary and so young, with the secret of secrets? Why? Small page walked home lost in thought, not even noticing that it was still raining. He knew that there was no-one in the castle to discuss with what was just told to him by Care Monster.

If he would say a single word about it, all would ridicule him saying he was a lunatic having hallucinations due to the lack of liquor in his blood. All people believe that to be interested in philosophy, and on top of that to be abstinent, is very harmful, especially at a very young age. But small page knew deep, deep in his heart that every single word said by was truth Care Monster and total truth; that he was not making fun of him but was only guiding him step by step towards the 'Ocean of Love' where there is no limit to the amount of the sweet nectar of Bliss one may drink. He also knew that from now on he would have only Care Monster as a guide, friend and companion; that, in fact, it would be a lonely trip and dangerous too. Until now he only knew a little, but even this already separated him from the mob, drunkenly singing their ribald songs and seated on beer barrels in the yard of the castle's only tavern. Now he would become even lonelier than he was before meeting Care Monster. But what would he miss? Would anyone from amongst the singers help him to reach the Ocean of Love? No! Definitely none! He was not sad because of this. On the contrary he felt ennobled; entering the Path he would become a chosen one. He was also tired. Never in his life had he used his brain so intensely.

But you, my children, must be tired too. The story is not the easiest one you have ever heard. It is even more difficult to follow than the one about the eccentric duck who once went to the doctor to post an unwritten letter, and then following her instinct inquired about the legal matters of her not-yet-born husband from a group of washerwomen working on the bank of a dried up river. Who is snoring? Is it you Kate, diving into the core of your existence? This is not the way, my darling! But now sleep children, sleep. See you all tomorrow night. I think that Love Dragon has a revelation for us. Good night. Good night and sweet dreams!!

The Declaration

Children dear, it is again time for us to translocate ourselves in duration and space to the country of Aham Ayam. There we will once again take part in the important meeting of a most mysterious creature, Care Monster, with the still miserable, and now badly confused small page, suffering because of his unfortunate love affair. Ready? Let us begin then, golden ones.

The teacher and the student met in the ornamental wooden bower standing at the crossroad of orchard alleys, as arranged. Care Monster looked this evening exceptionally majestic. His fur had the luster of a famous Australian, precious, opal. It shone, like a diamond, with the intensity of billions of microscopic sparks of all the colors of the rainbow, yet it still retained its pure clarity. Small page approached him with the reverence appropriate for a teacher and after he got warmly cuddled, he asked a question.

"Sir, I am now even more confused than before! You said first that I am the Awareness from which all is made and on the next day that it is you, Care Monster, who own and do everything. Please be kind enough to tell me who are you and who am I?"

"Excellent, splendid, remarkable my boy!! Although uneducated you still think quite well. There is no contradiction in my statements. It is only apparent disharmony. You do not understand correctly what I say because the Truth, which I teach you is not yet completely explained. In the light of your limited knowledge you can see only a distorted picture. When you see or know one fragment of a whole you can only incorrectly imagine how the rest looks. For example, you observe through the hole in a fence the tail of a pig. It moves and you guess that it must be a part of an animal unknown to you, as you are, let us imagine, only visiting this planet. How is it possible to imagine correctly the rest of its fat body? Most probably you would think that it must be a creature of the shape of a bristly, overgrown serpent. Just be patient and listen to the rest. Your fellow humans used to say, and not without good reason: 'He that can have patience can have what he wants.' So it is very important to learn to be patient. Patience is bitter but it has sweet fruits. The Truth I am trying to implant into your head is eternal, because it comes from the abundant well of My Wisdom. Wisdom and Truth are equal names for the same Ultimate Reality. I personally taught this Truth to God Sun in the beginning of the manifestation of this material Universe. From Him it was passed down through many millennia of the now mostly forgotten history of the human race in a perpetual succession of enlightened teachers and eager students, who in the fullness of their time became illuminated teachers themselves."

"Stop it, Care Monster!! I beg your pardon! How in heaven could you teach God Sun in the beginning of creation if you are here, right now, with me? This is impossible! It just doesn't fit together. Please, I am already quite confused. Do not joke anymore. This is enough! Tell me promptly the truth about who you really are!"

"Okay small page. You will have what you ask for. Just relax! All has to come at the right time. We can learn only step by step. How can you, who is tied up and directed by the consequences of your previous lives' actions, remember the past? You do not even know who you were a mere fifty years ago. But I, Care Monster, remember them all pretty well, yours and my past lives. My present statements are then made from the absolute standpoint. Please be seated! I do not want you to jump out of your skin, swoon and break your head when shocked. Who knows what is ahead. You may still need it occasionally. Then isn't it better to have it ready and in one piece, even if it is almost empty? Listen and try to be calm. I have to tell you the Truth. In fact without it we can't continue our teachings.

"I am the Absolute Reality. I existed from the time before I created time. That means Eternally. I am Infinite, All-pervading, Omnipresent and Omniscient Creative Intelligence. I am the only Principle. I set up and operate the Laws of Nature. I am the God of Gods. The Universe is pervaded by Me and has its existence in Me. I am all that can be thought of; I am this Awareness about which you worry so much. I am Existence itself. I am the common thought of all living beings: 'I AM'. I created everything from Myself. In fact only I exist. Uncountable suns shine throughout the Universe, but only I am truly bright because only I shine by My own light. Others are only reflecting My beacon. Now, I must tell you this too. In this body I look finite, but the truth is that this is Me, who is that Infinite Ocean of Love I told you about during our first meeting!

"You are my darling son. Eagles do not breed doves or chickens. Children are born with the same potential possessed by their parents. So . . . you are potentially Me. From Me you have emerged, in Me you have life and in Me you will dissolve after realizing who you really are. Now you are like this mad prince who left his father's palace and forgot who he was. He wandered around town begging for a penny when his vaults were filled with a treasure of gold and diamonds. The apparent difference between us is only in the intensity of manifestation of Divinity and not in its basic qualities. Are you satisfied with my answer? If so I will recite for you an amateurish poem which one of My sons and your brother will write in the distant future. Its words express partly the outlines of MY splendor and contain also a message for you."

Small page was as if in a dream state. He felt stupefied by the Care Monster's declaration. What he had just heard was shocking. From the beginning he had felt that behind the appearance of this incredible, six legged, friendly creature, was hidden some great mystery, but he would never have guessed that it could be The Highest Himself who had manifested in such an unusual form.

Then Care Monster assumed the pose of an experienced professional actor. He stood on His rear legs gently supporting Himself by His left middle leg and held His right front leg on his chest. The left front leg He used to reinforce the spoken words by gestures as He was fully aware that usually body language passes messages to the subconscious mind more successfully than spoken language, which is filtered by the critical faculty of the conscious mind. The recitation started. Love Dragon accented strongly some of the words. That was another advanced trick to say more than was said in the poem itself:

YOU AND I
Diving in an abyss of black holes
I explode in cascades of light
In super-novas.
Changing forms, I play
In all dimensions of Existence.
Space is contained in me,

Time I created as an illusion
To make the game more fascinating.
I am the Eternal
Changing, I am unchangeable.
I am alone.
Nothing exists as separate from Me.
I am the essence of all substances.
I am the life in all life forms.
I am the light in the suns
And the darkness in the nights.
I am the cold in interplanetary space
And the heat in the fire.
I am the feeling of surrender in love
And the feeling of possessiveness in hatred.
I am the doer of all—always doing nothing.
I am FREE!
I have neither beginning nor will I have end.
Even you are really not you!
You are me!
Wake up son! Try to see, to experience.
Do not dream anymore.
Just watch the play.
Just BE!
Be in now.
Only Now is real.
Ignore the time—and it will disappear!
But you are already FREE
Because you are ME!!
You were never bound,
You only took a nap
For a while and forgot your identity!
Come back home son, come
Come for a swim
In the Infinite Ocean
Of My Love
Come, come, come . . .
In this dimension we are playing in now,
It is most difficult

To find the way back home—
To ME!
It is a trip to the innermost SELF of you,
To ME!
The distance is enormous—
Because it is mental only.
Overcome the mind's limitations:
Attachments, desires and identifications
And you are instantly there,
As I never was away!
Dwelling everywhere—I reside in you, too.
I am only waiting.
I do not care.
I can wait millennia.
Time does not limit Me
As I am Him who created time.
But why wait?
Do it now!
Stop painting the picture
On the screen of space!
Open your eyes!
You are thirsty, being fully immersed in water.
Wake up and drink, drink, drink . . .
Your birthright is to be drunk from the Bliss.
Your duty is to realize your true identity!!
To live again as Me
To Be, Be, Be
Eternally Be
As Me . . .

"And what my boy? You probably again think that I am joking and wonder why I appear in such a strange body? Do not ask more questions please. I will tell you all Myself. There is a reason for this too and not a trifling one either. Whenever in space, those supposedly intelligent beings, poisoned by selfishness, divert shamelessly from the path of righteousness and start to neglect their amradic duties, ignoring the ancient Law of Nature and openly disrespecting the Only Truth. I incarnate Myself to make order of the spoiled affairs.

On different planets I assume different forms. They are always suitable for the occasion and the local conditions. Sometimes I am in a human body, sometimes in a serpent's, sometimes I am a huge electric amoeba or a White Eagle. Sometimes, but rather rarely, I become Love Dragon. I can even be in the form of super-conscious, colloidal, protoplasmic mist veiling the entire planet. I also can be simultaneously in few or many manifested forms in as many different locations as I like. It is no problem for Me as I have no limitations. Not all of My forms are recognized. Sometimes I work from a distance, staying unknown to the population of the planet, guiding its beings. Though in many forms, I always stay undivided. I never cease to be One for a second. On such occasions when I incarnate, my job is to perform a general cleansing of a degenerated population. It takes place on different levels of existence and in many often strange, but most effective, ways. The worst, evil beings I have to destroy completely, others I must remodel. Not always are my patients, on whom I perform an operation, aware of the process.

"The message I deliver is in differently wrapped packages and has a form of presentation depending on the needs of the times and requirements of the culture existing where I incarnate. The teachings are apparently different but it is always the same Only Truth that I explain. I never introduce any novelties as they can only cause confusion in the mind and can't add anything to the Only Truth, which is full in Itself.

"Also, My self-assumed duty is to meet all who have become worthy to be guided to the Ocean of Love 'for a swim', and show them a way and a means of travel. Congratulations my boy! You are one of those rare souls. You met Me because you became worthy of receiving My teachings. It happened according to a state, which I call the Law of Grace. It flows from Me without interruption but is not accessible to those who are like wet fuel. It can ignite in an instant for only those who have explosive minds like gunpowder. Listen to My words with attentiveness and assess them by the power of your intuition; practice in all sincerity using your will power; try to become more and more subtle, passionless, fearless, friendly disposed, even towards those rascals who are your opponents. Purify yourself by performing well the work given to you as your life's share, and finally merge in Me, become Me.

"Only those who comprehend Me at the end merge in Me and become amalgamated with the Infinite Love of Mine. They become Love Themselves. For those who succeed I grant as My legacy of Love— Divine Love. Eternal Immortality is their reward and they delight only in Pure Existence. This is the Ultimate Goal of all living creatures. It is yours too! Are you feeling dizzy? Maybe afraid? Most people are terrified at the prospect or unavoidable necessity of stepping outside and entering the frightening unknown, but at the same time they are equally or even more miserable and dissatisfied with their present state of affairs and surroundings which they, little selves reflected in their conventional life, claim as well known and consider as secure. They are afraid of taking actions and become inactive. Those who hesitate to act, to work, to fight battles, to love, are lost and become dead though still alive—inert. Inertia is a sort of illness and is a result of strongly predominant lethargic tendencies. It, just as every ailment, can be cured. The most effective medicine for it, which can do a world of good, is energetic activity. Those who, overtaken by laziness refuse to act, will live existentialistic lives in the misery of insecurity. In this state they will tremble, paralyzed by the fear of change, and lose themselves more and more in an artificial, mental, self-made prison of their own ugly Ogre. Bondage and liberation are nothing other than states of mind. Attached, full of fears and controlled by desires, the mind bestows on an unfortunate individual invisible chains of bondage. But when the same mind is relaxed, free of anxiety, detached, deprived of expectations and cravings, it will set that fortunate, lucky one free, and beyond external circumstances. So, my little page, do not drift into unconscious sleep but act energetically and fearlessly! Do principled deeds; do not dream them all day long, going into ecstasies of your non-existent grandeur. Instead of talking about great things, prove your worth by doing something even small but useful. Acts speak much louder than words.

"Everyone is born only for the purpose of fulfilling his previous life's desires. Unfortunately, the majority of people desired things or pleasures in the past and now are running after minor, short term benefits instead of trying to reach Me. So many do not even believe in My existence and think that they are the rulers of the Universe. They have eyes but do not see, they have ears but do not hear Me. Don't you think it is silly to do so? It is like saying with one's own lips: "I am dumb." Obviously it is much easier to attain mundane success is the world by worshiping one of My lower aspects, which are called Gods of Nature, than Me, the Absolute. What can I do? Whatsoever my children identify themselves with, I am bound to grant them the same, and in My mercy to fulfill their hearts' burning desires. All unknowingly yearn for unending union with Me, but being ignorant and not aware of their Real Nature they do it unconsciously, searching for Me in wrong directions: relationships with the objects of the external world and pleasurable pastimes. For those who search for Me using their physical senses, I have to appear as Nature with all its splendid beauty and sweet delights. I understand their limitations and know that they prefer the 'easy way' above the hardships on the real straight path towards Me. Their time will come too. Then, there is no need to worry. Obviously it is much harder to want nothing but Me than to chase the shadows of unending petty wants. It is more difficult to serve the World selflessly than to follow the pattern of working for the fruits of actions and excessively accumulate mostly useless, material possessions. The choice is yours. But why waste time, my boy? What can she, this silly girl, offer you in the long run? Only misery! Why not get into business, make order from the mess in your life and become Happiness itself? Do you agree that the only thing worth seeking is the Ultimate Truth of My Existence which I am trying to explain to you? There is no doubt that it is the hardest thing to get. Only a few determined ones want to become one with Me. Do not be silly!! Identify yourself with Me and attain Me. This is the way you should follow on the ascent from a miserable, mortal humanoid to a splendorous, immortal, Divine Being.

"But you must be alert! The Forces of Darkness operate to maintain balance. In spite of their negativity they too are manifestations of Myself. They are like the other side of a coin. They are also very powerful. Do not feel safe until you reach Me. It is very easy to slip, lose track and get lost for a long time in 'the woods of Existence'. You must also remember that your years are limited. Then hurry, but make haste slowly! In a rush it is easy to make an irreparable mistake. Work, think, but not too much, meditate on Me, contemplate on what I have told you and be constantly aware of the process in your mind. Watch this thief carefully. Be self-controlled and assess your chances before making the next step. Do not try to fly before you grow 'wings' or 'to cross a bridge' before it is built. Grow steadily! Be always humble! Do not dare to throw your weight about. Never swagger or pretend that you are a big wig. Have the dignity of a monarch, but blended with the utter humility of a beggar. Remember this lesson: Once a frog tried to look as big as an elephant and burst, making a mess on the stage. Do not imitate her.

"Be careful with praise as it can make a good man better but a bad one much, much worse. Refuse flattery as the worst possible hideousness. Those who need it like a drug, bolstering their self-image, are only puffed up emptiness in the form of an important bubble. One needle in the form of a word of truth can deflate them, bursting their pride and stinking and spoiling the air. As a result they will sink from their false, unjustified glory into the misery of their actual emptiness.

"Do not desire anything, as everything is Mine and only Mine. You do not own anything, you can't. I am only lending you My things for a short time to use. So you should not get attached to what is not yours. Be attached to Me! Desire Me alone! This is not creating any bondage. Aim for the Ultimate! I already told you; I am the Ultimate Reality. Ignore the empty, petty things of the transitory world. Do you see the difference? Your courtiers desire riches and delights of the flesh but you cry for love. This is already superior. But forget such love. Real Love is Me! Then cry for Me! If you want to become one with Me you must think of nothing but Me. Even love for her has to be abandoned as it is not only enslaving but also eating up your valuable life energy.

"Lofty emotions have a power much greater than thoughts, but an iron will is the strongest. Only from will are born applied reason, fearlessness and determination, which are so indispensable on the Path. My small page, no one can be in love and at the same time be wise because he automatically loses his reason. Look at yourself!

Who, being sane, sings love songs to an apple tree? I do not say that you have a loose screw in your brain, only that you are in extreme confusion as you are carried away by your exuberant imagination into the domains of fantasy. Do you follow Me? Lack of reason results in the deepening of ignorance. From ignorance doubts pop up like mushrooms growing in the woods after the rain. Ignorance is the real poverty. Pains of ignorance, as you well know from your own present experience, must be endured with a lot of tears. But there is a radical cure! This is the Knowledge, which destroys all doubts, as Knowledge and ignorance are not compatible and can't co-exist. Knowledge leads to detachment and desirelessness, which results in tranquility and equanimity. A tranquil person is content and this is his real wealth. We can call it more conventionally: Liberation.

"To become wise, to acquire Knowledge, a steady effort is necessary. This is the price to be paid by the spiritual seeker, but the truth is that efforts on the quest of Reality do not simply add up. They are multiplied by My grace. This is guaranteed. The wise person is never lonely though often alone. I, Love Dragon, am with him always. I walk the Path with all my students who struggle to reach Me. I bathe them daily with My grace.

"When all activities, physical and mental, are offered to Me as a sacrifice, My grace flows in abundance towards such a sacrificer. He effortlessly attains Wisdom and becomes Liberated while still living in the same body as before, and being, as before, here and now on this very Earth, or obviously on any other inhabited planet of the Universe on which he was born. I repeat again to make you highly alert: The Path is difficult, like traversing a razor-sharp, icy ridge on a Himalayan height. Only those who develop intuitive understanding, which will be the light on their way, can successfully cross it. Intuition is Divine in its nature as it comes directly from Me. Intuition and Knowledge spelled with a capital "K" are inseparable and are not gained gradually. They descend instantaneously and spontaneously as My gift onto those who are purified and serene, and who are prepared to accommodate them in their well cleaned minds. I bestow them only on those who surrender to Me completely and without reservation, who are humble, one-pointed in their devotion, who love

Me and respect Me with great reverence in all My manifested forms: worms, insects, reptiles, birds, animals, plants, humans, planets, stars, galaxies and the Universe. Knowledge of the Truth is most purifying from all accessible means, known and unknown by you. It removes the dirt of ignorance and deodorizes the rotten stench of egoism. This Super Detergent of God's can't be found on any stall of the castle market or in any external object or even thought. It is to be found in the Silence of meditation in the innermost enclaves of your own beingness, where I, Care Monster dwell and keep My store.

"By offering your small consciousness to Me you can almost elevate yourself to fellowship with Me. By killing this ugly Ogre, a Divinity is born. He who identifies himself with any of My aspects assumes those qualities which that aspect represents. But it is essential to be as innocent as a new born baby to assimilate some of My glory. I have given beings on this and other planets time to grow in Wisdom and not to accumulate transitory possessions and indulge in debauchery. Offer yourself on the sacrificial pyre of renunciation and total surrender and I will elevate you above the Gods. None of those sacrifices possible to perform are needed by Me, Care Monster, but it is for you, small page, the best way to get rid of your enemy: Ogre.

"Now I would like to recite to you another poem. Listen! It is summarizing all that I just told you about sacrifice.

SACRIFICE
There is no receiving
Without giving.
This is the Law of Nature.
Nothing can manifest itself from nothingness.
To get things—other things have to be sacrificed.
To get wanted experiences
We have to perform tapas:
To burn in the sacrificial fire
Our attachments, desires, habits.
Let us follow the Law!
Let us sacrifice our egos!
Let us give it as fuel

365

To the sacrificial fire!
Let the smoke from its destruction
Veil this world of illusion.
Tranquil our senses.
O Lord, we are offering You
All of the gross Universe:
You manifested in the forms
To You unmanifested.
We are sacrificing our egos
To experience our oneness with You,
To be as we should be:
Deathless, Unlimited,
Eternally FREE!!

"Humans, in their great arrogance born from egoism and ignorance of the natural hierarchy, forget who is in charge and think that they are holding the reins of their life's chariot and performing actions by their choice. Very silly!

"I am the performer of all actions. But nothing effects ME; neither actions nor the fruits of them. Those who realize Me are also not bound by their actions. Those who follow the example set by the ancient adepts, as I told you yesterday, act without a trace of egoism of harmful desires. There is one thing I must clarify, my small page. There are actions of different categories: right action, which benefits both the performer and the recipient of its fruits; evil action, which harms both of the earlier mentioned; inaction in action and action in inaction. This is the way work is understood by those who are mature in Wisdom. We will discuss this topic later. I want to mention now that we act not only in the so called waking state but also in dreams. Having in our mind a program of discrimination we are fully responsible for our choices made in the waking state. The actions performed in dreams are different. You are not in complete control of them so the responsibility is not executed. But please remember, I am the real performer of works on all levels in all dimensions of Existence as I am the Essence of It and action in acting.

"Don't you think that this is enough for one evening? Do not worry. It all sounds very difficult but in fact is very simple. Now have a rest. Go home. Do not talk to drunkards on your way. Contemplate first what you have learned under the spreading branches of the plum tree, which has listened to what we talked about and is feeling very uplifted. Now I will give you some time to absorb what I said and implement it in your day-to-day life. We will meet again after only forty years. From now on I am going to be invisible but when you call me for a help I will help"

Small page was so bewildered that he could hardly say anything. Forty years! Care Monster cuddled him, patted his head as if to check if it was still empty because it would then echo, and was gone before the boy managed to realize what was going on.

TALKS IN A QUEUE TO THE BATHROOM

Our Guru's ashram recently became too small for the residents and visitors. Many hundreds of people live there permanently and thousands are continually coming for a short stay. Especially crowded are the days of the famous Guru Bhava programs where all suffer some inconvenience: continuous all-night noise, poor food distribution and overcrowded bathrooms. Sometimes simply to pee is a major problem. Those well-connected to Western residents owning apartments in the high-rise buildings are sometimes permitted to use their friends' bathrooms; but only a very few chosen ones. To ease the ever worsening situation, new bathrooms were built on the roof of the ashram's East Wing. This totally solved the problem and helped a lot in many other ways; furthermore it also, unexpectedly, created a splendid and rare opportunity for one to become, from time to time, an involuntary listener to some highly enlightening conversations.

Once, after a whole day of running errands and working, one pretty dirty ashramite was having a well-deserved bath there. Energetically splashing cold water on his tired body, he overheard two people talking on the other side of his bathroom door about ashram life and its splendors and miseries, glitters and shadows.

"I have to go to the West soon to earn some money. I'm running short of cash. I haven't even had one beer in the last months, and now must borrow cigarettes from renunciate Gi-Tia", sounded the concerned and desperate voice of someone waiting in a queue to the bathroom.

"So do I," said another voice. "I will soon go to Europe and tour a few countries conducting seminars on spirituality and mental health. It pays well. People believe in all sorts of nonsense, literally in anything! I read a few books about spirituality and now I'm ready to instruct others on those matters. But after I return here, I would like to become a renunciate. It definitely pays out better in the long run. The initial investment of a donation to the Guru is substantial, but all together it's evidently cheaper if you want to stay here a few years. I bought an apartment in the new building and won't have to worry about living in a hut with spiders and rats as the brahmacharis do. I will definitely ask our Guru to be accepted."

"Maybe I should do the same. Being a resident is like playing a losing game," replied the first voice, a little unsure and with a dash of confusion.

One of the bathroom doors opened and the one, going to be a renunciate, left the stage to wash the worldly dust off his holy body. Soon another person joined the line. The conversation shifted to a different subject. An entirely new topic was now on the agenda. "You know, I am seriously thinking about moving to Puttaparti. On rolling stones, moss doesn't grow. Here it has become too crazy; twice a week the terrible noise of bhajans lasts all night, and there are thousands of visitors. There, in Puttaparti, the ashram is crowded too but better equipped and less noisy. It's organized more like in the West. The food too is so much better. Here, they rarely buy anything modern. Except for electricity, computers and the press, this ashram is like something out of Adi Shankar's times." The second man asked timidly,

"Don't you mind leaving our Guru? He is your Guru, isn't He?"

"It doesn't really matter! They are all one. Our Guru, Sai Baba or anybody else, in essence, are the same. Why should I suffer here? There, I can get what I want. It will be better for me. I know what I need. There is nothing wrong with living and working more comfortably. Just to be here in India is tapas enough" replied the first man.

His renunciation had obviously reached the climax of unimaginable heights, for us, the beginners. He had even managed to renounce his own Guru! Now he will have more comfort on this very dangerous spiritual path, the edge of a razor's blade. He was once told, by one initiated into the yellow robes of a sadhak, that a real Guru is inside of everyone. But the poor chap, being over-educated, misunderstood this statement. He thinks that he is already fit to make his own decisions, his own choices. Good luck brother! We can't even imagine how his ego is delighted, admiring whole-heartedly such an independent attitude.

Again the partners changed. A great yoga teacher arrived in an equally great hurry. Without hesitation he announced:

"I have to have a bath first! I am going to start my yoga class in fifteen minutes. You don't mind, I guess?!" The other person sounded not very unenthusiastic, but being less self-assured agreed in order to avoid a dispute. After a while, he inquired about his great yoga teaching career:

"Do you teach yoga?"

"Oh, no, not only yoga! In the West I have regular classes on self-development and spirituality, as well as my own school of modern yoga. Many consider me as their guru. I do not oppose it, as it is good for beginners to have faith in a teacher. I have a radical approach to all of this oriental junk. People read some ancient textbooks and start to believe in all sorts of superstitions. You know, the general public is made of laymen, and they can't distinguish between the Truth and religious symbolism. They need a professional person like me to guide them. For example, consider karma. Utter misunderstanding!

369

It only works on those who, in their ignorance, believe in such stupidity! Such beliefs act on people's emotions and erode their confidence. Everything in the universe is controlled by the mind. Stop believing in such nonsense and you are instantly a Free Man. People are victimized by all this rubbish, and later are afraid even to enjoy free sex and experiment with samadhi stimulants like LSD or Ecstasy," the yoga teacher replied. The questioner then asked:

"Have you considered giving a few classes here, based on your theories of real modern spirituality? Many Westerners would appreciate your approach."

"Yes," replied the yoga teacher; "I tried to give satsang, but the Swamis are not open to these Western ideas. They told me that ashramites follow only the Guru's teachings, which for me are too conservative and that, as a general rule, satsangs are given exclusively by the ashram residents. But don't worry. I don't waste my time here. I try to talk to Westerners, especially to those who are visiting India for the first time and whose minds are still unspoiled by all those out-of-date philosophies. Also, I found that many brahmacharis are interested in my approach to free sex." Soon thereafter, the yoga teacher's aerobic style yoga class started. He was a real professional! His students sweated, and were short of breath.

"Faster, deeper, deeper, faster. Don't be afraid to sweat!" he shouted. "It's the best method for cleansing the toxins from pot or a shot."

So . . . , my friends of the "Ashramitus Ignoramus" kind, we can relax, being assured that nothing is lost. The clever ego, to remain employed, can even assume the shape of a great yoga teacher and instruct innocent aspirants on how to evolve spiritually to the Ultimate State of Egolessness.

Is it all our Guru's lila? It is He who brings them here! What is the reason? First, He needs money; second, maybe He wants us to learn to separate the falsehood from the Truth? I am not sure! Maybe, by listening to such conversations, we will develop watchfulness and be able to detect more easily our own well-camouflaged deadly enemy, the ego, with its multiple desires, pride and anxieties. It is so well-hidden in the labyrinth of consciousness, often dressing up as a very spiritual entity. Only our Guru knows what is going on and why. We should not waste energy on criticism, only watch carefully, register what we notice here and there, and analyze it for our own benefit. These kinds of teachers too have their own very important roles in the game of life. Being exposed to them, we can exercise the usage of our *viveka*—power of discrimination. Let us learn as much as we can, to be able later to perform our roles at the peak of perfection. Let us be like swans that are able, as ancient scriptures declare, to separate milk from water. Let us not laugh, but think!

STARS

It was Monday, early afternoon. Under the green roof on the top of Guru's Ashram temple building, Guru had just started *darshan* for the residents. The air was humid, warm and felt like it had become semi-liquid, jellylike and opaque-transparent. It resembled the optical qualities of a clear quartz crystal held in the wrinkled hands of an ancient wizard trying to discover through this medium the secrets of Creation and who he is himself. His Golden Children were all seated tightly surrounding a Guru of gods and mortals. For innumerable cycles of creation and desolation, creatures from all four worlds, visible and subtle, one and multi-dimensional, appearing in various shapes, existing under many names and living innumerable cycles of long or short but always relative lives, recognized Him as their very own Divine Parent. He always was and is a central point of their life and a source of their vital force. In fact He is the sustainer of all lives in Existence. They all, small and big beings, emerged from Him at the beginning of time when He uttered the first Seed-Word. They have all had, for a long time, their little existences in Him, living only their separate lives, as His tiny extensions. One day, they all will eventually return to the Source and merge with Him for Eternity. When? Soon? Only He knows! But now for some the difference was really huge because some of them became partly aware of this most important fact that they eternally belong to Him and in Reality do not exist as individuals. In His presence the past and the future are condensed in timeless NOW. Gazing in silence at Him they enjoyed the Bliss of thoughtless Beingness.

The eyes of all hung on Him, hungry for Love Divine, which He was distributing amongst all present, along with motherly hugs and candies wrapped in colorful paper. He was giving His prasad and Grace in dozens, big or small, according to the readiness of people to accept it, who had capacity and free storage space in their minds and hearts to accommodate and retain those godly gifts. All were happy.

A Traveler felt like balancing on the edge of two realities belonging to very different dimensions. He clearly saw the people seated cross-legged on the floor and Him, a Guru, his 'Boat, River and Destination' on a couch. At the same time, looking at all of them he was aware that they are not only His children as humans, but also the stars from infinite space. Those stars, which pulsated with incomprehensible, indestructible life, are eternal Cosmic Consciousness and He is the very Source of this Light. They all are members of the Family of Immortals, beings created by His Divine Resolve for a mysterious and secret purpose. Here, on this green-blue planet, They were more familiar with the vast outer space saturated by various radiations than with this so beautifully-decorated-by-Mother Nature stage built for them with only one purpose of gaining first hand experiences. They were sent to this earthly primary school for an education and for a purifying treatment. They were all more or less successful, but in most cases there were no conscious attempts to reduce and finally eliminate their arrogant, selfish, angry, greedy, lustful egos and their most deathly self-made enemies, vasanas.

Stars!? Even these were not a final definition of their identities, even these were only temporary costumes used for the purpose of serving a Purpose. Suns, very well, but for how long? In Reality there was nothing at all, no bodies even as splendid as the suns. There was also no process of gaining their identity, as it was never lost. In Reality, what truly existed was only the magnificent, Silent, Eternal, All-pervading Presence of The Oneness.

He had an instant communication with them all as in fact they were as much parts of the Whole as he was. The feeling of belonging to the Totality, of living as one unlimited 'unit' was incredible. The inner makeup of Brother and Sister 'stars' was clearly visible. They did not have individual, separate existences but were all one eternal unlimited, interwoven Existence as rudraksha seeds on a cotton thread of a mala of wandering sannyasi. They were all temporarily wrapped in a cocoon of mental and emotional sheets, fears, likes and dislikes, all carrying smaller or bigger loads of desires. They were only phantoms dreaming their own reality. Their faults and sometime silly desires did not bother him as he was aware that they are only temporary and that he himself probably possessed many more faults than anyone else.

After billions of years spent serving in space as forms of secondary sources of light, they were all now given the privilege to incarnate in human bodies and personally meet the Incarnation of The Absolute. He was nothing else but their own Essence, which assumed a form looking similar to theirs. His only desire was to guide His Cosmic Golden Children to final Liberation; beings from all twenty-seven dimensions of Existence to Emancipation in The Oneness with Him; to help them to regain their actual and unquestionable Cosmic Royalty.

The game went on and on for eons. What was happening right now was only one mere act in the eternal performance of this divine drama. One after another, His children were coming, surrendering themselves, falling into His arms, thirsty for a sip of nectar of Real Love and to melt in a motherly hug of God Himself. Guru changed his facial expressions and voice; scolded some, cracked jokes with others, instructed, explained.

Through the Traveler's mind rolled, in slow motion, pictures of various parts of the Galaxy. He noticed one of his 'Sister Mice' wearing yellow clothes sneaking by to sit closer to Guru. She perhaps right now was not aware that just a few years back she had completed her service in the center of the Constellation of Ariadne as a Supernova, which exploded in massive gamma radiation. Her face still remained with maybe a trace of former cosmic splendor; or rather most probably it was a reflection of Guru's shakti, a shine of splendor of The Unlimited dressed in a human body.

Feeling overwhelming joy and happiness of fulfillment, he understood that now he didn't want anything, and is aiming nowhere, only hanging in the dense void of The All-pervading Presence. After traveling for Eternity through the Infinity of space he has finally found a resting-place at His Feet and surprisingly discovered that He was always everywhere. The search was only for understanding truth, but it was itself the Greatest Revelation! There was no need to be close to His humanlike form. So simple and at the same time it was all that any being could want. Now it did not matter if he was to come back to this planet to serve his four-dimensional relatives or not. Let Him decide. The readiness was there. A thousand more or thousand less incarnations sounds like nothing compared to inheriting Eternity of Immortal Existence. Even in higher mathematics infinity can't be manipulated by adding or subtracting petty digits as it always remains infinity; even an ancient 'Iśavasya Upaniṣad' says that: **"That is the Whole, this is the Whole; from the Whole the Whole becomes manifest; taking away the Whole from the Whole, the Whole remains . . ."**

Traveler joined the queue for a darshan. When he finally ended up on Guru's lap, time stopped, the world disappeared and Nothingness enveloped him in a shroud of Silence. He drank freely the sweet wine of His Grace and felt simply light; light as light can only be—nothingness.

"Every time you come to me you look younger," joked Guru.

"If I drink any more of this ambrosia I will soon become a baby" he replied laughing, and thought to himself: "A baby star, so, are we starting again this game? Let it be, if You Guru wants it this way!" He knew that there is no end to this drama. Even Liberation is not Real, as Reality is not something changeable and can't be gained or lost. Or, maybe He means emptiness of mind and a chance to absorb The Truth Itself? Let us see. Doesn't it feel like being a dirty, wealthy multi-millionaire and waiting as entertainment for one more drawing of a jackpot in the Ultimate Lottery of Freedom? Is it not like being a clown hanging head down on a high trapeze in the Grand Circus of Life without a net: "all or nothing" or playing a cosmic "Russian roulette" with a thermonuclear charge in the barrel? But here or there is no audience. The performer is simply dreaming. He is in fact the only witness. Also, there is no performance; only ripples on the surface of Eternity, dancing to the tune of the song of all-pervading Silence.

A MANTRA

The massive six-hundred meter high wall of Mount Gierlach, rising from the banks of the famous Tatra mountain lake called 'Morskie Oko' (Pol.:'Sea's Eye') dominated the Southwest, leaving its neighboring crag Mnich (Pol.:Monk) on the West, almost unnoticed. Mnich, a cone-shaped mountain, resembled a monk immersed in prayers, wearing a hood and kneeling humbly facing Girelach. Its Eastern wall has become a legend by providing one of the most technically difficult and spectacular solid rock climbs in this valley, with over one hundred meters of overhanging granite precipices three quarters of the way to its top. Andrew always dreamed about climbing it, but could not find a suitable partner for this adventure. He had just arrived from Central Poland where he worked, and was staying in a nearby chalet. In fact, it was his first time climbing in this area. Most of the time he climbed in his favorite location; the Valley of the Five Lakes. There he knew almost all the routes on all the slopes and rocky cliffs. There he had met not only with a good adventure but also with Raya, his extraterrestrial partner. There he met his first chance to leave Poland for the Free World. It came in the form of a Jewish girl, very intelligent and poetry-minded, who wished him to join her on a trip through Yugoslavia and Turkey, down to Israel. He liked her. She was a good, stimulating partner; but it was probably too early for him to desert this communist run 'kindergarten of life,' so he didn't leave. Maybe he had luckily escaped from trouble waiting for him in the Middle East. Who knows? Simply, there was no connection as they had entirely different backgrounds.

Now he was desperately looking for a partner to do a climb, any climb. He was on annual leave from his work. Time was running fast, like the sand in an hourglass. The days before return to work were becoming less and less in numbers. He walked to the rock climbers' camping ground and met there a girl called 'Kviatushek' (Pol.: Flower). She was a pretty girl but badly spoiled by her wealthy parents and very capricious in nature. As an old Polish proverb says: **"In the absence of fish even a lobster is a fish,"** which is equal to the English proverb: **"Half a loaf is better than none."** Anyway, they came to the mutual understanding that at this stage they should go together for a climb. She was not a good climber, and because of this their choice was fairly easy—the ridge of the 'Twelve Apostles' on the slope of 'Frog's Crags,' just opposite of Mnich, two kilometers across the lake. He didn't know the area well and when other rock climbers asked him how long the climb they were going to make would take them, he innocently said:

"One day, or maybe a day and a half if it's too difficult for her to do it faster." This answer caused an explosion of uncontrolled, gruff laughter, as the climb of 'Twelve Apostles' was classified as not more than four hours of easy exercise.

"Have you really been doing it for so long?" asked one of them. But, in spite of the difficulties and nasty comments they set themselves on the track towards the beginning of the ridge, sent off by the still laughing friends wishing them success in their climb to the peak of sexual fulfillment.

The weather was nice, with a clear sky and mild warm air. No wind at all, just a pleasant, fresh breeze from the Morskie Oko side. The climb proved very easy and extremely picturesque. The Apostles were tall, eight to twenty-meter pinnacles of different shapes, standing on the rising ridge of the lowest grade of difficulty. Kviatushek, a bit lazy, didn't climb all the Apostles, but Andrew did. The most spectacular was the fourth or the fifth in the row. It was over eighteen meters high, a narrow granite aiguille, which from a distance appeared solid, but during the climb it became evident that it was built from huge slabs and blocks of rock freestanding on each other. How it was possible for them to still stand firm, only its patron Apostle knew. Andrew climbed it and stood straight on its very peak, like a circus acrobat. There were at least three hundred meters of air between his feet and the surface of the lake. They climbed to the height of the seventh Apostle. Everything was going without the slightest problem, even Kviatushek wasn't complaining too much.

At one o'clock they stopped the climb and ate lunch. After the meal Andrew lay in the sun for a nap. Kviatushek walked away, and sitting on a huge boulder took out of her bag a flute and started to played 'El Condor Pasa,' a beautiful Peruvian melody composed especially for the flute and based on old Inca motives, describing through sound the experiences and feelings of the condor, the biggest bird on Earth, flying very high up to the stratosphere to enjoy a lonely glide in the infinity of space, and having a silent talk with God Sun. It was a very romantic moment. Kviatushek was sitting on a rock with the broad, deep valley, filled with a gentle mist, under her and Mnich in the background. Surprisingly, she was a very skilful flute player. The tones of this nostalgic melody, dreaming about Freedom in Unending Existence, spread far and were echoed by the mountains. Andrew, listening to it, thought that every single person has some good quality, talent or hidden skill, which is possible to be activated if stimulated by circumstances. Then he drifted into sleep and dreamt that he was entering the cave under Mnich.

On the walls, burning torches were attached to metal holders forged into the shape of hands. The entrance leads him to a huge vaulted hall. Covering the floor, between the rocks and sleeping in full armor, were knights, ancient hussars of the Polish Kingdom. He carefully walked around them, contemplating the beauty of the skilfully forged, long and heavy swords, axes and clubs, coats of arms on their chests and battle ensigns. Against the walls of the hall horses stood sleeping in full armor. Andrew picked up a soft leather container for carrying drinks, which belonged to one of the knights, and opening it he smelled the cork. It contained a liquid worthy of a King's throat. It was the Hungarian wine 'Tokay' stemming from at least the 16th century, and one of the best, heavy white ones ever made on this planet. Being thirsty after lunch he took a few good sips of it, and feeling sleepy sat on the ground near one of the warriors. Soon he drifted into a strange sleep. He dreamt a dream in a dream, being partly aware that he was dreaming. He dreamt that from behind him came a huge, white animal, at least five meters long, with the body of a weasel and the head of a flat nosed dog. His ears were long, broad and soft. He also had six legs and wings. Andrew, trembling from fear tried to run away, but found his legs weren't functioning due to the wine.

"Don't be afraid. I don't eat rock climbers for lunch. In fact I don't eat people at all", said the creature, pulling him towards its chest and smiling charmingly.

"I'm very pleased that you have come here. Now you are to become a Witness that Poland's freedom is not irretrievably lost. The Forces of Justice are waiting here ready for the right moment to restore righteousness and happiness to this land. Poles have to go through many painful experiences because such is their nation's collective fate due to some mistakes committed during the previous Wave of Life, when you all lived in Africa and misused, for selfish ends, the technological knowledge which was in your possession. But there is always hope; great suffering is always balanced by at least equally great joy. In the near future a man will come here and awaken these mighty knights, whispering a secret formula. Because I am a Care Monster, I would like to present to you, as the first visitor to this cave, a gift, which will make you akin to all creation. Don't be afraid. Eat this golden stone and experience in your heart the warmth of the Golden Light of Love. Saying this, the Care Monster handed him a huge, shiny oval stone. Andrew ate it and was surprised to find that it only looked hard like a diamond, but it was in fact soft and sweet like fruit jelly from the famous Warsaw based 'Wedel' factory.

After he finished eating the golden stone, he woke up from his dream in a dream and looked around to see what had happened to the sympathetic Care Monster. He had disappeared! He looked back and noticed at the end of the hall something fluffy and white disappearing into a cave corridor. Andrew jumped to his feet and ran to catch the Care Monster. He wanted to ask him a few very important questions.

But on the spot where the Love Dragon's tail had gone, there was now a solid rock wall!

"Where are you?" he shouted. Only an echo in the cave repeated his question:

"Where are you, you, you . . ." On hearing this spontaneous shout, the knights moved in their sleep, clanging and tinkling their armor. Andrew covered his mouth with his hand in fear that he might wake them up before the right time.

He was woken up on the slope of 'Frog's Crag' under the seventh Apostle by a distressed Kviatushek shaking his shoulder and crying,

"Wake up and look what's happening. We are going to die soon!" He was still half asleep but sat up. What he saw was a brownish gray, dark, dense cloud approaching them fast from behind Mnich. From it flashed blue zigzags of lightning and the entire valley echoed with the terribly loud thunder. The slopes of the mountains were repeating it in a multiple echo. It resembled the bang of big guns on the battlefield.

He realized the danger and jumped to his feet, deciding to give up climbing the other Apostles, and to move immediately toward the tourist track, by the shortest and easiest way possible. Being more experienced, he led the climb. He noticed blue auras of crawling sparks surrounding his hands and the edges of the rock he climbed. The auras were also on the carbines and pitons hanging on the sling across his chest. The cloud was now less than eight hundred meters away and, because of its electrical charge, everything became electrically charged. There was no time for longer contemplation of this spectacular phenomenon. He was aware that at any moment the lightning could convert them into ashes so he moved very fast. Being on the top he pulled on the rope, lifting Kviatushek up like an empty bag. They ran across the slope looking for a flat area where the rapid flow of the water from the rain would not wash them down, and where there was the least chance for the lightning to discharge. They found the right spot and Andrew hammered into the crack in the rock two pitons, attached to these two carbines and tied first Kviatushek and then himself on three-meter long slings quickly made from the belaying rope.

The downpour started rapidly and was so intense that even breathing needed skill. Kviatushek and Andrew lay face down on the hard and short high-altitude grass, covering their faces from the water running over their heads, trying to catch some air. The lightning around them was striking on the ridges and the top of the crag. The moving blue lines of discharged electricity decorated the slope like gigantic ribbons of not yet invented liquid neon lights. Somehow they survived unharmed. The storm ended as quickly as it had started. The clouds moved to the Slovak side across the country border, which was just on the top of 'Frog's Crags.'

Many years passed; Kviatushek immigrated to France after a disappointing, short marriage to a man whose family smuggled gold dinars from Austria. Andrew immigrated to the Southern Hemisphere and in his spare time taught Michael, his son, rock climbing.

Once, Andrew and his son went to the Cathedral Ranges, the closest granite hills of their town, which were suitable for beginners and intermediate-advanced rock climbers. The wall of the North Jawbone culminated over the valley, which was a tectonic depression formed many million years ago during a massive earthquake. From the car park on a road through bush land, where they parked car it looked impressive and almost vertical—a one-hundred-and-eighty meter cliff—but which in fact was only a sixty-five degree angled wall and fairly easy to climb. The weather was excellent, with a gentle breeze, clear sky, pleasantly warm air and, most important, no stinging flies. Flies were almost always annoying climbers, disturbing them during climbs, and tactfully stinging most painfully when climbers were in difficult positions or in trouble. The climb they chose started from the rocky gully, a few meters over the approach track. They unpacked the climbing gear and changed their hiking boots for special ones. Michael felt, for some reason, an unexplainable fear and asked if they really had to climb here and now. Andrew thought:

"No, we don't have to, but because the weather was more than favorable, and because we had come here just for doing so, we should climb!" Michael was not a novice. He had climbed many more difficult routes, but this time he was somehow not very confident, and when they started, he wore his harness and again said,

"Is it really a safe climb?"—"Yes, this is a climb for beginners," assured his father.

They climbed the first forty meters. Andrew set up a good belaying stand and Michael climbed as a second. He had just reached the spot where a eucalyptus tree, commonly called a 'Ghost Gum tree' grew in a huge crack of a rock, when a dark blue-gray cloud appeared as if from nowhere, though actually it had come from behind the North Jawbones. It started to rain. It was not just a rain; it was a downpour, so intense that the remaining one-hundred-and-forty meters of wall above them turned almost instantly into a white waterfall of icy cold water, falling down with the force of the famous Niagara Falls, and breaking into clouds of tiny drops on every imperfection or protruding stone. The father, attached to the belaying block on a short sling and being on a narrow ledge, was reasonably firm on his legs, but his poor son, still on a free rope going only from the eucalyptus tree to his father's belaying plate secured on a screw up carbine to his harness, was hanging almost upside down, already half drowned and trying desperately to catch his breath and find a support for his legs. His attempts to stand firmly were in vain. The water speeding down was constantly undercutting his legs. The father set up a system for his son to abseil down, but being stressed by the dangerous situation he made a very serious mistake. Michael picked it up immediately and pointed it out to his dad. Soon after correcting the fault, he was abseiling down. Below the wall in a gully their hiking boots and backpacks were floating. The protruding ridges glowed with the bluish light of electrical discharges.

"Don't worry Michael! Just relax and concentrate on abseiling! This is nothing! I went through much worse situations many times in the Tatra Mountains", said the father, trying to encourage his son while overcoming the roar of the water and the thunder. His voice probably sounded a little too self-assured because Michael only looked at him doubtfully, and not saying a word, continued his abseil.

The storm ended as quickly as it had started. They were alive but totally wet and very cold. Maybe the rain was mixed with hail. They quickly collected their belongings, fished out their boots from the water and, shivering with cold, started to walk quickly towards the tourist track. When they reached the track Michael asked:

"Do you know why we survived without any harm, Dad?

"No, I don't."

"Because, when the storm started and the waterfall fell on my head, I started automatically to repeat your Guru's mantra: 'OM NAMAH SHIVAYA.' I continued it until you had landed safely at the bottom of the wall." Andrew was silent, feeling deeply amazed. He thought, "What a mysterious person my son is. From where did this mantra appear in such a critical situation? Was it stored in his subconscious?"

They continued to walk-run down across the boulders and amongst the huge trees. Andrew was thinking to himself,

"Maybe this is just the formula needed to awaken the Knights of Justice sleeping in the cave in the Tatra Mountains, if they exist. But it was probably too late! Communism has already collapsed and Poland is now a Free Country. But are the Poles really free? People are demoralized by the earlier partition of Poland between Germany, Russia and Austria, and then by the long German occupation during World War II, and finally forty years of degradation under communism. People now have become very selfish and peremptory, and, in fact, live in the chains of material desires, greed and lust. Drinking, practised by almost all, destroys morale and families. Maybe the right time to awaken the ancient warriors is not so far away at all. Who knows? There is one thing known for sure to both of us though, that the mantra infused by a Mahatma or a Guru has power, and if used with faith can make the impossible possible, anytime and anywhere."

UNAVOIDABLE

D arkness is coming. Let it come. If the unavoidable must happen then let it happen. The balance is already lost. Darkness means no light. But for us, You are The Light. You will never fail. A Path to Freedom is open only for those who were growing in slavery chains. Then Darkness is only a prelude to Light.

If Transformation has to take place, let it be so. Fire or water? We don't care! Why should we? We are living only to be transformed by You. Afterwards, we can stay or go. Other forces can't touch the Real Us. We want to become dissolved in You; we want to disappear in a homogenous Existence of The Oneness, to become a ray of light playing freely in the infinity of space. When Darkness reaches its climax, and its bottomlessness in shameless falls, we will be cleansed; we will be ready for Your call.

To build the new, the old must be demolished. Let us make cobblestones for the road to a luminous future, which is due to follow the time of terror, the condemnation time. Let us become fireflies, tiny lamps helping those who want to see The Path; or we can grow to become trees. As You wish. We fear not and ask for nothing. We are the hosts of Your army. Surrendering to life, we become ready to die. For whom is dead? For the body? Then it is not for us! We are Your hosts, the Eternal Divine Hussars. Rustle and swish invisible wings as we are rising. Ensigns flutter as we are flying, to have a feast, as we are rushing to drink to our limit Your unique wine of amrita ambrosia. We are Your hosts. We are mighty armed with missiles of Love. A victory of Light over Darkness is as certain as life which always prevails over death. We are Your hosts. Darkness must fear, because we fear not!!

BLACKBERRIES

T raveler's steps were slow and wobbly. He was breathing with difficulty, almost totally exhausted and on the edge of collapse.

The temperature exceeded forty degrees centigrade and there was no moisture in the air. There was also no wind, and the air was like hot oil sizzling under the burning Australian sun, which was at its zenith in an incredibly blue sky. He whetted his lips which were dry and cracked from thirst and heat. Moving slowly along the bed of a small creek, his mind was entertaining a desire for fruit; any fruit, sweet or sour, but wet and refreshing. He was in a dream-like state. Unreal. Maybe it was delirium caused by heat, tiredness, thirst. He had no idea where he was and had almost forgotten who he was before he came here.

It was only two and a half months since he had asked his Guru for a blessing together with his lady partner. This was a relationship he had drifted into after a few years on a path leading toward renunciation. Guru's words still sounded fresh in his ears, "No, my son, Maha Maya caught you again. After a while try to free yourself." Guru's eyes were loving. In this moment Traveler's surrender was almost perfect. He accepted in advance whatever Guru would say. He dissolved his beingness in Him, experiencing only attributeless Existence. No desires. No thoughts. No wishes. Only the Bliss of Inexpressible Love.

Later, day by day, night by night, he experienced all this in memories so fresh that it was impossible to forget the smallest part of those few seconds with Guru. For the next two and a half months he went through an incredibly hard time renovating fourteen two-bed roomed flats for a client in the heat of Australian summer. He worked by himself. Being homeless after the separation from his partner, he slept in his van, every night on a different street to avoid being picked up by police. He ate rarely as he had very little money left from his savings, and this had been invested in materials for the renovations. Now the job was finished and he had been paid, but he had no cash on hand because the check deposited in the bank was not yet cleared. Having no food other than a little barley and Vegemite, he decided to go and spend a few days of rest on the beaches of the Peninsula, close to the town where he lived. For buying petrol he used his Visa Debit Card and luckily the transaction was processed despite the bank account being zero.

After four days of wandering along the coast and sleeping on the beaches, accompanied only by the sound "OM" of the ocean waves, he was in a state of dehydration. All that his body was demanding was fruit, fruit, just any fruit. It was like an obsession. Coming to a small clearing he noticed a gigantic bush of blackberries. He could not believe his eyes. It was not blackberry season but the bush was full of huge fully ripe fruit. A miracle! It was only the beginning of February. He didn't know whether it was happening in a dream, or if it was real but he started to eat the berries, slowly, with the fear that he would wake up. But he didn't. The blackberries were sweet and juicy. Life and energy were coming back to his body. He had the feeling that each of the berries was given to him by the Universe on his Guru's request. He was eating the fruit as if straight from Guru's hand. Presence of All-What-Is was in the air. Presence was in each fruit. He again experienced what he had two and a half months ago; a feeling of belonging wholly to the Totality of Existence and confidence that everything will always be taken care off. It was a state of no mind—only Bliss but in full awareness. Intuitively he realized that now, since he had surrendered to Guru who represents the Universe, he would never be left on his own. Whatever was necessary would be provided—sometimes in strange and unexpected ways—because such is the Law, the Law of Love, most powerful of cosmic laws.

THE EYES

A bove the warm Arabian Sea in Southwest India, massive rain clouds moved slowly, majestically, but steadily towards the Northeast. Their shapes were so fantastic and sophisticated, so extraordinary that, for those who were equipped with a vivid imagination, they supplied unlimited high-octane fuel to illustrate their thoughts and to decorate the stage for their lofty emotions. It was already monsoon time and frequently rained heavily.

They met unexpectedly on the reddish, muddy road of the coastal swamps. The Man was wearing, as all local people used to wear there, a colorful dhoti and a large plastic hat. It was hardly a substitute for an umbrella, but it left both hands free. The Traveler was clad in white. Their eyes dove into each other for a particle of a second. Startled, the Traveler recognized with astonishment the same Golden Light in the stranger's eyes, which always fascinated him so much in his Guru's dark, smiling eyes. There was a perfect nothingness, and at the same time a total, absolute fullness of Existence, pulsating uninterruptedly with Divine Love in the form of this precious sparkling Golden Light. The Traveler, under the tremendous impact of surprise, experienced for a blink of an eye his own non-existence as a separate, cognitive entity. He experienced for a moment the bliss of perceiving his identity with The Oneness.

The Man smiled towards the Traveler, like one does at the sight of his dearest relative. On his face, covered with wrinkled brownish skin and silvery-grey stubble, manifested a smile, which can appear only on the face of the Liberated Ones, the Light Bearers. His benign smile whispered silently with love:

"Welcome me in you. We are not two strangers as you think, but one. Try, my friend, to abide in the Natural State, to live permanently in the awareness of your oneness with The Oneness, as I do, only then will you fully understand what I am saying now."

The Man's legs and hands were covered in cement, as he was a construction worker. He raised his palms and saluted the Traveler in the traditional Indian way:

'Namaste'. The Traveler almost stopped. He mechanically returned the salute in the same way but walked on as if in a dream, with the action done in slow motion. He went to the canteen to have his morning tea. What could he have said? Hasn't everything that has any meaning already been told? He was very deeply moved by the unexpected experience with the unknown Man.

For the next few days the eyes of the Man were vivid and fresh in the Traveler's memory. He felt that they were still looking at him through everything he passed. Those eyes were surely The Universal Eyes, which manifest from time-to-time to radiate The Universal Light of Divine Love.

Under the influence of this experience, he thought:

"We can admit that those who manage to reduce their restless mind's activity become less self-centered and develop alertness and the ability to see what is happening a bit further than the tip of their nose. One can meet beings with the Golden Light in their eyes everywhere on earth. They are in the Gulag's hard labor camps in snowy Siberia, in the humid tropical jungles of Amazonia, in Himalayan caves, under the coconut palms of Southern India, on a Kevala bench in Kerala or in Hyde Park in London, and even on Third Avenue in NY City. They are Light Bearers, and some, like my Guru, are Super Light Bearers. We are all Travelers on a quest. Many of us are still unaware of where we are heading—it feels like being in a labyrinth. Maybe we don't know that we are all going back Home to merge for good with God, our Father. We are His darling children, but we're lost in the complexity of material existence. We are all in a state of auto-hypnosis, living unconscious lives. We think, but we think too much, and mostly in patterns. We think that we are awake, but in fact, we are in a deep sleep. In this sleep we are dreaming that we are going to sleep, and in these secondary dreams we sometimes have quite interesting dreams about awakening. But all of it is utterly unreal and has no real value at all. Our Father is patient; He is also very forbearing. He is silently whispering through our intuition His advice to help us find the Road, the Path back Home:

"Go straight; do not be diverted by transitory petty goals! What benefit do you get my Darling child by acquiring this or that object, by getting into this or that situation? Wake up, Golden Ones and stay alert. Aim only for the Highest! You are zero as an individual. Zero has no value. But zero attached to a number becomes important. I am number One. Be attached to Me!"

Do we ever hear Him? Do we ever follow HIS advice, which is full of Wisdom? Yes, but very rarely. We prefer to follow the advice of our wicked minds:

"A house of your own is what you need now. It will provide security for old age. She or he will make you happy . . . Do everything to make it happen . . . Don't listen to your intuition! Be practical! Think rationally . . . Spiritual mysticism will only lead you into trouble . . . Get those things which will make you somebody! Do it! Do it now. Tomorrow could be too late . . ."—Our Father will not force us to do anything. HE constantly watches us from everywhere as HE is in everything, but HE is giving us freedom to do it as we like; slow or fast. Ultimately all of us will reach our Eternal Abode, but it can take millions of incarnations if we don't understand why our life is in a mess, put our affairs in order, and start to work earnestly on self-improvement. Is it really worth it to spend our energy on pursuing endless, worthless, transitory goals, moving in circles, going nowhere, and in the end to experience only disgust and disappointment? What can give us permanent happiness, permanent Bliss? Why should we struggle hard to get this or that object, which we believe will make us happy only to experience after years of strenuous toil a short lasting pleasure at best, which we in our ignorance identify with happiness? Each pleasure has to be balanced sooner or later by pain and suffering. Because we are so badly attached to our material possessions, our relations and our feelings, even the smallest scratch on the surface, or any alteration in our relationships, causes us great mental agony. We often say:

"We are living in the Free World! We are free beings!" Are we really free? What do those chains of attachment, which we clearly see on us, mean? Do we not live animalistic rather than human lives? What predominates in our mental values? Is it not food, sleep and sex, with all the rest, and only to make our lives as comfortable and satisfying to our senses as possible? Do our eyes shine with Love Divine, as do the eyes of the Great Ones? Can we love unconditionally? Let us look into the mirror! What we see is a pair of frightened, insecure eyes anxiously looking for answers: Where to find happiness? How do we get what we want so badly? The picture is not too uplifting! Does it mean there is no chance to free ourselves from this wicked circle? No. There is hope! If we look intensely and deeply enough into those lightless eyes, deep, very deep and at the very bottom of them, under the many layers of memories of mental hurts, of ugly scars left by disappointments, under turbid filters of unfulfilled passionate desires and unmet unreasonable expectations, we will find a tiny spark of the Divine Golden Light of Love. It is hiding there, shy and overwhelmed by our self-assurance and selfishness. In quality it is exactly the same as the light in the eyes of the Great Ones, only its intensity is almost nil, because we are dimming it with the dense filters of our ignorance, and following it we live in a state of delusion.

It is up to us what we will do after this discovery! We can concentrate our energy on eliminating those filters in our eyes. They are not permanent. We can remove them one by one. If we learn to ignore our mind's demands they will gradually die from starvation. We can kindle this Divine Flame in us by acting selflessly, by being equipoised when facing the fluctuating experiences in our lives, by loving all whom we meet and rejecting none, by doing our hard work but not claiming its fruits . . . The Flame will gradually burst into that huge and powerful source of Golden Light, and we ourselves will find that so desired peace of mind and, following it unfailingly, reach that eternal happiness in Divine Bliss. After attaining this state we will not care what we do or don't do, what others will think about us or will do to us, what we will have or not have. There will be no others! Everything that exists would be ours. External involvement or non-involvement will have no meaning to us; just as it has no meaning to a homeless avadhuta beggar from Oarchira, a yogi in a Himalayan cave, a Free Man from the snows of Siberia's great nothingness, or a laborer—the Man from Kerala's coastal swamps. Who is really ready to try? Such difficult conditions! So frightening is the prospect of entering the Unknown! Maybe it is still better to try to get that new car which is obviously better than our best friend's. What about him or her? Is it not better to follow the example of the majority and enter into a bumpy relationship? When it becomes too much, we can always run away and get divorced. But now she or he is looking so nice and smiling so promisingly. She or he must be entirely different from the others. Perhaps she or he has already entertained the idea of getting happiness from being associated with us! But if we too want to allay our misery by being in this relationship, and we too expect to get happiness, then from where will this happiness come? What is the original source of it?

The first Law of Nature is: 'Nothing for nothing.' But everyone only wants to get without investing energy. Who is ready to give? We can easily guess the result:—suffering! It can't be different because there is no balance. No balance results in pain, pain causes unhappiness, and this in turn manifests as sickness. Most of the sick people are sick because they are immensely unhappy, because they want only to get, never ready to give. But our Father is still waiting. He can wait for eternity, as He is Him who created time. He wants nothing as all is created by Him from Himself. He can lend us what we ask for. Anyway, it's only for a few more years. What does it matter compared to Totality and Eternity? But Father is ready to give us all that He has. This can be given only to those who dispose of their own ugly, arrogant, deceiving egos, which have grown fat on the sweet but poisonous foods of desire, on attachment and dislike. He is willing to give those who are willing to enter into the sacrificial fire of surrender. Others, not able to destroy their greatest enemy can't receive even a little of the Father's riches. They are too full. There is no space in them. They would explode under its radiance like a thermonuclear bomb after being heated by the radiation of an atomic explosion.

Is anybody ready? None? Why? Get up and go! Go for the quest! Try to find happiness in the World, and when your hair becomes silver-grey, when you realize that you fruitlessly wasted all those precious years living like a beast in a human body, maybe luck will smile on you and you will become totally fed up with all of that, which before had such a charismatic magnetism for you. Maybe in this hour of dark despair you will meet one of the Light Bearers. He will seem to be a stranger with . . . shining eyes. Maybe if your suffering purified you well enough you will realize that nobody else but you are potentially Him. Maybe even elevated by the experience you'll find enough strength in your worn-out mortal frame to gather the fuel of devotion, renunciation and surrender, and will manage to light the sacrificial pyre and to offer to The Highest all that which until now you called 'you'. The smoke from this sacrificial fire will veil this Maya created world of illusion. Good luck! Be brave. Do not have mercy. Destroy it! Afterwards, as a Free Man, you may meet a Man from the coastal swamps on a muddy road. What a meeting it will be! You will meet yourself in a different manifestation. Let's do it; let's become Free and then roam among our still sleeping younger brothers and sisters, as long as our *prarabdha karma* allows us to be here on this blue planet called Earth. Go for it, go! He or she whom you've left unattended will soon find another being like you to charm, to offer that promise of happiness too. Do not worry. Nature can't tolerate a vacuum created by your absence in the game.

INITIATION

The midday sun was frying Kerala's South Indian landscape. Kanhangad Railway Station was almost empty. The rusty metal roof covering the concrete platform was radiating intense heat. Sitting under it was like being in a bakery oven. On a bench made of black granite an old man was sleeping, snoring loudly. A few villagers were sitting on the ground and eating homemade *uppuma* on banana leaves. Monkeys and stray dogs were digging in a pile of rubbish lying behind the platform. The air was saturated with the fragrance of sandal wood incense burned in the Control Room by the Station Master; the stink of rotting food leftovers on the line and urine as the bathroom was locked for renovation and travelers were relieving themselves almost everywhere. A gentle wind was bringing from a nearby dry meadow the smoke of burned cow manure cakes and wood mixed with the aroma of spices used in cooking by the tribal people from Western Ghats. They, being nomads, had erected there for a few weeks, their primitive tents made of coconut leaves and blue plastic sheets. Ladies were attending to their children, sprawled on the ground, hanging saris and other laundry on improvised clotheslines and preparing lunch. Men were busy making gypsum casts of Hindu Gods and painting them in vivid colors for the local market.

Traveler put his backpack on a bench close to the Waiting Room for Ladies and sat to wait on it. His train to Trivandrum was expected in half an hour. He was thinking about the mysterious tunnels with side meditation chambers, dug in a rocky hill on the order of late Swami Nithyananda, which he saw that morning. Traveler had spent a few days in meditation in peaceful Ananda Ashram of the late

Swami Ramdas and on the last day took a trip to this almost deserted Baba Nithiananda's place, which was not so far. Swami constructed these caves as homes for spiritual seekers and aspirants. The caves are meant for meditation. Carved out of a single laterite massive stony hill, without any civil engineering assistance, forty-three caves possess an unmatched acoustic curiosity, and when passages are clear of people and someone chants there the sacred syllable 'OM' the echo repeats for over a minute. The caves attract thousands of spiritual seekers and tourists from all over the world. Swami Nithyananda had an unusual way of delivering wages to his workers during the construction of these caves. Sometimes he used to take money out of his loin cloth, and at other times he told the workers to collect their pay from a package between the roots of a nearby neem tree or from underneath a stone. Surprisingly, the bundle always contained exactly the amount required to pay the wages. Swami Nithyananda believed that in future, great saints would live in these caves and inspire the birth of a new Golden Age, restoring *dharma* and revitalizing the eternal religion of *Sanathana Dharma*.

"Is this possible?" thought Traveler. "Humanity drifts these days at an alarming speed in totally different directions and the future of our race is very worrying. The uplifting of *dharma* is needed right now. Why wait for the future? Why spend so much energy in the form of labor and money and never put this to use now when transformation is most desirable?"

A small monkey approached and sat in front of him expecting an edible gift, anxiously rubbing her head. He opened his backpack and removed from it a 'ladies fingers' type banana and stretched his hand toward the monkey. The monkey was confused. Why doesn't this silly human throw the fruit toward her? Is it safe to accept it from his hand? She decided to use a trick: walked sideways, as if completely disinterested, and then suddenly ran straight to the fruit, grabbed it making an aggressive sound of warning and escaped in the direction of a semi-dried hedge, cautiously looking back at Traveler when running.

From the direction of the Ticket Office limped an old man wearing a, once white, dhoti and a *kavi* shirt faded by the sun. He sat on Traveler's bench and asked on which train he was waiting. After a while the man asked Traveler from which country he was. Traveler explained that it was a very difficult question as he was born in one country, raised in another and then lived in a few more. He told the man that he came from Australia as that was his last place of residence. The man said that he wanted to know Traveler's country of birth and that he has an important message for someone from a particular country, who is supposed to be traveling through Kanhangad today.

"Yes this must be you! Not very often do people from Lithuania pass through our town," whispered the man, almost inaudibly, when he heard the word "Lithuania". "Give me some money, as a messenger must be paid. If the amount matches what I was told, I will pass on the message." Traveler suddenly saw in his mind, in the blink of an eye—like a flash—a brownish, wrinkled hand accepting two pieces of bluish paper. He opened his wallet and took out two one hundred rupee notes. The messenger exclaimed in excitement:

"This is you! The recipient of the message is supposed to give me exactly this much! No one ever gives a beggar so much! One more correct answer is needed! Where do you live?"

"In Tiruvannamalai, I have there a thatched coconut-leaf hut."

"Yes you are the right person! Now listen carefully. Someone from the White Brotherhood wants to meet you. It is important that you do not miss this appointment, as the invitation will never be repeated in this life of yours. Go immediately back to Tiruvannamalai. Today is 21st. On the first Monday of next month go to Kannapa Temple. You obviously know where it is! Don't you? Be there before noon. Do not take with you a mobile phone or any other electronic gadgets. Do not wear or carry with you anything metallic. Do not eat anything on this day. No coffee! Only spring water is permitted. Wait there, doing your *japa*, and you will be called! *'Namaste'*" The messenger got up, saluted Traveler with folded palms and left in a hurry.

A computer generated voice of a young lady with a strong Indian accent announced: *'Attention please! Kanyakumari Express will arrive on Platform Number One in zero hours and ten minutes.'* The announcement was repeated in Malayalam, Tamil and Hindi. A policeman arrived on the platform with a huge mustache and his belly hanging down over his belt. He was holding in his left hand, close to his ear, a switched off CB phone, just to demonstrate his importance, and in his right hand a bamboo stick. He approached a sleeping man, hit his leg with a cane and when the man woke up, hissing from pain, he started asking inquisitive questions. A young couple entered the platform dragging their hysterically crying daughter wearing clothes like a Western doll. Traveler felt stunned. Everything swirled around him like in the vortex of a black hole. The memory of a strange book read once in Anti's house in the Polish mountains came to mind: '. . . White Brotherhood . . . Not one soul, deserving to be guided, will be left unnoticed . . .' "Me? Do I deserve? Why?"

On the train it was just time to serve lunch. Traveler purchased *'meals'*—wrapped in paper and banana leaf: rice, a tiny plastic bag of *sambar*, some vegetables, lemon pickle and another small plastic bag with *more* (*curd*—sort of yogurt with water and spices).

In Trivandrum Traveler rented a room in 'Vijaya Tourist Home' which is fifteen minutes walking distance from Trivandrum Central Railway Station. This was an inexpensive, clean, simple lodge managed by friendly people. For dinner Traveler went to a nearby vegetarian restaurant 'Mamma Mia'. The food was fabulous; *chappaties, allu masala, pacha pattani sambar* and *ladu* with spicy *chaya* for dessert. After dinner he took a short nap, then a cold-water shower, changed clothes—pants for a dhoti and at ten o'clock p.m. paid the lodge bill and slowly walked to the Railway Station, to board his train. On Platform One a policeman was chasing a dirty scoundrel and kicking him on the bottom. Traveler watched this for a while, admiring the scoundrel's skill in avoiding the force of kicks by bending at the right moment his body in a semicircle. Then Traveler climbed over the rails of a metal bridge stairs and walked to Platform Three, where his train was already standing. He had booked, before going to Kerala, his return ticket in a second-class sleeper—his favorite Upper Berth where there is much less disturbance. For a couple of hours he talked with co-passengers about the shortage of electricity in Tamil Nadu, unfair prices paid to farmers for agricultural produce, the rapidly growing cost of living and predictions of the possibility of American and Israeli war with Iran.

By late afternoon he was already in Villupuram. Traveler took a shared auto-rickshaw and went to the New Bus Stand. Shrinivasan Co. bus for Tiruvannamalai was already at the gate. It had stopped because of incoming traffic. Traveler boarded the bus. There were still a few seats empty. A young Muslim lady handed him printed in Tamil, English and Arabic a request card for financial support. He had seen her on a few occasions, as she had been begging on Villupuram New Bus Stand already for a few years. Someone told him that her husband went to Afghanistan to join the freedom fighters and had never sent a letter. He was either killed in battle or possibly sold by local warlords for a ransom to Americans and now kept captive and most probably tortured in one of their infamous 'black sites' – secret, lawless prisons floating on international waters or built in Poland, Lithuania and Bulgaria. Traveler gave her a fifty-rupee note. The lady looked, with great seriousness, straight and very deeply into his eyes; the way Muslim ladies never look at an unknown man, said nothing and immediately disembarked the bus. The bus video started to play a movie with a famous Tamil actor Vijay playing the part of a young undercover hero-policeman, fixing a gang of bullies who terrorized a small town. On the one and half hour trip to Tiruvannamalai this was repeated six times as the bus crew had no other movie to entertain the passengers.

Tiruvannamalai Bus Stand was, as usual, busy, dirty and crowded. Traveler narrowly avoided being hit by a government bus speeding in a cloud of dust towards Vellore and went down a street to choose a less rough and less corrupted auto rickshaw driver. All the auto rickshaw drivers looked very 'fishy' as they waited for customers. Traveler waited. One driver, who just arrived with a bunch of ladies, looked comparatively decent. Traveler asked how much he wanted to Arunachala Jewels Nagar. The driver did not know where it was.

Traveler explained how to get there and after a little bargaining they settled on a price of fifty rupees.

Nearing his hut, they passed his dogs, Raja and Sadhu, sitting under a huge mango tree where once upon a time he had entered into an agreement with an old Muslim to buy his building plot. Recognizing their master's smell and probably seeing in the darkness his aura, the dogs barked once and started to follow the auto-rickshaw, singing loudly their song of welcome. The place was empty but clean, as the cleaning lady had been informed that he was coming back. In a terracotta jar was fresh drinking water. He was tired. After drinking some water, he spread on the floor his rice straw sleeping mat and lay down. Big cobra crawled from a gap in a wall, hissed once, crossed the room and slowly climbed the hut's bamboo structure on the other side and disappeared into the coconut leaves of the roof. Traveler was very familiar with snakes and never feared them, knowing that as long as both parties have good intentions harm cannot be done to anyone. In Kerala in his hut lived a whole family of extremely venomous black snakes. Watching cobra and thinking what message is she bringing him Traveler quickly drifted to dreamless sleep.

Next day Traveler decided to go after breakfast in Sheshadri Ashram restaurant to Virupaksha Cave, where the late sage of Arunachala, Sri Ramana Maharshi lived for sixteen years, and spend there a day in meditation, trying to put the things which had recently happened to him in some sort of order. He walked along Chengam Road towards Arunachaleswaram Temple and after the transformer turned left. Passing by *Pandava Tirtham* he saluted '*namaste*' an old *sadhu* who was sitting there under a gigantic banyan tree. He looked like the *swami* who once stayed overnight in his coconut hut, when Traveler was staying for a few days in nearby Nanagaru Ashram and who left behind, cut from an iron tin, a sacred 'OM' now gold painted and installed on his *puja* table. The *sadhu* called him to come closer and smiling said:

"தம்பி—*Thombi* (Tamil: 'younger brother') do not forget about your appointment on the first Monday of next month!" Shock! "How does he know?"

"Do not worry brother! All is and will be fine. Go, go now and meditate!"

Virupaksha Cave was empty. No one inside! In the front garden a *swami* from a Ramanashramam, taking care of this place, was bathing, after breakfasting in the morning sun and drying his stainless steel plate and a cup on stones. Traveler entered the cave. Inside was silent as the noise of the busy town had been restricted by adding a front room to the cave. He sat, as he used to do, in the right-hand corner close to the doors, where there was more air.

Time stopped. Breathing slowed down. Traveler entered a state of 'no mind'. He was aware of his existence but it was not attributed to his body, not defined by his mind. He simply was as pure Awareness. Hours passed. He came back from his 'glide' semi intoxicated. It was difficult, almost impossible to get up. At least half an hour passed until he managed to rise and walk out limping, as his legs were still stiff. It was the middle of the afternoon. He sat by a stone wall surrounding the front garden and waited until his body regained normal strength. After some time he noticed the German lady Rita, whom he had known for a few years, passing by on her way up to Skandashram. He joined her. They walked maintaining *mouna* (M: silence—no talk) and in Skandashram split. Rita entered Ramana Maharshi mother's—(Tamil: திருமதி *Thirumathi* = Revered Lady, not exactly English Mrs.) Alagammal room to meditate there and Traveler went up the slope, and sat above the ashram building kitchen under a huge mango tree, a favorite spot of Ramana Maharshi. He watched monkeys playing on rocks and on an old mango tree. On a bend, visible in the distance, was Big Temple. A skinny young *swami* on duty from Ramanashramam came and asked Traveler to help him with making a drain of spring water that visitors can drink. They worked together without uttering a word for over two hours. After the job was completed Traveler went to the tap at the end of the water drain and drank until sated, then he set off on the return trip along a path towards Ramanashramam. Two hundred meters down on the left side was a big rocky platform hanging over Arunachala Southern slopes. From there was a fantastic view of Tiruvannamalai. Traveler sat there to gaze from this height on the town, which unexpectedly had become his place of permanent dwelling. After a while he noticed in the rock embedded massive dark brown intrusions. Immediately came to him the memory of his attempt to take to America a sample of this kind of stone to test its age by a friend from NASA. He expected that those lumps of rock, heavy in iron, were parts of Marduk, a natural satellite of Nibiru, unknown to present-day astronomy planet of Solar System—having a 3600 years long orbit, which according to Sumerian writings based on Anunakis' teachings in 'Enuma Elish' (Myth of Creation—a cosmological history of our planet), crashed into Tiamat (Earths' name used by Anunaki's before this cosmic collision). If so it should be much older than the Earth itself. Unfortunately the test never was carried out because he had to return urgently to India and left the stone together with a few of his belongings in the care of a friend. Later, one of his spiritual sisters, trying to be helpful, brought that sample back to India and Traveler never went there again.

Continuing on down Traveler passed a few stone carvers displaying their artistic merchandise: mini *Ganeshas, lingams* and *murtis* carved in gray, brown or black soapstone. Close to the Ramanashram back gate one of the Western *sadhus* passed him, running fast down the hill. This was the young man, Bruno, a French national already living in Tiruvannamalai for many years who was mentally unstable and believed that he was an incarnation of the God Shiva. He was barefoot, despite the hot stones of the path and had only a tiny loincloth covering his private parts. His face expressed a mixture of tension and anger partly covered by a bitter smile. (*Bruno, two years later, developed a bad infection on his leg and because he maintained his belief in his divinity, refused to seek medical help. After two weeks of struggling with pain and spreading gangrene he passed away in the garden of Ramanashramam where his already decomposing body was accidentally found.*)

On the appointed day, the first Monday of the following month, Traveler left his house at eleven am and walked along Inner Path of Arunachala *Giri Pradakshina* (which Inner Path is through jungle and Outer Path is on a tarred road.) through a jungle of bush-land with sparse trees towards Kannapa Temple. On a flat rock, about midway to Kannapa Temple, sat a group of Rajnish-Osho's disciples led now, after Master's *Maha Samadhi,* by one of Pune International Meditation Resort's community *sannyasin,* a middle aged man of German origin. He was a frequent visitor to Traveler's hut and they had in the past many interesting conversations. The group was singing: *"Shiva, Shiva, Shiva Shambo—Shiva, Shiva, Shiva Shambo—Máha Déva Shambo Máha Déva Shambo—Máha Déva Shambo—Máha Déva Shambo . . ."* When they noticed him, their singing subsided. One person from the group, an Israeli hippie girl, asked him, passing him a digital camera, to take a group photo of them. He took it, gave back the camera and slowly walked towards his destination to meet the unknown, pure mystery.

Kannapa Temple was closed. Also, no one was meditating on its terrace; only a few small monkeys were playing by climbing an ancient stone structure. Traveler walked around the temple, stopped on the left side of it where on a solid brownish stone, polished through the ages by feet of people, was an ancient Tamil writing chiseled long ago by an unknown monk-mendicant. Traveler tried to guess what it could mean. Maybe it is the declaration of the White Brotherhood that all deserving to be guided would be called at the right time. "Who knows?" He sat in the place where, in the past, a charismatic young lady from Chennai, used to sit with her spiritual partner, for her *satsangs.* This was during her short and tragic guru *bhava* performance for a few Westerners—mostly 'lost souls' addicted, as she was, to some substance. After a few years of this *leela* she committed suicide by burning herself with kerosene. Probably her lack of skills in the manipulating of a few Westerners who purchased land close to Tiruvannamalai in her name drove her to a point of such shame that there was no other way out except to quit the physical life and escape to another dimension. When she started to collect disciples and properties, people with predominant vibrations, matching hers, joined her group. Others left after seeing her a few times. Those who stayed enacted the drama of first 'surrendering' to her, then buying land in, supposedly, their guru's name. This was followed by constructing houses, a struggle for a control and an attempt to change ownership back to purchasers and finally beating her and even torturing her.

A priest, hired by the Shanthimalay Trust to perform daily *pujas* in this temple arrived. A person, dressed as lady, who was living in a nearby cave and who is known to be a hermaphrodite followed him. She approached Traveler, whom 'she' new from the time of a charismatic young lady's from Chennai *leela* as they had both a few times attended her *satsang*. She asked how things are now and waited. He gave her a fifty-rupee note—last item, before his secret meeting, from this world of grand illusion. The priest opened a metal door to Sanktum Sanktorum, lighted *deepam* on olive lamps and started worship. Traveler changed his place to be able to see it. From a distant mosque came the voice of muezzin, a Muslim reciter of midday prayers, which mixed with mantras chanted by a Hindu priest. When *puja* was over, an old *sadhu* came out from behind a temple idol. This was the same man Traveler met at Pandava Theertham.

"Come! It is your time now!" he said softly but authoritively. Traveler got up and waited to be guided. *Sadhu* did not leave Sanktum Sanktorum—only called him again:

"Come here! Go inside!" Traveler entered the temple. The priest stopped him and offered him on a small plate *vibuthi*. Traveler took some of this gray ash powder on his right hand middle finger and applied it between his brows where is supposed to be the 'third eye'. They passed *Shiva Lingam* on the left side and went through a small door leading to a staircase chiseled from solid rock. Six meters down was an ample size room. *Sadhu* invited Traveler to sit on a rice straw mat and went to a small side table standing against a wall. Northern, Southern and Western walls were part of a natural rock formation; Eastern was made of large stone blocks and had a small window in it. On the table were a stainless steel jar, a few half-coconut shells, a packet of incense, incense holder and a small alarm clock showing exactly 12 o'clock. *Sadhu* lighted a few incense sticks, put them into the holder and filled one coconut shell with something that was in a jar. He came back to Traveler with the coconut shell filled with some liquid.

"Drink this!" He commanded. "It will help you to separate from your body.'

"Is it my time to die?" asked Traveler a bit confused. "No. Do not worry. You are not going to die today. This is just water with some good herbs. It will not kill you. For us you are more useful alive than dead. You will only go for a small trip to higher dimensions, leaving for a while your body behind. No harm will be done to it." Traveler drank the liquid. It was fragrant, a bit sour but in fact tasted not too bad. Heat immediately spread all over his body. The room now looked like it had been built not from a solid rock but brownish mist. He lay down on a mat.

The landscape there was rigid; high cliffs, waterfalls, huge trees and everywhere gigantic boulders, but also the foliage was very rich with *sura param* berry bushes and marvelous tropical flowers—the kind he remembered growing in the Indonesian jungle of Sumatra where once he spent a month on a vacation. There was no visible sky—only hanging a few meters up a thin mist radiating gentle light. Between the boulders Traveler noticed a path made of reddish slabs of a soft material, like cork. He started to walk not knowing where he was nor what to expect on the path. After a hundred meters he noticed on his right side an entrance to a huge cave and entered it. Under the wall of solid stone overgrown by green moss sat cross-legged, a bearded old man wearing a white dhoti and a white shirt. His head was covered by a green turban. Traveler automatically saluted him in the traditional Indian way.

"Welcome *thombi*. I am one of the *siddhas* of Arunachala. I prefer not to use any name. So please, if you later choose to tell others about a few things we are going to talk about in our meeting do not create any name for me only call me simply Nameless Siddha. In fact it is my wish that you write down this part of our meeting which can be presented to the general public and make it accessible not only to spiritual seekers but also to those who want consciously to create their own Earthly reality. I know that you are very busy and so it may take you some time to complete it. I also understand that the situation on Earth is rapidly changing so I suggest that to make the story more accurate you include your later observations and conclusions. No need to strictly stick to our conversation. The important thing is to get the message through, make people aware who they are, how they relate to everything that exists and how they have allowed themselves to be conned. The Truth may shock some, it may taste bitter to many of those who are used to living with sweet lies. But it must be taken and digested as it is only medicine. Being venerable to the revelations of Truth, being open to love pouring from entire Creation is equal to permission to receive a gift of real existence, not a false way of life in the Matrix.

"We, the *siddhas,* live in Arunachala not in a physical dimension but in an astral one. Here is an entire vast town with many spiritually very advanced beings as residents. Not all are humans. We are guiding the spiritual advancement of this planet. I am appointed by the Council of White Brotherhood, to which I have belonged for more than the last seven hundred years, as your guide on The Path. I called you to come here because you have reached on your own the level of understanding, which qualifies for our acceleration. You, *thombi,* recently spent a few years in an ashram and left it disillusioned. No need to regret this. It was not completely wasted time. You had a fantastic opportunity to test yourself. Thanks to your earnestness and sincerity you had, during your stay there, many great and genuine spiritual experiences and, despite facing pervasive corruption and lack of substance, learned a lot by analyzing observed contrast. But, talking generally, ashrams are miniature, easy to manage communities where most residents share similar 'crazinesses' and limitations due to the common cult conditioning found there. Being an ashramite is in most cases a sign of people's insecurity to follow The Path on their own and a tendency to develop dependence on someone claiming to be fully realized or even God incarnated and who 'plays' the role of a Guru. This supposedly gives an aspirant freedom from *dharmic* duties, relief from making independent decisions, and imagined protection from evils of the world and, for those who expect it, spiritual guidance but not always genuine. Often for an initiation to meditation technique substantial payment is required and anyone having money can purchase it regardless of spiritual advancement. It is a perversion as from time immemorial spiritual guidance, instructions and initiations have always been offered to aspirants for free and only to those who were genuine seekers. During Vedic period even many wealthy kings were refused initiation because they wanted it only from curiosity. Thanks to an ability to think critically you survived there for a few years almost unharmed and without falling too deeply into this trap. What is most important is that you managed to preserve your independence. This secured you our guidance and protection. We do not want on Earth 'clones' of the same mentality and herds of blind followers. Individuality is what makes life worth living as it contributes to the expansion of the Universe bringing to the Oneness distinctive perspectives of each unique, autonomous and self-conscious projection of It.

"Now, before we start talking, I want you to see a few more of your past lives. This will help to understand the logic of the experiences in the present one. You are already familiar with a few of your incarnations as visions of them were given to you gradually before. Some, as being most significant, will be repeated now.

"Enjoy the 'trip'! Drink this now!" said Nameless Siddha passing to Traveler a small cup made of milky rock crystal. The liquid in the cup was sweet and spicy. Traveler was told to lie on a nearby flat slab of this reddish substance from which the path was made.

When the climate warmed up, the glacier era in Europe ended and a new cycle of life started. The barren landscape, covered by rocks, sand and clay carried in by the ice, was quickly overgrown by forests filled with a huge variety of trees suitable for the moderate climate. It became an ideal home for many wild animals: bears, elks, deer, lynx, wildcats and wolves, as well as for innumerable birds, with the mighty eagle as their King. In the clearing, Slavic tribes started to settle, taking their first steps in mastering agriculture and animal husbandry. The former glacier, many kilometers long and hundreds of meters deep, stayed for many years in the ground covered by several meters of rock, but gradually melted. The water from it created crystal clear so-called gutter lakes, abundant in rainbow trout, bream, trench, pike and perch. The climate was lively, very pleasant and healthy, with four well-defined seasons.

The Southern part of this vast country, which a few thousand years later was named 'Poland' and became one of the most powerful countries in Europe in the Middle Ages, was not directly affected by the glacier and was covered by ancient dense forests. Being formed on erodible limestone, it had a landscape with many valleys, ravines and huge rock formations.

In the meadow of one of its ample valleys, picturesque and peaceful just like heaven on Earth, a fifteen-year-old boy was living with his family and tribe. One day he stood under a twenty-meter high club-shaped limestone pinnacle. A wooden shepherd's stick, well polished by years of use, and with a waxy shine, glittered in his right hand. His long, straight shoulder-length hair resembled the golden color of the corn cultivated by his clan. His blue eyes were vigilantly scanning the valley. He was grazing a flock of sheep as he was in perfect tune with nature. Being a part of it, he felt instinctively that something was approaching. He knew that it wasn't dangerous, but rather something mysterious and exciting. He was very keen to meet the unknown. He was interested to know more about the world than his parents and elders knew.

The flat area of the valley was covered by moist, soft grass. It was like the expensive green rug which the chief of the tribe had bought last year from a traveling oriental salesman in exchange for seven bearskins and twelve big amber stones. This rug, the only luxurious item in the village, was used for special occasions: initiating young men into warrior-hood, making announcements about decisions in disputed matters, or sanctifying the marriages of young couples who fell in love.

The green rug of grass was decorated with white and black dots made of the sheep, which the boy watched over. To balance the carpeted landscape, the meadow was interspersed with white boulders of limestone, which stuck up like silent monuments of the not-forgotten glory of countless ancient warriors, whose blood fertilized this sacred land. Many skirmishes had been fought here with Germanic hordes invading it from the West, always greedily trying to conquer this Slavic heaven. The limestone rocks culminated on the border of the valley in high cliffs overgrown at the bottom by blackberries and hazelnut bushes. Higher up grew primeval forests of hundreds of years old oak, elm and beech trees, which rose up to the top of the hills. He could see in the distance the buildings of his village. Wooden log-huts stood in order, surrounding the central plaza where food was communally cooked on wood-fired clay and stone stoves. The village was encircled by a skillfully built high oak log palisade, with a few watchtowers around it. Below this fortification was a moat full of water surrounded by thorn bush branches and a drawbridge leading to the entrance gate.

The bluish smoke from the village was spreading towards the river where girls washed clothes and sang folk songs. Other girls were filling wooden buckets with the crystal clear water to carry to the village. He recognized the squirrel-like movements of his sweetheart and his heart started to beat faster. He thought with love that he did not have to wait much longer; next year he was going to be initiated into warrior-hood, and then they could get married.

The boy noticed a brown bear crossing the meadow. The bear was somehow also anxious. Walking slowly on all fours, the bear was frequently stopping and rising up on two legs, watching the road entering the clearing from the primeval forest, dense and humming from thousands of wild bees, bumble bees, hornets and other insects, tirelessly flying from flower to flower collecting golden pollen to make aromatic honey. The sun had already risen higher than the peaks of the hills. The boy looked back to check if the wolves were not creeping up to steal his sheep, and seeing the lime club-shaped pinnacle, remembered how last year during Autumn he had climbed its overhanging walls all the way to the top, and then found it impossible to climb safely down. The rescue expedition started immediately but, because of the approaching darkness, couldn't proceed as the gusty wind was blowing out their torches. He spent a very long, cold and sleepless night. It was too risky to drift to sleep, as the possibility of falling was almost certain. From that height it would mean instantaneous death. The following morning his relatives built a scaffold from alder tree sticks tied together with hemp ropes and led the boy down to safety.

He remembered how, during that long, long night, one of the stars on the black-black, infinitely deep sky had attracted his attention. It was blinking constantly, changing the color of its lights, talking to him with a strange, silent warmth and care,

"Wait. I am on the way. I am coming soon to Earth. We will meet face to face. I am not a star. I only assumed this shape to send my message to the chosen ones whom I will call. I am EVERYTHING. You are my son. I love you. Wait . . . Be patient!" It had really happened! It was not a dream! What was it? Who was HE? Now, on the very spot where he had spent the night shivering from cold stood a mighty eagle. He too was watching the road. He too was anxious. Why? What was going to happen? High, very high and motionless like a star in the sky floated a tiny lark, almost invisible against the deep blue background. The little lark filled the entire area with such beautiful trills of its amazingly loud song that even the tough old warriors, who in time of peace were the hunters, stopped from time to time on their way to the forest, secretly drying their teary eyes with their bushy mustaches. The lark was singing the song of love, love for the land, love for the Sun, and love for all the creatures living here in full harmony. This peerless song was making people cry with happiness. It was filling their hearts with the warm nectar of unconditional love for all manifested Existence. It was skillfully expressing their own feelings, which words in the human language cannot. The song expressed its own love towards The Oneness manifesting Itself in everything the lark knew, from the very day of its birth.

The hours were slowly passing. It was already afternoon. The boy ate the thick slices of dark rye bread with butter, and a piece of smoked sheep's cheese brought to him by his Little Sister. She stayed with him for a while and asked a few hundred questions, or maybe even more,

"Why do bears sleep all winter in caves? Why could birds fly and I can't? Why are the rays of the Sun warm and those of the Moon cool? Why are some sheep white and others black? Why did one girl, upon seeing him, become red in her face? Why, when this girl was around, didn't he hear or understand what people said? What are clouds?

What, what . . . ? Why, why, why . . . ?" He liked her very much and tried his best to answer all her questions, except those which made his face red too.

Suddenly Nature stopped its activities. Total silence covered the entire valley. The air was completely still. The sheep didn't move, and maybe even stopped breathing. It was completely silent; including the small lark that had stopped his song in the middle of a note. Perhaps even the Sun stopped His travel across the sky. The boy felt shivers crawling up his back. He had never experienced such a strange feeling or such deep, dense silence.

From out of the forest walked a man with a long stick in his hand. His hair was long, straight and black, like soot on the bottom of cooking vessels. His face, from a distance, also looked almost black, but really was brown, like the fertile soil of the valley dug out every day by the red-snouted moles and forming small hillocks in the green grass.

A few seconds passed in the dense silence. The first to break it was the lark, which started singing again in euphoria a song that was beautiful enough to be sung in the presence of God Himself. The entire creation almost choked itself in admiration of its song, and from inexpressible happiness and joy at the sight of the unknown Traveler. From the village a bunch of young children ran toward him. They wanted to be the first to greet him. They were attracted to him by some invisible pull, like iron rushes towards a magnet. What was so special about him? Who was he? No one had seen him before.

The Traveler stopped and waited patiently for them to come. On his face shone a smile, like that on the face of a happy father at the sight of his most beloved children. The children soon surrounded the Traveler and danced around him, singing and shouting in uncontrollable happiness. The man called them to him one by one and cuddled them like his own, gently caressing their golden hair with his brown skinned hands.

The boy didn't know what was happening to him. He forgot his sheep and himself and also ran toward the unknown man. He was for no

407

reason elevated and immensely happy. He felt that something, which he had been unconsciously waiting for all his life, was happening right now. He ran across the meadow as if in a trance, without care, over the stones and spiky weeds, feeling no pain. Just before reaching the man, whose eyes he could see glowing like two Golden Light stars, he lost his balance tripping on a crawling creeper, and he fell flat on the road, sliding in the dust towards the stranger. When his head touched the Traveler's feet, he experienced an incredible, unbelievable and unexplainable relief. He relaxed, like one who has arrived at life's ultimate destiny and, having nothing more to do with the world, is now resting horizontally after a long and dangerous journey, waiting for his soul to depart. The man lifted him up, looked straight into his blue eyes, smiled warmly and hugged him close.

"Son, I am so pleased that you are well. Why must you climb every rock, cliff and tree you meet on your way? You should be more discriminating. The time when you were incarnated as a monkey is long over, but you still have this deep-rooted tendency. I will teach you to climb to the top of creation, to reach the Highest Imaginable Peak. From there you will not want to be rescued nor need to come down again. In fact, from there, there is no return." The boy understood nothing. They walked together towards the village. The Traveler held the boy's hand throughout while looking at him from time to time, smiling.

The watchman on duty saw from the watchtowers everything that had happened, and the chief was informed. A replacement to watch the sheep had been promptly sent, and the chief managed to change his clothes into his leather armor and bull's-horn helmet. He waited for the Traveler's arrival standing in front of the guest-house. His wife prepared the linden wood bowl and poured lukewarm water into an oak bucket. She was waiting behind her husband ready to serve. The chief's bodyguards waited at his sides. All felt in a festive mood, but calm and silent, full of humble dignity.

The Traveler and the boy crossed the drawbridge and followed by the dancing children, entered the village plaza. The Traveler walked very slowly, smiling and looking at the gathered people. Every single person felt as if being seen by him in a very, very special way and felt happy. The Traveler came straight to the Chief. The old warrior, not knowing why, took off his helmet and handed it to his wife. The Traveler embraced him. Something broke open in the heart of this warrior, which had been hardened by difficulties and dangers on the battlefields and on hunting trips. He lost his strength and pride and slid down, kneeling in front of the unknown man and embracing his legs, he sobbed like a child. The Traveler lifted him up immediately and hugged him again, whispering softly,

"My son, my Darling son. All is well. Be calm."

The Traveler was offered a seat on a wooden chair covered with a brown bear skin and with the green Oriental rug spread in front of it. The chief performed the traditional washing of the revered guest's feet, done only to the most honorable visitors. First, he untied leather strings from the Traveler's sandals and then placed his feet in the wooden bowl. His wife assisted him by passing the wooden bowl and pouring water drawn from the bucket by a birch-wood pitcher. At the end she handed the chief a linen towel to dry the washed feet.

For the evening meal the chief ordered a feast. The chief's brother rolled out from the cellar a barrel with well-fermented barley beer, as well as a cask full of twenty-or-more year old mead. The chief's wife selected young goats to be slaughtered and roasted, and she baked a good supply of rye bread. Forest dwellers brought baskets of hazelnuts and wild beekeepers brought jugs full of fresh, golden aromatic honey. The Traveler ate only a little. He preferred milk with warm water and hazelnuts with honey to the roasted goat meat, beer, mead and rye bread. He talked the language of the Slavs but with a strange foreign accent. He talked to all present at the feast: men and women, adults, teenagers and children. He even talked to the trained hunting falcons sitting on pegs sticking out of the walls, and to the dogs crawling under the tables in search of leftover bones from the roasted goats which were scattered all over.

The next morning after sunrise, just before the orange-red disk of the Sun rose above the hills, the Traveler walked with the boy to the top of the highest hill and sat in silence on the soft moss. The boy had never before felt so peaceful. Sitting close to the Traveler, he almost effortlessly dove deep into a strange but comfortable, even joyful state of suspension. He simply forgot himself, his thoughts, his feelings, and delightedly abided in pure existence unstained by worldliness. In such spontaneous meditation more than one hour passed before they opened their eyes. The boy was surprised to notice that the Sun was already much higher than when they first sat down. He couldn't understand how he had not felt the passing of time; the experience of the Silence being beyond time, he felt the eternally long instant of NOW.

The Traveler pulled the boy toward him and embracing his shoulder he smiled and said,

"How was it there? Did you like it? It was only a small glimpse of what you will later experience. But for now, my boy, forget for a while your past and present life. Let us talk a bit about serious things. A big task is ahead of you my son. You were chosen, by the Council of the White Brotherhood, to be the first initiate in the land of Slavs. You will be a priest in the temple I am going to establish here on this land of impenetrable, primordial forests bordered by the sea, with its beaches covered with golden stones of amber. This temple will be the center of a faith in the Real God, based on the timeless Real Truth, taught by the Absolute Himself to the God Sun at the beginning of the creation of this Universe. The Real God is called by many names in many lands, but in spite of this He is always one and only one. HE is All-What-Exists. We will call Him Sviatovid. It means: HE WHO SEES ALL THE WORLD SIMULTANEOUSLY. We will introduce an idol carved in stone to create a concept for people to understand with ease. It will be a pillar, shaped with four human-like faces looking into the four directions of the world: North, South, East, and West. You will be taught all that can be said in the human language about the Truth. The most important part of this Wisdom will descend on you as an illumination after long years of rigorous meditation and other techniques I will explain to you later. After we build the temple, you will be the first priest. Your life's mission is to help others to grow in faith and to teach them to live according to the eternal laws set by God for Nature to follow. You will have to sacrifice your own personal goals and ambitions. The girl who is your sweetheart will not be able to marry you, for to have this inner power it is essential to live in celibacy in both body and mind. She loves you so much that she will not marry another man, but will stay near the temple and daily serve you, taking care of the premises and cooking. Your knowledge will be superior to all of your brothers and sisters, but you must remember never to feel superior. You have to adopt the humblest possible attitude of being a servant to all, great and small, humans and animals. You can't even hate enemies. This doesn't mean that you can't be firm and use your powers to support your brothers in their struggles to protect your fatherland from aggressive attempts by aliens to conquer it. From tomorrow you will start training. It is a slow process, as your personality will have to be rebuilt to make you suitable and competent for this new job. The sheep will be watched over by your younger brother. This has already been arranged with the chief. So what do you say? Agreed?"

The boy wanted very much to become a warrior and marry his little 'squirrel', but something inside of him whispered:

"Do not be afraid to give up this hackneyed life. He is offering you a unique chance to climb to unthinkable heights. Go for it! Go!" The boy looked around like a person who is departing, knowing that he will never return and said,

"I will follow what you say"

Days, weeks and months passed. The cold weather came. The boy stayed with the Traveler, serving him personally day and night. He was taught the mysteries of life, the universe, God, and he even learned amazing things about himself. He was pure in heart and his mind was empty like a freshly made vessel, which the Traveler was gradually filling with amazing knowledge about The Oneness. The boy identified himself with this teaching to such an extent that he almost started to see the four-faced Śviatovid in everything: in the trees, in the limestone pinnacles, in people and even in animals. He meditated regularly as instructed by the Traveler and repeated

411

a secret formula given to him as a personal password to the realms of God Śviatovid. Thanks to the grace of the Traveler and his own determined efforts, he very soon managed to enter the Silence of The Void, where his non-existence pulsated with the Presence of The Oneness. There he absorbed the Real Teachings about God directly from Him.

The following spring the construction of the temple started. Many people from near and far were involved, as the presence of the Traveler and his plans to establish a Natural Religion had become widely known and were supported by the people. By this time he saw many, many people from neighboring and distant villages and small strongholds and castles. People whispered a bit frightened that at night, when the last visitors coming for advice and blessings left, he welcomed the wild animals and talked to bears, wolves, deer, elks, lynxes and foxes, and even to eagles, hawks and owls which came just before sunrise. When the boy was asked if it was the truth, he kept quiet, never confirming or denying this mystery. The news about him had even reached the Germanic lands.

The very top of the highest hill had been cleared of trees. Only near the very summit, one huge oak tree was left. Perhaps it remembered the end of the glacier era. The diameter of this many thousand year old giant was such that it needed seven warriors holding their arms stretched and joined together to embrace its trunk. The temple was constructed just under its branchy crown. It was not a huge object: Six-by-six steps of the warrior at the base and double the average human height tall. The walls were made of white limestone and had four oak timber doors facing the four directions of the world. The door seals and portals were made from dark, gray sandstone. On the corners of the temple had been installed outlets for water and milk used during the worship of the idol. They looked like the open mouths of bears and were carved in the same sandstone as the portals. The structure stood on a limestone-paved platform, ending with three steps also made of sandstone. On top of its shingled roof, shining in the sun was a polished top-piece made from four brass weaponry axes joined together by the village smith. Inside stood an idol of Śviatovid carved in light gray granite. The stone had been transported with great difficulty through road-less forests and across huge bridge-less rivers from the Tatra Mountains, which guarded this land in the South from Asiatic Turkish hordes, which frequently attacked the Southern part of Europe. Lower down on the slopes of the hill, the Traveler pointed to a spot where, after digging, an abundantly flowing spring had been found. Its waters were diverted by stony gutters to the feet-washing stands located at the entrance to the temple compound, which was surrounded by a stone wall. Outside of it, the builders erected solid log huts for lodging pilgrims, storing foodstuffs and housing a kitchen. The Traveler supervised all the work, demonstrating both engineering and architectural skills. His simple-to-follow common sense suggestions saved the workers many hours of hard labor. He showed them how to use wooden logs as rollers to easily move heavy stones, how to use a simple lever to lift things, and many other unknown tricks and secrets of the building trade.

The opening ceremony brought a massive attendance of warriors, forest dwellers, fisherman and wild beekeepers. One week before the inauguration there arrived a large number of foreign delegates from the land of Russ and the land of Czech. From sunrise on, the well-trained young boys and girls chanted special formulas in the original, perfect language, which long ago was given to humans by God Himself, later evolving into all the now existing languages and dialects. Exactly at noon the Traveler entered the temple and closed the four doors. This day he was dressed for the first time in a pure white garment, with a red cloth band around his head. The gathered people were also dressed in their best clothes and leather armors, while the women hung strings of amber beads around their necks.

Minute after minute passed. The gathered people waited patiently, standing or sitting around the temple. Above, in the blue sky, a mighty eagle was seen. But it was not an ordinary eagle of brownish-gray color. It was a huge, pure white bird. Nobody had ever before seen an eagle of such size and color. It was flying in circles above the oak tree and the temple, without moving its wings, as if suspended on the invisible energy emanating from below. After a while, the intense silence was broken by the sound of a brass bell. It was coming from inside the temple. The doors opened and the gathered people saw the Traveler kneeling in front of the North side of Śviatovid waving a flame on a piece of birch tree bark. Then he moved to the West, South, and East sides. While waving the flame, he repeated some formulas in the God given original language. His face was as still as stone and resembled the image of the God Śviatovid. Everyone felt that something very great, very special was happening, although they didn't understand what. They felt that God Sun had come down, and from now on would invisibly reside in the granite idol. The boy also wore a white robe. He stood nearby and blew the horn of the aurochs, just like on the battlefield when they used to blow it before the warriors locked together in combat with their enemies, or to announce their victory after defeating alien hordes.

The Traveler placed the still burning flame in a bowl made of malachite, brought as a gift by the Russ warriors, and started to pour milk mixed with water and honey on the idol. Then he offered a big bowl of hazelnuts mixed with honey to Śviatovid. Now the boy was assisting inside. They both decorated the idol with garlands made of wild flowers, and burned some incense prepared by the chief's wife made from spruce tree needles, aromatic wood powders, dried flower petals, cherry tree resin, juniper berries and a crushed reddish variety of amber. Its sweet fragrance covered the compound of the temple. All present then walked around the temple in a procession and were given milk and honey with hazelnuts in wooden mugs as God's treat. The Traveler made a short speech explaining that Śviatovid was not limited to the temple; that as His very name indicated, He was everywhere and at all times. He explained that worshiping the just installed idol is easier than worshiping an invisible God, and that the idol will help the people remember His unlimited formless aspect. He explained in simple words the philosophy of this religion. The Traveler warmly encouraged them to faithfully follow the newly re-established religion, as it would help them to live in tune with the laws of Nature and also result in uninterrupted contentment. The people, being pure-hearted, childlike, and living close to Nature, effortlessly understood the logic in the principles of Śviatovid and felt it to be very obvious and natural. The inauguration ended in the village with a splendid feast. There was an ample supply of delicious food as well as plenty of barley beer.

The boy, now sixteen and a half, had not been initiated by the chief into warrior-hood as the other boys of his age. He was instead initiated by the Traveler into the secrets of God, and became the first priest in the temple. His blonde haired 'squirrel' sweetheart, from the day of the inauguration, stayed in the temple compound buildings and assumed the duty of the temple housekeeper. She was proposed to by one of the young warriors, but humbly refused, saying that she was already married to God Śviatovid. From that day until her death she never again uttered a single word. She did her work in silence and communicated with the people by finger gestures and facial expressions.

The Traveler stayed for a few more months, helping the young priest to establish the routine of daily worship, setting a time for special celebrations at festival times, making some astronomical calculations, and still continuing the teaching about The Oneness and the timeless Truth about IT. He formulated one hundred and eight proverbs covering the entire philosophy of this new religion. Soon it united the separate tribes and family clans, making the country stronger and the people much better, not so accessible to potential aggressors.

One day after the midday worship, the old Traveler and the young priest were sitting on the wooden bench just in front of the temple compound entrance. The Traveler was preparing for his departure, and they discussed the details of spreading Śviatovid doctrine to other Slavic lands. Suddenly from out of the forest came two Germanic assassins on galloping horses, sent by their knight to stop this religion, which was making the hated Slavs too strong. They charged with their high brass axes raised high. Their roar was almost paralyzing, and certainly promised a very quick death. There was no escape. The distance was very small and the horses were fast. The young priest jumped to his feet in fear, but the old Traveler said calmly:

"Sit down son. Do not be afraid. We work for Him and it is His job to protect us. With His will even a single hair will not fall from our heads. Wait!" The assassins were no more than ten steps away when thunder clapped and lightning struck a nearby elm tree, breaking its top. It fell straight onto the galloping alien warriors, smashing their heads, breaking their necks and killing their horses. The boy looked up at the clear sky above them. There was not even a single cloud. From where had the lightening come? It was obvious—from Him, from Śviatovid! He looked at the old Traveler. He was sitting motionlessly on the bench. His face showed no emotion. It was as if carved from dark brown basalt. Through the young priest went an electrical charge like lightening. He realized for the first time the old Traveler's oneness with Śviatovid. He fell on his knees embracing his teacher's legs and prayed silently, his mouth hanging open from amazement and admiration.

The Traveler lifted up the right arm of the young priest to the sky, and looking penetratingly into his eyes said:

"I am giving you the power to stop evil, and even to kill instantly with only a look any number of opponents if necessary. You are now stronger than an entire army. But remember, never use this power for selfish ends or demonstrate it for show. It is being given to you only to help in the beginning, to protect this new religion while it formulates itself into the structure of the country. It will not be passed on to others who will continue your work."

Years were passing fast. Around the year 950 of the Common Era a new epoch began in this country. Christian missionaries started to visit settlements and small towns in primordial Slavic forests. They were spreading their new faith, which was already adopted by most of the Western European countries. They were trying to spread the teachings of Jesus Christ, but being often ignorant themselves, they didn't fully understand the message of their own Master, nor did they recognize the basic unity between Śviatovid and the Christian faith. The Catholic Church, with its Pope in the Vatican, had become a very powerful political factor on the stage of Europe. Seeing it, and understanding the benefits of belonging to the European community controlled by the Pope, Prince Mieshko, then ruler of the country, decided to get converted to Christianity and forced his subjects to do the same. He was officially crowned by the German Cardinal, who represented the Pope, and became the first king of Poland, named Mieshko I-st. The statues of Śviatovid and His old temples, standing under the ancient trees on the hilltops, gradually fell prey to the fanatical and narrow-minded Christian missionaries and priests. They considered them as a dangerous remnant of a primitive, old fashioned, pagan cult and used brutal force to introduce what they claimed was 'a message of love and compassion'. The old cult of Śviatovid was mercilessly attacked and priests killed by swords or arrows.

One day a priest and his serving lady, whose hair by this time had turned silver-white, were cleaning oak leaves from the path to Śviatovid temple. From the forest came on horses a missionary with a group of soldiers. He was wearing a long black cassock and on his neck hung a huge silvery cross. They were killed without exchange of words. Death from an arrow of a soldier accompanying a Christian missionary was sudden and unexpected. He entered foggy tunnel and met Light-Being.

※

After eight months of defending the fortress, Ben Yair, a leader of Hebrew rebels opposing Roman occupiers was very tired. When his rebellion was defeated he, with the remaining warriors and their families, took over the fortress of Masada which became their last stance. Occupiers surrounded the fortress with a mighty army, set up camp and waited until the rebels would run out of food and then surrender. It was the feared Legion X called 'Fretensis'. The Roman army was well trained and numerous. To the rebels' advantage was the inaccessibility of the Masada fortress, (Hebrew: מצדה = metzada = fortress) built by King Solomon due to its location on the top of a hill surrounded by almost vertical high cliffs. They had sufficient storage of food and an ample quantity of water in underground tanks. Thanks to this, the zealous band of freedom fighters was able to survive a few months' long siege. They had only three hundred and twenty men able to fight; the rest were ladies and children that numbered six hundred forty.

Now the Romans' patience was exhausted. It was taking too long without any progress being made. In the eyes of the Palestinians it was even seen as humiliation. During the last two months the Romans had been building a ramp from stones and soil, and planned to bring a battering ram to smash the fortress' fortification wall. The ramp was now completed. Under the cover of darkness, the Romans drove up their machine of destruction—a mighty ram. A few hundred slaves were involved. The zealots' archers killed some but after a long siege the arrows were scarce so it had practically no impact on the Romans' task. Ben Yair was aware that if the Romans entered the fortress there would be no chance for a successful defense; all his people who had been captured would be tortured to death in order to terrorize the country's population not to follow their example and rebel again. He called the elders and proposed to commit mass suicide, in this way to save honor and escape the cruel treatment by the enemies. All agreed. It was decided that a man who was an expert in the ritual killing of animals dedicated for burnt-offerings to God Yahweh would train four others and then they would start killing the ladies and children, after that the warriors, and at the end they would kill themselves.

Ben looked around for his companion Aviva. She was, as usual, in service to people, this time consoling other ladies who were terrified by the prospect of being killed. Ben asked her to come to the Northern Palace where he would be waiting. When they met, Ben took Aviva's hand and they walked towards the external wall of the palace from where, through the windows, the Dead Sea was visible from a distance of four miles. It was a Full Moon night. The Moon was on the other side of the Dead Sea and the waters were reflecting its light straight into their faces. In this blue-green light they looked more like ghosts than humans.

"Are you, Aviva, afraid to die?" asked Ben softly.

"Yes, I am! I would prefer to live. For many years I had a dream, a vision for our future together and now all is in ruin. Is it not natural to want to continue life, to have a family, a good husband and a few children?" answered Aviva in a crying voice. "Do you think, Ben, that we lost our fight for freedom because God was not supporting us? How was it possible if the learned men of our nation say that He, Yahweh, declared us as His chosen people? Is it true? Do you, Ben, know what our mistake was?"

"Aviva, I am not sure about the validity of our nation's status as chosen ones. Anything can be written in books as only people write those books and later declare them sacred and even words of God. Some people like to manipulate other peoples' beliefs because they have hidden agendas to promote. From my understanding it is very questionable. How God can be impartial and discriminate against the bigger part of His own creation? I think that all people are equal. We lost our cause not because God did not support us, but because the majority of our people had selfish attitudes and didn't support us or support enough. Only a small number of the population joined us in fighting. Many even refrained from providing us food and unfortunately chose to continue life in the chains of slavery. They ignored our call for support hoping that they could avoid the risk of being killed. But the Romans killed many non rebels anyway, to terrify the population, many who were not even a part of our uprising.

"Long ago when I was a boy I met an old hermit living in a cave. He had a huge collection of scrolls. Some were very ancient, some were written on thin copper plates. He claimed that he could even read writings from the time before the Great Flood when people knew more about the Truth than now. He told me that God never directly interacted with people, as He is not a person but a primordial, eternal energy from which everything was created and lives in each as his innermost Self. He told me that the singular God is quite a recent invention and the old text always used plural when talking about our creators. Hermit told me that those who interacted with people and are called in our sacred writings Gods were not Gods, but visitors from other worlds who had a vested interest in implanting in peoples' minds some unreasonable beliefs."

"Ben, tell me the truth! Are we going to meet after death? Is there any continuation of life after this or will everything be over forever? I always hoped that one day you would cool down from this rebelling and settle with me. I love you very deeply."

"Aviva I also love you but could not give up our struggle for freedom. I thought that we could be a family only after we were completely free. How could it be possible to live happy lives as slaves? I believe that our lives are not limited to these bodies, which we are now using. Hermit also told me that life continues forever, that we are like droplets of water coming out of the waves and returning to the sea. Soon we will find out. We were born to be free so we cannot accept slavery. There is no other option. Let us now go to meet our destiny. We will meet again and create a family if this is what you want. Believe me, all the energy of the Universe is activated by your intent so it must be as you wish. Hermit told me that our thoughts are very powerful and we create our reality. Do not be afraid! We will meet again and be a family."

Ben and Aviva made an agreement to continue their connection in following incarnations. He went to join the others. Killing started. Ben scribed on a slate of chip his name. Bleed to death when chanting his mantra, enter a foggy tunnel and met Light-Being.

After midnight all Ben Yair's people were dead except two ladies who were too cowardly to escape slavery and hid themselves. Early morning when the Romans entered the fortress there were no defenders. They found only the corpses of the self-slaughtered warriors and their families. The Governor of Judaea, Lucius Flavius Silva, who commanded the legion during the siege was a warrior but not a barbarian, so in appreciation of the heroism of the rebels and to show the population his respect of their bravery and determination, arranged for a splendid funeral for most of the bodies by cremation near the Romans' camp. Only 29 leaders' remains were left in the fortress' territory. Ben Yair and a few of his lieutenants were put into a mass grave each holding a slate plate with his own name.

∴

The morning started for him as always, very early. It was well before sunrise when, after having had a bath and already dressed, he entered the small temple attached to the palace. It seemed there was no one inside. Olive lamps were burning in front of a large bronze statue of Buddha sitting cross-legged. The smile on his face seemed to express peaceful contentment. The air of the temple was saturated with the fragrance of sandalwood incense. He prostrated fully in front of his beloved Lord. In the middle of the temple, in front of the statue, a small rug was spread for him. He sat on it for his morning meditation. His mind, trained for years by rigorous spiritual practices, was easy to control.

After chanting a peace invocation, he started to imagine worshiping the Holy Feet of the Lord. First, honey was applied with great reverence and devotion. Then, petals of a red rose were spread over the Lord's Feet. He washed off the honey and the petals with milk and then with clear spring water. He mentally kept all the ingredients in separate vessels on a round alabaster tray: honey in a copper bowl, milk in a silver jar and water in a golden goblet. The white alabaster tray was decorated with a carving of a snake swallowing its own tail.

When the washing was over, he dried the Lord's Feet with a very fine cotton towel. Embroidered on the edge in gold and red letters were sacred mantras. After the Lord's Feet were dried he placed on each a beautiful gigantic lotus flower, cream colored with a dash of pink. He was opening its petals one-by-one while simultaneously chanting the Lord's one-hundred-eight names. When he was finished with the chanting, he lit camphor from one of the oil lamps on a small golden spoon. He then rose up to a standing position and, bending forward, started to wave the burning camphor in a clockwise direction, starting from the feet of the Lord and moving up to the head. He did it with such concentration that, after a while, all the world ceased to exist for him. Now only he and the Lord existed. Then, even this merged into The Oneness. There was no longer One who was worshiped and the other who worshiped Him. There was only One who existed and who was being worshiped by Himself. Even the act of worshiping merged also into The Oneness.

When the camphor had burned out, he regained a bit of external consciousness and fell on the stony floor in full prostration, crying uncontrollably for the Lord, lost in the ecstasy of the bliss of love. Sometime later, he again sat cross-legged on the rug saying his mantra. His disciplined mind mentally repeated slowly and rhythmically sacred words, those words which only he knew.

The mantra was given to him in a dream in his youth by a Divine Being, which manifested itself as a blazing Golden Light. No sidetracking thoughts entered his mind as he lost himself entirely in the mantra. He again lost body-consciousness. The mind and the intellect automatically stopped functioning. He himself became the mantra. There was nothing more remaining, only the mantra. Mantra alone was filling the entire Universe, pulsating with the vibration of Love and shining with the Golden Light of its Giver. He was intoxicated and had no awareness of his surroundings. He did not know where he was or who he was. He experienced only awareness of pure Existence. He was experiencing Bliss beyond words, beyond any possible mental structure and beyond even imagination.

Two hours passed. He did not feel it because time had disappeared along with the mind. Tears of Bliss were rolling down his face, creating a little pool on the stony floor of the temple. Gradually he regained consciousness, returning to the so-called normal state. His body was still stiff. Slowly and gently he started to move. First he moved his hands, then his head, legs and so on. After some time, he managed to prostrate again to the Lord's statue and rose from his seat.

He walked slowly towards the palace. The feeling of intoxication did not leave him completely. While walking he showed respect towards servants, the King's court officials and country visitors alike. Often, while passing, he stopped to ask about their health, family matters and business problems. They all loved him—he was a Prince by birth, but unbelievably humble in his nature. He was a counselor, friend, confidant and moral supporter to all: the beggars, shopkeepers, soldiers and visiting peasants. Dressed in simple off-white clothes, he did not look like the successor to the throne. Rather, he looked like one of the peasants who had come to town for shopping or temple worship.

Inside the palace it was peaceful, like in the temple. Not too many people had managed to get up this morning as early as usual. All were exhausted as the previous night there had been a long and splendid reception for the King. It was a celebration of his sixty-five years on the throne. During the feast, the King had publicly expressed his desire to retire soon and pass the duty of ruling the Kingdom to his eldest son—him. The Prince was walking barefoot on the polished marble and granite floor, making no sound. His private apartments were on the ground floor, quite close to a passage leading through a small courtyard to the temple.

Upon opening his door, he was surprised to see his mother giving orders to the servants on how to prepare new clothes for an approaching coronation ceremony. It shocked him deeply. The Prince knelt in front of his mother and kissed her feet. She smiled at him and quickly lifted him up, asking about his well-being. Healthy as always, he ignored the question as rhetorical, and having an opportunity to talk with the Queen alone, as all the servants had left the room, he started to explain his plans, never before having spoken of them to anyone. In simple words, he explained to the Queen what his spiritual path meant to him; what the ultimate goal of it was.

He told her that compared to the possibilities of spiritual growth; the Kingdom offered to him by his father was nothing but a handful of dust. All the riches of the world and all positions are transitory, but the Bliss of union with The Oneness is everlasting. He told her that it is the only way to transcend this worldly existence and enter the realm of Immortality. He said that he didn't want to offend his father by refusing to take over the King's responsibilities, but he had decided to follow his intuition and act according to his inclination. He had decided to renounce worldly life and join one of the semi-secret monasteries hidden in the rocks and sands of the Great Desert.

The Prince fell on the floor again, asking his mother to support him and diplomatically explain his intentions to the King—his father.

He did not want to run away from awaiting duties, but due to his spiritual inclinations, he did not feel fit to take over the Kingdom. He was too gentle, too feminine to be the executor of laws, lead wars and be in charge of the lives and deaths of millions of people. His younger brother, however, was ideal for the position. He was fond of his physical strength, mastery of arms, bravery and desire to lead; to be great and powerful. He was always jealous about the first-born right to the throne—now he could have it.

The Queen was an intelligent and farsighted woman. She understood him perfectly. She loved both of her sons and was sad that her older one wanted to become a monk. If that happened, she would never have a chance to cuddle both of her children again. But the aspiration to grow from dust to the Divinity of Godhood was not foreign to her. Her own brother had long ago become a renunciant, and after many years of wandering all over Asia and staying in a few monasteries in the Great Himalayas, had attained the state of Sage-hood. He then traveled far to the North, to the cold countries, where dense and beautiful green forests, thousands of years old, covered most of the land. He traveled through virgin forests full of unknown wild animals. He met people, the innocent and childlike, who collected from the seashore light-yellow stones of amber which they valued more than gold. There he established a religion based on the eternal Sanatana Dharma. For them it was the most suitable religion, blending naturally with their existing local beliefs. Its philosophy was intuitively understood by the unspoiled minds of the forest dwellers, hunters and beehive keepers, who were slowly learning the art of farming on small clearings in the forest. The Queen perceived the logic in her elder son's explanation and agreed to prepare the King— her husband—for the surprising news.

A few days later the King called the elder Prince to the court hall. There they officially met as King and Prince. There was nobody else, only the two of them. The young Prince fell at his father's feet and begged him not to feel offended, but to understand his soul's cravings, his desire to become a Free Man through renunciation. The worldly-minded King could not comprehend his son's plans and aspirations. He had never been interested in any particular religious practices or spiritual disciplines, but being compassionate, and deeply loving his sons, he did not want to act against their will and make them unhappy. In fact, the King often worried as to how such a gentle, meditative Prince would manage to do the King's tough job. He agreed for the Prince to become a monk and pursue his path, but on the condition that first he would be formally crowned, as tradition demanded. Then, during the same ceremony, pass his office with all its accoutrements to his younger brother. Both the old King and the young Prince fell crying into each others' arms. The solution was found; a solution suitable to all parties, one not involving a compromise.

One month later, after the coronation ceremony, small groups of people on horses were seen early in the morning crossing the gates of the capital town. All of them wore plain gray robes and all covered their faces. Nobody knew who they were; but the guards at the gate saluted them with royal respect. The small group of riders directed their horses towards the Great Desert. A week later they arrived at their destination. Leaving the horses in the care of a spring-keeper, they started to climb, on foot, the rocky hills surrounding Golden Canyon, where the monastery was located. Just before the forged Iron Gate they uncovered their faces. They were the old King, Queen, First-born Prince and his niece: a young and beautiful Princess who was supposed to be his fiancée. No words were spoken amongst them. The royal parents, by their movements, facial expressions and eyes, were showing nervousness, sadness and anxiety. The Prince was calm and withdrawn, looking through everything as though non-existent, a transparent mirage. The Princess, poor thing, was silently shedding tears and looking from time-to-time with silent adoration upon the Prince's face. She had loved her uncle, the Prince, all her life. From early childhood she had hoped that one day she would become his wife and be able to serve him, please him and bear his children. Now her dreams were unexpectedly ending. She would not see him again in this lifetime. She loved the Prince so much that she accepted his decision to become a monk without protest or rebellion. She wanted him to be happy in the way he chose for himself. In such a turn of events, she decided not to marry at all and, though staying in the world, she would yet be out of it.

The Prince rang the bell. The sound of it repeated a few times, echoed by the walls of the Golden Canyon. The gate was solid and installed in a stony arch, chiseled out of native rock from the cliffs surrounding the canyon. But nobody came to open the gate and welcome the royal family. The Queen spread a rug and, tired after the travel, they sat on it to rest while awaiting the gate-keeper. Only the Prince remained standing straight and facing the canyon, calm, withdrawn, already belonging to a different world. It looked as if no one were alive in the monastery—deep silence was all pervading.

Two hours passed in waiting. The King, already agitated by such a reception, wanted to ring, ring and ring until someone came. The Prince managed to calm him down, saying that they knew they were down there, but the time was not yet right to open the gate and accept him. At the same time they were giving him a final test. Soon after he said this, an old man in camel-wool clothes appeared on the other side of the gate. He saluted the waiting party by humbly bowing and saying:

"Let peace be always in your hearts and minds." He opened the gate, and with a gesture invited the Prince to enter. The Prince turned back and knelt on the stones in front of his parents and fiancée. He prostrated fully and repeated the words of the monk.

"Let peace be always in your hearts and minds." He looked at each of them separately, and then crossed the gate which was immediately locked behind him.

Without saying more, the Prince started to walk slowly towards the steps carved in the solid rock, which led down to the bottom of the canyon. Shocked and dumbfounded, the old King, Queen and little Princess watched the drama while hanging onto the bars of the gate. When the Prince, now monk, reached the first step, he stopped for a moment, turned back and sent them, whom he had loved so much all his life, a warm look and benign smile. This smile and look had an amazing, instantly calming and tranquilizing effect on the poor, shivering Princess. Looking straight back into his eyes, she had a glimpse of The Oneness. She realized her oneness with him and with all existence. This particle of a second in the midst of emotional agony became a blissful experience, totally changing her attitude towards their relationship. She decided to follow her spiritual path, and in the next incarnation meet him not as a wife, but as a sister in The Oneness.

With each step down, the Prince-monk experienced the growing silence of the canyon; deeper and deeper, step-by-step. He counted eighty steps. When he reached the bottom another monk approached. The monk saluted him with a gesture—putting his open palm on his chest where the heart is located. It was like silently saying:

"My heart loves you, brother." He gestured the Prince-monk to follow him toward the rock formation at the very bottom of the canyon. The Prince soon saw some openings into cave-like dwellings. The monk showed him the door to the first of the caves. The Prince-monk entered and at the entrance turned back to the guide with a silent question,

"And what now?" The monk-guide understood his need for explanation and said,

"Brother, despite your never having contacted us, or making arrangements beforehand, we have been waiting for you. This humble dwelling was prepared especially for you. After you enter it, the door will be permanently sealed. Food and water will be delivered daily. You will not see or talk to another human again in this life. At the right time you will meet your Guru who lives in total oneness with Lord Buddha, whom you worship. They are merged in The Oneness. You do not need any changes in your spiritual practices. Continue all as before. Your meeting with your Guru will not necessarily be on this plane of existence. Let there be peace in your heart and mind." Saying thus, he turned back and slowly walked away, not waiting for the Prince-novitiate to enter his new and last dwelling. There was no initiation, no ceremony or elaborate instructions; nothing. He was left on his own to follow only his intuition.

The cave was small but very well designed. Beyond the door on his right was a bathroom from which sewage was directed by ceramic pipes towards far away parts of the canyon, where a septic tank was probably located. Straight in from the entrance was a room with a floor on two levels. The right side was higher, with a bed, which also served as a sitting bench. Everything was carved in solid rock. On the left lower side were a small, low table-altar and a shelf. There were no idols, no symbols on the altar. In the middle of its clean, smooth, surface there was only a burning olive oil lamp and underneath there was a box filled with wicks and a copper jug filled with oil. In the front of the altar he noticed on the floor an asana, with a folded woolen blanket underneath. That was all. No vessels, books, pictures, clothes, nothing. On the bed there was a bamboo sleeping mat and another woolen blanket.

The rock from which the room was carved was golden yellow and seemed to be a sort of well-cemented sandstone. The room was rounded; only the altar top had a straight front. On the wall above the bed, the builders of this dwelling had made a round tunnel-like opening for a sort of window. Through it he could see the cliff walls of the canyon and a bit of sky. The walls of the canyon, as everything here, were golden yellow.

The Prince-monk prostrated to the lamp and sat for his first meditation. He went, as usual, through the process of imagining the worship of the Holy Feet of the Lord Buddha, and afterwards dived into his mantra while gazing at the flame of the oil lamp. Hours passed. After sunset, he heard a noise at his door. A small flap at the bottom had opened and through it a bucket of water for a bath was given. Then came a one-gallon water jug made of unglazed terracotta, an earthenware glazed mug, and a good-sized pewter bowl containing food. It was covered with a round straw mat. No words were spoken. He saw only the hands of the person bringing the food and water. The man's skin was very dark, much darker than his own. When the flap was closed, he heard the sound of a metal bar sliding across the door, then another one. He realized that he was now locked in for life. His body would one day be carried away, on the day after the delivered food remained in the vessel. The game for Freedom started from being voluntarily imprisoned. So strange!

The Prince-monk lifted the round mat from the bowl. There was some rice, cooked vegetables, beans and, in a separate small bowl, inserted into the rice, curd. He sat on the bed-bench and loudly, but in a low-pitched voice, repeated the prayers he used to say before meals. Then he started slowly to eat, chewing each portion of the food many times before swallowing it. While eating, he was mentally repeating his mantra. He tried not to think about his past life, nor imagine the future. After the food he waited about twenty minutes and then had some water. The taste of the water was so incredible that, instead of repeating his mantra, he had a thought:

"I have never before in all my life had such tasty and refreshing water."

After his meal, he walked around his apartment for at least two hours doing japa mantra. He then did some Qi Gong exercises, which he had learned in the Himalayas from a Tibetan mendicant when he had unsuccessfully tried to reach India. The exercises lasted only 30 minutes and were done very slowly with proper breathing while chanting mantras suitable for each posture. He did not want to awaken his body-consciousness, only keep it fit and healthy. Afterwards he had a bath in almost total darkness, as the only light was from the olive oil lamp on the altar. After the bath, he checked the oil in the lamp and filled it with oil from the jug to keep it burning throughout the night. The Prince-monk then knelt in front of his altar. Finally, he said his prayers for the night, ending with a peace invocation for the well-being of all the beings in the three worlds which he repeated three times.

The nights on the Great Desert are chilly. He covered himself with a blanket and drifted into deep sleep while repeating his mantra. He was relaxed because there was nothing on Earth he wanted. He had arrived at the place of fulfillment of all his desires, gross and subtle. The rest was not up to him. Now he would continue his routine and leave the rest in the hands of his unknown Guru.

Morning was just a routine: bath, meditation and japa. He met the sunrise seated in front of his altar. The light of the sun, reddish in color, came through the round window of his simple dwelling. It projected the round red circle onto the stony wall exactly in the middle of his altar, forming a spectacular background for the olive lamp. Seeing it he drifted into a deep meditative state. He intuitively understood that the reddish circle was a sign from The Oneness, accepting him as an aspirant who wanted to merge in It. He did not regain his external consciousness until midday, when he again received a meal and when the previous day's meal-bowl, which he had washed last night, was taken away.

Weeks, months and years passed. The routine was established so firmly that it became his second nature. He did not receive a single bit of information about worldly affairs. He was not aware that a war was fought, that the rulers of the neighboring countries had been changed, or that his brother, the King, had been seriously injured but was again fit. He didn't know that his fiancée, the Princess, had died in an accident. A landslide had covered her body with more than seven meters of soil and rock while she was sitting in deep meditation under the hill near her parent's palace. In fact, he was not interested in anything. He was not even interested in attaining Liberation. He was just abiding in his peacefulness, totally content and desire-less.

One full moon night he was sitting as usual for meditation in front of the olive oil lamp. He was deeply submerged in Peace, with his eyes wide open, but not perceiving any external objects. Suddenly, he started to feel the light of the flame growing. It was not perceived by his eyes, but throughout his whole body. Each cell of his body became receptive to this light. After a while a golden orange light engulfed the entire room. Now he saw it even through his physical eyes. He was gazing at the phenomenon, but remained calm and detached. He felt that something was going to happen and he was prepared for anything. He had no fear.

In the flame, on the right side of his altar, a door manifested. It was a door with a portal, carved in a similar way as in the temple of his parent's palace, but this time it was made of the flame. The door was slightly open. He understood that it was an invitation for him to enter. He got up from his seat, walked towards the wall of flame and opened the door fully. He registered in his mind that the flame was not hot and was not burning his body or clothes. It did not affect him in any way.

Slowly, with respect for the unknown awaiting him, he crossed the doorway and found himself in a garden full of flowering bushes and a great collection of beautiful, enormous and fragrant flowers. The garden was maybe one hundred meters in diameter and was surrounded by a high compound wall made of stones. In the middle of a central lawn he noticed a pedestal called peetham made of the same stones as the fence, and in front of it a stony semi-circular wall. Current, like an electric shock, went through his body at the sight of that wall. Attached to it were gold, silver and bronze letters, forming his mantra. The place was as his very own was. It was his place!

When he looked again at the *peetham*, he experienced another shock. There was now seated a man, old, with long hair and beard. He was wearing clothes exactly like his. It was him! He recognized himself, but not without difficulty as he had not seen his face for many years, only in the reflection in the water in the dark bathroom. He walked towards the peetham. His double opened his eyes, coming out of meditation and, turning his head in the Prince-monk's direction, said in a soft voice,

"Welcome. Now we are ready to meet our Guru. Please go through the gate, which is behind the Mantra Wall. There He is waiting for us. Go, go, it is our time now."

"Who is He, this Guru? Is He not the Lord Buddha?" he thought but could not ask, because his replica had dissolved in the light of the sun. The Prince-monk walked around the Mantra Wall and, as told, discovered a gate. He opened it and walked through.

He immediately found himself in the middle of a huge meadow. The intensely green grass went half way up his calves and covered the entire area like a soft juicy carpet. The meadow was vast indeed.

Some fifteen kilometers away he noticed a range of high snow and ice covered mountains encircling the meadow. Through the meadow ran a crystal clear creek. The sky was intensely blue with a few white clouds. When he turned back he noticed a small group of people scattered in the grass around the central figure of a man in white, sitting cross-legged. They were all sitting or lying, relaxed and looking towards Him. The Man in white called him with a gesture. When he walked slowly toward the group he noticed he couldn't see the people clearly. They were somehow out of focus, like looking through wet glass. Some of them were males, some females. Most of them were wearing white clothes, but some wore yellow, some kavi. They looked more like symbols of existence than individuals, more like wild flowers growing freely in the grass. One of them resembled the little Princess, his fiancée. She smiled towards him as if saying,

"You see, I managed to come first, but never mind. You too will be here soon. Please hurry!"

The Prince-monk knelt in front of the Man in white. The Man reached for him and pulled him towards Himself. He ended up on His lap, being cuddled like a little child.

"It is good that you came." He said. "You are my son. You belong here. This is your real family." The Prince-monk was in Bliss. He enjoyed belonging to Him; he enjoyed the glimpse of his oneness with Him, his oneness with The Oneness, because he felt that The Man in white was Its total manifestation. The Man in white started to talk again and said in a soft voice expressing Divine Love,

"I am your Guru. Son, you will join me soon, but now you have to go back to the world. You still have some *vasanas* to exhaust. You will do it in three lifetimes and in the fourth I will see you again. For then you will be sitting amongst us. Go and grow strong. You have much work to do in the future. You have earned, through your disciplined *sadhana*, the right to be guided to Freedom. Don't worry. I will take you Home. Be patient. I will help you to go through any difficulties. It will not be long. Now go back. Be brave. Do not fear to enter the Unknown. I am with you always."

The Prince-monk, moving slowly as in a trance, prostrated and touched His Holy Feet, then walked back towards the gate. After a while he stopped and turned back. There was no longer a Man in white seated in the middle of His children. Behind him on the grass was a huge ball of Golden Light and, connected to it by golden threads were small lights lying in the grass. There was no difference in the quality and characteristics of those lights. They were all the same in nature. The difference was only in the intensity of the manifestation. The Prince-monk, full of energy and feeling charged by his Guru, was happy that he was on the final path towards permanent merging in The Oneness, in Him, whose love he felt in all his beingness. He crossed the gate.

The next day the bowl of food and the bucket of water were found untouched behind his flap door. The following morning a small group of people carried his body to the end of the Golden Canyon where a bottomless cliff began. It was cremated without any ceremony or ritual. They left the remaining ashes on a stony table, built just on the very edge of the cliff. The life of the gentle Prince-monk ended immediately after the incredible experience and outer-dimensional meeting with his mysterious Guru. Now his soul was busy getting ready to incarnate again. He was not afraid. He was assured by Him that he would be guided. Suffering would come and difficulties also, but he was already on the highway to Freedom and only three lifetimes distant from the Goal Supreme.

During the day, the wind spread the ashes of his mortal form. What was born had died. From dust it emerged, to dust it had returned. But he was still unaffected; he still existed. He was very much alive. He was not a Prince-monk any more. That was only the name given to his body. He was the spark of Golden Light, eternally connected with his Guru. He was the son of Him. He was the son of The Oneness, an extension of IT sent down only for the purpose of growth, of learning to love, for finding his way back Home in the labyrinth of manifested Existence, to rediscover his oneness with The Oneness.

Prince-Monk entered a foggy tunnel and at its end met Light-Being.

The golden orange sunset once more stained the yellow walls of Golden Canyon in the color of renunciation, the color of clay, the color of dust, the color of Freedom from earthly bondages. Our monk this time was not seeing it through his window, as he was already free, but only from his body. Yet he was on the way to Eternal Freedom, on a way to permanently experiencing his beingness in The Oneness.

From this day onwards, every morning, a mighty eagle was seen flying in circles above Golden Canyon. Maybe the soul of our Prince-monk entered the body of the King of birds and was gliding motionlessly in the clean desert air, continuing his *sadhana*, and doing *japa* mantra. Or maybe The Oneness appointed one of Its sons to make this silent salute to him who surrendered everything to the Path leading to The Oneness.

⁖

Medieval town. Life as a lady. Murder of a husband by poisoning as revenge for an affair with a servant girl. Punishment. Public flogging. Pain. Life in the body of an old woman living in an iron cage in the middle of a town's central plaza. People throwing into cage food leftovers. Cold. Humiliation. Burning stings of lice. War. 'Liberating' arrow from an anonymous invader. Entering a foggy tunnel. Meeting Light-Being.

⁖

Small town in Persia. Sandstone cave on its outskirts. Big, very big body of a bold man. A Sage-hood. Totally sublimated mind. Abiding in uninterrupted Peace. Two dedicated and loving disciples. Traveler realized that he knew those men in his present life. They were now Indians, *brahmacharis* in Kerala, in the ashram where he spent six years. Entering a foggy tunnel. Meeting Light-Being.

⁖

Ukrainian planes of loessal. A deposit of fine yellowish-grey loam which occurs extensively from north-central Europe to eastern China, in the American mid-west, and elsewhere, esp. in the basins of large rivers, and which is usually considered to be composed of material transported by the wind during and after the Glacial Period.) black earth. Digging out potatoes. Tractor, which is supposed to take them from work to barracks not arriving. Rain mixed with snow falling down, making clothes wet. Cold, hunger and anger. Arrogant guard, also wet and hungry, is shouting something. Arguments. Guard hitting his head with an iron pipe. No pain, no cold or hunger. Relief. Entering a foggy tunnel. Meeting Light-Being.

"And what do you think *thombi*? Are you happy?" said Nameless *Siddha* to Traveler who had just opened his eyes. "There were, in the last few past lives, some mistakes but generally you were progressing steadily in the right direction. Use experiences of your remote past for the benefit of your present life. Any time when you feel stressed you can shift yourself mentally to Golden Canyon monastery or the time in Persia when you were immersed in impenetrable Peace. But generally you now host peace in your heart, know that The Universe is taking care of you and that you possess guaranteed security and there is no need to worry about the future. You wake up daily with anticipation of new adventures and see everything with the wonder of a child. This is good for a start!

"We have to talk now about a few things, most of which you already know, just to put them into the right perspective. So I will ask you a few questions. Do not be afraid to be completely open. It is not an examination, which you must pass. Just tell me in the simplest possible way how you understand what I ask. You also can make comments and digressions.

"Do you, *thombi*, believe in God? Tell me please who is God," asked Nameless *Siddha* looking with mischief on Traveler.

"It is very tricky question, Sir. It all depends on one's definition of God. Why do you, Sir, use the pronoun '**who**' and the verb '**is**' asking about God? It implies first that God is a being and second that God exists! Do I have it correctly?" asked Traveler.

"It seems to me that you do not easily take 'baits'! So tell me then what your definition of God is!" said Nameless Siddha.

"I think that the word 'God' is the most misunderstood, misinterpreted and most unfortunate term in the human language. According to the assumption I identify with there is no personal God, no Divine Being, no Creator who dwells somewhere and remotely controls his creation. From ancient records we know that on Earth in the distant past were some 'gods', but they were in fact only technologically advanced beings from other planets in our and other galaxies, and it was simply that the first, created by them primitive humans, in their ignorance, elevated those aliens to the status of divinity. We can only imagine how an isolated tribe of Indians, living in the Amazonian jungle, would react if suddenly a vertically landing military jet came from the blue sky, landed on their glade in assault gear, shot a few most impudent youths and announced through loudspeakers that they came to introduce democracy and freedom. They would prostrate and worship those commandos as 'gods'. In my understanding, Sir, only Eternal Energy, which is Self-Conscious and super Intelligent exists. It created and continuously creates from Itself All-What-Was-What-Is and What-Will-Be. This energy manifests itself to us as material Universe including all biological beings. Non-biological beings, which are very intelligent and also conscious, are suns, planets, comets, moons and so on. Our science says that our visible, physical universe contains only a small percent of the energy in existence. Some estimate it as only 4%. From the balance of energy are built other realms with more dimensions than in ours. Scientists, having no way to directly investigate them, call those domains 'black energy or 'black matter'. Matter in this physical, heavy density of our world is nothing more than light 'frozen' into slow vibrations. So I can say, if we still decide to use the word 'God', that '**God Is Everything That Exists in All Worlds Visible and Invisible—Totality of Energy manifested − dynamic and not manifested—potential, The Ultimate Principle which creates from Itself The Multidimensional Universe, sustains and recycles it**.' This is my definition. So I can also say that **there is no God or that everything is God as only He exists as Real**. Also the genius scientist Nikola Tesla understood that everything that exists is created from primordial energy and said: **'If you want to find the secrets of the universe, think** [only] **in terms of energy, frequency and vibration.'**

"But the majority of people are so obtuse that they can't understand this and prompted by priestly castes build temples, churches and mosques to worship in them 'gods' of their liking, giving them names and assuming they have certain attributes. They imagine that God must be a Supreme Being looking similarly to us because the Bible said that God created humans in His image. It is an insult to All-What-Is to be represented in stones and paintings and worshiped when we are having our existence in It and being ourselves nothing else but It, only temporarily individualized. It is ridiculous, purely insane! I wonder if there is on Earth even one sane person who would like to be abused and disrespected (Nature) and at the same time worshiped by his children (us) in temples built for this purpose and stored within his stony idols or paintings?

"People are advised by religious leaders to search for a God and after finding Him be blissful. Some follow this recommendation and end up disillusioned, not finding Him, and become even more miserable and unhappy than at the beginning of their search as Bliss eludes them also. The reason is that they search in the wrong way. Only those who aim to attain Bliss will find this 'God' by experiencing The Oneness as He is in everything as He is not a separate entity but the very Totality of Existence. I tried to specify this in my definition of 'Him'.

"I am a bit embarrassed and feel uncomfortable because, despite my deep love and reverence towards Sri Ramana Maharshi, I, who am a very beginner seeker, can't agree with some of his statements which simply do not resonate positively in my Inner Being. For example in his gospel Maharshi says: **'Nothing happens except by Divine Dispensation . . .'** and later: **'What is destined to happen will happen.'** I also once believed in this kind of stuff, but not anymore. He also said in the same book: **'God has created**

the world; it is His business to look after it, not yours.' As far as I understand Sri Ramana was promoting *Advaita Vedanta*—a philosophy of no-duality but these kinds of statements, I consider, as not in tune with *Advaita Vedanta* because they clearly indicate dualism: Him a powerful Creator and the Universe—His choice-less creation with us as only puppets without any right to co-create, even to look after this planet which He has given to us as custodians. It also encourages passivity and suggests accepting a lot, which life provides by default as He, Creator already 'preset' everything in our lives and we have no free will or choice and no rights to make any choices and evolve in consciousness and Wisdom. If I accept such statements as valid spiritual advice I would completely lose the drive to live a conscious life by making those choices I at this moment consider as correct, learning from mistakes, sending into the Universe my deliberate intentions to create my life experience as I design and as a result stagnate. I can't accept suggestions that the present obviously fundamentally wrong direction of our 'civilization' suffering severe value disorder of messed up priorities is in tune with a will of some 'God' who, as scriptures declare, is supposed to be nothing but pure perfection, but **this way** is 'looking after His creation, blaming us for His faults of creating us far from being intellectually and morally perfect.'

"I also respect and admire the spiritual teachings of Osho/Rajnish. His insight into 'science of life' is so close to my heart and to my rebellious mentality, but he also made statements which repel me. He was frequently talking about the existence of God as something obvious and about Christ as an actual, historical personality when there is not even one authentic record from the times when he was supposed to roam the plains of Judea and perform miracles on the banks of the Galilean Sea. Jews and Romans were very efficient in recording each event and everything was precisely archived. A teacher of Love and Peace followed by twelve disciples and admired by crowds is not mentioned even once in the records of both parties. Also executions of most petty criminals are recorded but there is not a single word about the crucifixion of a 'messiah' who claimed to be a king. All 'proof' of his existence is based on earlier assumptions which are based on nothing. If this has any basis of truth then all his disciples were illiterate and did not bother not to record their master's teachings. The New Testament is a compilation of not always consistent stories written down 200-350 years after the date of something which did not happen.

"Bertrand Russell—British philosopher and social reformer—1872-1970: **'What a man believes upon grossly insufficient evidence is an index into his desires—desires of which he himself is often unconscious. If a man is offered a fact which goes against his instincts, he will scrutinize it closely, and unless the evidence is overwhelming, he will refuse to believe it. If, on the other hand, he is offered something which affords a reason for acting in accordance to his instincts, he will accept it even on the slightest evidence.** The origin of myths is explained in this way.' I have also personal experience. I witnessed in one of South Indian ashrams how the myth of the divinity of the person in charge was created and details increasing devotion added freely to this guru's biography and other book so I think that this was practiced from the beginning of humanity. I only wonder if those mentioned and many other Gurus, 'avatars' and philosophers are afraid to 'break a spell' of religious conspiracy and try to avoid ending in trouble and denial because of their condemnation of commonly accepted false beliefs and legends or simply do they pretend to know but actually they do not know?"

"*Thombi,* you are a localized, individualized 'projection' of the Unlimited, which gradually grows into Divinity. Never take anything for granted or literally even if it is said or written by someone respected or considered as an unquestionable authority. Also, do not take for granted my statements. Any statement's validity depends on the accuracy of its definitions. Testing everything and experiencing it personally is needed, which in fact you are actually doing. Some great Sages simplified their teachings by coming down to a contemporary level with their aspirants, telling them for example what brother Ramana said; **'Everything is according to the will of God'** or **'God never forsakes him who has surrendered.'** Do not be confused. They knew The Truth, but the times and their listeners were not ready to be told **the naked Truth**. Follow only your intuition, follow

The Path your unique way, and never imitate others. If you want to find The Truth, then never become a believer of others' revelations. Accepting beliefs without checking and cross checking their validity can only restrict and restrain your ability to think and you must think, as thinking is your most powerful 'tool. That's why Buddha said to His students: **'Believe nothing, no matter where you read it or who said it, not even if I have said it unless it agrees with your own reason and your own common sense.'** Sages speak from their own, personal truth but it is their truth, their personal spiritual asset. The beliefs of followers are only credits of trust of other people's claimed revelations, which are not always correct nor always reflect personal experiences. Remember what Ramana Maharshi told you in a dream: **'. . . remember son, please find your own Path, and do not follow others.'** I also like to put more stress on this subject because you already once forgot this advice so now you must get the message! Never follow the crowd and accept its beliefs because those who do usually go no further than the crowd. Follow your own Path, The Path towards Source as our Brother Ramana told you and you will have a chance to 'visit' realms never visited by those from the crowd.

"Now, I must say that you have done some homework boy! Congratulations! You were probably born or at least raised not under an ordinary star but under a comet. But you must be aware, *thombi,* that you may lose your dear life for having such radical beliefs. On Earth, to which soon you must return from here, are narrow-minded religious fanatics in plenty and they would be very happy seeing you being 'crucified' or burned. But never-the-less even this does not matter as you already know that your body is not the real you, only your temporary 'hiding place' in matter. But Truth is Truth and our duty, after knowing Truth, even partly, is to tell It to others even at the cost of life. Tell me now what you think about evolution. Darwin became famous after he published his 'The Origin of Species'."

"In my opinion there is only evolution of consciousness in beings which through experiencing contrast increases their intelligence and growth in Wisdom. Physical evolution of species is limited to adaptation to changing physical conditions. Therefore it is impossible for atoms to be first randomly synthesized by nature into organic molecules; secondly, molecules to form a cell, which is already immensely complex. Only intellectuals with no common sense can believe in such a possibility. Even more impossible is for a one-cell organism, supposed to be our common ancestor, as Darwin claims, to evolve to a mammal, a reptile or even a fish since it is as impossible as for atoms to spontaneously unite to create an automobile, which is definitely less complicated than any smallest living thing. Never have atoms united themselves spontaneously to form even a simple nail or a nut because for this basic task intelligence and creative thought are needed. Also, never was observed the mutation/evolution of bacteria to something more complex like amoeba for example.

"The chromosomes can't result from random reactions of molecules and later the number of chromosomes can't be altered by also random mutations. DNA is an extremely sophisticated language of life. It also cannot be created by random events. It is a result of creativity of super intelligent energy. To say, as contemporary scientists are saying, that our DNA resulted thanks to random chemical reactions of organic molecules; and that genes formed sequences due, also, to random mutations, is like cutting out the individual letters of 'Mahabharata' and then expecting to get this grand epic back in order; chapter by chapter, verse by verse after the letters had been exposed to the wind. All beings were created by intelligent resolve of Source Energy, of All-What-Is and do not have a common ancestor. All life forms on Earth possess the same non-coding DNA sequences but in different combinations. Recently a group of genetic scientists made an amazing discovery: 97% of the non-coding sequences in human DNA, which are common to all living organisms on Earth are no less than the genetic code of extraterrestrial life forms as they are unknown in other species. In human DNA, they constitute a larger part of the total genome so the overwhelming part of our DNA is 'off-Earth' in origin, which means we are actually aliens to this planet.

"Exactly! You are quite inquisitive. Tell me how, according to your knowledge, humans came into existence," asked Nameless *Siddha*.

"After Earth was created from a mega eruption on our sun, Galactic Root Race of bodiless super intelligent beings initiated on our planet the first Wave of Life. It was composed of etheric beings, as there were not yet physical conditions to sustain biological life. This first civilization concentrated on developing creative mental powers to manifest physical things. In the following three Waves of Life beings had bodies. They in time became very advanced, lasted millions of years but got exterminated by natural cataclysms. Not much remains, even to prove their existence. There are only rare artifacts that do not match the official science of our past. For example, the monumental stone of over 1000 tons, abandoned in the remote past in a wilderness near Balbek in Lebanon. It is so heavy that our present technology could not transport it even if a road existed. Another known artifact is a golden chain embedded in a lump of coal, found in an American mine which is a silent witness to our glorious past now lost in the darkness of millennia. There are also a few other startling examples of proof but not too many. We are the Fifth Wave of Life. The Pentagram is a symbol of our period. As such we have five senses; five fingers and five extremities. We were created by advanced beings visiting Earth in the remote past.

"Zecharia Sitchin, who studied in depth Sumerian records written on clay tablets found detailed descriptions of visits by 'gods'/spacemen, some 450 thousand years ago, who were searching for gold. Their planet, Nibiru, had been exposed to deadly cosmic radiation in the aftermath of a nuclear conflict, and had lost its natural protection. The only way to fix this problem was to suspend in a deteriorating atmosphere tiny flakes of gold. They had only little of this element but on Earth they found it in plenty. Sumerians called them Anunaki and spelled An-Una-Ki a name given after their planet ruler—Anu. Their life span was enormous. A Nibiru year, called 'sar', was approximately 3600 Earth years long and they have a genetically preset life span of around hundred twenty years, but Nibirian years. So in Earthly standard they were almost immortals living on average 120x3600=432,000 years. After some time, over thirty thousand of our years, the 'gods '—miners got tired of the continuous toil of mining gold and mutinied. Anu visited Earth, assessed the situation and instead of punishing his workers decided to create a race of hybrid beings—primitive workers that would, as bio-robots, relieve his subjects from laboring. After many trials and attempts, which took over ten thousand years, the first examples were created using the already available genetic pool of Earthly creatures; namely goats and the now extinct tribe of monkeys and genes of the 'gods', as is written in Sumerian clay tablets. Being such a composite product of genetic engineering we are, as I already mentioned, partly extraterrestrial. They called the new hybrids 'A-Da-Mus'—'Earthling' in their language. Those creatures were pre-humans and had no self-awareness. From this probably originated the Biblical name of the first man 'Adam'. Many years passed and two of those aliens— genetic engineers from the royal family of their planet, who were leading this project on Earth—Enki and his sister Nin-Hur-Sag felt uneasy seeing their creations on an animalistic level; so they, without authorization of their father Anu or even Nibiru Council of Elders, upgraded the original design granting Earthlings consciousness and self-awareness. This created problems for the exploiting Earth visitors as humans possessing genes of their creators became in a short time very resourceful. In the beginning our creators were interbreeding with humans, as it seemed that we were compatible. This is described in the Bible which says *(Gen 6:1-2, 4): 'When man began to multiply on the face of the land and daughters were born to them, the sons of God saw that the daughters of man were attractive and they took as their wives any they chose . . . . When the sons of God came in to the daughters of man, they bore children to them. These were the mighty men who were of old, the men of renown.'*

"Born from those unions, the secondary hybrids were appointed later by aliens/creators as ruling classes; pharaohs, emperors, kings and so on. Contemporary aristocracy descends from the children of those hybrids. That's why, to maintain genetic superiority, so called 'blue blood', they mostly interbred between members of their own clans. As administrators of a 'herd'—us − they created secret societies, which exist from the most ancient times until now and are often embedded in multinational corporations. They passed a selection of the truth and knowledge of Cosmic Laws to their high initiates but this is kept secret from the general public as this knowledge, when applied, secures highest power.

"I believe also that those 'gods' who were knowledgeable and technologically advanced, but not so ethical, long ago altered the humans' original genetic code to restrict our memory, intelligence and life span. It was done probably only for a selfish reason as in the Golden Age humans became too competitive for them and were living too long. This was done because to control beings with limited intellectual capacity is much easier than beings representing the full potential of Creative Source. The first humans, as the Bible and inscriptions on varied copies of stelas of 'Sumerian Kings List' say, lived many hundreds and even thousands of years and we now rarely live to one hundred. According to old records our history started in antediluvian times with A-Da-Mus —the first of the seven of human Patriarchs, Enoch the seventh. Enoch was taken for an educational trip to 'alien/gods' space station—a mother-ship. Following him was a Dynasty of Gods. First eight 'god'—kings lived over twenty thousand years each; first Divine Kings: **Alulim** reigned **28,800 years** = 8 sars—orbits of Nibiru; **Alalngar** reigned **36,000 years; En-men-lu-anna** reigned **43,200 years; En-men-gal-anna** reigned **28,800 years; Dumuzid** reigned **36,000 years; En-sipad-zid-anna** reigned **28,800 years; En-men-dura-ana reigned 21,000 years; Ubara-Tutu reigned** 18,600 years (5 sars and 1 ner) They were pure aliens but humans called them 'gods'. After the Great Flood, rulers were human-alien hybrids; the first rulers were from a Dynasty of the Demigods of Kish. They lived only a few hundred years each except the first one, **Jushur,** who reigned 1,200 years. **Kullassina-bel** reigned 960 years; **Ningishlishma** reigned 70 years. The 27th of the postdiluvial kings was **Gilgamesh** who was from Uruk Dynasty and ruled for only 126 years (circa 2600 years BC).

"Genetic engineering programs and attempts to create more superior hybrids have been going on continuously for thousands of years. I believe that a few groups of extra-terrestrials are still on this task, with each group doing this job independently and with very different motives on their minds. I have very personal experience with aliens, which looked like humans and seemed to be benevolent. I participated in a genetic experiment and do not regret it. But, unfortunately, there are here other groups who have an agenda, which does not match our interest as a race. So called Grays are artificially created soulless bio-robots to serve the purpose of an, unknown to present man, advanced alien race of reptilians, possibly actual 'owners' and Overseers of Earth. Grays possess neither the ability to reproduce naturally nor the capacity to experience emotions. They are programmed for certain tasks and cannot divert from their paradigm, as they have no free will. They try to hijack human bodies and occupy them by merging both systems to survive as a race. Probably already walking among us are hybrids from this amalgamation. A few years back I met in Australia a lady who had no emotions but whose intelligence, memory and capacity to calculate was amazing, computer like, super human. Once, I with her husband, who was my client, tested her. She could divide or multiply in a split second a ten digit number (the capacity of the calculator we used to check her), and could remember the amount of all bills for electricity, phone and other utilities for all the years since they got married. She could tell which day of the week was on any particular date when she was a high school student. In high school she scored top marks in all subjects without even reading textbooks. She only played tennis.

"I also suspect that those uninvited visitors to our planet, certainly having advanced mind control technology well mastered, programmed humanity in a few aspects of our behavioral and inter-racial relations. Maybe our aggression and tendency to wage wars is artificially implanted in us, as it is not natural in any other species of mammals. Animals do not have this tendency. They fight only to protect their territory, choose a clan leader or to get food, but this is different from attacking a country on the other side of the globe to control its resources or to topple a non-cooperative leader. Another possibility is that we, as a hybrid race, having huge genetic input of our creators got this tendency of waging perpetual wars and massacring our brothers and sisters directly from them—those alien 'gods'. They, according to Zecharia Sitchin were constantly in conflict between themselves and the struggle for the influence over different continents and regions of Earth. The renegades, who lost a major conflict, were sent in exile to Asia and in time became to be known as fierce 'gods' of India, China, Japan and a few other Asian countries.

"Racial segregation is also somehow encoded in humans' mentality despite that it is against our biological interest. I have noticed that the offspring from inter-racial relationships are physically strong, mentally stable and brilliantly intelligent. But this is, for some reason, not encouraged in so called 'sacred writings', which were probably influenced by aliens, and in national or racial traditions culminating in racial discrimination. It seems to me that aliens want to have for their selfish genetic projects pure races to work with. Unfortunately, it is against our interests because the closer the parents' genetic setup, the more faulty are their offspring. This is most obviously visible in the case of marriages between members of a very close family—commonly practiced in some communities—where as a result unhealthy weaklings and mentally retarded children with learning disabilities are often born.

"Life was created for the purpose of self-perpetuating growth in Wisdom, in developing intelligence to the point of merging with Cosmic Mind of All-What-Is. Cosmos is teeming with life. It is as common as light. We humans, when compared to the vast Universe seem to be tiny and insignificant specks of cosmic dust but in truth we are infinite, eternal and very powerful beings and all of us are equally needed in Totality of Existence. Despite the harm done to us by those 'gods', each human, who is a unique 'projection' of All-What-Is, is equipped with individual talents and the infinite potential of expressing itself. We belong to this Totality and must only marvel at the immense magnificence of entire Existence with Its diversity in unity of The Oneness and respect everything equally. We must forget limited beliefs which restrict us to space and time in this dense, material realm with all its illusionary dramas and sagas. The entire Universe was created only for a purpose of boosting our intelligence by expanding our understanding. We should not imitate nor follow those few who, forgetting the 'Win-Win' principal of mutual respect and cooperation, enthusiastically use their intellect to create barriers, setting taboos for the purpose of control and by doing so block their own and others' progress. We are free, unlimited, spiritual beings of light, children of the Oneness of Energy, and Eternity is our domain of never-ending existence. Humans were fashioned from eternal Energy of All-What-Is as a result of thought manifested in It and by a desire of this enormous Intelligence to become a multitude of individualized thinking beings seeing and experiencing Creation from unique perspective of each. How wonderful!

"Jane Roberts, when channeling body-less entity, a teacher called Seth, said that we should remember that our thoughts become sooner or later manifested, that there is no division between physical and spiritual realm as through us, physical beings spirit speaks and we are nothing else but its manifestation.

"It is highly possible, I would even say almost certain, that Earth still is a sort of 'farm' or 'colony' maintained by clandestine extra-terrestrial Overseers, but not directly and openly like in ancient pre-deluge times, but, rather, secretly through ruling classes controlled by them by creating our so called reality, a secondary illusion.

"*Thombi,* now please tell me why you say 'so called reality'? What did you mean by this?"

"Well, all this that we see, all this physical manifestation is not real at all. *Advaita Vedanta* calls this *Maha Maya* – Grand Illusion. Those objects, which the majority considers as 'solid' are only appearances and 'exist' only in our brains. As I already said, everything is made of energy, which carries information. This energy vibrates at different frequencies. Depending on the frequency of a vibration, we see different colors, which are only different vibrations decoded by our brains. The same is with sounds. Our ears pick up vibrations and the brain decodes them into sounds. Some vibrations are beyond the capacity of our senses to be recognized. Our senses can process only a tiny part of a probably infinite spectrum of vibrations. For example ultrasounds, ultraviolet, radio waves, X-rays are not perceivable by humans. Our senses were programmed by the designers to protect the physical bodies from basic dangers but not to see the full picture of manifested energy in the existing and the surrounding material Universe. For example, if someone came across a lump of plutonium or uranium lying on a road, his senses would not warn him about its lethal radiation because those elements are not supposed to exist in

Nature in a pure/concentrated form and the designers of our senses hadn't made provision for detecting this kind of danger.

"In reality, vast distances exist between the parts of an atom forming a solid object. If we compare a proton to a tennis ball and electrons to mustard seeds then the distance between those two would be the length of a football ground. There is nothing solid in an apple in someone's hand or even in the stainless steel knife he has to cut it. It is only 99.99999% of empty space. In reality it is not really empty but filled with 'black matter' which escapes our perception. One physicist calculated that the energy contained in one cubic meter of total vacuum can boil and evaporate all Earth's oceans, rivers and lakes. Even those subatomic 'particles' called quanta, occupy only 0.000001% of its volume. If we start to investigate deeper, solid things are not as they look, only vortexes of pure energy, which disappear from our physical dimension and appear again with such frequency that it looks as if they are always here. The human body has a frequency of 'ins' and 'outs' of 35 trillion cycles a second. So we are also not always here but spend a considerable amount of time in other than physical reality. The same 'trick' of the senses is used on a grosser scale in movies where a film with twenty or more still pictures changing in one second in front of our eyes creates an illusion of movement. In such a way people are 'chained' by the great illusion of *Maha Maya* to believe in reality of unreal.

"Another revelation of present day's quantum physics science is that those most miniature quanta exist in our dimension only when they are **consciously observed**. So where is the foundation of reality of our world, our physical realm? That's why I call it **'so called reality'**, which really means 'perceived by us as reality'."

"You, *thombi,* when young, used to drink wine and beer. Is that correct? So you know first-hand, from this practice that, for a connoisseur, a glass of decent Australian Cabernet Sauvignon or a mug of German Pilsner or DAB has seven heavens bigger value than a PhD on the subject of wine or beer testing or a hundred books read, where the art of wine and beer sampling is described most scientifically. You are getting 'high' by having first hand glimpses.

Even the tiniest glimpse has tremendously transforming power. It wakes the spiritual seeker up from a dream of *Maha Maya,* it makes him Free, limitless and powerful—a co-creator of experience of his own existence. What you know from experiencing glimpses is yours forever. The mind of an individual that experienced Bliss, even once, can never return to its old limited disposition.

"Follow your own 'legend' and grow in Wisdom. Many imagine that they are spiritually growing by feeding the intellect with second-hand philosophical ideas, by reading classical scriptures and attending discourses of pundits and gurus. What can I say? Writings, even most advanced, are only sign-posts on a road of spiritual growth. Who knows about Bliss only from books can't imagine the real experience of merging in The Oneness of Existence. You have been a mountaineer and a rock climber and understand that only rock climbers who have been in a difficult spot on a brittle rock, for example in the New Zealand Alps, having no means for decent belaying, can know how it feels. The same is with spiritual experiences. Those who only study spiritual writings will gather knowledge but stay 'dry' and empty, having no chance to experience Bliss because it does not belong to the domain of intellect. The same is with glimpses. Beliefs which are not based on personal knowledge only restrict our intellect and prompt us to make wrong choices. If someone's personal or borrowed beliefs are not in tune with Reality then unavoidable suffering will result, as there is discord between the right way and the way this person follows.

"On a path of scriptural study there is also a great danger to develop pride—'spiritual *ego*'. This 'ego' is very canny and always trying to be, at any expense, right, to control everyone or to win an argument in an attempt to be seen as superior, as more intelligent, as more educated or more powerful and even as more 'spiritual'. Be yourself! Do not try to find, with people who are not ready to reset their world-view, a common platform of understanding. It is impossible. Very few, if any, will understand what you say anyway, because there are vast differences of perspectives. It does not matter—not at all! Why even bother? It is explicable because most people measure the level of others' advancement by the prism of their own limitations, imagining that other, higher planes of understanding cannot exist. Allow them to be what they have chosen for themselves to be and inner peace will be your reward," said Nameless *Siddha*.

"Tell me now, *thombi,* what love is and what function it has."

"Sir, love is the most creative force of The Universe. Love can be also called attraction. It is love/attraction allowing oxygen to join with two atoms of hydrogen and form water, the most important substance for our life, substance of miracle, substance which is able to store *prana,* substance having memory and the ability to react to sounds, thoughts and even images. Gravity is also a form of love/attraction. If the Sun is not pulling the Earth toward itself and we got free from orbiting it then all life forms, in no time, would get frozen in interplanetary cold space.

"As a first step, interaction with other projections of All-What-Is creates a magnificent opportunity to develop love to entire Existence by first experiencing love towards those chosen projections. Ultimately love is a means by which All-What-Is, that Eternal, Intelligent, Resourceful and Conscious Energy can experience Itself by creating illusionary duality, uncounted myriads of individualized projections of Itself and then love them and be loved. Also, us humans were created to learn to love each other and things were created to be used. Now priorities are twisted, things are commonly admired and loved and people used. Love functions by binding together those manifestations of All-What-Is, which have similar vibrations. It functions according to the rule: **'Like attracts like'**. People who vibrate on the same frequency resonate, develop friendship or fall in love. That's why a thief never develops friendship with a *sanyasin,* nor does a boy without integrity establish a lasting relationship with a sincere girlfriend. Unmatched people simply repel each other and continuously attract similar. So to change a pattern of repeating the same actions, projecting the same vibrations and by doing so, creating similar results, one must first change oneself, raise oneself to a higher frequency. This realization, when properly understood, empowers people assuring them that they are not left to the unpredictable mercy of circumstances or an angry God but are free beings having inborn ability to create what they desire: abundance, health, peace and Bliss—and that all of it is their very birthright which only has to be claimed. We, as co-creators of this 'reality' living in expanding Universe, also should follow paths of expansion. We should expand our consciousness, grow in understanding interactions of mind and matter and eventually merge with Cosmic Mind—Universal Consciousness.

"Law of Attraction—Law of Love a First Principle is the most important Universal Law governing entire Creation. Thanks to it, we humans, as conscious beings, can create our 'reality' by attracting what we choose. By focused thinking we activate forces in invisible dimensions and if we persist and allow the process to grant us our desires and by believing that we deserve it—materialize what we want. But to start this process a person must establish firmly what he really wants. Otherwise energy will be dispersed and results simply ZERO. In Russia children are told a very old story which illustrates the need for directed exertion. *'Once upon a time animals started to move a sledge with food supplies for the winter. Bull was pulling it forward, donkey in opposite direction, eagle up, a bear sideways and pig, being most clever, refused to participate and started to eat what was loaded. They struggled all day but the sledge did not move an inch. Job started to progress only after wise fox came and ordered all of them to pull sledge forward – in one direction.'* To illustrate this from my own perspective I will narrate a story: Once I met on the Internet a young lady who, after reading a few books on the above mentioned subject, became very enthusiastic and decided to guide humanity towards happiness and prosperity. Even though she failed her high school final exams at the first attempt, she dreamt about creating worldwide centers of self-development and international travel for workshops as a guru of success. In the meantime, she was doing a cosmetic course because there is money in this occupation. When she finally got her High School Certificate she immediately applied to University for a pharmacy course knowing nothing about 'Big Pharma', but knowing only that big money was there so better to get involved. Self-development program and guiding humanity to happiness and prosperity 'starved' from lack of energy input and was swapped to program of drugging humanity for profit. My point is that a person who has no firmly established goal will achieve nothing and he who does not stand up for himself will fall for anything propaganda promotes or greed for money suggests. Buddha once said: **'He who aims at nothing surely will arrive there.'**

"An old proverb says: **'As man thinketh, so he is.'** But humanity is continuously living in its own mental prison, not even noticing that its door is wide open as always was. Our external world is an exact mirror reflection of our inner world—no exceptions. We are like droplets of ocean water, having been created from the same energy as entire Existence, having the same power of creating desired things and conditions, so we are co-creators of our lives and by this expanding The Universe. We are not victims of circumstances or 'fate' but in charge of it all. Energy strings connect everything in this multidimensional creation forming The Oneness. The Universe is an unlimited reservoir of a quantum soup of energy possessing unconstrained possibilities of self-transformations. It is a Being/Universe, we could say, in which galaxies are like molecules in our bodies. Every and each unit/part of this immense Being is instantly aware of what is happening to all other parts of It regardless of how distantly they are located but still maintaining its unique energy 'signature'. Exactly the same is with our body cells. Our body is built from approximately 300 trillion cells and each one is aware of what is going on with every other cell.

"Our DNA not only stores the blueprint for life but also serves as a two-way transmitter sending and receiving vibrations of our intents and reading the intents of others. So our every intent activates entire Creation to support our endeavor and by rearranging this quantum soup brings things and circumstances we want (or do not want if we concentrate on negativity or fear of lack) to manifestation in our lives. Our predominant thoughts are results of our beliefs accepted as truth. So if someone is not pleased with their present situation they must examine their beliefs, change them and by doing this alter their internal self-talk, which would alter their intents and finally send out by DNA vibrations. This will result in external changes.

"Unfortunately people mostly feel and act according to their personal beliefs, which they take mistakenly as universal truths. So poor people stay poor even after winning a jack-pot because they harbor limiting beliefs—they have the shortage and the limitation mentality. Successful people on the other hand, even if they end up broke, soon regain their wealth using failure as a lever for rising even higher. Each of us, as we are today established in life, is the result of our own past thinking. The same applies in the field of spirituality.

"We believe that the reality of what we see, hear and observe with our physical senses is truth but, in fact, a major part of what we perceive is a result of a function of our brain which is editing entering information from our senses according to 'filters' of our beliefs. We see and hear mostly what supports our world view—what we would like to see and hear. Some neurologists estimate that over half of perceived 'reality' is a result of this editing and only less than half comes from actual data received by our senses. Even 'external reality', perceived by us, is nothing more than a creation of our very own DNA, which is projecting to The Universe our intents, desires and corresponding thoughts, which are also a result of our beliefs. This creates a catch 22. **We are seeing what we believe and we believe in what we see.** This is a self-perpetuating and self-reinforcing cycle from which it is difficult to free ourselves without radically resetting our beliefs. And there is more to this story—a very important revelation: our DNA is not set in stone. Dr. Bruce Lipton, the author of 'Biology of Belief' discovered that by altering beliefs we change the structure of DNA and so change its signals sent to the Universe. So there is only one logical alternative; learning how to adopt progressive and beneficial beliefs.

"Many people develop the art of quoting uncountable reasons to justify their unhappiness and dissatisfaction. Many master the skills of perpetuating their lives of misery because they accept as truth that things must be the way they are observed. So All-What-Is accepts each person's beliefs and choices and by the power of the Universal Law of Attraction/Love make it their reality. I believe, Sir that those of us who are afraid to take responsibility for their lives stay where they are, indefinitely waiting for God, Shiva or Arunachala to grant them usually undeserved boon of success and happiness. The Spiritual Path is for those few who are brave enough to face their own personality and have the determination to eliminate unwanted 'weeds' from their set up. To do this one must voluntarily cross the boundary of one's personal safety zone and enter The Unknown where one will find a domain of wonder and 'miracles'.

"Strangely, many spiritual seekers, who consider themselves advanced, are afraid of the word 'love' because they associate this word with sex not knowing its real meaning as an abstract quality or a principle. Unfortunately, in English language there exists the most ridiculous expression for sexual intercourse: 'making love'. So sad! Not knowing what love is, those people cannot use this most powerful Universal Law to their advantage because they shove love out from their lives as something fearful, something which requires commitment and responsibilities or even something that is 'dirty'. But love can be experienced continuously if one maintains awareness. Nature is abundant in hidden chances; love can be felt when watching an insect crawling along the grass, bliss of love can be felt when gazing on the rising Sun or drinking a glass of life supporting spring water. This is excellent initial practice to activate love to entire Existence. Each moment spent on contemplating beauty and the perfection of Nature automatically induces a state of thoughtless meditation.

"Love is also the only 'medicine' for a deviation of our 'civilization', a culture of intimidating. A famous American singer and songwriter Jimi Hendrix said: **'When the power of love overcomes the love of power, the world will know peace.'** Power and love do not mix like water and fire. That's why long ago Plato said: **'Power should be confined to those who are not in love with it.'"**

"Good! I am so pleased that you got it right. I'd like to add here a few points: Love does not require an object of love as it is not an action but a state of mind, a way of experiencing Existence. Love which demands something from someone is not true love but a celebration of *ego* as all demands and cravings originate there. Love requires surrender. Surrender is the death of *ego*. The only means of eliminating *ego* is to practice meditation. Meditation is the only 'road' to the answer of the most important question 'Who am I?' It is the only way to activate awareness of our magnificent Inner Being. Meditation is not a way of destroying thoughts but rather of transcending them and by doing so creating inner space in a state of Stillness. Thoughts are like expensive clothes on a beggar, creating a false personality—*ego,* so to starve *ego* they must be transcended. When *ego* dies and love overcomes a person he starts to have glimpses of The Truth. A person overtaken by Love towards all Creation and 'drunk' from intoxicating Bliss of The Oneness is called an 'Enlightened One'. In this state loving merges with loved and even with the act of loving. Love living! So simple! Is it not so? But it needs practice not discourses! When Buddha was once asked what he had gained from the practice of meditation He replied: **'Nothing, but let me tell you what I lost; Anger, Anxiety, Insecurity, Fear of old age and Fear of death.'**

"Now tell me, *thombi,* if, according to your knowledge 'free will' exists or are some events in people's lives predestined and if so by whom?"

"Sir, if there would be no free will then all this incarnating on Earth, as individualized 'projections' of The Oneness, for a purpose of learning and gradually returning to the Source would have no sense. Only when we can decide how to act, what to say and what to accept and what to reject, does it make sense because all our choices bear consequences. If we enjoy the results it means that we have made the right move, chosen correctly. If we suffer, it indicates the opposite and we eventually learn not to repeat the same mistake in the future. But still it looks like some events are predestined. But it is only illusion. In fact all major events of our lives are also chosen by each of us. Before incarnating on Earth we decide, in astral realm, on the pattern of our future life. Always we have a few options to choose from but the accent is always put on going into situations which will help us to progress in understanding who we are and what we are supposed to do to grow in Wisdom. In each option are the most important events and people of greater significance than others. We have the freedom to accept them or postpone them until the next incarnation. After approving our next life we enter into agreements—contracts—with those who are going to be our partners, relatives, mates, lovers, friends and associates and set 'key signals' to help us to recognize people with whom we made agreements when the situation presents itself. In most cases a 'game' of each incarnation is played with the same souls who enact different roles in different lives; sometime as parent, mate, friend or sometimes even as an enemy.

"So we have complete, uncompromized responsibility for everything going on in our lives because we agreed beforehand to go through it and accepted the freedom to make choices in each coming situation. There is no Higher Power, no Authority and no God to decide for us. We are those who consciously choose but there is a catch. Our choices are determined and restricted by the scope of our intellect, which can be developed only though stimulating education. That's why the Controllers see control of education as their first priority. They act according to the motto: 'Who controls the past, controls the future: who controls the present controls the past.' So our history is manipulated to serve their agenda.

"Cowards and weaklings cannot be truly spiritual and aim to The Truth by a direct path. They need 'walking sticks' in the form of intermediaries: 'sons of God', avatars, priests, gurus and 'fortifications' of temples, churches or mosques believing that God is there more present than in the rest of His Creation. Most people even hate the idea of taking responsibility for their own lives so they need, more than anything else, God or another 'authority' like Shiva, Allah or Christ to blame for the trouble of sending them 'tests', for their chosen unhappiness and dissatisfaction in their present status quo. Others are passing it on Arunachala, Mount Kailash, Fuji Yama or whatever they consider as suitable for this purpose. Worldly people and unbelievers blame bad luck, fate or other people like government officials, own spouses, parents or even children."

"Good! Now explain to me please what your view on organized religions is."

"A spiritual aspirant who is really brave and wise, is not a follower of any cult or profession of faith but follows a 'religion' of unconditional, unassociated with any object, Love, love so powerful that there is no 'space' for fear. If one uses Love as a torch on The Path one will never get lost and will gain Wisdom and attain Freedom. The road from slavery in fear, due to ignorance, to Freedom in Wisdom is through meditation and not through churches, temples or other religious organizations and their rituals. Practicing religious rituals of worshiping symbols can help in the very beginning to develop basic concentration but after that is achieved, must be dropped as they lead nowhere. In fact there are much better ways of developing concentration, than mystical practices, like *japa,* for example, or watching the second hand of a wrist watch or counting to a hundred, then back, then again but missing the even numbers. The Truth can only be known when our inner world is calmed though meditation and, as such, is in harmony with Totality of Existence. A really Free person is wise, whole and continues without interruptions experiencing belonging to the Totality of The Oneness. Organized religions have given in rare cases a spiritual boost to very few, already advanced humans, but have never elevated the masses whose morals did not change in time and whose greed, envy, intolerance, jealousy and violence continued through the ages. Hypatia of Alexandria, a famous mathematician in Egypt and 'pagan' philosopher who got into trouble with Christian clergy for her radical teachings, long ago said: **'All formal dogmatic religions are fallacious and must never be accepted by self-respecting persons as final.'** And this is now no less valid than it was in her times.

"Religions have not solved any of man's problems. In the name of God many bloody wars have been fought under the banners of religious organizations. The most outstanding in their cruelty were the Christian Crusades and this insanity continues to this day because it serves the intentions of few who want to take over the wealth of the Middle East. And the sheeple buy it!

"Millions of Muslims were slaughtered in the name of Jesus Christ. To suppress knowledge and avoid disclosure of dogmatic fraud the Catholic Church tortured and executed in the Middle Ages many free thinkers and arranged the genocide of Cathars who believed that there was no reason why ordinary people could not communicate with God directly, without an artificial intercessor. A bloodbath endorsed by

457

the Church resulted in over 20,000 people being slaughtered and burned at the stake.

"It seems to me that from all existing religions Buddhism is on the highest moral level and its teachings closest to the Truth. It is not introducing God as an entity in charge of creation, if I understand it correctly knowing about it only very little. Also Chinese Falun Gung, which is an offspring of classical Buddhism is a peaceful movement and harms no-one but helps its followers to grow spiritually. Unfortunately, recently Buddhist mobs attacked Muslim communities in Myanmar and in Sri Lanka Buddhists are attacking and demolishing Hindu temples. So even this peaceful, until now, spiritual movement is becoming more and more in tune with other faiths' aggressive and intolerant trends.

"All religions were either established or later overtaken by extra-terrestrial Overseers of Earth. They are all based on modernized older faiths, adapted to presently existing mentality. It was always done not for the liberating of but for the purpose of controlling the population through fear of an angry God which could only be pacified by rituals and sacrifices, by creating dependence on a priestly cast; by fear of a sin or eternal condemnation; by fear of possible schism as a result of independent thinking.

"Creating religions was also the agenda of certain rulers who saw in creation of new faiths a chance of political advancement. This was the case of British born Roman Emperor Flavius Constantinus and the creation of Christianity. He ordered the writing of compilations of the Gospels by pundits gathered from his vast empire. It was a blend of Mithreaism, Druism, Culdees, Egyptian Book of Revelation—the Mysteries of Osiris and Isis—Greek philosophy and selected aspects of Hinduism. Included in the final product of the 'New Testament' were, among others, quotations and extracts from the Hindu epic 'Mahabharata', passages from Greek statement Artus of Sicyon (271-213 BC) and also passages from 'Hymn of Zeus' written (c.331-232 BC) by Greek philosopher Clamenthes and 'Thais' of Menandar (c. 343-291 BC) which were written in gospels as sayings of Jesus Christ. Those books, claiming to contain 'words of God' were written three hundred and fifty years after the events, which were never proved as historical and supposed to have taken place. This resulted in a book full of contradictions and geographical inaccuracies. I cannot say that they do not contain wise advice and insights but, however, they are forgery. Later, Emperor Flavius Constantinus decided on the name of a new God. It was created from blending the name of the Druid god—Hesus and the Hindu god—Krishna, which in Sanskrit means the name Christ. The new god was proclaimed and officially approved by decree: Acta Councilii Nicaeni. In those days there was no letter 'J' in the alphabet until the ninth century when 'Hesus Christ' evolved to the presently used name—Jesus Christ. Eastern European countries adopted Christianity to enhance the rulers' power by banding together with rest of Europe, which was under Roman management. The conversion to Judaism of Khasars, I already mentioned earlier. Communism was also a religion, thought totally materialistic and created on bogus reversed principal that 'existence creates consciousnesses (they meant; from proletariat life hardships revolutionary ideas are born) only for political gain and as a sociological experiment of the Cabal.

"As far as I know, none of the existing religious movements empower people; only maintain feelings of guilt, inadequacy and servitude to an inaccessible God through servitude to a priestly caste. I like a saying, which I heard once in America: **'God save us from religion and grant us ability to see the Truth'.** Mahatma Gandhi said: **'The most heinous and the cruelest crimes of which history has record have been committed under the cover of religion or equally noble motives.'** Also Pascal said: **'Men never do evil so completely and cheerfully as when they do it from religious conviction.'**

"All religions are designed to bring under control human individuality and independent thought, and restrain awareness that both life and death are part of the great illusion as well as all material existence. They hide from followers the truth that eternal life does not have to be earned but it is that which we are living right now and our presence on Earth is only a small trip to this dimension for training purposes. They hide the knowledge that humanity has been for a purpose separated from its Source by artificially created Matrix

---

in which religions are a very important component. People go to churches, synagogues, temples and mosques prompted by the hope of finding emotional comfort by immersing themselves in an illusion that a loving God is taking care of them, and that they can dream about freedom; forgetting present miseries and emotional anguish. So I completely agree with statements I heard repeated endlessly as propaganda against Catholic Church when I was living in communist countries: **'Religions are opium for ignorant masses.'** Only in this were communists right. Religion is the only human to human contagious psychosis known to modern medical science which can't be cured even with famous 'Prozac'!

"No-one can explain the Truth to others. No religious institutions can help. It cannot be found in books either, even ones believed as most sacred. It must be discovered by each aspirant on his own, in the innermost part of his own Being."

"Very, very good! In worldly standards you, my dear Traveler, qualify without a slightest doubt, even without a trial, as it becomes now very trendy in some countries, for burning at the stake of not-too-dry wood − slowly. I am proud of you! All my favorite students are notorious rebels. Welcome to our 'classroom'! You are accepted! Tell me now what do you want for yourself? Any idea?"

"Yes Sir. I have a few ideas. Oscar Wilde said: **'An idea that is not dangerous is unworthy of being called an idea at all.'** So, I as a notorious rebel, have a few ideas. I would like, Sir, to improve myself. I would like to eliminate as many of my negative tendencies as possible, to be a conscious architect of my life and build it like a wall made of bricks, one brick at a time, until it is completed and perfect. I want to change myself; I want to progress, to grow in Wisdom and strength of knowledge because I have come to this World to contribute to its changes for the better and I can contribute to its changes only by starting to change myself. I believe that I can, so know that I will! I would like to understand better the teachings of Nature, to clearer hear the voice of Silence. I would like to make choices, to decide how I live, in which direction is good for me to focus attention and how to evolve as a spiritual entity. I want to serve those who are open to accept my help. I would like to be free to say what I want to say because my heart dictates it even if others do not like my 'truth' because I believe in The Oneness of Existence and 'others' I consider as different aspects of me, which sometimes are under development and need correction. Now, Sir, the biggest thing! *Advaita Vedanta* statement of one of Upanishades says: **"By knowing that one thing, everything else is known."** "I want, Sir, to know It!"

"Nothing more?" asked Nameless Siddha. "No, Sir, that is all. There **IS nothing more**."

"Accepted! Done! It is your choice. Let it be as you wish!" said Nameless Siddha. "Tell me, *thombi,* what has to be done to reach Enlightenment?"

"Nothing, Sir. Enlightenment is not achievable by effort. It is just a phenomenon of perceiving and experiencing the Reality when the mind is still. When the mind subsides, the inner light of the Self— Inner Being, which was always there can be seen. That is all as far as I understand."

"Now, *thombi,* we will meet your brother who is anxious to tell you his story." Out of the mist came a young man wearing white clothes and a gold embroidered white cap on his head—the typical outfit of Tamil Muslims.

"Greetings my brother from one of our past lives together," said the man, folding his palms on the front of his chest and bowing forward three times. "I was ruling our country when you passed to me a kingship. Our lives continued along completely different paths. Your aim was to grow spiritually and I, as a warrior by nature, continued confronting my enemies real and imagined. My brother, I am so happy to meet you again. Now I rest in astral realms. In my last life my name was Abdul. I was a Muslim; the son of a prosperous rice merchant from Villapuram—a medium size town in the Indian state of Tamil Nadu. You must know where it is, as you frequently pass it on your way to Kerala's capitol Trivandrupuram. I married Sabeeha (Arabic: صبيحه = Beautiful) She, the daughter of a hardware shop owner was really beautiful as her name indicated. My father-in-law promised me a nice dowry: a new house in Villapuram, a Tata Sumo Jeep, 950 grams of 24K Dubai gold in ornaments, furniture, linen, a paid trip to Mecca and much more. But, being always adventurous and enraged by the frequent news about unbelievable crimes committed by Western military and their intelligence organizations in Muslim countries, I joined a small local group of radical *jihadists*. For six months we exercised guerrilla techniques and combat strategies learned from a smuggled leaflet from South Arabia. A small, uncultivated bushy farm close to our town, belonging to one of my old relatives was excellent for this purpose as no one was around to watch us. After our training was completed, and all of us felt fit to fight we decided to fly to the Pakistani capital, Islamabad, then go by bus to Peshawar, cross on a ferry the Tochi River and join a caravan sneaking through the Waziristan mountains to Afghanistan and there help, for some time, the Talibans to fight American and NATO coalition forces—occupying country aggressors.

"In Islamabad we rented a room in 'Jyoti Family Hotel' and bought clothes suitable to blend in with the locals. On the third day of our stay at three o'clock in the morning someone knocked on the door. One of our team opened it. In no time the room was filled by men wearing black balaclavas and camouflage uniforms, holding in their hands machine-guns, which were immediately pointed at each of us. They were from ISI—the Pakistani dreaded spying agency.

"We were arrested without any explanation of our crime. Our personal belongings were searched thoroughly and then confiscated including passports and money. We were transported in a closed boxed lorry to some sort of base or a prison. Interrogations started almost immediately after our arrival. All interrogators were Pakistani. First there was a lot of shouting, pointing a handgun at the heads of each of us. When this did not give the expected results, the beating started. First they beat us with bamboo sticks while we were sitting on chairs. Again more shouting and coercion.

"Somehow our oppressors deduced that I was the team leader and hung me up by my handcuffed hands on rings attached to the ceiling.

Six hours later, while I was still up, another session of questions. I had nothing to say so they started to beat me on my legs. It was really very painful and I felt totally hopeless.

"The next week they transferred me to some place in Afghanistan. This I learned from other prisoners who shared a small cell with me. This prison was in the hands of the Americans. Later, other prisoners told me that we had ended up in a place called Bagram. Interrogations started like in Pakistan—with threats and shouting. After half an hour came a blond lady wearing casual clothes like those who work in Western offices. She was a foreigner and probably in charge of interrogations as everyone in the room stood up and saluted her. On her face were no emotions. She looked like a life—size artificial doll. She checked my file lying on the desk, said something to one man and left the room not even looking at me. They started to hit me with a sort of rod connected by wire to some machinery. It was terrible. The rod gave me electric shocks. I lost consciousness. Someone poured water on me. I was taken down and driven on a trolley to my cell. The torture was repeated twice a week. After a month of torture they took me somewhere on a 'plane, with twenty others. We were hooded with black bags, which were almost hermetic and only a little air entered them. They placed us in a lying position on the floor, tied to ropes going across and along the cargo plane. Our flight lasted over twelve hours. I know this because the soldiers were talking about a long flight. From the airport, where we landed, a helicopter immediately took us to an old cargo ship, which had been converted to a floating prison. It was one of the 'black sites', those secret prisons, which were placed by America in international waters so not to be accountable to any laws. Prisoners kept there had no personal rights, no access to defense lawyers, and even charges were never specified. They called us: 'enemy combatants'. Sometimes, someone, after a prolonged suffering of torture was found innocent, and when assessed as a useless source of intelligence released. Others, even if they had been arrested by mistake and had never been involved with resistance forces, died from the torture and were disposed of in the sea.

"I was placed in a caged cell close to a deck from where I often overheard guards talking. Once, two guards, hiding from the sun came close to me, and, unaware of my presence, chatted: complaining of the boredom on this isolated post where nothing was available to play with. One of them who looked a bit overweight was slow talking and slow thinking like a typically overfed son of a potato farmer from Utah. It was Private Mark. 'You, John, never were in Afghanistan,' said Mark. 'It is tough up there, very dangerous but there are also many opportunities to have some fun. We were controlling Kunar province. Each day a few helicopters flew over this province to check on the movements of insurgents. We were careful not to be shot by the Taliban when approaching settlements. Often, when we spotted in a remote village a young girl we landed and took her aboard our RAH-66 Comanche. After all of us had raped her to satisfaction she was usually disposed of, most of the time already unconscious, from a high altitude flight, sometimes on her own village. Sometimes we had such fun with a young shepherd boy but to be honest I always preferred young nomadic girls.'

'Do you, Mark, consider this as fun? It was a terrible crime!' responded the other guard, John, in a disturbed voice. 'I won't do it! Never! Never!'

'Oh, No? Then, buddy, you may have a nasty accident. Some guys were shot for not co-operating, as the chance of a report to the high command was real. In the battlefield there is always a chance to eliminate such cowardly guys. Most blokes participated and now have good memories.'

"I thought: 'Real courage and a way to live a life of integrity is in having the backbone to say: 'no', even if all your other mates say: 'yes' and try to force us to do what they do by making threats'. How many of those brainwashed military men can practice integrity by doing right things because it is right even when all the others do just the opposite because in the military 'herd mentality' prevails? On what moral level are those Junkies? They started out on a false pretext; by the canny deception of this illegal war. They can't even respect civilians, ladies in occupied countries; raping and killing them when there is opportunity and dehumanizing the natives of occupied countries. They are lower than wild animals which do not kill their own kind, nor kill for any other reason than to satisfy their hunger, and they newer torture their victims.

"Interrogation started next day by hanging me up for eight hours before the first questions were asked. Afterward, when I did not reply for ten minutes for every question asked, the interrogating civilian left the room saying something to Private Mark. Mark, who liked so much to rape Afghan ladies and kill them afterward by dumping them from a helicopter, started to beat my legs with a polymer rod. I screamed in severe pain, as my legs had very sensitive bruises from earlier beatings. He did not take any notice of my screams. After a while I lost consciousness. Mark, not being very observant and almost brainless continued doing his 'job'.

"Half an hour later John entered room. 'What are you doing Mark? Are you mad?' shouted John. 'He is unconscious and his leg muscles are already lacerated. Are you a human or a machine? Maybe you are a devil?' he shouted terrified. 'What do you want? I am just doing what I was told to do! In the army we are not supposed to think, only follow orders. Am I not right?' Mark defended himself.

"Private John poured some water on me. I opened my eyes. It felt like hell. It is impossible to imagine the pain when all your nerves are exposed in muscles, which are almost minced meat, and on top of that, the pain of parts of the body that have been stretched by hanging for so many hours.

"'Water!' I whispered. John went to a side table and took a huge waxy paper cup like those in which popcorn is served in American cinemas. He filled it with tap water, and came very close to me. I noticed, with surprise, a very warm and loving look in his eyes mixed with the disgust of witnessing my suffering. It was clearly visible on his face. I opened my mouth. John suddenly put the cup carefully on my mouth and hit it with his other palm. Water violently entered my lungs and after a few convulsions I was dead.

"There was no pain. I was free to move. I was hovering just below the ceiling and looked down with surprise on those two soldiers standing in the middle of the torture room, staring at my hanging dead body. The interrogator returned and, seeing me dead, scolded Mark for losing a subject, but he did this without any visible emotions. I saw their auras. Only John and Mark had distinctive auras but of very different hues. The interrogator's body was covered by a sort of cocoon of grayish-brown mist, like a dead person. Then I started to rise up. After a while I entered a tunnel at the other end of which was a strange Light. When I reached this Light I realized that it was a Being radiating loving, Golden Light. From behind Him came our great Sage, *Haji*, beloved in Tamil Nadu. (For Glossary: Who took *Maha Samadhi* in Tiruvannamalai on 5th of December 1888). He embraced me lovingly and took me away for a talk. We analyzed together my life and I was permitted to stay there.

"But I must also tell you, my brother, something more. When I was hanging upside down in the torture room I had a vision. In beginning of the XII c. I was one of Genghis Khan's messengers and was captured and executed by Polish hussars on the steppes of Podole. They were very cruel and did not respect the fact that I was on an official diplomatic mission. First they dragged me behind a horse through wilderness by ropes attached to my legs. The thorny bushes and stones injured my legs and back terribly. Almost all the skin from my back was removed. After my head hit a rock I lost consciousness. When I came to, Polish soldiers were adjusting a sharpened pole in order to drive it into my body though my rectum. Horses pulled the ropes attached previously to my legs and I felt the burning pain of wood pushed by force into my body. When it reached my rib cage they stopped and put me, pinned by the pole in vertically position, securing it by rocks in a small pit, which was earlier dug for this purpose. I stayed on this pole in unbelievable agony and in the burning sun all day. In the evening a Being of Light came to me and took me to heaven.

"When time passed I understood that from the times of making wars as a king of our country until the present time I had been controlled by anger and rage and, as a consequence, suffered the whole time.

I realized that problems cannot be solved by using brute force and that there is no point in escalating violence. I understood that peace is a state of harmony between people and countries where all warfare is completely absent. I understood that there is no way to fight for peace. Violence in a world filled with weapons of mass destruction will ultimately lead to the self-destruction of all life. It was my mistake in my last life that I decided to join the Taliban fighters. They had an unquestionable right to defend their country from aggressors who had no legal or moral right to be there but I should not have got involved just because of my boiling anger. I think that by now I have learned this lesson."

"That was a very sad story, *thombi*. Wasn't it?" said Nameless *Siddha* looking at Traveler and his brother Abdul with deep sympathy. "These kinds of lives are now not exceptions. Human cruelty has reached a level and scale never in the past practiced nor even possible. Very good, Abdul, that you understood the correlations between thoughts charged by emotions and their fruits. You, *thombi,* should tell others about it, as they have the right to know what is being done in their name and then, later, on the TV news called 'bringing democracy' and 'liberating'. Also those who follow *jihad* propaganda should realize that this is not the way to peace and independence. All humanity must wake up and put a full stop on all kinds of violence. It is up to people to change the course of humanity from technologically advanced totalitarian barbarianism to spiritual democracy. Staying home and just doing one's job is not going to help anyone get out of this torpor and, in fact, is not much better than what Mark did to your brother.

"But now watch out! I'd like to ask you, *thombi,* a very personal question. Your spiritual sister, a princess who wanted to be your wife, but you chose the path of renunciation and became a monk, your darling 'squirrel' from the times you served in the temple of Śviativid as a priest, and later your companion during the defending of Masada, has incarnated on Earth again. She is already a Free Being but has decided to come to Earth to help others, particularly you, who are still struggling to try to find a way to permanent Freedom, and also for a personal reason. Recently, after you became single and also left the ashram, she approached the Council of White Brotherhood, under which direct supervision she now works, with a request to grant her permission to spend a few years with you, since your and her mutual contracts from a few thousand years back have not yet been completed. Her request was granted on the condition that you, as a being having free will, would agree too. Do you?"

Something broke in the tough, hardened by many 'life battles' interior of Traveler. Events from the past, always considered as only dream fantasies, flashed in front of his eyes. He suddenly saw again the thread of golden light binding them for Eternity. He understood that permanent feeling of oneness with The Oneness could be secured only by forming oneness with her who is his Twin Flame and that they never can be whole, living as separate existences, separate projections of The Oneness. Tears of love rolled down from the eyes of Traveler creating a pool on the reddish surface of the slab on which he was sitting. Nameless Siddha got up, walked to him and paternally patted his shoulder with encouragement.

"Let it be as she wishes!" whispered Traveler. "Her wish can only be my will, Sir."

"Good on you!" Nameless *Siddha* exploded with happiness. "I am so happy that you are now more open. In a few lives you sacrificed your love for ambition of spiritual growth, which was a good way but also ultimately not very correct. Good that you understand now that it is not possible to complete your quest on The Path without fulfilling once accepted contracts. Your Teacher, Swami Chinmahananda has done a great job because you understand now that the *sannyasa* path is not superior over the *grahasta* one. Now you are not afraid to become a householder. Be blessed, you two! You will have the best possible teacher we can provide! She is an exceptional being! Congratulations on the way to Freedom."

Out of a milky mist came a young lady wearing a blue sari. She was short and dark skinned, as dark skinned as are Tamil people. She first saluted *'namaste'* to Nameless Siddha and then the Traveler.

She was surrounded by a strong aura of confidence, dignity and an impenetrable peace charged with spiritual power.

"Be blessed my spiritual brother for allowing to happen what must happen because long ago we agreed that it would happen. Be ready as I am, to face whatever life will grant us. I will meet you in a month's time and you will recognize me when I wave towards you my palm, holding my hand high above my head. In this life I am not going to be a royal, just as you are also not. We will be by worldly standards low profile people – servants of servants. My name is Viji." Saying so, she broadly smiled, saluted Traveler with folded hands and faded in mid-air before Traveler managed to utter a word.

Traveler woke up on the rice straw mat in the room under the Kannapa Temple. He sat up and looked all around. Old *sadhu* was sitting as still as a statue in a corner and looking at him with a smile.

"How was your 'trip', *thombi*?" asked *sadhu*, softly. "Would you like to have some pure water? No need now for any herbal concoctions." Traveler was not yet fully alert. He looked around again as if seeing this place for the first time. "Am I dreaming?" he thought. Then he noticed on the table an alarm clock. There, on it was the time: ten minutes after twelve PM.

"Sir, I went there through a few lifetimes, had long talks with Nameless Siddha who asked me many questions and I met my brother from the remote past and later Viji and only ten minutes passed? How is it possible?" asked Traveler, looking for an explanation from the old *sadhu*.

"My boy, there time is entirely different than in our dimension. You could experience in those ten minutes even many thousands of years. It simply is as it is. In fact it does not exist at all but there is no need to dwell on it now. Even in the Bible it is said that 'with the Lord one day is like a thousand years, and a thousand years like one day'. Have you heard this? The Bible talks about time operating in astral. Experiences are only valid, no agreements about measuring mind activities—called time. Go back to your house now and think about what you saw and heard over and over. You will be called two more times."

Traveler went home. He felt dizzy and decided to have a nap. It was three o'clock PM Friday. When he woke up it was already after sunset. He went to the kitchen to get something to drink, as he felt thirsty. On his cell phone, which was lying on the side cabinet the day was Tuesday. He checked the Internet. Yes it was Tuesday! So he had been in a coma-sleep for more than three days.

Days, weeks passed on *sadhana*. He decided to put in writing his experiences and started to formulate stories. On the first Monday of the next month DTDC Couriers called, informing that printer cartridges, which Traveler had ordered from a Bangalore Co. had just arrived and asked if delivery could be done after 4 PM. With Traveler it was OK as he was in his hut and immersed in his writing. At a quarter past 4 PM in Traveler's house the bell rang. He opened door. A lady—a delivery person from DTDC Couriers brought him his expected parcel. She was rather short, beautiful and wearing a blue sari. She was a low status employee but he noticed that a strange aura of confidence, dignity and peace surrounded her. He automatically signed her delivery records book, took the parcel and looked at her as if waiting for something more. It was a very strange feeling for apparently no reason as this simple business was already completed. She was also standing and waiting, as if something more should be said. After while she left, walking slowly towards her TVS Scooty. Just before reaching it she lifted her hand quite high, much above her head, and waved towards Traveler, still standing in the doorway.

"Is that YOU Viji?" He asked involuntarily as if in a trance, trying to bring back to memory something known, something obvious but long, long ago forgotten.

"You got it first time! Good on you! Yes, I am Viji! *Namaste-vanakam.*" said the lady in the blue sari, turning back and walking slowly towards Traveler's hut, which from this moment became their house. The final 'game' towards Freedom had started. Each day Traveler learned from her more than many others rarely learn in a whole lifetime. She was, by her own example, a most gentle but also a most uncompromising teacher of The Truth. Vijis' and the Traveler's lives started working their way through each other to complete the remaining *karmic* stages of the journey on The Path and later to continue in the realm beyond.

Three more times Traveler was invited to meet Nameless *Siddha* but this time always together with Viji. On the second visit he was initiated. For this they were instantly transported to the Himalayas by going through a sort of crystal gate. There he met all the members of the White Brotherhood. No introduction. Initiation was simple but profound. He was immersed in the cold waters of the rapid Gaga River close to its source in Gangotri and some mantras were said by a *Siddha* who was clearly the oldest since he looked the most ancient of them all. All members of the White Brotherhood stood silently in a semicircle. Viji also watched it from their right side, standing next to Nameless *Siddha*. After this short ceremony was over Nameless *Siddha* took Traveler to a nearby cave and granted him there many spiritual blessings and also empowered him with a proficiency in creating his own destiny. Details of this cannot be passed on, readers, as total confidentiality is required and only those who, through their *sadhana* and a life with total integrity, earn the right to know this, and can then be told, at the right time, directly by one of the White Brotherhood members.

On the third visit Traveler met again his former brother Abdul who asked him to help his wife in Villupuram. She was sick from unhappiness and now dying of cancer.

Traveler, without much difficulty, found the small house of Abdul and Sabeeha. All auto rickshaw drivers from New Bus Stand knew them. It was a one-room cottage in the poor Muslim neighborhood of South Villupuram. Saba's father had still not built them the house he had promised before their wedding, and, after Abdul left for Afghanistan, disappointed he took back the entire dowry making her very poor. Abdul's father passed away from a heart attack a week after Abdul left for Afghanistan so from this side also was no help. She was not surprised to see him. A week before she had a dream in which *Haji* told her that she would soon join her husband in heaven and that a Westerner would take care of her and Abdul's son.

Traveler told her about his relationship with her husband, about their meeting in the astral interior of Arunachala but skipped the details about the torture. It surpassed that she already knew from *Haji* how they were related and, on top of that, she was told that she was their mother, a Queen in this remote past incarnation when the Traveler had become a monk. The same day Advocate Rajram filed in the Villupuram District Court an adoption request, which was approved in a week, as priority was recognized as obvious. The day after Saba's funeral Traveler took the boy Basha to Tiruvannamalai.

Now, at the time of writing this story, Basha is a student in the second year of a course of Mechanical Engineering in Anna University in Chennai. He is a very peaceful person and has an exceptionally brilliant mind!

الله هو العظمى Allahu Akhbar!—Allah is the Greatest!

أننا نريد شيئا سوى السلام. We want nothing but peace.

LAST DARSHAN

Two old men appeared at the forged iron gate and crossed it confidently, like those who know the way. Now they were walking slowly under the cover of an arcade, hiding in its shade from the burning sun. The air there was pleasantly cool. The medieval building breathed antiquity from every stone and brick.

They were wearing plain, brownish robes. The Companion was a bit younger, probably in his seventies, and much taller. The Traveler was nearing his eighty-fifth year. He had a fine build. Despite his age, which had put limitations on his body, he was still walking upright, and radiated an inexhaustible energy. His face was glowing with contentment and serenity. They entered the building. The interior was of gray and beige sandstone; it was much cooler than outside.

Their sandals clapped on the stony floor tiles; the walls repeating the echo. It sounded like a mantra chanted monotonously: "Om Ram, Om Ram, Om Ram . . ." Otherwise the place was totally silent. There were no other people in the building. Everything was more like a symbolic stage decoration than a real thing. They entered a huge hall. Everything here looked exactly as it had a few hundred years ago when the building was erected. Arched ceilings were supported by rows of slim columns made of stone, decorated on their crowns with tasteful simplicity, and bearing in style a dash of oriental influence.

They left their sandals at the door and walked across the hall. Now inside, barefoot, there was no sound at all. There was such a dense silence that they even started to hear their own hearts beating and feel the blood moving in their veins. There, He was waiting for them.

They could not see Him as the columns were in the way, but they felt His presence very strongly. His powerful energy vibrations saturated the air of the entire hall. It was pulsating with Divine Energy. The Companion started to shrink. His body was bending down and down, diminishing. He could not bear this energy. It was as though he wanted to disappear, to vanish under the floor. Then they saw Him. He was standing on a little plain rug, wearing a modest robe similar to theirs. Very tall and slim, but muscular and rugged, he looked ninety years old, with silver hair and a long beard. His face was extremely serious and strict, as well as smiling, radiating love and compassion. In His right hand He was holding a long, craggy stick, similar to those used by Middle Eastern shepherds. He was the MASTER SHEPHERD HIMSELF!

The companion could not to go any further. He simply fell on the floor, being unable to even look at the Master's face. He felt that if he went closer he would be turned in an instant to ashes.

The Master made an inviting gesture with his left hand toward the Traveler. The Traveler approached Him with appropriate respect and made an attempt to kneel on the floor, to prostrate and worship His Holy Feet, but his body refused to bow. It was stiff and full of pain.

"Don't worry my son", the Master Shepherd said softly. "I know that your body is worn out. There is no need for it. You have already given me all necessary respect. All your life you worshipped me by your work." Then He stepped forward, putting His arm around the Traveler's shoulder bringing him to His chest.

The Traveler sank with relief into the Master's torso. He felt very clearly that his Earthly wanderings were over. He, at the end of his long and very intense life, had come back home—to Him. His mind was at a total standstill. After a while, the Traveler lifted his head and looked with devotion and admiration straight into the Master's face. He was shocked, as if hit by a thunderbolt. In the glowing face there was only the left eye. In the place where the right one should have been was a large opening, like a round window! It was opening into Eternity, to Infinity of endless space. It became obvious that the Master's body was only a thin, balloon-like temporary manifestation, enveloping His Real formless aspect. The Traveler intuitively knew that he could instantaneously acquire any knowledge he chose to possess. Anyone who gazed into that window would know all the secrets of creation, the past and the future. But he refused to gaze. He didn't want to know anything. He was at the conclusion of his life and ultimately satisfied. His perfect surrender was satisfying him much more than any knowledge could. But . . . in the fraction of a second that he had looked into the Window of Knowledge, he had the chance to notice that the dark infinite space was pulsating with an all—pervading bright Golden Light. He was astonished, as he found himself identified with this Light. He felt that he had no limitations, and that he was ever-present, existing eternally as Awareness, as Consciousness, as Love Divine.

The Master smiled warmly and said in a kind voice,

"Now, my darling son, you know who you are, don't you? Are you happy?" A strong charge of energy passed through the Traveler's body like lightening. He answered automatically without thinking, like one answers about something obvious and evident,

"I know. I am YOU. I am Love." Then he entered a state of Bliss Absolute, ceasing to exist as an individual. He merged in the Master. He became Him. He became that Golden Light of Love. He became Immortal.

After some time, when the Companion raised his head, there was not a trace of the Master or the Traveler. Only as before, in the middle of the hall, a small plain rug laid on the tiled floor. They both had turned into light and merged in the Totality of The Oneness, and were now permeating the entire creation as its substratum, as the Golden Light of Love.

The Companion felt Them in his heart and was happy.

Glossary

Advaita Vedanta	Hindu philosophy of non—duality. There is nothing apart from God or, we can say, Conscious, Eternal and Super-Intelligent energy.
Allu masala	Spicy cauliflower stew.
Atma Vichara	Inquiry into one's own being by asking the question as a mantra but not automatically with a desire to know; 'Who I am?' as advised for advanced seekers of Truth by Sri Ramana Maharshi of Tituvannamalai.
Avatar	Incarnation of God or an aspect of God.
Ashramite	An inmate of a Hindu ashram—monastery

Avathut | A wandering, often naked *sadhu—renunciate,* in most cases self-realized—liberated. Usually free to disregard any conventional rules of conduct.

Bajan | A devotional song.

Bhagavad Geeta | Divine Song–a part of epos Mahabharata. Teaching of Lord Krishna on a battlefield to his disciple Arjuna. One of the most important scriptures of Hinduism applicable to all humans. Note of interest: Hitler was always known to have close by, and was often observed reading, its German translation.

Bhakti | In Sanskrit: devotion

Bhakti | Yoga Yoga of devotion; singing bhajans, offering to chosen aspect of God flowers, performing pujas and so on . . .

Bhava /Guru Bhava/ | Sanskrit: bhava = mood./ Guru Mood— Exhibiting all the splendor of self—realized personality of Guru. Krishna Bhava—total identification during Krishna Bhava program with Krishna.

Brahma | The Hindu God of creation and one of the Trinity.

Brahmaloka | A realm of Brahma. It is considered as Hindu Heaven.

Brahmacharia | Conduct of celibacy; physical and mental.

Brahmachari/-rini | A person who practices *brahmacharia.*

Brindavan	A place in Gujarat where was born Krishna.
Chappaties	Indian flat and thin bread made of 'Atta', a whole-grain wheat flour.
Chandanam	A sandalwood round mark on the forehead.
Chaya	Indian spicy and sweet tea with milk.
Darshan	Seeing or being in the presence of a Saint, Guru or a religious person. Can be silent, but with dialogue or teachings then becomes *satsang*. It influences the vibrations of the person attending *dharshan,* which automatically attune to a saint's.
Dharma	In Hinduism it is understood as human conduct and behavior that are considered to be in accord with the natural order.
Sanathana Dharma	'Eternal religion' (usually referring to Vedic philosophy).
Ganesha	One God of Hindu pantheon.
Giri Pradakshina	Walking around Hill of Arunachala.
Gopi	Cow/s attending girl/lady.
Gulag	An extensive system of Hard Labor camps for dissidents and criminals, mainly in Siberia which existed during the times of the Soviet Union.

Guru	A spiritual teacher, often self-realized who leads aspirants of the Truth from darkness toward light—that is, from ignorance to knowledge and wisdom. Around some Gurus ashrams are formed as was the case with Sri Ramana Maharshi. Not all those who call themselves (or who are referred to by others as) "Guru" are in fact 'real' Gurus, but the title has become misused over time, so that in many cases today it simply refers to someone who has a strong hold/influence over his/her followers.
Hanuman	A legendary warrior, a Monkey King, disciple of Sage Rama (see epos 'Ramayana')
Hatha Yoga	Yoga of physical exercises—stretching postures activating glands and nervous system.
Homa	Vedic fire ceremony / ritual performed by Brahmin priests for intentions, such as blessing a newly built house and so on.
Japa Mantra	Repetition of *mantra*.
Karma	A result of personal choices and actions, either physical or mental, made in waking state. Dream actions can have (dream) results but do not result as karma in walking state.
Kavi	From Sanskrit: color of fire, red bricks— the color of clothes worn by Hindu *sannyasis—Swamis*.
Kama Sutra	A Vedic text of sexual instructions of intimate conduct.

Kumkum	A red powder made from turmeric and saffron used for social and religious markings in Hinduism; often applied by Hindus to the forehead.
KGB	An abbreviation for *Rus. Fon.: Komitet gosudarstvennoy bezopasnosti (Rus.: Комитет государственной безопасности (КГБ)*, Eng.: 'Committee for State Security' existed in communist Russia during Soviet Union times.
Ladu	Indian sweet ball made of milk, sugar and spices like cardamom and turmeric.
Leela	Divine play of hide-and-seek in illusionary reality. God is hidden in Creation.
Lingam	Symbol of penis of God Shiva in a form of low, usually black pillar with three vertical lines—worshiped in Hindu Temples for blessing of fertility.
Loess/Loessal	Geol.: A very fertile soil created on a transported by winds microscopic mineral particles. In China are regions where this is over ten meters up from original bedrock.
Mantra	A word or formula for repetition as a spiritual practice aiming in controlling the mind by concentration. Examples: OM, Om Namah Shivaya, So Ham—a natural mantra repeated when breathing by all humans; **So**—breath IN, **Ham**—breath OUT—means in Sanskrit: **I am That**.
Maha	Great.

Maha-Avatar	Great Incarnation of God or aspect of God, usually on Earth for extended period of time. Babaji described by Yogananda in his 'Autobiography of a Yogi' is presented there as an Avatar for this Wave of Life.
Maha Maya	Great Illusion of reality of physical world.
Maheshvarah	One of the aspects/manifestations of God.
Maya	Illusion.
Math or Mutt	Hindu ashram—monastery.
Meals	Name for SOUTH Indian lunch of rice, *sambar* and selected vegetables.
Mouna	Sanskrit: Silence.
Mouni	Silent /for example Mouni Sadhu a disciple of Sri Ramana Maharshu, author of 'In Days of Greate Peace' and 'Concentration'/.
Mudra	A gesteure, a palm sign like a popular sign 'V' for victory. Diferent mudras are used by saints for different purposes. Illuminati and it's Camal also use mudra as a sign of power: index and small fingers pointing up other fingers folded—imitate a head of an owl.
Murti	A carving in stone of a cow—used for altars and in temples.
Namaste	Hindu greeting. Means: **'I salute you'**.

NKVD	An abbreviation of Engl.:'People's Commissariat for Internal Affairs (Russ.: Народный комиссариат внутренних дел, Fon.: *Narodnyy Komissariat Vnutrennikh Del*).
OM	Sacred syllable representing the sound which initiated the manifestation of the physical Universe. It can be heard coming from roaring ocean waves.
Pacha	patani Green pea.
Pandava Thirtam	A water tank where, according to legend, Pandava Clan rested when on exile as described in epos Mahabharata.
Peetam	Elevated seat usually made of stone and covered by tiger skin on which the Guru sits when teaching his/her disciples.
Politruk	During Soviet times an official guardian of political morale of a group of workers or soldiers.
Prasad	Offering of a Guru or a Saint to his/her disciples, devotees or visitors—usually as a blessed food, often with *sankalpa.*
Puja	Hindu ritual like Christian mass. Can be performed in Temples by priests but also in human residences by house-holders of both sexes.
Puja table	A low table on which to perform a *puja.*
Ravana	Legendary God-Demon of Sri Lanka. He kidnapped Sita, the wife of Sage-King Rama (See epos 'Ramayana').

481

Sadhana	Spiritual practices: singing *bajans*, praying, meditating, *yoga nidra*, doing *japa mantra*.
Sadhu	A wandering *renunciate* who perform *sadhana* on his own—not being an *ashramite or Sannyass Order initiate*.
Sahaya Nirvikalpa	The highest form of Samadhi above a 'trance' and is not associated with any particular 'subjective' state. "Remaining in the primal, pure natural state without effort is ***sahaja nirvikalpa samadhi***"— Sri Ramana Maharshi. There is no sense of a barrier between our world and the energy called God. It is perpetual experience of the Oneness when being active on the physical plane.
Samadhi	A state of illuminating trance, or the grave of a person.
Sambar	South Indian spicy soup, vegetarian or non-vegetarian (fish *sambar*, egg plant *sambar* and so on).
Sankalpa	A saint's or Guru's silent pledge, directed towards a visitor or his/her disciple often during *dharshan or* when giving *prasad* containing the intention to give him/her support on the Path.
Sannyasa	One of the ancient Hindu Orders of formal/ initiated *renunciates*.
Sannyasi	A member of the *Sannyasa* Order.
Satguru	Self-Realized Guru.

Satsang	Meeting with a saintly person to listen to a discourse. Being in a holy person's presence.
Seva	Expected or voluntary work of inmates or/and visitors dedicated to Guru or ashram.
Siddha	A self-realized adept living in the physical or Astral realm, possessing superpowers. For example, being physically present in a few places at the same time, ability of physical translocation over vast distances, often extraterrestrial, and assuming invisibility at will.
Shambala	A mytical, hidden Kingdom of Sages. Possibly located in Himalayas. It is protected by a subtle energy fieldand only invited people can enter.
Shanti	In Sanskrit: Peace
Shloka	A Verse from sacred writings.
Shraddha	A Hindu ritual performed for one's ancestors, especially deceased parents.
Surya Namaskaram	Sun Salute. A cycle of Yoga postures.
Swami	A monk of *Sannyasa* order.
Śhastra /course/	A basic study of Hindu scriptures to understand the philosophy, customs and way of conduct offered by some ashrams to those who wish to convert to Hinduism.
Upanishads	A vast collection of texts from Vedic period which contain the central religious concepts of Hinduism.

Uppuma | A popular South Indian breakfast dish, cooked as a thick porridge made from dry roasted semolina with onion, green chili and carrot, capsicum.

Vasana | A behavioral tendency like bursting into anger, 'chasing' opposite sex, drinking or hoarding money, possessions or gold, even excessive reading.

Vedas | A large body of the most authoritative Hindu sacred texts composed in Sanskrit, originating in most ancient India probably in Indus Valley civilization and gathered into four collections: The Rig Veda, The Yajurveda, The Samaveda, The Atarveda. Difficult to interpret by contemporary scholars because they were written down from thousands of years of oral transmission when the way of expression abstract ideas was entirely different and because in Sanskrit many words have multiple meanings. So each translation is different. Only a self-realized person can interpret the Vedas correctly because they are part of his being.

Vedic | Knowledge and beliefs of *Vedic* religion, Vedic astrology based on Vedas, also time when Vedas were written down from most ancient oral transmission. Adjective describing any aspect of the Vedas; eg Vedic religion.

Vedanta | 'End of Vedas'. Explanation. Hindu philosophy based on *Upanishads*.

Vibuti | Sacred ash of cow manure applied on forehead and body as a symbol of us being dust in comparison to glorious God.

Vishnu	One of Hindu Gods of trinity.
Vishnu Tirtha	A water tank dedicated to God Vishnu.
Viveka	In Sanskrit: discrimination.
Viveka Chudamani	Most famous writing of Adi Shankara 'Power of Discrimination' which explains how to discriminate between real and illusionary, between truth and falsehood.
Yoga Nidra	A yogic 'sleep', a conscious deep sleep-like state where full awareness is maintained and 'glides' to other realities controlled. It provides extreme relaxation and the possibilities of subtler spiritual exploration. It provides such rejuvenation of the body that advanced practitioners can reduce normal sleep to two hours as does the Dalai Lama for example.
Yuga	According to Hindu cosmology an epoch or era within four age cycles: Kali Yuga, Satya Yuga, Dvapare Yuga and Tetra Yuga. Total length of those cycles is approximately 4,320,000 years. We are now in **Kali Yuga** which is the shortest period of only 432,000 years. In this period there is in human conduct prevail 25% of high merit, 75% of wrongdoing. In This period human lifespan rarely exceed 100 years, intelligence and memory are poor and health fragile and easy to spoil by negative thoughts and emotions and incorrect diet. According to some Vedic pundits we are in the middle of it, others claim that Kali Yuga will end in 2025.

485

Credits Of Photos And Quotations

page—vii—Author on Kannapa Temple terrace—a photo from author's family collection.

page—viii—Author on slopes of Arunachala—a photo from author's family collection.

page—xiv—Swami Chinmayananda—reproduced with permission of Chinmaya Mission—Mumbai, India.

page—134—Sri Ramana Maharshi—reproduced with a permission of Ramana Meharshi Ashramam—Tiruvannamalai, India.

page—138—Darghar (Samadhi) of Muslim Saint Syedini Bibi—photo by author.

page—143—Niches for olive laps at Darghar of Syedini Bibi.—photo by author.

page—144—Darghar (Samadhi) of Haji—photo by author.

page—170—Arunachala—reproduced with a permission of Ramana Maharshi Ashramam—Tiruvannamalai, India.

page—172—Samadhi of Sri Ramana Maharshi—photo by author.

page—212—Swami Sivamurty Saraswaty—reproduced with a permission of Satyananda Yoga—Greece.

pages—437-438—Quotations from Ramana Maharshi 'Gospel' reprinted with permission of Ramana Maharshi Ashramam—Tiruvannamalai, India.

Title page—by Dan Drewes

OTHER BOOKS BY ANDREW M. BUKRABA.

The Birds Colony—This is a story of a spiritual search - through the enlightening contrast between truth and deceit. A memoir of a 'bird' seeker who spent a few rewarding years among a strange collection of 'birds' from many countries who all most probably had only good intentions.

Smashwords Edition 2014
© 2014 Andrew M. Bukraba a.k.a.—Woodpecker

FREE download - available on: **www.smashwords.com** and from: **http://bukraba.wix.com/woodpecker-traveler**

'The Birds Colony' is a metaphorically presented account of years spent in service to a believed-to-be enlightened guru. It is about cult mentality, corruption, bullying, sex and misuse of donated funds all in the name of declared spirituality & charity. This story is a must read for all those who want to get involved in any ashram, or are considering contributing substantial funds to its charity.

Andrew a. k. a. Woodpecker dedicated a major part of his life to an uncompromising search for Truth – which is still on-going. Of the many places visited during this search was a famous ashram founded and run by an equally famous "Guru". Sadly, the Truth Woodpecker sought was not the "truth" being offered there. It took him some time to fully realize & believe that this is a sad reality and even longer to collect data to prove it.

"The Birds Colony" is a tale of classic cult mentality, fanaticism, ego games, corruption, manipulation, bullying, sex, abuse of power and misuse of generously donated funds all in the name of declared spirituality & charity. It is not a Hollywood (nor even a Bollywood) blockbuster, but a metaphorically presented, true account of his years spent in service to a being he believed, on the basis of statements from many seekers, to be 'enlightened'; but realized, it was just the very opposite. The situation described is not unique but, unfortunately, common in many 'spiritual' organizations which divert their energy towards business.

Zawartość tego zbioru, z wyjątkiem trzech wierszy, nie jest przekładem angielskiego tomu 'Poems' i jest głównie adresowana do Polskich czytelników.